# SWINBURNE

## THE PORTRAIT OF A POET

PHILIP HENDERSON

# SWINBURNE

## THE PORTRAIT OF A POET

ROUTLEDGE & KEGAN PAUL
LONDON

*First published in 1974*
*by Routledge & Kegan Paul Ltd*
*Broadway House, 68–74 Carter Lane,*
*London EC4V 5EL*

*Printed in Great Britain by*
*The Camelot Press Ltd, London and Southampton*



*ISBN 0 7100 7734 3*

# CONTENTS

# ILLUSTRATIONS

# ACKNOWLEDGMENTS

My principal debt – and it is a large one – is to the six volumes of Dr Cecil Y. Lang's monumental edition of *The Swinburne Letters* (1959–62) and I am most grateful to Dr Lang and the Yale University Press for permission to quote extensively from these. Next in importance is Edmund Gosse's *Life of Algernon Charles Swinburne* (1917). Gosse was a fairly close friend of Swinburne during the 1870s and his book is, after the *Letters*, the main source of our knowledge of him, though Gosse later modified and enlarged the portrait drawn there by his supplementary essay bequeathed to the British Museum and published for the first time by Dr Lang in his 'Appendix'. Gosse and Wise also published an expurgated, two-volume edition of some 325 letters in 1918 and these were included in vol. 18 of *The Complete Works of Algernon Charles Swinburne* (1925–27) (the Bonchurch edition). The publication in 1952 by the late Randolph Hughes of the unfinished semi-autobiographical novel called *Lesbia Brandon*, with its enormous 'Commentary', has still further clarified the poet's image in several respects.

But it is to the two volumes of Georges Lafourcade's *La Jeunesse de Swinburne* (1928) that we must still turn for the most illuminating analysis of the essential character of the man and his work. Subsequently, the most important contributions towards an understanding of the central tragedy of Swinburne's life have been made by those ardent Swinburnians, John S. Mayfield[1] and Dr Lang[2]. Further support for their conclusions is to be found in Miss Jean Overton Fuller's biography of 1968. There has also been a recent and most welcome reprint of T. Earle Welby's critical study, originally published in 1926.

Among those who have given me valuable assistance I should mention particularly: Lady Swinburne, who received me at Capheaton with all the charm and courtesy of her ancestor; Captain Browne-Swinburne; Mr Geoffrey Trevelyan, for his introduction to his sister Mrs Pauline Dower, who not only entertained me hospitably at her home at Cambo, Northumberland, but took me on a most illuminating tour of Wallington; Miss Kathleen Farrell, who put me in touch with Mr Raleigh Trevelyan, currently at work on the Trevelyan Papers; Mrs Virginia Surtees, who generously allowed me to reproduce the photograph of Swinburne, D. G. and William Michael Rossetti and Fanny Cornforth, given to her by Sir Sydney Cockerell; Mr E. V. Quinn, Librarian of Balliol College, Oxford, who arranged for William Bell-Scott's portrait of Swinburne to be specially photographed; Professor Oswald Doughty, who sent me valuable Swinburne material; April Fitzlyon, who drew my attention to the Swinburne references in the only complete edition of the Goncourt *Journals* (Monaco, 1957) and kindly sent me translations of a relevant extract from S. Usov's article, 'Mozaika', published by the Russian journal *Istorichevski Vestnik* (1912), as well as the references to Swinburne in the latest edition of Turgenev's letters (Moscow, 1961– ); Quentin Keynes, the owner of the largest collection of Sir Richard Burton's manuscripts; Mr Frank Wilson, who communicated to me his illuminating analysis of Mary Gordon's novels; Dr Alex Comfort, who enlightened me about the habits of monkeys; Colin Franklin, who originally asked me to write this book and was instrumental in obtaining for me an Arts Council Award; and, finally, my eldest son, John, who was my guide to Newcastle and the surrounding countryside during two very stimulating visits to the University of Newcastle. But especially I should like to express my feelings of gratitude to my wife, my publishers and my brother-in-law, Mark Hamilton of A. M. Heath, without whose patience, sympathy and encouragement I could never have carried this book through to completion. I am also once more much indebted to the expert typing of Mrs R. Kloegman, who dealt so efficiently with a somewhat chaotic manuscript.

In addition, for permission to quote from copyright material, I am indebted to: Macmillan & Co. Ltd, London and Basingstoke (Edmund Gosse, *The Life of Algernon Charles Swinburne* and Sir Harold Nicholson, *Swinburne*); William Heinemann Ltd (Max Beerbohm, 'No. 2 The Pines' from *And Even Now*, and Gosse, *Portraits and Sketches*); the Trustees of the estate of the late George du Maurier, and Peter Davies Ltd (Daphne du Maurier, *The Young George du Maurier*); Professor John D. Rosenberg and Random House (*Swinburne: Selected Poems and Prose*); Faber & Faber, and New Directions Publishing Corporation (*Literary Essays of Ezra Pound*); Hamish Hamilton Ltd (Helen Rossetti Angeli, *Dante Gabriel Rossetti: His Friends and Enemies*); Chatto & Windus Ltd, and New Directions Publishing Corporation (William Empson, *Seven Types of Ambiguity*); John Murray Ltd, the Society of Authors and the *Cornhill Magazine* (A. E. Housman's lecture on Swinburne); the Trustees of the Hardy Estate, the Macmillan Company of Canada and Macmillan, London and Basingstoke (Thomas Hardy, 'A Singer Asleep'); and the Department of Manuscripts, British Museum. Finally, I should like to pay tribute to the courtesy and helpfulness of the Librarian and Staff of the London Library, the Department of Manuscripts, British Museum, and the Library of the Victoria & Albert Museum.

# ACKNOWLEDGMENTS

The illustrations in this book are reproduced by courtesy of the Master and Fellows of Balliol College, Oxford; the National Portrait Gallery, London; the Trustees of the Tate Gallery, London, the Estate of Sir Max Beerbohm and William Heinemann Ltd; the Victoria & Albert Museum; the Detroit Institute of Arts; Mollie Panter Downes and Hamish Hamilton Ltd; Mrs Virginia Surtees; the Fitzwilliam Museum, Cambridge; and Elliott & Fry (Bassano & Vandyck Studios, London).

The quotations from Swinburne's poems and plays are taken from the edition prepared by Swinburne himself (Chatto and Windus, 1904) as being in general more reliable than the Bonchurch edition of Gosse and Wise; *A Year's Letters* (*Love's Cross-Currents*) and *Lesbia Brandon* follow the holograph manuscripts in the British Museum.

*We shall hear, as one in a trance that hears,*
*The sound of time, the rhyme of the years;*
*Wrecked hope and passionate pain will grow*
*As tender things of a spring-tide sea.*

'THE TRIUMPH OF TIME'

# INTRODUCTION

'Swinburne has hitherto been fortunate in his biographers,' wrote Sir Harold Nicolson in 1926, 'for it would indeed have been regrettable if the life-story of one who, although surpassingly strange, was yet so exquisite a gentleman, had been marred from the outset by any ungentle handling. In Edmund Gosse, Swinburne found a historian such as the fates accord but rarely to the inheritors of fulfilled renown.' And he went on to forecast that 'there will be those, doubtless, who will one day explore the intricacies and causes of his non-existent sexual repressions, and will trace depressing and essentially erroneous analogies to Dr Masoch or the Marquis de Sade'.[1] Depressing, maybe, but certainly not erroneous, as Georges Lafourcade amply demonstrated only two years afterwards in *La Jeunesse de Swinburne*, and as is still more apparent from Dr C. Y. Lang's edition of *The Swinburne Letters.* In fact, Gosse himself felt qualms about the reticence of his *Life*, and subsequently deposited in the British Museum a typescript containing supplementary material which he rightly judged unsuitable for publication at that time, together with the letters of those to whom he had sent it for their opinions.

But times have changed and Swinburne studies have advanced a long way since Gosse and Nicolson. Indeed, as Dr Cecil Lang wrote in 1959: 'So far Swinburne's life has hardly been penetrated. The biographer who attempts it will have to deal more intimately and perceptively with his "autobiographical writings".'

If the resultant portrait is sometimes less than complimentary, the strange charm and complexity of Swinburne's personality as revealed in his letters, the perfection and beauty of so much of his poetry, and the brilliance and wit of his earlier prose, will, it is hoped, go a long way to dispose of Nicolson's fears of 'ungentle handling', should the full truth of his life ever be known. 'The impression I have retained from my several meetings with him,' wrote Guy de Maupassant, 'is perhaps of the most extravagantly artistic person alive in the world today.'[2]

It is also time that something like justice was done to the man who rescued Swinburne from a squalid and ignominious death and gave him thirty more years of healthy, vigorous life – the devoted, much-maligned Theodore Watts-Dunton. But whether the later Swinburne is as interesting as the earlier Swinburne is, of course, another matter. There is a direct relation between the mechanical regularity of his life at Putney and the mechanical regularity of the verse he produced while living there under the watchful eye of his friend. But that is not to say that the gradual waning of his creative powers during the last half of his life was due to his removal to Putney: they had begun to wane before that. As the poet in him declined, the scholar and man of letters took over. This was only natural, since, having lost touch with nearly all his more stimulating friends, through whom he had earlier lived, he was now practically confined to the companionship of Watts. But Watts gave him stability, and curbed his excitability. Swinburne's excitability was manic and self-destructive; it had to be curbed if he were to live, just as pale ale had to be substituted for the immoderate doses of brandy with which Richard Burton had supplied him.

From one thing Watts could never wean his 'dear old friend', namely, the inflamed interest in flagellation, which recurs so monotonously throughout Swinburne's earlier correspondence and spoils, for most readers, his second novel. It was a taste he shared with a number of his friends, notably Lord Houghton, Simeon Soloman, and his cousin Mary Gordon. But it is significant that the spate of letters to Houghton dwindles to a thin trickle during the second half of his life. 'It is curious that though Sade is the author who most influenced Swinburne,' A. E. Housman wrote to Gosse in January 1919, 'and though Swinburne's writings are full of Sadism properly so-called, his own propensities were those of Rousseau and Sacher-Masoch. It is true that these are cheaper to indulge, but that does not seem to have been the reason. . . . Judging from the dates drink had a great deal to do with his best poetry, though the poetry declined before the drinking stopped. The history of the Mohammedan world confirms Horace's opinion of the connexion between the two.'[3] But when the drinking reached the stage of alcoholic dysentery it had to be stopped.

For some time now, Swinburne has been among the most neglected of our poets. The enormous bulk of his work is partly to blame, and also the habit of judging him by his worst poems. The chief reason, however, is that our whole approach to poetry has changed, though for long he was regarded as one of the finest lyrists in the language. 'None of the more important Victorian poets is more difficult to read, with any pleasure, today, than Swinburne,' wrote John Heath-Stubbs in 1950. 'His rhythms are mechanical, his heavily stressed anapaestic and dactylic metres vulgar, his use of pause often lacking in subtlety; though a certain facility in the melodic arrangement of vowel sounds must be granted him.'[4] Such has been the view for some time now, and one suspects that it is based on a reading of 'Dolores' and 'The Hymn to Proserpine', and little else. It is usually coupled with the charge of imprecise writing, and leaves out of account the infinite variety and rhythmic subtlety of so much of his work. Swinburne is often extremely precise in his observation of nature, to take only such poems as 'The Sundew', 'Relics' or 'At a Month's End', and the later descriptive verse is often Wordsworthian or Turnerean in feeling. There are, too, the superb elegy on the death of Baudelaire and the magnificent Villon translations. Again, few novels have more clarity and concision than *Love's Cross-Currents.* As for his letters, though they may suffer by contemporary standards from long-windedness, they are the letters of a man of immense learning and wit. Many of them bear witness, also, to a delicious sense of the absurd, as does his parody of French novels about English society, *La Fille du policeman*, which so amused his friends, and the spoof reviews of imaginary French poets with which he pulled the leg of the editor of the *Spectator*, with their masterly parodies of Hugo and Baudelaire. There is, too, his almost forgotten pioneer work on William Blake, his review of *Les Fleurs du Mal* which he said was written in a Turkish bath in Paris, his fine essays on Chapman and Ford and on the work of his elder contemporaries, Arnold, Rossetti and Morris, which caused such excitement when they first appeared in the *Fortnightly Review* in the 1860s, not to mention the excellence of much of his *Study of Shakespeare.* Nor is it recognized any longer how much Walter Pater was indebted to Swinburne's 'Notes on the Designs of the Old Masters in Florence' of 1864, for both the style and the method of his *Renaissance* – an indebtedness acknowledged by Pater himself. These 'Notes' are evidence of an intense sensitiveness to drawing and painting which was never developed, just as his feeling for character and drama, shown in his early novel and the fragments of *Lesbia Brandon*, went into the composition of more or less unreadable (and certainly unactable) plays on the Elizabethan model. Thanks largely to his family, who were very musical, and to his Welsh friend, George Powell, Swinburne discovered Wagner when his music was little known in England. Evidence of this is to be seen in *Tristram of Lyonesse*, which he intended to be his masterwork. In the same way, he was well before his time in England in his knowledge and appreciation of French poets and novelists, of Laclos, Stendhal, Hugo, Balzac, Baudelaire, Flaubert, Gautier, Latouche and Léon Cladel. He was also widely read in the medieval French romances, in Brantôme and all that had to do with Mary Stuart, to whom he had a romantic attachment. The scholarship that went into the writing of his enormous drama *Bothwell* was immense. Above all, he was a Greek scholar, as is shown by *Atalanta in Calydon* and *Erechtheus* and many of the shorter poems. He even assisted Jowett in his translation of Plato. In short, Swinburne is one of the most learned and richly endowed poets in the language. And since the *goût de l'horrible* is once more in fashion, then why not such poems as 'The Leper', 'Les Noyades', 'Anactoria' and 'Faustine'? For there, in the mid-nineteenth century, will be found all the elements that were to be taken up and developed by the symbolist and *fin de siècle* writers and painters all over Europe.

At the height of the clamour provoked by *Poems and Ballads, First Series*, the ever-perceptive Ruskin wrote to J. M. Ludlow, the social reformer, who had asked him to add his voice to the general protest: 'He is infinitely above me in all knowledge and power and I should no more think of advising him than of venturing to do it to Turner if he were alive again. As for Swinburne not being my superior, he is simply only one of the mightiest scholars of the age in Europe. . . . And in power of imagination and understanding simply sweeps me away as a torrent does a pebble.' In a letter to Swinburne himself, Ruskin compares him to 'a deadly nightshade blossom' and 'a thunder-cloud'.

The comparison with Turner has been developed by Professor John D. Rosenberg of Columbia University, himself the author of a fine study of Ruskin, *The Darkening Glass*, in an essay which is perhaps the best contemporary analysis of Swinburne's poetry yet written: 'Swinburne's love of mixed effects gives to his descriptive verse much of its Turnerian quality. His poetry is charged with the tension of delicately poised opposites: shadows thinned to light, lights broken by shade, sunset passing into moonrise, sea merging with sky. He is obsessed with the moment when one thing shades off into its opposite, or when contraries fuse, as in "Hermaphroditus". . . . Yet apart from his profound aesthetic affinity with Turner, there is the unique idiosyncrasy of Swinburne himself, who was equipped with superb senses, each of which must have transmitted a peculiar counterpoint. This basic, polarizing rhythm runs through his being and manifests itself in his compulsive use of alliterating antitheses in prose and verse. Much in Swinburne that has been criticized as mere mannerism – paradox, alliteration, elaborate antithesis – strikes me as deriving from his deepest impulses, although the question of "sincerity" is always vexing in his verse. In a sense, Swinburne *perceived* in paradoxes, and his recurrent synthetic images express perfectly that passing of pain into pleasure, bitter into sweet, loathing into desire, which lay at the root of his profoundest experiences.'[5]

The reputation of Swinburne reached its nadir in the 1920s and 1930s after the revolution in poetry brought about by Ezra Pound and T. S. Eliot – a revolution which has now, perhaps, spent its force by making poetry often almost indistinguishable from prose. There is now evidence of the beginning of a new and more discerning interest in Swinburne in the second half of this century in the United States. Edmund Wilson demonstrated this trend with his appreciation of the novels and the letters,[6] though he fails to appreciate the poetry. But Edith Sitwell had already produced her *Swinburne: a Selection* in 1960, with an introduction distinguished for its creative insight. It is to be hoped that this new interest may not be confined to the better known, somewhat brassy Dionysian side of this extravagantly gifted being, who was once felt to be the liberator of a whole generation in revolt against Victorian pieties and repressions, but, now that we no longer need liberating, may lead to a deeper knowledge of the man who, in his less febrile moments, wrote some of the most exquisite poetry and the finest criticism of his time.

## CHAPTER ONE

# 1837–49
# SEAGULL

Algernon Charles Swinburne was born during a visit of his parents to 7 Chester Street, Grosvenor Place, London, on 5 April 1837 – 'almost by accident', says Edmund Gosse, as though there were something peculiar in his having been born at all, as perhaps there was. Later, he said of himself that he was born 'all but dead, and certainly not expected to live an hour'. Though nervous and fragile in appearance, he was fundamentally healthy, with a wiry strength of constitution that made him seem almost tireless, for the Swinburnes were a tough and long-lived stock. In the portrait with his two sisters painted by George Richmond in 1843, he appears at the age of six a perfectly normal, well-proportioned child with a serene and lively face. More revealing, perhaps, is the miniature painted two years earlier, with its sharply intelligent little face already showing signs of a malicious wit.[1]

His father, Captain (later Admiral) Charles Henry Swinburne, had married Lady Jane Hamilton, the fourth daughter of George, third Earl of Ashburnham of Ashburnham Place, Sussex, in 1836. They were second cousins, their maternal grandfathers being brothers. Algernon was the eldest of six children.

The Swinburnes were a Northumberland family of some antiquity. William de Swinburne held the lordship of Chollerton, where the little Saxon church still stands, in the reign of Henry II. In 1274 Sir Adam de Swinburne, whose descendants lost Swinburne Castle, acquired from Sir Thomas de Fenwyke the domain of Capheaton, near Newcastle, which is still to this day the family seat. The present house was built soon after the Restoration by the local architect Trollope in a style of provincial baroque. It is approached by a splendid avenue of ancient trees. With the wide horizons, woods, streams, rocks and moors of the surrounding countryside it stands in the very heart of Northumberland, which Algernon always regarded as his homeland. The house dates from the time of John Swinburne, 'the auld carle of Capheaton', rewarded at the Restoration with a baronetcy for his services to Charles I in the civil war.

John Ashburnham, the poet's ancestor on his mother's side, was the intimate friend of Charles I himself and suffered imprisonment and the loss of his estates under the Commonwealth. At the Restoration he managed to recover them, with the help of his brother William, cofferer to Charles I and Charles II, and he rebuilt Ashburnham church, which still stands in the grounds with its original box-pews and flamboyant family tombs. It was William who rebuilt Ashburnham Place after his elder brother's death in 1671. Since then the house has undergone many transformations and, except for part of the central block, refaced in 1850 with peculiarly unattractive red and grey bricks, it has been largely demolished. Together with modern extensions, it is now the centre of the Ashburnham Christian Trust. The remarkable collection of pre-Renaissance paintings accumulated by George, the third Earl, and the magnificent library of illuminated manuscripts and early printed books in which Algernon delighted, collected by Bertram, the fourth earl, was sold to pay crushing death duties when the Ashburnham line came to an end with the death of Lady Catherine, daughter of the fifth earl, in 1953. Half the estate, amounting to some 8,500 acres of farms and woodlands, was sold at the same time.

Algernon's great-grandfather on his father's side, Edward, was living at Bordeaux in the mid-eighteenth century, having married Christina Dillon of the Dillons of Roscommon. He is described by the governor of Bordeaux in 1756 as one 'Edw. Swinburne du Northumberland, fils cadet du baronnet John Swinburne d'une famille catholique et zélée pour les Stuarts'. The connection of the family with Bordeaux goes back to Thomas Swynbourne, who received the Château de Guines from Richard II in 1396 and was eight years later appointed Mayor of Bordeaux. He was, however, buried in England and his epitaph may be seen in the church of Little Horkesley in Essex: '*Icy qist Monsr. Thomas Swynbourne. . . . Mair de Bordeaux et capitaigne de Fronsak qu mourut dans la veile de Saint Laurence l'an de grace Mill CCCCXV*^e^ *de qy Dieu eyt pitee et Mercye. Amen.*'[2] It was the Swinburnes, rather than the Ashburnhams, who retained their romantic attachment to the Stuarts, a tradition carried on by Algernon's lifelong fascination with the figure of Mary, Queen of Scots.

Swinburne's grandfather, Sir John, who became the sixth baronet and inherited the domain of Capheaton, was born at Bordeaux in 1762. Educated in France, he was the friend of Mirabeau and Wilkes and was painted by Gainsborough.[3] Strikingly handsome, Sir John had in his manners much of the urbanity and grace of the *ancien régime*, and it was for him that the poet reserved his greatest admiration as a boy. On acceding to the title at the age of twenty-five, he renounced the catholic Jacobite traditions of his family and became Member of Parliament for Launceston, Cornwall, in 1788 as an ultra-liberal. 'It is absurd,' he wrote in a letter of 30 July 1786, 'to sacrifice my consideration in my own country, my prospects in life, to condemn myself to eternal insignificance and oblivion for Tenets I did not believe and Ceremonies I never practised.' According to Swinburne, he attacked the Prince of Wales in one of his parliamentary speeches and when Leigh Hunt and his brother were imprisoned for libelling the Regent, he wrote expressing his 'sorrow and indignation' and offering from two to three hundred pounds towards the payment of the fine. He was, according to Swinburne again, 'one of the most extreme politicians as well as one of the hardest riders and the best art-patrons of his time. . . . It was said that the two maddest things in the north country were his horse and himself. . . . He was the friend of the great Turner, of Mulready, and of many lesser artists; I wish to God he had discovered Blake.'[4] Sir John's mother, Swinburne always insisted, was 'a lady of the house of Polignac'. But both Swinburne's sister Isabel and his cousin Mary Gordon, later Mrs Disney-Leith, denied that there was any foundation for this claim and that Swinburne had no French blood in him though he always liked to think so. As Gosse remarks dryly: 'The poet, although so great a republican, was no democrat.' Nor, for that matter, was Sir John, as he grew older, for we find him writing to Leigh Hunt in 1858, ten years before his death: 'The Socialist section in France I consider as the most dangerous enemies of liberty, both civil and religious.' Their aim was nothing but 'the complete unhinging of society'.

At Capheaton Sir John possessed one of the finest libraries in the north country, particularly rich in French literature of the eighteenth century. At the age of eighty-eight he took his daughter Julia to London to see an exhibition of paintings and works of art, 'of which', he wrote, 'she is a very competent judge having attained no common skill in painting under the long and competent instruction of my valuable friend Mulready'. Until 1837 Sir John was President of the Literary and Philosophical Society of Newcastle, and had been at one time President of the Society of Antiquaries.[5] He lived on until his ninety-ninth year, and survived being trepanned after a shooting accident, which, says Swinburne, 'happened to blow away his right eye with a good bit of the skull. . . . An ancestress of his (i.e. a Lady Swinburne), bore thirty children to one husband; people thronged about her carriage in the streets to see the living and thriving mother of thirty sons and daughters. I think you will allow that when this race chose at last to produce a poet, it would have been at least remarkable if he had been content to write nothing but hymns and idylls for clergymen and young ladies to read out in chapels and drawing-rooms.'[6] Indeed, Sir John remained the idol of Swinburne's childhood, the first of that gallery of grand old men, among them Landor, Victor Hugo and Mazzini, whom he particularly revered. By nature a rebel, it was always necessary, it seems, for him to have someone before whom he could abase himself, his nature swinging perpetually between the twin poles of revolt and submission.

Swinburne's father, Charles Henry, was Sir John's younger son by Emilia Elizabeth Bennet of Beckenham, a niece of the second duke of Northumberland. Born in 1797, he entered the Royal Naval College in 1810, and, after sailing 'all the seas of the world', became a captain in 1835. Towards the end of his life, the poet wrote to Thomas Hardy that his father had served as a midshipman under Collingwood – a typical romantic exaggeration, for Collingwood died six months before the future admiral had even started his career at the Royal Naval College. In 1857 he was put on the reserve list with the rank of rear-admiral. Swinburne's mother, Lady Jane, had been brought up partly in Italy, spending much of her youth as one of the English colony in Florence. She had some knowledge of the literatures of both Italy and France, and also read Bowdler's *Family Shakespeare*, Scott and Dickens to her family, though Byron, being notoriously cynical and irreligious, was not read; she made Algernon promise that he would not read him until he was grown up. Both parents were ardent Anglo-Catholics and much affected by the Oxford Movement, Algernon himself early falling into 'unaffected and unashamed ecstasies of adoration'[7] at Mass.

The greater part of Algernon's childhood was spent in the gentle environment of the Isle of Wight, at East Dene, Bonchurch, near Ventnor, where his father had rented a large house, with long holidays at Ashburnham Place and Capheaton. Sir Henry and Lady Mary Gordon, the poet's maternal uncle and aunt, lived not far from East Dene at their seventeenth-century mansion of Northcourt, Shorwell. Algernon also frequently visited the Orchard at Niton, the house of Sir James Willoughby Gordon, his cousin Mary Gordon's grandfather. Here he might be seen 'riding on a very small pony, led by a servant'.

Edmund Gosse has written:[8]

> The rambling gardens and lawns of East Dene descend southward to the sea-shore, divided from it only by the masked path that leads to Luccombe, and so they practically shelve from the great trees in the shadow of the undercliff down to the shingle and the sea-weed. The view from the house south-east is over limitless ocean. Close by, to the east, is the wonderful chaos of the Landslip with its tangled lianas and romantic chasms, and to the west, the shores of Monk's Bay and Horseshoe Bay, with their groynes and their fishermen's boats, so that on each side there lay an enchanted Tom Tidler's Ground for emancipated children through the blissful and interminable seasons of seventy years ago.

Algernon, in fact, spent so much of his time playing on the shore and in and out of the sea that he came to be known in his family circle as 'Seagull'.

In *A Year's Letters*, later published as *Love's Cross-Currents* in 1905, he has himself given a picture of the great households and their environment between which he grew up in the Isle of Wight and Sussex:[9]

> They were to have enough to do with each other in later life, these three scattered households of kinsfolk; but the mixing process only began on a late spring day in 1849, at the country-house which Mr John Cheyne had inherited from his wife. This was a little old house, beautifully set in among orchards and meadows, with abundance of roses now all around it,

under the heavy leaves of a spring that June was fast gaining upon. A wide, soft river divided the marsh meadows in front of it, full of yellow flag-flowers and moist fen-blossom. Behind there slanted upwards a small broken range of hills, the bare, green, windy lawns of them dry and fresh under foot, thick all the way with cowslips at the right time. It was a splendid place for children; better perhaps than Ashton Hildred with its huge brick-walled gardens and wonderful fruit-trees blackened and dotted with lumps and patches of fabulous overgrown moss, and wild pleasure-grounds stifled with beautiful rank grass; better decidedly than Lord Cheyne's big, brilliant Lidcombe inspite of royal shooting-grounds and the admirable slopes of high bright hill-country behind it, green sweet miles of park and embayed lake, beyond praise for riding and boating; better incomparably than Captain Harewood's place, muffled in woods, with a grim, sad beauty of its own, but seemingly knee-deep in sere leaves all the year round, wet and weedy and dark and deep down, kept hold of somehow by autumn in the midst of spring; only the upper half of it clear out of the clutch of winter, even in the hottest height of August weather, with a bitter flavour of frost and rain in it all through summer.

Comparatively little is known of the details of Swinburne's childhood, though it seems to have been an unusually happy one. When drawing a picture of English aristocratic families in *Love's Cross-Currents* and *Lesbia Brandon*, it would be natural for him to base it upon his own particularly close-knit family, but in later life he denied that this was the case. Nevertheless, it is evident that a great deal in these novels is autobiographical. Comparing his own childhood with Shelley's, Swinburne in a letter to William Rossetti of 15 January 1870, admits that, like Shelley, he was an 'afflictive phenomenon' to his father, 'before, during, and since my Oxford time', adding: 'but I do not think you make allowance for the provocation given (as well as received) by a father, who may be kindly and generous, to a boy or man between seventeen and twenty-one or so, with whom he has no deep or wide ground of sympathy beyond the animal relation or family tradition. You will allow me to say that I am sure you can never have felt at that age the irreparable, total and inevitable isolation from all that had once been closest to the mind and thought, and was still closest to the flesh and the memory, the solitude in which one passes from separation to antagonism of spirit (without violent quarrels or open offense, but by pure logical necessity of consequence) the sense that where attraction gradually ends repulsion gradually begins, which many besides Shelley, and as affectionate and faithful by nature and temperament as he, *have* felt at that age.'[10]

Evidently some such alienation from his own father occurred during Swinburne's adolescence, though, unlike Shelley, he never openly quarrelled with him. Mrs Disney-Leith, the cousin to whom, as Mary Gordon, Swinburne was closest of all, tells us that the admiral was 'a stern disciplinarian'. The photograph she gives of him in his old age, in her book of sentimental reminiscences, *The Boyhood of Algernon Charles Swinburne*, shows a finely-featured face somewhat bewildered and worried, as well it might be, for all its tight-lipped control. After all, his father paid for the publication of Swinburne's first two books – though he heartily disliked them – and his treatment of him, throughout all his later excesses, was consistently generous. But then as an adult Swinburne always behaved like an angel at home, after he had reduced himself to illness and exhaustion by his wild life in London, and was only too glad to be looked after by an affectionate family – at least for a time. His feelings for his mother were always very affectionate, as they were for his sisters – Alice, the eldest; Edith, his favourite, who died in 1863; and Charlotte and Isabel. Of his brother, Edward, the youngest of the family, very little is known, except that he married 'the worst of wives' (according to Swinburne), had a passion for the music of Schumann and Wagner, and died in 1891 of heart-failure, when his wife married again. It seems that no love was lost between the two brothers.

A semi-autobiographical passage in *A Year's Letters* tells us that:

> Reginald was growing visibly mutinous and hard to keep down by preachings and punishments; had begun evidently to wince and kick under the domestic rod. His father and the clerical tutor who came over daily to look after the boy's holiday task could hardly keep him under by frequent flogging and much serious, sorrowful lecturing. He was not a specially fast boy, only about as restless and insubordinate as most fellows of his age; but this was far more than his father was prepared to stand.

It was unlikely, from what we know of Swinburne's relationship with his father, whom he always addressed in his letters as 'Darling Pino', that this can be taken as a true picture of his own childhood. But a parallel passage from *Lesbia Brandon*, written shortly afterwards, dealing with the childhood of Herbert Seyton – Reginald again under a different name – has an undertone of resentment and bitterness:[11]

> Sensitive by nature, and solitary by accident, a child will taste as keenly and judge as justly as few men can do. . . . Not incompetent to think, he is incompetent to make use of his thoughts: fancies may fill him as perverse and subtle and ambitious as a grown man's dreams and creeds. His relish of things, again, will probably be just and right, his faith and his taste wholesome, if not twisted round and disfigured by the manipulation of fools, preached out of heart and moralized out of shape.

It is noticeable that in both passages there is an emphasis on preaching and lecturing. But Reginald's father is represented as a sadist and Herbert is at the mercy of a sadistic tutor. By the time that both these novels came to be written in the 1860s, Swinburne himself was obsessed with sadistic fantasies of flagellation. Of Herbert Seyton we read just before he went to Eton:[12]

> Few children had ever enjoyed eleven years of such idleness and freedom and no seagull likes to have his wings clipped. The scissors must cut close that were to fit this bird for a perch in the school pen.

This refers to the arrival of the tutor Denham, who was to wield the 'scissors' in the most painful manner imaginable. But one has to remember that the cruel whipping of children was still all too common in the Victorian age, as one gathers from other novels of the period, not least from Samuel Butler's autobiographical *The Way of All Flesh.* Moreover, flogging in the army and navy, in prisons and at public schools was regarded as a perfectly normal method of punishment. It is only today, with the wisdom of hindsight, that the result of such treatment on a nature so sensitive and abnormal as Swinburne's can be gauged. And doubtless, the admiral, though kindly enough by nature, had naval notions of discipline.

Although Algernon grew up as part of a large family group of sisters and cousins, uncles, aunts and grandparents, he was essentially in his poetic nature what 'sun, and wind, and waters made him'. The earliest and most powerful influences came to him through nature, above all from the wild moorlands and seas of Northumberland, as may be seen from the splendid passages of natural description in *Lesbia Brandon*, where Capheaton appears as Ensdon:[13]

> A shrill wind shook the trees and bushes about the old house as they started: the day was sharp and the light hard and fitful. No rain fell, but the flooded burn had not yet gone down; the long reeds sang sharp in the wind, the flowerless heather heaved and quivered under it by fits. Following the water-course they passed out of the line of moorland and under the grey and yellow crags that faced the low barren fields beyond; dividing these and twice crossing the border stream, their road rose again over green hills and between small wayside rocks, formless and weather-scored. After miles of high lonely land it went down among sudden trees and out into a land of old woods and swift streams, backing and doubling, crossing and mixing; and over copse and down from the right hand came a sound and smell of the sea. At the next turn they were in sight of it; a spring-weather sea, grey and green as leaves faded or flowering, swelling and quivering under clouds and sunbeams. . . . The water moved like tired tossing limbs of a goddess, troubled with strength and vexed with love. Northward and southward the grey glitter of remote foam flickered along the extreme sea-line, marking off the low sky so that water and cloud were distinct. Nearer inshore, the sea was as an April field of sweet and pale colour, filled with white and windy flowers.

When he was not riding over the moors, Algernon, like Herbert Seyton, would wander alone along the beach for hours:

> he could have gone blindfold over miles of beach. All the hollows of the

> cliffs and all the curves of the sandhills were friendly to his feet. The long reefs that rang with returning waves and flashed with ebbing ripples; the smooth slopes of coloured rock full of small brilliant lakes that fed and saved from sunburning their anchored fleets of flowers, yellower lilies and redder roses of the sea; the sharp and fine sea-mosses, fruitful of grey blossom, fervent with blue and golden bloom, with soft spear-heads and blades brighter than fire; the lovely heavy motion of the stronger rock-rooted weeds, with all their weight afloat in languid water, splendid and supine . . . the hard sand inlaid with dry and luminous brine; the shuddering shades of sudden colour woven by the light with the water for some remote golden mile or two reaching from dusk to dusk under the sun; shot through with faint and fierce lustres that shiver and shift; and over all a fresher and sweeter heaven than is seen inland by any weather; drew his heart back day after day and satisfied it. . . .

Here Algernon played like a sea-bird:

> Here among the reefs he ran riot, skirting with light quick feet the edge of the running ripple, laughing with love when the fleeter foam caught them up, skimming the mobile fringe that murmured and fluttered and fell, gathering up with gladdened ears all the fervent sighs and whispers of the tender water, all delicate sounds of washing and wandering waves, all sweet and suppressed semi-tones of light music struck out of shingle or sand by the faint extended fingers of foam and tired eager lips of yielding sea that touch the soft mutable limit of their life, to recede in extremity and exhaustion. At other times he would set his face seaward and feed his eyes for hours on the fruitless floating fields of wan green water, fairer than all spring meadows or summer gardens, till the soul of the sea entered him and filled him with fleshly pleasure and the pride of life; he felt the fierce gladness and glory of living stroke and sting him all over as with soft hands and sharp lips, and under their impulse he went as before a steady gale over sands and rocks, blown and driven by the wind of his own delight, crying out to the sea between whiles as to a mother that talked with him, throwing at it all the scraps of song that came upon his lips by chance, laughing and leaping, envious only of the sea-birds who might stay longer between two waves. . . .

This ecstasy in the presence of nature is strangely enough to be found rather in Swinburne's prose than in his poetry. But it is an ecstasy that is, as usual, closely linked in his imagination with cruelty:[14]

> The winter dangers of the coast were as yet mere rumours to him; but the knowledge of how many lives went yearly to feed with blood the lovely lips of the sea-furies who had such songs and smiles for summer, and for winter the teeth and throats of ravening wolves or snakes untamable, the hard heavy hands that beat out their bruised life from sinking bodies of

men, gave point to his pleasure and a sheathed edge of cruel sympathy to his love. All cruelties and treacheries, all subtle appetites and violent secrets of the sea, were part of her divine nature, adorable and acceptable to her lovers. Why should the gods spare men? or she, a sure and visible goddess, be merciful to meaner things?

Here we are already in the world of *Atalanta in Calydon*.

'It is a daring but not untenable paradox to contend that Swinburne's emotional receptivity began to ossify in 1857, that is, in his twenty-first year,' writes Harold Nicolson in his elegant biography of the poet. 'The experiences which he had by then absorbed became his future attitudes: all subsequent experiences were little more than superficial acceptances or . . . special kinds of belief. . . there was no stimulus after 1857 that became really essential.' There is no doubt that some such process took place in Swinburne's emotional development. But it is equally certain that it did not begin until some years later and arose from the climacteric experience of 1863–64, which, he says himself, 'reduced his young manhood to a barren stock'.[15] This experience seems to have exhausted his emotional reserves; but as a child and a young man he responded passionately to the world about him, and both his novels show a sharp and witty observation of character. An estimate of Swinburne based entirely on his poetry is inevitably misleading, for it is clear that he had in him the makings of a considerable novelist. It is true that he virtually withdrew from social life in early middle-age and that in time his response to literature, passionate as that was, became a substitute for his response to life. Subsequently, he lived on memories.

In 1848, Swinburne was sent to be prepared for Eton by the Reverend Foster Fenwick, Vicar of Brooke, a small town in the west of the Isle of Wight some twenty-five miles from Bonchurch. Here he had his own room and did not return home for the night. The Reverend Fenwick gave him instruction in the rudiments of Greek and Latin, without, it is hoped, too much of the preaching and moralizing of East Dene.

# CHAPTER TWO

# 1849–53
# ETON

When, at the age of twelve, on 24 April 1849, Algernon Swinburne arrived at Eton with his father and mother, his Bowdler's *Shakespeare* under his arm, his cousin Bertram Mitford, later Lord Redesdale, saw him as 'strangely tiny. His limbs were small and delicate; and his sloping shoulders looked far too weak to carry his great head, the size of which was exaggerated by the tousled mass of red hair standing out almost at right angles to it. Hero-worshippers talk of his hair as having been a "golden aureole". At that time there was nothing golden about it. Red, violent aggressive red it was, unmistakable, unpoetical carrots. His features were small and beautiful, chiselled as daintily as those of some Greek sculptor's masterpieces. His skin was very white – not unhealthy, but a transparent tinted white, such as one sees in the petals of some roses. His face was the very replica of that of his dear mother, and she was one of the most refined and lovely of women. His red hair must have come from the Admiral's side, for I have never heard of a red-haired Ashburnham. . . . Another characteristic which Algernon inherited from his mother was the voice. All who knew him must remember that exquisitely soft voice with a rather sing-song intonation.' It was a voice later copied by numerous Oxford undergraduates in the years of Swinburne's fame: 'His language, even at that age, was beautiful, fanciful and richly varied. Altogether my recollection of him in those schooldays is that of a fascinating, most lovable little fellow.'[1]

Yet this sprite-like little figure, with his huge head of carroty hair and his dancing step, had a strange dignity, an elaborate courtesy, and there was already something a little formidable in the level gaze of his green eyes. It never occurred to anyone to bully him – for bullying, like beating, is one of the oldest traditions of our public schools. Lord Redesdale remembers him reading in the boys' library in Weston's Yard: 'I can see him now sitting perched up Turk-or-tailor wise in one of the windows looking out on the yard, with some huge old-world tome, almost as big as himself, upon his lap, the afternoon sun setting on fire the great mop of red hair. There it was that he emancipated himself, making acquaintance with Shakespeare (minus Bowdler), Marlowe, Spenser, Ben Jonson, Ford,

Massinger, Beaumont and Fletcher, and other poets and playwrights of the sixteenth and seventeenth centuries. His tendency was greatly towards Drama, especially Tragic Drama. He had a great sense of humour in others. He would quote Dickens, especially Mrs Gamp, unwearyingly; but his own genius leaned to tragedy.'[2]

In fact, after reading *The Revenger's Tragedy* at the age of twelve in his tutor's Dodsley, Swinburne wrote a gruesome tragedy of his own in four acts, influenced also by Massinger's *Virgin Martyr* and Webster's *Duchess of Malfi*. This was *The Unhappy Revenge*, into which, as he wrote to Churton Collins on 11 December 1876, he 'contrived to pack twice as many rapes and about three times as many murders as are contained in the model.... It must have been a sweet work and full of the tender and visionary innocence of childhood's unsullied fancy.'[3] Swinburne adds that he had the sense to burn it at the age of sixteen, but it has survived in a manuscript notebook.[4]

It deals with Eudoxia, a sister of the late Roman Emperor, who, to avenge her violation by the Emperor Maximus, betrays Rome into the hands of the Huns. The most important character, however, is Eroclea, a Christian virgin, who manages to preserve her virginity, until she is martyred and dies by torture. It is through her mouth that Swinburne expresses his own religious faith, intact until he reached Oxford. The play actually contains only one rape, one suicide, two murders by poison and four executions, though it is unfinished and the final act would have provided an opportunity for further horrors. Even as it stands, it is an astonishing achievement for a boy of twelve. Lafourcade detects in *The Unhappy Revenge* 'une sensualité déjà forte et déjà subtile', particularly in the speeches of the Christian martyrs. In such speeches as that of Pulcheria, Swinburne has achieved, through his extraordinary imitative faculty, a style already mature:

Must my quick youth
Be withered in thy wrinkled barren arms?
Can I not find to quench my hot desires
Some lusty and fit limbs for strong embraces?

This maturity is more evident still in the speeches of the Christian martyr Eroclea, which reflect the style of Massinger:

What is that death they boast but a frail pageant,
A shade that falls and passes? 'Tis a cloud
That but dissolves in rain, sweet Nature's tears,
And leaves a rainbow, shaded with each hue,
Of varying light, to make a blessed arch
That opens our way to Heaven.

And in the funeral chant of the Christians may be heard the voice of

Webster's fools and pilgrims. But from Scene II of Act 3 a pious hand has torn out three pages.

Sir George Young says that Swinburne read him at Eton three complete Elizabethan tragedies – but then he had already written pseudo-Shakespearean dramas and fragments of dramas before going to Eton. Shelley's atrocious play *The Cenci* was one of his early favourites.

At first, Algernon felt completely lost at Eton. We can gauge his feelings from his account of Herbert Seyton's first term there in *Lesbia Brandon*:[5]

> he left Ensdon in a blind passion of pain, and like one born alive out of life, or all that was sweet in it. It was rather a physical than a sentimental pain, he felt the sharp division and expulsion, the bitter blank of change, like a bad taste or smell. Away from home and the sea and all common comfortable things, stripped of the lifelong clothing of his life, he felt as one beaten and bare. . . . It was very bitter and dull to him, to be taken up and dropped down into the heart of a strange populous place, beautiful and kindly as he like others should have found it. . . . No possible training for a schoolboy could have been worse than his had been: and it now bore him painful and unprofitable fruit. He had a dear and close friend or two, with whom he rambled and read verse and broke bounds beyond Datchet or Windsor; dreaming and talking out the miles of green and measured land they tramped or shirked over. It was a new country to his eyes, veiled with light pendulous leaves and inlaid with sleepy reaches of soft water: pleasant and close and sweet and wearisome. The seagull grew sick in an aviary, though (it may be) of better birds. Instead of tender hanging tendrils of woodland he desired the bright straight back-blown copses of the north: and instead of noble gradual rivers, the turbid inlets and wintry wildnesses of the sea. Child as he was, and foolish, the desire of old things was upon him like a curse. So his first half came to an end sadly enough: and the next somewhat worse.

Gosse says that Algernon did not distinguish himself particularly at school work, which, of course, consisted chiefly of Greek and Latin, though he won the Prince Consort's prize for modern languages. Lord Redesdale tells us that 'his memory was wonderful, his power of quotation almost unlimited', as it remained for the rest of his life. He used to take long walks in Windsor Forest and in the Home Park, and as he walked along 'with his peculiar dancing step, he would pour out in his unforgettable voice the treasures which he had gathered at his last sitting. Other boys would watch him with amazement, looking upon him as a sort of inspired elfin – somebody belonging to another sphere. None dreamt of interfering with him. . . . He carried with him one magic charm – he was absolutely courageous. He did not know what fear meant. . . . Swinburne's pluck as a boy reminds me of Kinglake's description in *Eothen* of Dr Keate. . . . "He was little more (if more at all) than five feet in height, and was not very great in girth, but within this space was concentrated the pluck of ten battalions." That was Swinburne all over. . . . Of games he took no heed; I do not think that he ever possessed a cricket bat, but of walking and swimming he never tired. . . . He was no horseman. . . . But in the matter of horses he was absolutely without terror. He, unskilled though he was, would ride anything as fearless as a Centaur.'[6] Later, of course, riding became a passion.

During the summer holidays of 1849, Algernon's parents took him to Mount Rydal to see the aged Wordsworth, who recited Gray's *Elegy* to him – a poem which Swinburne ever after thoroughly disliked. The Laureate then took his visitors on a tour of inspection of his house, showing them some tokens of royal recognition of his genius. At their departure, he said that Algernon would never forget the interview in so dismal a voice that the boy burst into tears. Somewhat later, Samuel Rogers proved more encouraging and, laying his hand on Algernon's carroty head, pronounced: 'I prophesy that you, too, will be a poet.' In 1851, Queen Victoria and Prince Albert visited Eton and Algernon celebrated the occasion by writing 'The Triumph of Gloriana' with easy accomplishment in the manner of Pope.

It would seem fairly obvious that Swinburne's lifelong obsession with flagellation had its origin in the beatings he both witnessed and received at the notorious Eton flogging block. We are told that his tutor, the Reverend Jim Joynes, in whose house he lived, was not a particularly stern disciplinarian and A. C. Benson gives an affectionate portrait of him in *Memories and Friends*. Nevertheless, Swinburne's description of his methods *seem* circumstantial enough. 'I have known him (I am really speaking now in my own person) prepare the flogging room (*not* with *corduroy* or *onion*) but with burnt scents,' he wrote to Lord Houghton on 10 February 1863, 'or choose a *sweet* place out of doors with smell of fir-wood. *This* I call real delicate torment. . . . Once, before giving me a swishing that I had the marks of for more than a month (so fellows declared that I went to swim with), he let me saturate my face with eau-de-cologne. I conjecture now on looking back to that "rosy hour" with eyes purged by the euphrasy and rue of the Marquis de Sade and his philosophy that, counting on the pungency of the perfume and its power over the nerves, he meant to stimulate and excite the senses by the preliminary pleasure so as to inflict acuter pain afterwards on their awakened and intensified susceptibility . . . but he was a stunning tutor; his one pet subject was *metre*, and I firmly believe that my ears for verses made me rather a favourite. I can boast that of all the swishings I ever had up to seventeen and over, I never had one for a false quantity in my life. . . . One comfort is that I made it up in arithmetic so my tutor never wanted reasons for making rhymes between his birch and my body.' And in the last paragraph he assures Houghton again that what he has told him is 'the experience of a real live boy'.[7] But was it? When reading his recollections one can never be quite sure how much is based on actual fact and how much is fantasy. A. E. Housman, for instance, wrote to Gosse that he found Swinburne's anecdotes of being flogged by his tutors 'perplexing because Etonians tell me that the only person privileged to flog is the headmaster'.[8] On the other hand, A. C. Benson tells us: 'There is a well-known caricature in *Vanity Fair* of Joynes standing in cap and gown, brandishing a birch and pointing with an air at once sinister and pastoral to the flogging block: he at least was prepared to do his part! The half-closed eyes, with their dull shadows, the big devouring mouth, give the picture a grim quality. . . . It was like the original in a sense, but only in one, and that a rare mood.'[9] Rare or not, Eton evidently had a good deal to answer for in the development of the morbid side of Swinburne's character.

A writer in a recent number of the *Listener*, during a lengthy correspondence on Wagner, pointed out that if Nazi tendencies can be found in *The Ring*, then *The Messiah* should be considered a sadistic work on the evidence of the aria which describes with relish the punishments in store for the enemies of the Lord – 'He shall break them with a rod of iron', and 'dash them to pieces'. But it is *Israel in Egypt* which exultantly describes the plagues visited by the Lord upon the Egyptians. Swinburne has told us himself that many of the choruses of *Atalanta in Calydon* were directly inspired by Handel's choruses played on the organ by his cousin Mary Gordon. Moreover, it has been shown by Lafourcade, who has undertaken the closest analysis of Swinburne's work, that underlying *Atalanta* may be found the essential philosophy of de Sade, which he had then only lately discovered. This did not become so apparent, however, until the publication of *Chastelard* and *Poems and Ballads*, *First Series*, many of which were written before *Atalanta*. Of 'Faustine' Ruskin wrote to the author that 'it made me all hot, like pies with the devil's fingers in them. It's glorious!'

At Eton, Gosse tells us that Swinburne's appreciation of Latin poetry was 'less cordial' than his love of Greek. But Catullus 'gave him pleasure of an ecstatic kind', also Sappho, both of whom he discovered for himself, for when he wrote a poem in the same metre as Catullus's 'Atys', he tells us that he was beaten by Joynes for impertinence. So both Sappho and Catullus, as Nicolson remarks, 'retained for him ever afterwards the attraction of forbidden fruit'. Swinburne left Eton with only an average knowledge of Greek and the success of his elegiacs, when he was 'sent up for good' to the Headmaster, was probably due more, Gosse thinks, 'to his extraordinary gift for imitation than to any precocious knowledge of the Greek language. The mediocrity of his record, on arriving at Oxford, bears this out.' But, from what we know of Swinburne's rare intellectual endowments, this can only be accounted for by assuming that he simply did not bother to exert himself to his full capacity. Even so, he remains one of the most highly endowed poets in the language, drawing upon the traditions of not only English, but French, Italian, Greek and Latin literature. In this respect he was almost as learned a poet as Milton. Landor's *Hellenics* remained an abiding influence throughout his life. In 1852 he read Hugo's *Notre Dame de Paris* and, in the following year, *Les Châtiments*, which produced in him 'a sort of rapturous and adoring despair'. During the holidays, he used to wander along the beach between Bonchurch and Shanklin declaiming Hugo's rhetoric to the waves and, while riding over the downs with Mary Gordon, he would recite long passages from Macaulay's *Lays of Ancient Rome*.

The records of Swinburne's behaviour at school represent him as 'unaggressive and self-contained, gentle, courteous and gay'. Being of a highly nervous disposition, Lord Redesdale tells us that 'the smallest obstacle ruffled him'. From earliest childhood he had the trick, whenever excited, of stretching down his arms from the shoulder and giving quick vibrating jerks with his hands, a habit to which his family attributed his sloping shoulders. If he happened to be seated at moments of excitement, he would jerk his legs and twist his feet also. 'At such times,' says Gosse, 'his face would grow radiant with a rapt expression.' A specialist his parents consulted about his odd, jerking movements and fluttering hands gave it as his opinion that these symptoms were due to 'an excess of electric vitality' and that it would be most dangerous to attempt to correct them.

At the age of sixteen or so, Swinburne became difficult to deal with and his tutor complained of increasing idleness and lack of discipline. It is possible that at this stage he may have been beaten more frequently. He said later that he much preferred a beating to spending hours writing out 'lines'. For one thing a beating was soon over and, like other boys, he also took pride in it as a test of his courage. It was and probably still is at most English public schools the custom for boys to compare notes on their ability 'to take it' without breaking down. Most boys at that time seem to have taken corporal punishment as a matter of course and to have soon forgotten about it. Unfortunately, in Swinburne's case, the effects of being beaten and seeing others birched were not so transitory: they warped his nature and developed into an obsession that remained with him for the rest of his life.

To everyone's surprise, Swinburne was removed from Eton in July 1853 at the age of sixteen. After the summer holidays at East Dene, he was sent to Cambo, Northumberland, to be prepared for Oxford by the Reverend John Wilkinson, vicar of his grandfather's parish. Wilkinson complained that the boy was too clever by half and would never study. He seems to have spent most of his time out riding on the moors, swimming in the cold Northumbrian seas and visiting Wallington, the Georgian family seat of the Trevelyans. At Wallington, he came under the benign influence of Lady Pauline, the friend of Ruskin and patroness of the Pre-Raphaelites. In a letter to Edmund Gosse of 8 June 1916, printed as 'Appendix II' of the *Life*, Sir George Otto Trevelyan, the historian, describes Lady Pauline as 'a woman of singular and unique charm; quiet and quaint in manner, nobly emotional, ingrainedly artistic, very wise and sensible, with an ever-flowing spring of the most delicious humour. No friend of hers, man or woman, could ever have enough of her company; and those friends were many, and included the first people of the day in every province of distinction. She was Algernon Swinburne's good angel; and (to quote one of his letters) he regarded her with "filial feelings".' In 1854 she was thirty-eight, twenty years younger than her husband, Sir Walter, who spent most of his time in geological and botanical research. He was an unbending Puritan. One day, finding a novel by Balzac, which Swinburne had given to his wife, lying on the drawing-room table, he took it up and threw it into the fire. Swinburne immediately walked out of the house. No decent person, let alone a lady, in those days read French novels. It is unlikely that Sir Walter approved of Swinburne, or that he ever heard him reading any of his poems. But Swinburne had his revenge upon him later in the ironic portrait of Ernest Radworth in *Love's Cross-Currents.* It has been argued that in Lady Midhurst, Swinburne also drew a portrait of Lady Pauline Trevelyan.

It was on Ruskin's advice that in 1855 the central court of Wallington was roofed over by Dobson, the Newcastle architect, and William Bell Scott was engaged to decorate the walls with scenes from the history of Northumberland from Roman times. The most interesting of these is 'Iron and Coal', done in 1861, representing the Quayside at Newcastle shortly before the building of the High Level Bridge. It must be about the first representation of heavy industry in Victorian painting and contains a portrait of Sir Walter Trevelyan, in peaked cap and leather apron, as one of the workmen, wielding a large hammer. In the foreground is a careful painting of a Newcastle newspaper and a little girl sitting on an iron girder, reminiscent of one of the figures, in Madox Brown's *Work.* Bell Scott himself was not a particularly agreeable character and soon became jealous of Lady Pauline's affection for Swinburne, a feeling frequently displayed in his slyly censorious letters. He recalls seeing Swinburne riding over to Wallington from Capheaton on a long-tailed pony, a bundle of books strapped to his saddle, and he pointed out his close resemblance to Galeazzo Malatesta in Uccello's *Battle of San Egidio.*

That Lady Pauline was herself a gifted amateur painter may be seen from her floral panel in the great hall at Wallington. Ruskin did an exquisite companion panel of oats and blue corn flowers, which he insisted upon calling 'corn cockles'. It is, however, uncompleted, and the story goes that when his hostess told him that corn flowers were not the same as corn cockles, he threw down his brush in a pet and left the house. In August 1853 Ruskin had visited Capheaton to see Sir John Edward's Turners. If he had not already met Algernon at Wallington, he may very well have done so then.

News of the madly heroic Balaclava Charge – when a company of English lancers charged the Russian artillery at point-blank range along a narrow defile in the Crimea – reached East Dene in October 1854, and Algernon was fired with the romantic ambition to become a cavalry officer. The idea may seem to us absurd, but it is nevertheless a testimony to his courage, and his parents did not like to refuse outright. Instead, they took three days to think it over before gravely vetoing the request. In his disappointment and to prove to himself that he was not a coward, during the Christmas holidays Algernon climbed the practically vertical Culver Cliff, ten miles to the north of Bonchurch. Many years later, he wrote a detailed account of the exploit to his cousin, Mary Gordon, who quotes him as saying that 'my never having heard of the occurrence showed that he was not a boy to brag or swagger'. In the first few sentences Swinburne refers to himself in the third person. The letter is undated:[10]

> If you really want to know about my doing Culver, I don't mind telling you. . . . But he didn't care to talk about the great disappointment of his life. After leaving Eton near the end of his seventeenth year he wanted to go into the army. Didn't he, poor chap! The Balaklava Charge eclipsed all other visions. To be prepared for such a chance as that, instead of being prepared for Oxford, was the one dream of his life. I am sure you won't deride it because he was but a little, slightly built chap. My mother was not altogether against it, and told me that they must take three days to think the matter over. I never said a word even to A. [his eldest sister, Alice] about it, but at the end of three days they told me it could not be; my father had made up his mind. I dare say now he was quite right. But then I couldn't and didn't say anything. It was about the middle of the Christmas holidays, and I went out for a good hard tramp by the sea till I found myself at the foot of Culver Cliff; and then all at once it came upon me that it was all very well to fancy or dream of 'deadly danger' and forlorn hopes and cavalry charges, when I had never run any greater risk than a football 'rooge'; but that there was a chance of testing my nerve in face of death which could not be surpassed. So I climbed a rock under the highest point, and stripped, and climbed down again, and just took a souse into the sea to steady and strengthen my nerve, which I knew the sharp chill would, and climbed up again, thinking how easy it would be to climb the whole face of the cliff naked – or at least how much more sure one would feel of being able to do it – if one did not mind mere scratches and bruises; but to that prehistoric sort of proceeding there were obviously other objections than the atmosphere of mid-winter. So I dressed and went straight at it. It wasn't so hard as it looked, most of the way, for a light weight with a sure foot and a good steady hand; but as I got near the top I remember thinking I should not like to have to climb down again. In a minute or two more I found that I must, as the top part (or top story) of the precipice came jutting out aslant above me for some feet. Even a real sea-gull could not have worked

its way up without using or spreading its wings. So of course I felt I must not stop to think for one second, and began climbing down, hand under hand, as fast and as steadily as I could, till I reached the bottom, and (equally of course) began to look out for another possible point of ascent at the same height. As I began again I must own I felt like setting my teeth and swearing I would not come down again alive – if I did return to the foot of the cliff again it should be in a fragmentary condition, and there would not be much of me to pick up. I was most of the way up again when I heard a sudden sound as of loud music, reminding me instantly of 'the anthem' from the Eton College organ, a little below me to the left. I knew it would be almost certain death to look down, and the next minute there was no need: I glanced aside, and saw the opening of a great hollow in the upper cliff, out of which came swarming a perfect flock of 'the others' [seagulls, of which he loved to speak as being his brothers and sisters – the 'others', in home parlance, writes Mrs Disney-Leith], who evidently had never seen a wingless brother so near the family quarters before. They rose all about me in a heaving cloud – at least, I really don't think the phrase exaggerates the density of their 'congregated wings' – and then scattered. It did flash across me for a minute how nasty it would be if they flew at me and went for my indefensible eyes; but, of course, they never thought of anything so unnatural and unfraternal. I was a little higher, quite near the top or well within hail of it, when I thought how queer it would be if my very scanty foothold gave way; and at that very minute it did (I assure you on my word of honour that this is the exact truth, strange as it sounds and is), and I swung in the air by my hands from a ledge on the cliff which just gave room for my fingers to cling and hold on. There was a projection of rock to the left at which I flung out my feet sideways and just reached it; this enabled me to get breath and crawl at full speed (so to say) up the remaining bit of cliff. At the top I had not strength enough left to turn or stir; I lay on my right side helpless, and just had time to think what a sell (and what an inevitable one) it would be if I were to roll back over the edge after all, when I became unconscious – as suddenly and utterly and painlessly as I did many years afterwards when I was 'picked up at sea' by a Norman fishing boat upwards of three miles (they told me) off the coast of Étretât, and could just clutch hold of the oar they held out; 'but that is not in this story' – which I hope is not too long for the reader. On returning to conscious life I found a sheep's nose just over mine, and the poor good fellow-creature's eyes gazing into my face with a look of such kind pity and sympathy as well as surprise and perplexity that I never ought to have eaten a mutton-chop again. I couldn't help bursting into such a shout of laughter (I did the same thing when I 'came to' in the boat . . . ) that the sheep scuttled off like a boy out of bounds at sight of one of the masters. I don't think I was

1 Swinburne aged 23, from the painting by William Bell Scott

2 Sir John Edward Swinburne, 1785, from the painting by Thomas Gainsborough

ever so hungry as when I got back to East Dene, and found that everyone was out looking for me (or so the servants said). After eating and sleeping I had an interview with my mother, of which I should not care to write except to the daughter of yours. Of course she wanted to know why I had done such a thing, and when I told her she laughed a short sweet laugh most satisfactory to the young ear, and said 'Nobody ever thought you were a coward, my boy.' I said that was all very well: but how could I tell till I tried? 'But you won't do it again?' she said. I replied, of course not – where would be the fun? I knew now that it could be done, and I only wanted to do it because nobody thought it could.

A great deal of the young Swinburne comes out in this letter, though it was written in later life a good many years after the event. But the essential youthfulness of spirit, which he never lost, is still there, as is the ambition to prove himself, impelled by what Harold Nicolson calls his 'virility complex'. For by imprisoning this dauntless and defiant spirit in so apparently helpless a little body, nature had played him a particularly scurvy trick.

Early in 1855 Swinburne left East Dene to prepare finally for Oxford with the Reverend Russell Woodford, who had just been appointed Vicar of Kempsford, near Lechlade, Gloucestershire, and who later became Bishop of Ely. Woodford had settled for a time near East Dene and is probably to be identified as the tutor who visited the house daily to coach Swinburne after he had left Eton. Thomas Snow, who shared in the duties of coaching at Kempsford, remembers how Swinburne would 'declaim Greek poetry to a late hour of the night'. Woodford took him through most of Juvenal, which Swinburne thoroughly enjoyed, Juvenal being on the syllabus of the Oxford entrance examination, though he disliked Horace.

During the summer holidays of this term he visited Germany with his uncle, Major-General the Hon. Thomas Ashburnham. The general, an old Indian army officer, was on his way to drink the waters at Wiesbaden, and evidently found the enthusiasm of his young companion rather tiring. On 18 July Swinburne wrote the first of a series of long letters to his mother from Cologne:[11]

We have come thus far on our way safe and well, though Uncle Tom seems rather tired. Last night we slept at Liège, and the night before at Calais. Lord Sandwich accompanied us from London to Aix-la-Chapelle, and was very good-natured; he walked with me over Liège and showed me the old Bishop's Palace, with its great cloisters. I liked the old city very much; it is so beautifully placid. . . . The whole way from Liège hither was so perfectly lovely that I grudged the speed of the railway by which half the beauty was lost. . . .

Now I have got the coast clear for the Cathedral here, and really now I am come to it I don't know what to say. Such things are not to be *jabbered* of. The magnificence bewildered me on entering, the large

> arches and beautiful windows and the enormous size of the whole building; it was worth coming from anywhere to see. Uncle Tom was so good as to come with me to the Cathedral as the guide spoke only German, though I don't think he wanted to come: and waited while I saw the relics and crosses, &c. in the Sacristy and the Shrine of the Three Kings. . . . But I trust some day that we may all come here and see everything!

During the service he 'felt quite miserable, it was such a wretched feeling that while they were all praying, old men and tiny children kneeling together, I was not one of them, I was shut out as it were. I could have sat down and cried, I was so unhappy.'

They arrived at Wiesbaden on 23 July and Swinburne says that he would have enjoyed the journey down the Rhine much more had it not been for the 'muddle of smoking and jabbering fellow-travellers, and missing half which was worth seeing on board a noisy crowded steamer. . . . I can't say either that I like the prospect of a month here, though the gardens and lake are very pretty.'[12] He was soon reconciled, however, by meeting a Captain Joliffe, who had fought in the Crimea at Alma and Balaclava. Tirelessly he visited all the surrounding sights and attended a performance of Kleist's *Katchen von Heilbron*, carrying away 'a chaste and delightful impression', which, he says, 'will never vanish from my heart or my mind'. He went to Mayence with Uncle Tom's servant and was much impressed by the effigy of a crusader in the cathedral, who 'had the loveliest face you can think of, a smiling still expression, and the figure so perfect that it might move and not surprise one. . . . I then went up the tower to the belfry; saw the city and view of the country, with the junction of the Rhine and the Maine below; and then up a ladder above the belfry into the highest point, a round gallery within the upper dome, with open-work sides, to the horror and alarm of the showman, who assured me that people hardly ever went up; but of course this determined me to go, and I did, whereof I am rather conceited, especially as the great clock struck four, making the most awful noise just as I was halfway up the ladder, and made the whole place shake and rattle. The view was very fine.'[13]

On 13 August they left for Wartzburg, and spent the inside of a week at Nuremburg. During the night of the twenty-third, while crossing the Channel to England from Ostend, their boat was caught in a great storm. Uncle Tom swore that he had never known anything like it outside the tropics. To Swinburne's delighted imagination, it suggested Victor Hugo. Fourteen years later he recalled it vividly in the opening paragraph of his review of *L'Homme Qui Rit*:[14]

> Once only in my life I have seen the likeness of Victor Hugo's genius. Crossing over when a boy from Ostend, I had the fortune to be caught in midchannel by a thunderstorm strong enough to delay the packet some three good hours over the due time. About midnight the thundercloud

was right over head, full of incessant sound and fire, lightening and darkening so rapidly that it seemed to have life, and a delight in its life. At the same hour the sky was clear to the west, and all along the sea-line there sprang and sank as to music a restless dance or chase of summer lightenings across the lower sky: a race and riot of lights, beautiful and rapid as a course of shining Oceanides along the tremulous floor of the sea. Eastward at the same moment the space of clear sky was higher and wider, a splendid semi-circle of too intense purity to be called blue; it was of no colour nameable by man; and midway in it between the storm and the sea hung the motionless full moon; Artemis watching with a serene splendour of scorn the battle of Titans and the revel of nymphs, from her stainless and Olympian summit of divine indifferent light. Underneath and about us the sea was paved with flame; the whole water trembled and hissed with phosphoric fire; even through the wind and thunder I could hear the crackling and sputtering of the water-sparks. In the same heaven and in the same hour there shone at once the three contrasted glories, golden and fiery and white, of moonlight and of the double lightenings, forked and sheet; and under all this miraculous heaven lay a flaming floor of water.

# CHAPTER THREE

# 1856–60
# OXFORD

Swinburne went up to Balliol in January 1856, matriculating on the twenty-fourth. Robert Scott was Master and Jowett Professor of Greek, though it was not until later that he became an important influence in Swinburne's life. Three months after his arrival, in May, Birkbeck Hill wrote that he had 'dined at the Observatory and met a Balliol friend of mine – Swinburne – with his father Captain Swinburne'. Hill was at Pembroke and was a friend of Edwin Hatch and the members of the 'Birmingham set', which included Burne-Jones (then still plain Jones) and William Morris. Another friend of Swinburne was Walter Sewell, Warden of Radley, the brother of Elizabeth Sewell, the Bonchurch schoolmistress. But after his defence of Tennyson's *Maud* at the school debating society and after Sewell had been told that he had developed 'theories of free-thinking in religion', Radley was closed to him.

Apart from the fact that the theological atmosphere of the university in the aftermath of the Oxford Movement, when Jowett was still being attacked for heresy, became increasingly repellent to him, Swinburne's free-thinking derived directly from the Old Mortality Society, founded just about this time by John Nichol, in whose rooms the statutes of the Society were drafted, and who was to play an important part in the formation of Swinburne's opinions. Birkbeck Hill was also a member. The object of the Society was 'stimulating and promoting the interchange of thought among the members on the more general questions of literature, philosophy, science, as well as the diffusion of a correct knowledge and critical appreciation of our Standard English authors'. The Society derived its somewhat depressing name 'from the consideration that every member of the said Society was or has lately been in so weak and precarious a condition of bodily health as plainly and manifestly to instance the great frailties and so to speak mortality of his own human life and constitution'. Swinburne was, as far as we know, then in an excellent state of health. The same could not be said of Nichol, who drank, and was three or four years older than the other members, none of whom were partial to taking any form of exercise. We hear that they were 'a revolutionary set and read Browning'. The Society was later to publish a monthly journal, *Undergraduate Papers*, in which Swinburne's projected long poem *Queen Yseult*, written in close imitation of William Morris, began to appear from 1857–58, as well as a number of his essays. The Society was dominated by Nichol, who, at the age of fifteen, had been an undergraduate at Glasgow University, where his essays had won prizes. He was a considerable help to Swinburne in his university work in the study of logic, for which he had little aptitude. Nichol was also responsible for finally destroying Swinburne's religious faith and confirming him in atheism and republicanism.

Swinburne put up in his rooms a portrait of Orsini, who had attempted to assassinate Napoleon III, and by the autumn of 1856 had written his *Ode to Mazzini*, in which he abuses Ferdinand of Naples as 'Bourbon's murderous dotard' and calls for English intervention in Italy against Austria, and *The Temple of Janus*, an apology for tyrannicide and liberty.

*The Temple of Janus*, presented as a Newdigate prize poem in 1857, was preserved by Isobel Swinburne and deposited in the British Museum (B.M. Add. MS. 40888) in 1915. It is written in heroic couplets, as required, and is in praise of republican Rome, from the time of the expulsion of the Tarquin to the early days of the empire and the revival of the republic by Rienzi. The history of Rome is then carried forward through 'the silent years' of those who ruled 'By fraud and force and the blind strength of fears', to Ferdinand, 'the crowned snake of Naples'. It ends with the prophecy of 'The visioned Rome that nobler hours shall bring', the new Rome of Mazzini, more beautiful, with Liberty crowned at her side and the serpent of evil crushed beneath her foot. The vision fades and the poet finds himself alone by the sea at dawn. For Swinburne, the idea of liberty was ever associated with the great forces of nature, the seas, the stars, the irresistible flood of great rivers, recalling Byron, Shelley, Dante, Victor Hugo and Landor. In *The Temple of Janus*, the fervour of his love for Italy and Mazzini, which was to find more abstract and rhetorical expression in *Songs Before Sunrise*, is already apparent.

The poem, though a considerable *tour-de-force*, did not win the Newdigate prize, the judges probably being repelled by its outspoken republicanism and the insulting reference to Ferdinand of Naples, who was, after all, still reigning. The dominant influences throughout are Aeschylus, Dryden and Shelley:

O ye whose snow-white plumes
Winnow the illimitable wastes of air. . . .
and ye
Whose viewless footsteps whiten the dim sea
With gleaming foam and rainbow lights of spray,
And ye whose unimaginable way
Is past the starry watch fires of the night. . . .
O children of the many-coloured year,
Wild hours that speed the unslumbering seasons, hear!

Certainly *The Temple of Janus* is far more than a brilliant mixture of influences and at times one can detect accents prophetic of the mature Swinburne of *Atalanta in Calydon*, *The Garden of Proserpine* and *Ave Atque Vale*.

> I stood in thought among the buried years;
> I saw the daily veil of things undrawn
> And the grey gleam of immemorial dawn
> Upon the shoreless waters of the Past. . . .

And:

> and where he stood
> Swift ripples whispering through the lighted flood
> Filled with low sound that glorious solitude,
> Whose echoes died of their divine delight. . .

At the same time, Swinburne was writing, for his tutor at Balliol, calmly judicious political essays on such subjects as 'The Constitutional Influence of Small Republics' and 'English Government in India'. Of the mutiny and its effects, he observes:

> No man could wish to stand between them [the rebels] and retribution, but retribution will no more regenerate Indian politics than it will bring back the dead. How, we repeat, is this problem of adapting governments and reconciling nations to be finally settled, when the question lies once more between conquerors and the conquered? On that solution will depend, whether (as our political enemies affirm) English power will perish and be forgotten, or whether centuries hence a great Indian Empire will dwell under the shadow of the banner of our native land.

In the light of history, this observation is remarkably prescient. Swinburne condemns English repression in India in the light of his republican principles.

In support of the same principles, he contributed to *Undergraduate Papers* of March 1857 an article on 'Church Imperialism', an attack on Napoleon III's French Empire and its clerical supporters with many violent quotations from Hugo's *Les Châtiments*, and it is remarkable for its intimate knowledge of French politics. Swinburne's hatred of Napoleon, inflamed of course by Hugo and the massive deportations of 1852, was expressed in his poem *A Song in Time of Order*, first published in the *Spectator*, 26 April 1862, and reprinted in *Poems and Ballads, First Series*, but written at this time, with its savage lines: 'We shall see Buonaparte the Bastard/Kick heels with his throat in a rope.' In the event, Napoleon III ended his days peaceably at Chichester. The essays are contained in a notebook of forty-eight pages, with Swinburne's signature, in the T. J. Wise Collection in the British Museum. Some of them are initialled 'R.S.' – that is, Robert Scott, Master of Balliol. It was not generally realized, until Georges Lafourcade pointed it out in his *La Jeunesse de Swinburne*, how politically conscious the poet was during his Oxford years. Another essay, 'Foreign Intervention', castigates 'the cowardice of England' for not re-establishing order and justice in Naples.

To another number of *Undergraduate Papers*, Swinburne contributed the mock-censorious review, which curiously anticipates the sort of reviews he was to have himself for his own poems, of *The Monomaniac's Tragedy and Other Poems* by Ernest Wheldrake, author of 'Eve: A Mystery'. He quotes passages from the imaginary *Eve* to show how the author dwelt upon 'unbecoming topics' like 'wine-dishevelled tresses' and 'globed sapphires of liquescent eyes, warmed with prenatal influx of rich love'. The hero of *The Monomaniac's Tragedy* is writing 'Iscariot: A Tragedy' and, in order to gain experience of the feelings of thieves and murderers, has broken into his brother's house and wrung his nephew's neck. The work is an early example of Swinburne's peculiar sense of humour. He was to repeat the same sort of hoax in his two reviews of the works of imaginary French poets for the *Spectator*, though the editor's suspicions were aroused by the exaggerated obscenity of the passages quoted.

Meanwhile, in the autumn of 1857, another powerful influence was to divert Swinburne temporarily from his political preoccupations, when he met Morris and Jones, late of Exeter College, during their decoration of the walls and ceiling of the Union debating hall under the aegis of Rossetti, with frescoes of subjects from the *Morte d'Arthur*. He was already familiar with their work, which had begun to appear in the *Oxford and Cambridge Magazine* in January 1856. In November, Edwin Hatch took him along to be introduced to the artists at work. Morris had finished his picture of Sir Tristram among the sunflowers, called 'How Sir Palomydes loved La Belle Iseult with an exceeding great love, but how she loved not him but rather Sir Tristram' – a subject that was to be tragically prophetic of his own emotional life – and was already at work with Charles Faulkner painting the ceiling with heraldic beasts. Rossetti and Jones were similarly engaged, with other of their friends, in the gallery that ran round the great circular room between the cinquefoil windows, their pictures gradually emerging with a brilliant freshness of colour that was soon to fade into the damp brickwork. The work proceeded amid shouts of laughter, obscene jokes and the popping of soda-water bottles. Thus 'dear little Carrots', as Burne-Jones called Swinburne, was suddenly introduced, from the earnest political world of Nichol and *Undergraduate Papers*, to the 'jovial' campaign of later Pre-Raphaelite medievalism – not that these artists were less earnest and dedicated than Nichol himself, though they managed to combine their medievalist ideals with a riotous horseplay which Swinburne found quite enchanting.

William Morris himself, known as 'Topsy' to his friends, with his powerful physique, fair beard and fine features, despite his shortness of stature, must have seemed the very incarnation of medieval chivalry and knightly prowess, especially when he donned the coat of mail, the casque and sword he had had designed and made for him by a local smith. The spectacle as a whole must have been sufficiently astonishing, especially when the visor of Morris's helmet got stuck and refused to open and he was left dancing with rage and roaring inside. There was a native innocence, a modesty and humility about Morris which endeared him to his friends and made him the constant butt of their practical jokes. Though at this time, under Rossetti's influence, he intended to devote himself to painting, he had already written most of the poems published in the next year in *The Defence of Guenevere.* Swinburne was soon writing his *Queen Yseult* on all-too-close imitation.

In contrast to the florid, ebullient Morris and the pale, elfin-like Edward Jones, even more impressive perhaps was the dominant figure of Dante Gabriel Rossetti – burly, stocky, full of slang, with his dark hair and olive complexion and his fanatical devotion to art. But between Jones, known as 'Ned', and 'little Carrots' there was an immediate sympathy. 'Now we are four and not *three*,' he exclaimed on being presented to Swinburne. It was to Burne-Jones that Swinburne dedicated his *Poems and Ballads* (1866), and to Rossetti that he posed in the act of kissing Fanny Cornforth for the cover-design of Rossetti's translations of the early Italian poets. Morris read his poems to him and Swinburne came to love him as an elder brother. Morris's poems, though all founded upon recognizable medieval models, have a startling force and richness of colour comparable to thirteenth-century stained-glass, at once more virile and more clumsy than Tennyson. When Swinburne, in his turn, read the first canto of *Queen Yseult*, Morris characteristically exclaimed that it was much better than his own poems – 'which opinion I took the liberty to tell him was absurd', Swinburne wrote to Nichol on 13 December 1857. But then he always derived satisfaction, when he was not in open rebellion, in subjecting himself to a stronger nature than his own.

In *Queen Yseult*, Swinburne was not imitating the poems published in *The Defence of Guenevere* so much as the early poems which Morris did not publish, though his principal source was the thirteenth- and fourteenth-century English metrical romance *Sir Tristrem.* He also seems to have known the *Tristan* of Béroul and some fragments of the English *Tristram* of Thomas.[1] But, of course, Morris had himself been following medieval romances, such as *Sire Degrevant*, scenes from which Burne-Jones was to paint on the walls of the great room at Red House.

When Morris said that Swinburne's *Queen Yseult* was better than his own poetry, he was, in a sense, right. Morris's lines from *Blanche*, which he did not publish, suggest nothing so much as George du Maurier's parody of Pre-Raphaelite verse, *A Legend of Camelot:*

Many flowers grew around
And about her is the sound
Of the dead leaves on the ground.

There she knelt upon her knees,
There between the aspen trees.
O! the dream right dreary is.

Now Swinburne's *Queen Yseult*:

A great wonder took him there,
For her face was very fair
Under all her gathered hair.

At her side no queen might stand,
Was none like her in the land,
Golden hair and arrow hand. . . .

Clothéd queenlike sate she there,
Sate she in the moonlight bare,
Golden light and golden hair.

Pre-Raphaelite pastiche or not, such lines have an individual charm and accomplishment. Swinburne is less successful in dramatic narrative, when compared to such poems of Morris's as 'The Defence of Guenevere' itself, or 'Concerning Geffray Teste Noir', or 'The Haystack in the Floods'. There is a passion and drama in such poems which is absent from Swinburne's early imitative verse. Moreover, Miss Jean Overton Fuller has pointed out that Tristram plays a peculiarly passive role in Swinburne's poem. As he does not know the way to Iseult's bed-chamber at Tintagel, she carries him there on her back:[2]

she raised him tenderly,
Bore him lightly as might be,
That was wonderful to see.

So they passed by trail and track,
Slowly in the night all black,
And she bore him on her back.

As they twain went on along
Such great love had made her strong,
All her heart was full of song.

This episode Swinburne took, as Lafourcade shows,[3] from the twelfth-century *Chronicle of Charlemagne*, where a page, Eginhard, is carried in the arms of Emma, which event is neither peculiar nor out of place. The interesting thing is that in his poem Swinburne reverses the usual sexual roles, unconsciously seeing Tristram as small and passive as himself. The imagination boggles at the thought of such a scene taking place in the second act of Wagner's *Tristan and Isolde*!

After *Queen Yseult*, Swinburne was to develop along quite different lines, and so was Morris after *The Defence of Guenevere*. Indeed, Morris was never again to recapture the glowing colours and sharp visual impact of his first volume. Swinburne also wrote another long fragment in an entirely different measure, *Joyeuse Garde*, which forecasts some of the pieces in the first *Poems and Ballads*. He was to return to this theme on a grander, more rhetorical, scale in 1869, when he wrote the *Prologue* to *Tristram of Lyonesse*; but he was not to take it up again and complete it until the 1880s. As with Morris, the larger and later version compares somewhat unfavourably with the experimental pieces of this early period, which have much of the moving simplicity of their medieval sources. There is indeed much the same difference between them as between a *trouvère*'s recitation to the lute and the thick *impasto* and orchestral splendour of Wagner's *Tristan*, which Swinburne said that he found 'stimulating' when writing *Tristram of Lyonesse.*

Another early piece of this time is *Lancelot*:

Very long and hot it was
The dry light on the dry grass
The set noon on lakes of glass
  All that summer time. . . .

For the ship that seemed to pass
Through the sea of fiery glass,
That strange ship my own soul was,
  And my life the sea.

The same form is used by Morris in 'The Chapel in Lyonesse' and derives from medieval miracle plays, especially *Noah's Flood.* Swinburne also imitated Morris by writing a ballad with a French refrain in 'My Lady':

Long ago I sent to her
River blossoms wet and fair,
And meadow-lilies for her hair,
  *Qui bien ayme tard oublie.*
All who see her feel a light
That changes their sense and sight
As autumns change a petal's white,
  *Qui bien ayme tard oublie.*

He recaptures the same airy delicacy in the French songs in *Chastelard*, which are, perhaps, the best part of that particularly perverse play.

Meanwhile Swinburne was pursuing his intensive study of French literature. Lafourcade has shown that between March 1859 and May 1860, he borrowed from the library of the Taylorian Institute works by Stendhal (*Chronicles*), Dumas (*Souvenirs et Mémoires*), Balzac, Ronsard, Michelet, *Lettres de Marie Stuart* in eight volumes, *Les Gloires du Romantisme*, Gervais, *Les Croisades de Saint-Louis*, and other works. To this list must be added Hugo's *Les Châtiments* and *La Légende des Siècles*, Gautier's

*Mademoiselle de Maupin* and Choderlos de Laclos's *Les Liaisons Dangereuses*. Baudelaire he read a little later. At the same time, he was a regular reader of the *Revue des Deux Mondes*. He wrote two acts of an Elizabethan drama, *The Laws of Corinth*, which he attempted to pass off as a genuine work of its period, noting: 'The first edition of this rare play was printed in quarto, 1609, the second in 1622. I have noticed their variations in the footnotes. Following these copies I have retained their divisions into Acts only.' He also wrote the first draft of a play, *Rosamond*, in which the Swinburne that we know begins to appear.

Ruskin had been so struck by Swinburne when he met him at Wallington that on his visit to Oxford in 1858, when he stayed with Dr Acland, Radcliffe Librarian and Reader in Anatomy at Christ Church, he asked to meet him again. Acland was very hospitable and Swinburne used to describe his house as full of bores, who stood about in groups and made fatuously 'aesthetic' remarks. Burne-Jones said that 'Acland's pulse was only really quickened when osteologists were by, who compared their bones with his till the conversation rattled'. Both Swinburne and Burne-Jones derived much wicked amusement from teasing the doctor. 'On one occasion,' Gosse tells us, 'when Dr Acland was so kind as to read aloud a paper on sewage, there was a scene over which the Muse of History must draw a veil.'

In January 1858 Swinburne and Edwin Hatch, who was staying at East Dene, visited Tennyson at Farringford. They called in the morning when the Laureate was busy with a poem, but he asked them to dinner that evening and read *Maud* to them until long after midnight, 'in his glorious little room', as Hatch notes in his diary. It must have been a memorable experience. Afterwards Tennyson wrote to Dr J. R. Mann that Swinburne had impressed him as 'a very modest and intelligent young fellow, but what I particularly admired in him was that he did not press upon me any verses of his own'.

On his return to Oxford, Swinburne wrote to Hatch on 17 February:[4]

> Morris's book [*The Defence of Guenevere*] is really out. Reading it, I would fain be worthy to sit down at his feet. . . . Such however, is the invincible absurdity of all poets, that he ventured to prefer *Rosamond* to 'Peter Harpdon' in a repeatedly rebuked and resolutely argued statement. It appears to me simple mania; but certainly I am glad of his words, for Rosamond is about my favourite poem, and is now verging on a satisfactory completion. The first scene as rewritten is an acknowledged improvement. But after all – I long to be with you by the firelight between the sunset and the sea and have talk of *Sordello*; it is one of my canonical scriptures. Does he sleep and forget? I think yes. Did the first time Palma's mouth trembled to touch his in the golden rose-lands of Paradise, a sudden power of angelic action come over him? . . . Who knows these matters? Only we keep the honey-stain of hair.

I write more folly to you than I dare read over, because I think you wise. So take my stupidity as a compliment. If you like it and if it prospers I will send you specimens of a new *Tristram* I am about. . . . I should like to review myself and say 'that I have an abortive covetousness of imagination in which an exaggeration of my models – i.e. blasphemy and sensuality – is happily neutralised by my own imbecility'. I flatter myself that the last sentence was worthy of the *Saturday Review*.

One evening when the *Union* was just finished – Jones and I had a great talk. Stanhope and Swan attacked, and we defended, our idea of Heaven, viz. a rose-garden full of stunners. Atrocities of an appalling nature were uttered on the other side. We became so fierce that two respectable members of the University – entering to see the pictures – stood mute and looked at us. We spoke just then of kisses in Paradise, and expounded our ideas on the celestial development of that necessity of life; and after listening five minutes to our language, they literally fled from the room! Conceive our mutual ecstasy of delight.

All my people desire to be remembered to you. I had a long letter from Edith [his sister] the other day: I know you will be glad to hear this, as I am to think of Morris having that wonderful and most perfect stunner of his to – look at or speak to. The idea of his marrying her is insane. To kiss her feet is the utmost man should dream of doing.

Mind you send for his book at once; read it, and repent your former heresies, or I will review it somewhere and say that he is to Tennyson what Tennyson is to Dobell or Dobell to Tupper.

Morris married his 'stunner', Jane Burden, the daughter of a Hollywell Street groom, next year in April and was to find, during the course of an unhappy and frustrating marriage, that Swinburne's semi-serious words were prophetic. A postscript to this letter mentions that 'The Albigenses' are not yet organized. 'I must read more, and then dash at it in wrath' – indicating that Swinburne was contemplating an epic poem on a subject which would have given him plenty of scope for sadistic description. But he did write next year a Renaissance drama, *Laugh and Lie Down*, in which he gave full expression to the sexual ambiguity of his nature. The heroine, the courtesan Imperia, cossets and whips her page, Frank, only to have him finally whipped to death. Frank and Fred, his brother, appear alternately as boys and girls.

Writing to J. C. Collins on 14 October 1873, Swinburne says: 'I suppose you can tell me nothing of the *other* comedy attributed to C. T[ourneur] by Lowndes, with the charming title of "Laugh and Lie Down". I was so delighted with the name that in my last Oxford year I wrote in three days three acts of a comedy, after (a long way after) the late manner of Fletcher, under that title; but I shall take good care that this one never sees the light!'[5] The three acts were to survive, however, with the fragment of a fourth act in the collection of T. J. Wise, among the papers doubtless sold to him after

Swinburne's death by Watts-Dunton, and now in the British Museum. There are passages in the play which forecast the mature style of Swinburne, even though it is mostly still Elizabethan pastiche:

Thou art so fair
That in this woven wonder, your wrought hair,
Love lies and laughs, beholding his bound hands;
In your white brows his planted ensign stands
Over blue veins; your temples are smooth lands
Wherein he walks with print of quiet feet;
Your throat is tender-coloured, your breast sweet
As the first fruit the year lies down upon
To sleep a spring through till his queen be gone.

The movement of the verse is felicitous enough, but it was evidently written at high speed and left unrevised. Frank–Francescha is a unique creation, a product of the ambiguous dreams of Swinburne's adolescence, an ideal he later found embodied in the Louvre 'Hermaphrodite'. The fertility of his creative impulse was already amazing.

Edwin Hatch, who meanwhile had been ordained, was at that time preaching and teaching in East London. He arrived at Oxford on 17 April, and noted in his diary: 'Called on Swinburne, talked in his window seat in the sunset, and then went to Morris' – who could not tear himself away from Oxford because of Jane Burden. Next day Hatch 'Breakfasted with Swinburne – then Morris came – read together'. On 20 April, he noted: 'Poor Swinburne fearfully depressed, seemingly knowing little of trouble, even the slight one of having to read what is disagreeable – pleasant talk with him down the High at night.'

Swinburne's next letter to Hatch begins: 'I am very sorry to have missed you before you left us for the improving recreation of canes and chemistry, Gregorians and castigations.' He continues gaily:[6]

> Item, a review of Guenevere in the Tablet – I believe by Pollen: certainly the best as well as the most favourable review Morris has had. The party has given us no signs of life as yet: in vain has the 'Oxford County Chronicle' been crammed with such notices as the following:
>
> 'If W.M. will return to his disconsolate friends, all shall be forgiven. One word would relieve them of the most agonizing anxiety – why is it withheld?
>
> 'If the Gentleman who left a MS. (apparently in verse) in George St. will communicate with his bereaved and despairing Publishers, he will hear of something to his advantage. Otherwise the MS. will be sold (to pay expenses) as waste paper, together with stock in hand of a late volume of Poems which fell stillborn from the press.'

– which, unfortunately, was all too true.

> The town crier is to proclaim our loss to-morrow. 'Lost stolen, or strayed, an eminent artist and promising *litterateur*. (The description of his person is omitted for obvious reasons.) Had on when he was last seen the clothes of another gentleman, much worn, of which he had possessed himself in a fit of moral – and physical – abstraction. Linen (questionable) marked W. M. Swears awfully, and walks with a rolling gait, as if partially intoxicated.'

Such jokes at Morris's expense were common currency among his Oxford friends.

During his third year at Oxford, under the stimulus of Jowett's conversation, Gosse tells us, Swinburne 'paid a closer attention to his studies than he had hitherto vouchsafed'. In June 1858 he took a second in Moderations and the Taylorian Scholarship for French and Italian a few days later. In the Easter vacation he had, according to Gosse, accompanied his parents to Paris, and before going 'gave them a solemn promise' that he would do nothing while there 'to undermine the authority of Napoleon III'. Lady Trevelyan was so amused by the solemnity of the undertaking that she did a water-colour of Swinburne stripped to the waist, his red hair flying in the wind, a blunderbuss in either hand, striding across a barricade. 'He handsomely kept his word not to endanger the Empire by any overt act,' says Gosse, 'but his republican spirit boiled within him. One afternoon, driving in an open carriage in the Champs Elysées, Algernon being on the box beside the driver, the party met "the Accursèd" in his imperial person. Admiral and Lady Jane Swinburne stood up and bowed to the Emperor, who very politely raised his hat in response. "And did you take your hat off to him?" I asked. "Not wishing," the poet answered slowly in an ecstasy of ironic emphasis, "Not wishing to be obliged to cut off my hand at the wrist the moment I returned to the hotel, I did *not*!" On his reappearance at Balliol, Swinburne's rites of incantation before the portraits of Mazzini and Orsini became more extravagant than ever.'[7]

In the previous year, Matthew Arnold had been appointed Professor of Poetry at Oxford. Swinburne found his lectures cold and uninspiring, especially as he had greatly admired his lyrical poetry while at Eton, remarking: 'the "Reveller", the "Merman", "The New Sirens", I had mainly by heart in a time of childhood, just ignorant of teens'. At Eton, too, he had read 'Empedocles on Etna' on its publication. His early enthusiasm was now modified by the prejudice of Nichol, who 'full of ardour for Carlyle, deprecated the Hellenism of Arnold'.

After the departure of most of his older friends from Oxford – Rossetti, Morris, Burne-Jones, Hatch, Nichol and Spencer Stanhope – Swinburne's conduct, Gosse tells us, became turbulent and unseemly. He was looked upon as 'dangerous' by the college authorities and Jowett became anxious lest he be sent down for some extravagance – 'Balliol thereby making itself ridiculous as University had made itself about Shelley'. Swinburne would enter the Union debating hall, his head held to one side, his tie blue, as a contemporary remarks 'stepping on the toes of the principal speaker'. His friend A. V. Dicey of the Old Mortality was President of the Union and favoured his passionate interjections. Lord Sheffield recalls hearing him 'reading excitedly but ineffectively a long tirade against Napoleon, and in favour of Mazzini'. It must have been in the same speech that he delivered a Landorian oration on tyrannicide, to coincide with the Prince of Wales's arrival as an undergraduate in November. This, however, was received indulgently by the audience, which contained, as Swinburne said, several 'grave and reverend seniors'. He was following with 'frantic interest' Italy's war of liberation against Austria, but we do not know what his other extravagances were, except that they caused the authorities considerable annoyance. His most serious offences seem to have been neglect of his work and a refusal to attend morning chapel. Having been 'gated' by the Dean for non-attendance, repeated after many admonitions, he was debarred from accompanying the Old Mortality Society on an annual excursion to Edgehill in 1859. On their return, Lord Bryce told Gosse, one of the members said, '"Let us condole with poor Swinburne," and so we went to his rooms to cheer him up. He launched into a wonderful display of vituperative eloquence. He was not really angry, but he enjoyed the opportunity, and the resources of his imagination in metaphor and the amazing richness of his vocabulary had never, I think, struck us so much before.'[8] This explains the zest with which in later life Swinburne never failed to throw himself into controversy with much the same gusto as he threw himself into the sea.

The story goes – Gosse attributes it to Morris – that Swinburne thought that there were only two cab-fares, a shilling for a short drive and one-and-sixpence for a long one. On one occasion, a cabman who had been underpaid began to abuse Morris and Swinburne, 'when the latter instantly replied with such a torrent of abuse that the cabman drove off at full speed'. That trait in Swinburne would have appealed to Morris particularly, as he was himself in the habit of losing his temper and letting fly on such occasions. The difference was that Swinburne did not really lose his temper; he enjoyed giving vent to abuse for its own sake – for its aesthetic effect, so to speak. In the same way, he worked himself up into a passion over Napoleon III because Victor Hugo had done so in *Les Châtiments*. But for all that, everyone who knew Swinburne at Oxford was struck by his admirable manners and courtesy, when not over-excited. Unfortunately, he was apt to become excited rather too easily, and the majority of the dons regarded him as half-mad.

As Swinburne's behaviour became more and more extravagant and he failed to pass his exam in classics, Jowett, in consultation with the admiral, decided that it would be better if he left Oxford for a while. In November 1859, he wrote to his mother, who was abroad with the family:[9]

I have myself been rather busy since I last heard from A. and E. at Tours, in working (unhappily too late) for my first examination in Classics – which turns out a failure. I *had* hoped to get it done, and have my way clear to work for honours in the spring. As it is, I shall have them both on my hands at once, and I need not add, feel ashamed of myself.

But the claims upon him of Shakespeare's Sonnets, Marston, Fletcher and the Border Ballads proved stronger than law and political economy.

Jowett's attitude seems to have been extremely enlightened. Though he admitted that he did not understand Swinburne and described him as 'in some respects the most singular young man I have ever known' with 'extraordinary powers of imitation in writing . . . he composes (as I am told) Latin mediaeval hymns, French vaudevilles, as well as endless English poems, with the greatest facility'. While deploring the influence of the Pre-Raphaelites, Jowett concluded: 'I incline to believe that the greatest power older persons have over the young is sympathy with them. If we don't allow enough for the strange varieties of character, and often for their extreme, almost unintelligible unlikeness to ourselves, we lose influence over them, and they become alienated from fancying that they are not understood.'[10] This, from mid-Victorian Oxford, is remarkable enough!

Accordingly, it was arranged in November to send Swinburne to read modern history with the young Reverend William Stubbs, the future Bishop of Oxford and learned medieval historian, at Navestock in Essex, where Stubbs had recently married the village schoolmistress. Swinburne's stay at Navestock vicarage was to be short, but dramatic. He arrived on a Saturday evening, and Mr and Mrs Stubbs, thinking he must be tired after his journey, advised him to go to bed, saying that his breakfast would be sent up to him in the morning. Next morning, after the vicar had left the house for church, it being very fine and sunny, Swinburne came downstairs and stood at the garden gate to watch the village assemble for divine service. But, with his bush of red hair, scarlet dressing-gown and vermilion slippers, he was such a flaming apparition that the villagers, thinking that they had met the devil in person, dared not pass the vicarage gate. Since the path to the church led past the vicarage, a crowd of people gradually built up along the lane. Swinburne became more and more interested in this curious spectacle, and as his interest in them increased, so did the alarm of the villagers. 'Not a worshipper appeared in church,' writes Gosse, 'until Stubbs, at a loss to account for the absence of his parishioners, bade the clerk ring again. Still no parishioners! But at last the boldest man in Navestock, fixing his eyes on the poet and hugging the further hedge, made a bolt past the churchyard, and the entire congregation followed him in a rush. Swinburne reflected, "how oddly the Essex yokel takes his Sunday service", and then strolled back to the vicarage for luncheon.'[11] This, at least, is the version of the incident that Stubbs used to relate.

Stubbs, with the amused affection for his pupil which he never lost, used to tell another story. 'Finding Swinburne passionately devoted to the poets and remarkably learned in their works', Stubbs asked if, by any chance, he had ever written any poetry himself. Learning that he had indeed, Stubbs pressed him to read some of it to them. Thereupon, Swinburne produced the manuscript of *Rosamond*, his play about Henry II's mistress, and, beginning early in the evening, read it right through. Stubbs was much impressed, but, says Gosse, 'felt obliged to say that he thought the amatory passages somewhat objectionable'. The result of this remark was 'a long, silent stare from Swinburne, followed by a scream that rent the vicarage, and by the bolt upstairs of the enraged poet, hugging his MS. to his bosom'.

Presently, we are told, Mrs Stubbs 'stole upstairs, and tapping gently at Swinburne's door, entreated him to come down to supper. There was no reply, but an extraordinary noise within of tearing and a strange glare through the key-hole.' Strange noises continued to be heard from the poet's room all night, and in the morning Swinburne appeared 'extremely late, and deathly pale'. Stubbs, by this time feeling rather guilty, was moved to say how sorry he was that he had so hastily condemned the drama, and hoped that Swinburne had not been discouraged by his criticism. Swinburne replied: 'I lighted a fire in the grate and burned every page of my manuscript.' Stubbs was horrified. Swinburne went on: 'But it does not matter; I sat up all night and wrote it right through from memory.'[12] It is a good story!

Otherwise Swinburne's stay at Navestock was very pleasant; he apparently got on with Stubbs very much better than with Jowett, though the latter always treated him with tact and consideration. Nevertheless he did his best to discourage him from writing poetry, and particularly deplored the influence upon him of the Pre-Raphaelites.

On 16 December 1859, Swinburne wrote to William Bell Scott from Navestock parsonage:[13]

> You may suppose that your letter of the sixth was some time in finding me here, where I am staying for some weeks to read law and history for my degree, which comes on in the spring. I have got nothing ready for publication yet, and when I have I see no chance of getting funds to defray the cost – much less of discovering a judicious publisher to take the risk. Such is life! I had a jolly fortnight in London – left the Hogarth [Club] very flourishing – and saw D.G.R.'s new poems and pictures. I daresay you have heard of his head in oils of a stunner with flowers in her hair, and marigolds behind it [*Bocca Baciata*, a portrait of Fanny Cornforth]? She is more stunning than can decently be expressed. I read my 'Rosamond' to the party in question and he was pleased to approve of it much more than it deserves. Besides this, and some more of that interminable 'Catherine' [*The Queen Mother*] I have written a new ballad so indecent that it beats all the rest and is nearly up to Blake's

Klopstock – I have got *Blake's Dante* – seven plates – stunners. Also his Job. I shall bring them north next year. I wish to goodness I was going up this winter but I shan't be let, with that blessed Oxford ahead. . . .

Item – I have got the immortal Whitman's Leaves of Grass and there are jolly good things in it, I allow. Do lend yours to Lady Trevelyan. . . .

Don't you think a good dramatic subject would be Mary Stuart's amour with Chatelet? one might end with cutting off his head on the stage. . . .

Have you begun Balzac yet? I found Gabriel Rossetti in the thick of him and appreciating him very justly. You would delight in the Etudes Philosophiques which I have just purchased. . . .

Will you write to me again, when you have time? it is a true work of mercy, shut out as I suddenly am from Society except that of a very passable parson I admit (For he worships Sidonia).

Meinhold's *Sidonia von Bork*, an early-nineteenth-century Gothic novel, was much admired by Rossetti's circle in the translation by Oscar Wilde's mother.

In January 1860 Swinburne was staying with the Bell Scotts at Newcastle, and returned from the Tyne to the Thames by sea. On 8 February at Navestock he came upon the following passage in the *Guardian*:[14] 'The Vice-Chancellor of Oxford has received from "a non-resident member of the University much attached to her interests" the sum of £50, for a prize to be awarded to the writer of the best English poem on "The Life, the Character and the Death of the heroic seaman Sir John Franklin, with special reference to the time, place and discovery of his death".' The poem was to be in rhymed verse 'to be recited during the meeting of the British Association at the time and in the place which the Vice-Chancellor may appoint. All members of the University whatsoever to be at liberty to compete for the prize. The composition to be sent to the Registrar of the University on or before the 1st of June, 1860, the usual course for concealing the name of the writer and distinguishing the compositions to be followed. The judges are to be the Vice-Chancellor, the Dean of Christchurch, and Lord Ashburnham, of Christchurch.'

Swinburne decided to compete and, with Stubbs's encouragement, spent two mornings writing his fine 'The Death of Sir John Franklin'. It was to be his first original poem, linking up the tragic nineteenth-century expedition with the heroic exploits of the Elizabethan seamen who first discovered the North-West Passage:

Where the slow shapes of the grey water-weed
Freeze midway as the languid inlets freeze. . . .

What praise shall England give these men her friends?
For while the bays and the large channels flow,
In the broad sea between the iron ends

Of the poised world where no safe sail may be,
And for white miles the hard ice never blends
With the chill washing edges of dull sea –
And while to praise her green and girdled land
Shall be the same as to praise Liberty –
So long the record of these men shall stand,
Because they chose not life but rather death
Each side being weighed with a most equal hand,
Because the gift they had of English breath
They did give back to England for her sake,
Like those dead seamen of Elizabeth
And those who wrought with Nelson or with Blake
To do great England service their lives long –
High honour shall they have; their deeds shall make
Their spoken names sound sweeter than all song.

Had the judges the wit to perceive it, here was not only a new voice in English poetry, but a fine poem in its own right. It is the only poem of Swinburne in which arctic imagery predominates; it is also the first poem of his directly inspired by the sea.

For the laborious time went hard with these
Among the thousand colours and gaunt shapes
Of the strong ice cloven with breach of seas,
Where the waste sullen shadow of steep capes
Narrows across the cloudy-coloured brine,
And by strong jets the angered foam escapes;
And a sad touch of sun scores the sea-line
Right at the middle motion of the noon
And then fades sharply back, and the cliffs shine
Fierce with keen snows against a kindled moon
In the hard purple of the bitter sky.

But the prize was given to one Owen Alexander Vidal of Trinity, of whom nothing was heard again. It must be admitted, of course, that Swinburne's poem does not deal with the life, death and character of Sir John Franklin, nor with the time, place and discovery of his death, as stipulated. Nevertheless, he came second. Carried away with a characteristic afflatus, Swinburne went on to contrast the 'disastrous north' with the mariners' recollections of:

How in soft England the warm lands were starred
With gracious flowers in the green front of spring,
And all the branches' tender over-growth,
Where the quick birds took sudden heart to sing;
And how in meadows in their sweet May sloth
Grew thick with grass as soft as song or sleep.

He also, most daringly, prefaced his poem with the marvellous lines from *Pericles*:

> The unfriendly elements
> Forget thee utterly –
> Where, for a monument upon thy bones,
> And e'er-remaining lamps, the belching whale
> And humming water must o'erwhelm thy corpse;
> Lying with simple shells.

On 11 March Swinburne wrote to his mother:[15]

> I have the honour to announce that the one really awful piece of work before me is now behind me. I have completed my analysis of Blackstone's law. All that remains is by comparison to the hard parts of that work as pleasant as reading Dumas. . . . As to my Oxford sojourn I can tell you now. About a week after Easter I go up. If all is well I shall have to stay the whole term. For the little examination is at the beginning and the great one at the end.

He wrote to his mother again on 15 April, not too encouragingly:[16]

> When I have done with routine work I think of taking *periods* to read contemporary books if I can keep up with my present leaning towards history. I got out (the last time I was at Wallington) all sorts of things about Mary Stuart of the most exciting kind, down to an inventory of her gowns, which gave me great satisfaction, as they were very nice colours, and showed she had an eye for painting. I am in the meantime taking in (at Oxford) either Charlemagne or St. Louis – possibly both. That is the sort of history I like – live biographical chronicle not dead constitutional records like the respected Hallam's, over whom Mr Stubbs and I (neither without execrations) have been breaking our teeth more or less for months.

Swinburne returned to Oxford later in April 1860 to re-take his 'little examination' in classics and an honours degree in law and modern history, for which he had had to read Blackstone's *Real Property*, *The Origin of Equitable Juristry in Chancery*, Justinian, Adam Smith, the life of Louis IX and, in particular, the history of England from Charles I until 1642. In May he took a pass in classics. In June he was faced with the dreaded examinations in law and history. But a riding accident interrupted his studies, which were in any case not far enough advanced, and he hesitated whether to go in for his finals or not. Instead of working, he was writing another Elizabethan pastiche, *The Loyal Servant* in five acts, completing the first four acts and five scenes of the fifth act. Gosse describes it in a letter to Wise as 'a close, an astonishingly close and even slavish imitation or pastiche of the style of Beaumont and Fletcher'. The plot, however, was almost exactly copied from Marston's *Antonio and Mellida*. Otherwise there is the perceptible influence of Marston's *Malcontent*, of *Hamlet* and *Timon of Athens*. The piece as a whole, as Lafourcade has pointed out, marks the transition between Swinburne's early handling of Elizabethan dramatic forms and the first drafts of *Rosamond* and *Chastelard*.

'At the beginning of last week,' Swinburne wrote to his mother, 'I had a bad fall from a horse in leaping a gate. It was in the end lucky that I alighted full on my chin and the lower part of my face – but as some teeth were splintered, the jaw sprained and lips cut up it was not pleasant. For a week I have been kept in bed and fed on liquids, and still I can eat nothing but crumb of bread and such like. But I am up today and able to write, and quite well otherwise (jaws excepted) only of course not very strong. The Dr *did* last week prohibit ideas of trying to bring my ill-fated work through to some end or other (certainly the Fates *are* against my reading for honours in history), but I must stay a day or two longer to try. If I really *cannot* do enough to get fairly through and take a decent place in the list – then of course I shall not try but come up to London this week. . . . If I don't try (as everybody advises me not to) I shall be able to travel this week.'[17]

In the event, Swinburne did not sit for his finals, but joined his family in London, where he had further medical treatment for his injuries. Gosse says that he went to stay with his grandfather in Northumberland, whence he negotiated with his father who was 'deeply incensed by his son's failure at the university'.[18] He may have done so, but Sir John was in very poor health at this time, having reached the age of ninety-eight. His father's feelings may be reflected in a bitter passage from a letter of Captain Harewood to his son Reginald, in *A Year's Letters*, which is crossed out in the manuscript of the novel:[19]

> At the end of last autumn, I had the pleasure of reflecting, as I looked back over my son's school and college days, on three memorable features in them of which his friends could justly boast: that he had got himself constantly flogged, twice plucked, and once rusticated. The distinction was noble and well-merited; any boy and any father might be proud of it for life.

But Swinburne's original notes for the letter, contained in a fragmentary plan of the novel, discovered by Lafourcade in a first edition of *Poems and Ballads* – 'Summary of Redgie's character and conduct – moral and religious blow-up. Style muscular-christian' – suggest that the letter as a whole is not so much an original document as an original creation, like many of Theobald's letters to Ernest in *The Way of All Flesh*. This is made clearer still by Swinburne's letter of 21 August 1905 to William Rossetti, written when the novel appeared in book form as *Love's Cross-Currents*, in which he says of Redgie Harewood 'who (though nothing can possibly be more different than his parents from mine) is otherwise rather a coloured photograph of yours A. C. Swinburne'.

There is no doubt that Swinburne felt humiliated, for he wrote later: 'My Oxonian career culminated in total and scandalous failure,' and on 25 November 1902 he wrote: 'I was not formally but informally expelled'. It may well be that he preferred to think of himself as another Shelley, sent down for his revolutionary opinions and rebellious conduct. According to Gosse, his Broad Street landlady complained to the authorities about his late hours and 'general irregularities' and later said: 'I've had me fill of them troublesome Balliol gentlemen.'

Swinburne never forgave Oxford for a humiliation which, in actual fact, he had brought upon himself. But at least Oxford had given him the opportunity to meet such men as Nichol, Rossetti, Morris and Burne-Jones, as well as unlimited leisure in which to read and to find himself as a poet. As he remarked, 'Oxford has turned out poets in more senses than one.'

It is just as impossible to think of Swinburne as a clergyman or a lawyer, as a lighthouse-keeper or a cavalry officer, though the last two were his own choice. But, once, at Capheaton, seeing him flash past the windows on his horse, his red hair flying in the wind, one of his grandfather's friends had remarked: 'That boy is a flame of fire.' But it was a flame which, all too soon, was to burn itself out.

# CHAPTER FOUR

# 1860–63

# CHELSEA: *A YEAR'S LETTERS: JUSTINE*

'I am leaving for Mentone in a fortnight for the winter,' Swinburne wrote to John Nichol on 18 September 1860, from East Dene. '(Now had you and I learnt the use of rifles, we might go together and be of some use at Rome and Venice) . . . I wish you could have looked me up in London, where I fell under medical hands. I am very well now.'

But Sir John Henry Swinburne died on 25 September at the advanced age of ninety-eight and the family went north for the funeral. There is no mention of this in Swinburne's letters, but he stayed for a time at Wallington, where a certain coldness had developed between him and Sir Walter Trevelyan. Next month he was in Newcastle again, staying with William Bell Scott, who finished his remarkable portrait of him begun in January. Bell Scott describes Swinburne's company at this time as 'like champagne or a ray of sunlight', but says that he was 'excessively idle and emancipated from the demands of ordinary life, his pockets stuffed with manuscripts'.

The journey to Mentone being temporarily postponed, Swinburne managed to persuade his father to let him remain in London on his own. The admiral generously agreed to allow him an income of £400 a year, and Swinburne immediately took up the threads of his old friendships with Rossetti, Burne-Jones and Morris. He visited Madox Brown in Kentish Town, Rossetti and Lizzie at Chatham Place, Jones and Georgie at Russell Place, Great Russell Street, and Morris and Jane at Red House, Bexley, where they all spent hilarious weekends. He took rooms at 16 Grafton Street, Fitzroy Square, to be near the British Museum reading room, and resumed work on *Chastelard. Rosamond* and *The Queen Mother* were now finished, and his father, though heartily disliking both of them, agreed to pay for their publication.

Georgiana Burne-Jones has left a vivid account of Swinburne's visits to Russell Place in the *Memorials* of her husband published in 1905: 'he had rooms very near us and we saw a great deal of him; sometimes twice or three times a day he would come in, bringing his poems hot from his heart and certain of a welcome and a hearing at any hour. His appearance was very unusual and in some ways beautiful, for his hair was glorious in abundance and colour and his eyes indescribably fine. When repeating poetry he had a perfectly natural way of lifting them in a rapt, unconscious gaze, and their clear green colour softened by thick brown eyelashes was unforgettable. "Looks commercing with the skies" expresses it without exaggeration. He was restless beyond words, scarcely standing still at all and almost dancing as he walked, while even in sitting he moved continually, seeming to keep time, by a swift movement of the hands at the wrists, and sometimes of the feet also, with some inner rhythm of excitement. He was courteous and affectionate and unsuspicious, and faithful beyond most people to those he really loved. The biting wit which filled his talk so as at times to leave his hearers dumb with amazement always spared one thing, and that was an absent friend.

'There was one subject which in these days he raised our hopes that he might deal with; but the time passed, and now we shall never see his proposed Diary of Mrs Samuel Pepys, kept concurrently with that of her husband'[1] – which is certainly a pity.

A letter to Lady Pauline, written from Maison Laurenti, Mentone, on 19 January 1861, contains a curious diatribe against the Provençal hinterland, which was then part of Italy:[2]

> It is more like the landscape in Browning's Childe Roland than anything I ever heard tell of. A calcined, scalped, rasped, scraped, flayed, broiled, powdered, leprous, blotched, mangy, grimy, par-boiled country, *without* trees, water, grass, fields – *with* blank, beastly, senseless olive and orange trees like a mad cabbage gone indigestible; it is infinitely liker hell than earth, and one looks for tails among the people. And such females with hunched bodies and crooked necks carrying tons on their heads and looking like death taken seasick. Arrrrrrrr. Grrrrr. . . .
>
> I am very glad you like my book [*The Queen Mother* and *Rosamond*]; if it will do anything like sell I shall publish my shorter poems soon: they are quite ready. I have done a lot of work since I saw you – Rossetti says some of my best pieces: one on St Dorothy and Theophilus (I wanted to try my heathen hand, you comprehend, and give a pat to the Papist interest); also a long one out of Boccaccio, that was begun ages ago and let drop ['The Two Dreams']. Item – many songs and ballads. I am trying to write prose, which is very hard, but I want to make a few stories each about six pages long. Likewise a big one about my blessedest pet which her initials is Lucrezia Estense Borgia. Which soon I hope to see her hair as is kep at Milan in spirits in a bottle.

It is strange to hear echoes of Mrs Gamp in such a context. These stories included 'Dead Love', in which a woman falls in love with the dead body of her husband's murderer and brings it to life by kissing it, 'The Chronicle of Queen Fredegond', 'The Marriage of Mona Lisa' and the sadistic

*Lucretia Borgia: The Chronicle of Tebaldeo Tebaldei.* Swinburne's intention was to complete a *Triameron* after Boccaccio, but the stories for the most part were not published until 1909, and then privately. 'Dead Love', however, appeared in *Once a Week* in October 1862. *Tebaldeo Tebaldei* was edited by Randolph Hughes in 1942 and published by the Golden Cockerel Press. Some of the quite masterly Northumbrian ballads were included in *Lesbia Brandon*, others appeared in *Ballads of the English Border*, edited by William A. MacInnes in 1925; while others, such as 'The Leper' and 'Les Noyades', were included in *Poems and Ballads* (1866) and evidence a curious taste for necrophily. This was a taste Swinburne shared to some extent with Rossetti, who, a year after her death in 1863, painted his wife as 'Beata Beatrix' in a 'death trance', and some years later opened her coffin to recover his buried poems, which had become entangled in her hair. Of the beautiful, ecstatic *Beata Beatrix*, Rossetti made in all six replicas, two in crayon, one in water-colour, and three in oil[3] – in itself a strange thing to do, comparable to Swinburne's lover in 'The Leper' amorously tending the body of his beloved for six months after her death:

> Six months, and I sit still and hold
> In two cold palms her cold two feet.
> Her hair, half grey half ruined gold,
> Thrills me and burns me in kissing it.
>
> Love bites and stings me through, to see
> Her keen face made of sunken bones.
> Her worn-off eyelids madden me,
> That were shot through with purple once.

One should add that Rossetti did not actually open his wife's coffin himself. He felt intensely guilty about the whole grisly procedure and got Charles Augustus Howell to superintend it. In 'Les Noyades' the peasant lover of a noble lady is bound to her face to face and drowned in the Loire, achieving in death the fulfilment of a love that had been denied him in life.

> 'For never a man, being mean like me,
> Shall die like me till the whole world dies.
> I shall drown with her, laughing for love; and she
> Mix with me, touching me, lips and eyes.'

The letter to Lady Pauline of 19 January continues:

> I wish I *had* anything to do besides my proper work if I can't live by it . . . but what *is* one to do? I can't go to the bar: much good I should do if I did. You know there is really no profession one can take up with and go on working. Item – poetry is quite work enough for any one man. Item – who is there that is anything *besides* a poet at this day except Hugo? . . .
>
> I am in love with Paris – you know I never saw it before. What a

stunner above stunners that Giorgione party with the music in the grass and the water-drawer is – that Gabriel made such a sonnet on.

The picture was *Le Concert Champêtre* in the Louvre and Rossetti's sonnet 'For a Venetian Pastoral' was written as early as 1849. It had a considerable influence on Swinburne.

Water, for anguish of the solstice: nay,
  But dip the vessel slowly. – nay, but lean
  And hark how at its verge the wave sighs
Reluctant. Hush! Beyond all depth away
The heat lies silent at the brink of day:
  Now the hand trails upon the viol-string
  That sobs, and the brown faces cease to sing,
Sad with the whole of pleasure. Whither stray
Her eyes now, from whose mouth the slim pipes creep
  And leave it pouting, while the shadowed grass
  Is cool against her naked side?

In January also, Swinburne wrote to William Bell Scott: 'I have just got your letter which has made I may say a green and gushing spot in the dullest of lives. I am very glad you approve the Queen Mother on revision. (What did Rossetti say of it to you? You say you heard from him about it.) I quite give in about the style: the amount of fine talk is awful and quite wrong. I think of going over it and crossing out what I find faulty, but am afraid to begin. The two scenes I prefer myself are Act Four, Scene two, and Act Five, Scene three: and the best part I fear concerns the luckless M. de. Soubise. On the whole I like Rosamond better than the five acter. But I rejoice that you approve of Denise. My father's criticism is that it is altogether far worse than useless – most pernicious. I quote literally. Need I add that I have grave doubts as to the authenticity of the fifth commandment in the superannuated series of Jewish axioms vulgarly known as the Decalogue?

'For my work here I have done three prose stories of a mediaeval kind, about as long and as moral as those of Boccaccio's – seven chapters. Item – about three fourths of Chastelard in the rough. Item – furnished and corrected all loose (in either sense) poems lying by me. Item – nearly completed my French novel by way of relaxation – don't talk of French horrors till you have read the hideous disclosures of English society contained therein! Rape, perjury, murder, opium, suicide, treason, Jesuistry, are the mildest ingredients. The atrocious conduct public and private of Prince Albert is branded with scathing and deserved indignation. As for the clergy – Should it come forth and be read, I would follow it up by a tale which I have vaguely conceived already. A twin sister of Queen Victoria, kidnapped on her birth by consent of the late Sir R. Peel and Lord Chancellor

Eldon for political reasons – to remove a rival candidate for the throne – grows up a common prostitute – is discovered in The Haymarket by the *Lor Maire* on a profligate excursion – informed of her origin claims her rights – is confronted with queen – queen swoons – the proofs of her birth bought and destroyed – the Apb of Canterbury solemnly purjures himself to the effect that she is an imposter – finally consumed by an ill-requited attachment to Lord John Russell, the heroine charcoals herself to death. There! At this rate I shall have a series of historical romances of the Victorian period rivalling Dumas.'

The French novel is *La Fille du policeman*,[4] a skit, as Dr Lang has shown, on Paul Feyal's *Les Mystères de Londres* (1844) and *Les Mémoires d'un policeman* (1859) edited by Alexandre Dumas. *La Fille* was a great success with Swinburne's friends, when he read it to them. Meredith described it as 'the funniest rampingest satire on French novelists dealing with English themes that you can imagine. One chapter, "Ce que peut se passer dans un Cab-Safety", where Lord Whitestick, Bishop of Londres, ravishes the heroine, is quite marvellous.'[5] Prince Albert, who pretends to sympathize with the insurgent Chartists in order to secure the throne for himself, is known as 'le prince prolétaire'. When the mob gathers in 'la grande place Wauxhall' and moves on 'Buckingham-Palace, le vieux palais gothique', he throws open 'les immenses magazins Alsopp-Barclay' and demoralizes them with unlimited supplies of beer. The second tale became the play *La Sœur de la reine*,[6] dealing with the adventures of 'Miss Kitty', an illegitimate daughter of the Duchess of Kent. Queen Victoria appears as a debauched and cruel tyrant, who gives vent to her feelings in tirades in the manner of Victor Hugo's *L'Homme Qui Rit*. When Lord John Russell, one of her former lovers, threatens to expose her scandalous life, she threatens in turn to have him executed, like the headmaster of Eton, who had had the temerity to tell his boys about Messalina, who she too much resembled. Only two acts of this play survive, although John Bailey remembers hearing a scene in which the queen confesses to her mother another lapse from virtue: 'Ce n'était pas un milord, ni même Sir R. Peel. C'était un misérable du peuple, en nomme *Wordsworth*, qui m'a récité des vers de son *Excursion* d'une sensualité si chaleureuse qu'ils m'ont ébranlée – et je suis tombée'[7] – which sounds even more delightful. Some years later Swinburne also read to Georgiana Burne-Jones the first act of another tragedy, *Sir Brown*, based on Queen Victoria's *Leaves from the Journal of our Life in the Highlands from 1848 to 1861*.

Swinburne's first published plays, *The Queen Mother* and *Rosamond*, exhibit the same qualities of Elizabethan pastiche as his other undergraduate dramas. *Rosamond*, however, is more Pre-Raphaelite in feeling. Henry II's mistress appears as a sort of vampire image that has seduced and destroyed men through the ages. It is an image which had an especial appeal for Swinburne:

Yea, I am found the woman in all tales,
The face caught always in the story's face:
I Helen, holding Paris by the lips,
Smote Hector through the head: I Cressida
So kissed men's mouths that they went sick or mad,
Stung right at brain with me; I Guenevere
Made my queen's eyes so gracious and my hair
Delicate with gold in its soft ways
And my mouth honied so for Lancelot.

For Swinburne, love is always inseparable from sadness, cruelty and often death. It is the note of *Tristan* – passion felt in its original sense of suffering, as a madness and a subtle poison, usually doomed (as in his own case) to frustration. At the same time it was a literary convention, reaching right back to the twelfth century, to the romantic view of love involving martyrdom, since carnal love was seen essentially as sin. It was exemplified in his own time in the sad, brooding sensuality of Rossetti's women, *La Belle Rosamond*, the paintings and drawings of Jane Morris, and the entranced damsels of Burne-Jones. In the 'Dedicatory Epistle' to his *Collected Poems* (1904) Swinburne wrote: 'My first ambition was to do something . . . not unworthy of a young countryman of Marlowe the teacher of Webster the pupil of Shakespeare.'

Such lines from *Rosamond* as:

I whose curled hair was as a golden gin. . . .
Wherein the tawny-lidded lions fell

hold the essence of the play, which is not so much a play as an extended lyrical poem. In striking contrast, we read of Queen Eleanor:

Frenchwoman, black-haired and with grey lips
And fingers like a hawk's cut claw that nips
One's wrist to carry.

Rosamond appears clearly as one of Rossetti's women in such lines as:

how she went
Holding her throat up, with her round neck out
Curdwise, no clot in it not smooth to stroke –
All night I shook in sleep for that one thing.

Her beauty is, needless to say, a cruel, tormenting beauty. Henry exclaims:

God help! your hair burns me to see like gold
Burnt to pure heat: your colour seen turns in me
To pain and plague upon the temple vein
That aches as if the sun's heat snapt the blood
In hot mid-measure; I could cry on you

Like a maid weeping wise, you are so fair
It hurts me in the head, makes life sick
Here in my hands. . . .
Your beauty makes me blind and hot, I am
Stabbed in the brows with it.

which strikes one as being unlike Henry II, but very like Swinburne.

In *The Queen Mother*, Swinburne chose like Marlowe before him the massacre of St Bartholomew for his subject, which evidently filled him with the same sort of exhilaration as his predecessor, with whom he shared what he himself called 'the hideous lust of pain'. It is a more ambitious work than *Rosamond*, closely following Brantôme and other contemporary French historians. Catherine de Medici he describes as 'That woman with the reddish blood-like lips.' The sadistic monster Charles IX is most vividly presented, and his obscene delight at the height of the massacre. 'Il prist fort grand plaisir de voir passer soubz ses fenêtres par la rivière plus de 4,000 corps ou se noyans ou tuez,' Brantôme tells us. Predictably, his mistress Denise says to him, as they make love, in the language of Cyril Tourneur:

Now I could kill you here between the eyes
Plant the steel's bare chill where I set my mouth
Or prick you somewhere under the left side. . . .
Yea I could search thy veins about with steel
Till in no corner of thy crannied blood
Were left to run red witness of a man. . . .
Sooner than lose this face to touch, this hair
To twist new curls in: Yea prove me verily,
Sift passion pure to the blind edge of pain,
And see if I will.

When Charles asks to see the bullet that had killed Admiral Colingy in his bed and the blood stains on his shirt, the Queen Mother remarks:

All's clear again: he smells about the blood
That shall insense his madness to high strain

meaning that the massacre will now go well, for Denise had tried to dissuade him from it. It reads almost like a parody, though Swinburne had history to support him. As usual, the play was exhaustively researched, but the evident desire to load the lines with psychological analysis and historical fact is inclined to retard the action – a failing seen at its worst in the huge historical drama *Bothwell*. Swinburne is at his best in the tumult and fever of the actual massacre by torchlight in the streets of Paris, when the ladies of the court – 'twenty with sweet laughing mouths' – gather about a Protestant corpse to insult it with 'fleers and gibes that made the murder merry'.

Stylistically, *The Queen Mother* in the main follows Chapman's French plays, though it exhibits an extraordinary virtuosity, establishing its author as a true late-Elizabethan alongside Beddoes. The play is no more pleasant than the characters and actions that motivate it. Of the court, Swinburne said later that 'it would be flattery to call [it] a brothel or a slaughter-house'. But on its appearance the book was ignored. The *Athenaeum* reviewer simply said that he could not read it on account of its dullness. But dull, one would have thought, is the very last thing it is. Swinburne said afterwards that 'of all still-born books *The Queen Mother* was the stillest' and accepted the situation with his usual stoical courage. He always felt a certain contempt for Keats for taking his early critical drubbings to heart: for himself he regarded reviewers as *canaille* and beneath his notice. *The Queen Mother* volume was affectionately dedicated to Rossetti, who wrote of it judiciously on 13 November 1864 to the Scottish lawyer John Skelton:

> I think I agree with every word you have said on Swinburne's first vol.; but no doubt you with me are astounded that with all its faults it should have hitherto had no justice done to its beauties. It was published when he was not much more than 20 [i.e. 23], and mostly written even earlier. He has since written an abundance of things of many kinds, and of quite another order from those early ones as regards perfection. His principal fault now is perhaps abundance – exuberance it hardly is, for no one has more real command of style than he has now acquired, and is daily further acquiring. Among the mass of works he has in MS is a tragedy on the subject of Chastelard and Mary Queen of Scots which I believe you would admit went far to answer your requirements, having been written and rewritten to avoid the faults of the other two early plays. But he finds the greater difficulty or indeed hitherto impossibility in getting his work accepted by a publisher. M. [Moxon] took them into consideration, but ended by funking them. Everyone finds them too outspoken on the passionate side. I think nothing could please him better than such an article as you would be likely to write in Frazer, giving the first full recognition he has obtained in print, though of course not slurring . . . the shortcomings of his early volume: of which he himself is well aware. In private he has made so large a circle of admirers that I cannot doubt his public reception would eventually be most enthusiastic, though not a universal one.

Skelton's article duly appeared in *Frazer's Magazine* in June 1865. But by then *Atalanta in Calydon* had appeared and Swinburne was famous.

Swinburne left his family at Mentone in February 1861 to pay his first visit to the north of Italy. He went to Genoa, Turin, Milan, Brescia, Verona, Vicenza, Padua and Venice. He was interested principally in the art galleries and monuments, dutifully enraptured by the earliest masters and disgusted by the 'sugared' painting of Raphael. He gives a list of all the galleries and churches he visited in a letter written in December 1863 to his sister Alice, when she herself was visiting Italy. Apparently he was also greatly impressed by the beauty of three women, as when writing to Watts on 24 January 1875:

> As to women, I saw in Venice one of the three most beautiful I ever saw (the other two were one at Genoa, the other at Ventimiglia in the Riviera); by her gaze I thought I might have addressed her, but did not, considering that we could not have understood each other (verbally at least); so caution and chastity, or mauvaise honte and sense of embarrassment, prevailed. – But I must not begin on Italian things or people, or I shall never stop.

The impression made upon him by these women remained with Swinburne all his life. He celebrated their beauty in three little poems, 'Three Faces', published in 1883 in *A Century of Roundels* at a time when he was living at Putney with his memories.

Perhaps it would have been better for Swinburne had he stayed a little longer in Italy, until the beauty of these women overcame his 'sense of embarrassment'. However, by March or April he was back in London. On 5 June he breakfasted with Richard Monckton Milnes at Upper Brook Street in the company of Richard Burton, Coventry Patmore and Aubrey de Vere. In August he spent a fortnight at Fryston, where he met Burton again. Milnes's house-parties were deliberately arranged so that the most contradictory types should be brought together for his amusement. Nothing could apparently be more opposite in character than the burly traveller and orientalist Burton and the little poet with the fluttering hands. But, against all expectation, Swinburne's and Burton's natures proved to be complementary. Burton admired Swinburne as a poet and was enchanted by his conversation and wit; Swinburne, with his capacity for hero-worship, admired Burton's great knowledge of oriental life and literature, and was particularly intrigued by his wide acquaintance with oriental sexual practices. The other members of the house-party were Carlyle, Charles Kingsley and Froude – none of whom could be expected to approve of either Swinburne or Burton. Milnes had already presented them with copies of *The Queen Mother*, in preparation for Swinburne's arrival, with the remark: 'I am giving you this little volume because the author arrives this evening, and so that you should not regard him as an absurdity.' Unfortunately no details survive of this particular party, but Swinburne's later antipathy to Carlyle may have had its origin there. Nor could he have found the 'muscular Christian' Charles Kingsley particularly sympathetic.

A letter of 15 October to Milnes from his rooms at 10 Grafton Street, Fitzroy Square, tells us that Swinburne had spent a week on his return journey in September with his cousin, Lady de Grey, Countess of Ripon, and continues: 'Since I came back to London about a fortnight since, I have done some more to "Chastelard" and rubbed up one or two other things; my friend George Meredith has asked me to send some to "Once a Week" which valuable publication he props up occasionally with fragments of his own. [He sent the ballad 'Fratricide', reprinted as 'The Bloody Son', and the necrophilic story 'Dead Love'.] Rossetti has just done a drawing of a female model and myself embracing – I need not say in the most fervent and abandoned style – meant as a frontispiece to his Italian translations. Two mornings of incessant labour on all hands completed the design, and the result will be, as everybody who knows me already salutes the likeness with a yell of recognition – that when the book comes out I shall have no refuge but the grave.'[8]

*The Early Italian Poets* came out this year (1861) without the frontispiece, though it is one of Rossetti's most charming designs. The model was the vulgar Fanny Cornforth, whom Rossetti had lately picked up in the Argyle Rooms and who revolted Swinburne. The lovers are seen kissing against the background of a rose trellis, with hearts in their interstices. Swinburne's letter concludes by reminding Milnes of his promise to allow him to 'look upon the mystic pages of the martyred marquis de Sade; ever since which, the vision of that illustrious and ill-requited benefactor of humanity has hovered by night before my eyes, and I run the risk of going as mad as Janin's friend, but with curiosity alone'.

By this time Swinburne had already written his French poem 'Charenton', an imaginative portrait of de Sade (quoted by James Pope-Hennessy in the first volume of his life of Milnes) and had begun work on his epic of flagellation, *The Flogging Block*, in which his imagination played delightedly round the subject of the whipping of small boys at Eton, and which was to engage him at intervals for the rest of his life. He had also already written many of the poems that were to appear in *Poems and Ballads* (1866). In December, William Hardman met him at Rossetti's house and wrote that though 'almost a boy, he upholds the Marquis de Sade as the acme and apostle of perfection, without (as he says) having read a word of his works. . . . The assembled company evidently received Swinburne's tirades with ill-concealed disgust, but they behaved to him like a spoiled child. He has a curious nervous twitching, resembling or approaching St Vitus Dance.'[9] If Hardman was disgusted, this was unlikely to have been the case as far as Rossetti was concerned, for next year, when Swinburne read passages from *Justine* aloud to him and some of his other friends, the 'assembled company' could not contain their uproarious amusement at the monstrous absurdity of the book, which doubtless lost nothing by Swinburne's rendering. After that, *Justine* became a standing joke between them all; for years, there is hardly a letter of Swinburne's to his more intimate friends without some humorous *Sadique* reference. This does not mean, however, that *Justine* and de Sade's other works did not add fuel to the fire that was already smouldering in the

3 Elizabeth Siddal, from the drawing by Dante Gabriel Rossetti, 1860

4 Swinburne, Dante Gabriel and William Michael Rossetti and Fanny Cornforth, *c.* 1863, in the garden at Cheyne Walk

depths of Swinburne's own nature, the very jocularity of his references being merely the mask beneath which he attempted to conceal their irresistible appeal to him.

A more attractive aspect of Swinburne is seen in his attachment to Elizabeth Siddal, whom Rossetti had at last married in 1860 and who Swinburne described after her death as 'that incomparable lady'. Both of them were small, pale, red-haired and high-spirited, almost like brother and sister. Swinburne was a constant visitor to Chatham Place, where Rossetti was painting him, and he would read Elizabethan dramas (suitably expurgated) to the already ailing Lizzie for hours at a time. The two of them would play together and romp about the studio like children. 'Rossetti was much entertained by their innocent intimacy,' Gosse tells us, 'occasionally having to call them both to order, as he might a pair of charming angora cats.' And when Burne-Jones joined them, the fun grew more boisterous than ever. The three of them, Rossetti, Swinburne and Lizzie, sometimes dined together at the Sablonière Hotel in Leicester Square. On 10 February, after a dinner during which Lizzie was 'in a peculiarly excited condition',[10] Rossetti took her home and went out again at nine o'clock, probably, as she doubtless guessed, to visit Fanny Cornforth or another model – as tradition asserts – though William Rossetti says that he went to the Workingman's College. On his return, at about eleven o'clock, he found Lizzie lying unconscious from an overdose of laudanum. She never regained consciousness. The doctors, called in by Madox Brown, to whom Rossetti had at once appealed for help, could not save her, and she died at 7.20 the next morning. Swinburne gave evidence at the inquest, dwelling on the devoted affection between husband and wife, and a verdict was returned of accidental death, though Rossetti was to be tormented by feelings of guilt for the rest of his life. In later years Oscar Wilde declared 'the truth was that Lizzie under the influence of laudanum had acted so foolishly while dining at the Sablonière, that Gabriel, very angry at her behaviour in public, took her home, and when she demanded more laudanum despite his protests, thrust the bottle roughly into her hands, saying: "There, take the lot!" and then went out with Swinburne.'[11] Doughty omits to give a reference for this story, though it sounds plausible enough and, if true – coupled with Rossetti's infidelities, would account for his crushing remorse. It is highly unlikely that Lizzie's death was 'accidental', as claimed at the inquest.

On 13 March 1862 Swinburne wrote to his mother:

> I am sure you will understand how that which has happened since I wrote last has upset my plans and how my time has been taken up. Till last week when I was laid up with a bad turn of influenza I have been almost always with Rossetti. For the last few days I have been with a friend in the country and am nearly quite right again.

I would rather not write yet about what has happened – I suppose none of the papers gave a full report, so that you do not know that I was almost the last person who saw her (except her husband and a servant) and had to give evidence at the inquest. *Happily there was no difficulty in proving that illness had quite deranged her mind* [my italics], so that the worst chance of all was escaped. . . . I am only glad to have been able to keep him company and be of a little use during these weeks.

The 'worst chance of all' suggests that Rossetti might have been charged with manslaughter, or even murder. As an act of retribution, he buried the only existing manuscripts of his poems in Lizzie's grave at Highgate cemetery.

'Rossetti and I are going to live together as soon as we can move,' Swinburne's letter continues. 'Of course he could not stay in the old house, and asked me to come with him. . . . In the autumn we get into a house at Chelsea – in Cheyne Walk, facing the trees and river – with an old garden.'[12] This was before the construction of the Chelsea Embankment, and the splendid seventeenth- and eighteenth-century houses of Cheyne Walk, with their front gardens behind high ornamental iron gates and railings, were only separated from the river by tall trees and a towpath, beyond which might be seen the tawny sails of the slow-moving Thames barges. Today Cheyne Walk is a deafening inferno of heavy traffic. When Rossetti, his brother and Swinburne moved into Tudor House, there was little to disturb its peace, except the wild and irregular habits of Swinburne himself and the strident cries of the peacocks and the other exotic birds and animals which Rossetti began to collect. He even had a kangaroo and at one time suggested adding an elephant to his private menagerie, so that it might be trained to clean the windows by squirting water from its trunk. In 1862, however, he was in no mood for such levity.

In an account of his friendship with Rossetti found among Swinburne's papers, we read of Lizzie's death and 'the anguish of her widower, when next we met, under the roof of the mother, with whom he had sought refuge. . . . With sobs and broken speech he said that he had lost the only woman he had ever loved; . . . he appealed to my friendship, in the name of her regard for me – such regard he assured me, as she had felt for no other of his friends – to cleave to him in this time of sorrow, to come and keep house with him as soon as a residence could be found.'

At first Rossetti took a studio at 77 Newman Street, but, growing dissatisfied with it, made it over to Swinburne. Then in October 1862, Swinburne moved into Tudor House – if it can be called 'moving in', for he was more often than not absent – together with William Rossetti and George Meredith, who had rooms assigned to them which they were to occupy two or three nights a week. Originally, Rossetti had thought of asking his mother and sister, Christina, to share the house as well. But, on second thoughts, he realized that the presence of Swinburne in his wilder moods would scarcely accord with their devotional gravity.

At Tudor House, between 1862 and 1864, Swinburne met Frederick Sandys, the painter of *Medea* and *Cleopatra* – on which subjects he wrote poems; Frederick Leighton, representative of the 'classical' school, who, though utterly opposed to the Pre-Raphaelites, remained on very good terms with them; Alphonse Legros, the friend of Whistler and Baudelaire, who became Slade Professor of Fine Arts; Whistler himself; Joseph Knight, who introduced him to John Morley, later editor of the *Fortnightly Review* to which he was frequently to contribute; Augustus Sala, the journalist and flamboyant man-about-town, for whom Swinburne had an immense admiration; Thomas Purnell, later drama critic of the *Athenaeum*; the landscape painter J. W. Inchbold, who became a close friend and with whom he was to spend holidays in Cornwall; and 'Dickie' Doyle, the cartoonist of *Punch.* Treffry Dunn, Rossetti's assistant, in his reminiscences, recalls hearing Swinburne declaim his poems one afternoon during a thunderstorm – the flashes of lightning seemingly coming from his hair, so passionate was his rendering. Other frequent visitors were, of course, William and Jane Morris and 'Georgie' and 'Ned' Burne-Jones. Over all these people Rossetti presided as undisputed master, like some Renaissance prince. Through his friendship with Morris and Burne-Jones, Swinburne became very intimate with the young painter Simeon Solomon, who designed panels for the stained-glass windows of Morris & Co. Swinburne, Burne-Jones and Solomon formed a trio, exchanging riotously obscene drawings, verses and letters. Solomon was an effeminate character with whom Swinburne formed a semi-homosexual relationship, introducing him to de Sade and teaching him to drink and being partly responsible for his rapid degeneration. This responsibility he shared with Pater, John Addington Symonds and Oscar Browning.

A different circle was to be met at the studio of Madox Brown in Fitzroy Square. As Whistler comments in his journal:

> There was always [at Brown's in 1863] the most wonderful people, the Blinds [that is, Karl Blind, the German anarchist, and his sister Mathilde, the poetess], Swinburne, anarchists, poets, and musicians, all kinds and sorts, and in an inner room Rossetti and Mrs Morris sitting side by side in state, being worshipped, and fluttering round them Howell with a blood red ribbon across his shirt-front, a Portuguese decoration hereditary to his family.

It was to Charles Augustus Howell, an ambiguous Anglo-Portuguese figure among the Pre-Raphaelites, that Swinburne later entrusted his negotiations with his publisher, John Camden Hotten. Then there was Red House at Bexley, where Swinburne was a frequent visitor, being present at the christening of Jenny Morris in 1861, when Rossetti sat silent and apart, 'eating raisins out of a bowl' while, as Arthur Hughes remembered, Lizzie 'snarled at him'. Four months later she gave birth to a dead child.

In October 1862, Swinburne began to work at his 'commentary' on Blake. Rossetti, who, with his brother William, was editing Gilchrist's unfinished *Life of Blake*, had asked Swinburne to write the missing chapters on the 'Prophetic Books', but he said that he would rather do an essay of his own. He worked at it intermittently until 1867. Not only is it the earliest serious attempt to interpret Blake, but is also distinguished by the complete originality of its approach and by the magnificence of its descriptive passages which contrive to recreate in words the visual effect of Blake's designs, as in the following passage:

> Dante and Virgil, standing in a niche of ribbed rock faced by another cliff up and down which a reptile crowd of spirits swarms and sinks, looking down on the grovelling and swine-like flocks of Maleboge; lying tumbled about the loathsome land in hateful heaps of leprous flesh and dishevelled deformity, with their limbs contorted, clawing nails, and staring horror of hair and eyes; one figure thrown down in a corner of the crowded cliff-side, her form and face drowned in an overflow of ruined raining tresses.

Such a passage might be compared to Swinburne's evocation of Rossetti's *Lilith* from *Essays and Studies*:

> Clothed in soft white garments, she draws out through a comb the heavy mass of hair like thick spun gold to fullest length; her head leans back half sleepily, superb and satiate with its own beauty; the eyes are languid, without love in them or hate; the sweet luxurious mouth has the patience of pleasure fulfilled and complete, the warm repose of passion sure of its delight. . . . The sleepy splendour of the picture is a fit raiment for the idea incarnate of faultless fleshly beauty and peril of pleasure unavoidable.

'Peril of pleasure unavoidable' might be the last line of a sonnet in Rossetti's manner. The whole passage, in fact, shows how strongly Swinburne was still under Rossetti's influence in 1868, when these 'Notes on Some Pictures' exhibited in the Royal Academy were written.

Even more characteristic of Swinburne are the impressions of a woman's head by Sandys in the same essay:

> a woman of rich, ripe, angry beauty, she draws one warm long lock of curling hair through her full and moulded lips, biting it with bared bright teeth, which add something of a tiger's charm to the sleepy and couching passion of her fair face.

Admittedly these are purple passages, but they reflect not only contemporary reactions to Rossetti's and Sandys's work, but also the tone and imagery of the poems Swinburne was writing at this time.

What is extraordinary is that the author of such lush descriptive prose could also write that little masterpiece of psychological subtlety, concision and restraint, the epistolary novel *A Year's Letters*, begun at this time, later republished in 1905 as *Love's Cross-Currents* and modelled to some extent on Laclos's *Les Liaisons Dangereuses.* In a letter to his sister Isobel of 21 June 1905, Swinburne says: 'The letters are dated just about the time I wrote them or perhaps a year earlier.' The first letter is dated 'Jan. 12th, '61'. He tried the book on several publishers without success, because as it was more or less about his own family he could not put his name to it at that time. It was serialized in Purnell's review, the *Tatler*, in 1877 under the name of 'Mrs Horace Manners'. The novel exists in three separate texts: the manuscript in the British Museum is more complete than the version published in 1877, which again is more complete than the 'official' version of 1905 with its dedicatory letter to Watts-Dunton.

The Cheyne–Harewood–Radworth relationships of the novel are very complicated. After a 'Prologue' outlining the earlier history of the families involved, the novel, as Swinburne himself realized, 'stands or falls with Lady Midhurst' – a subtly-drawn Machiavellian character who cleverly manipulates the members of the younger generation so that their adulterous love affairs shall not bring disgrace upon the family. Swinburne put himself into the novel under the name of Reginald Harewood, of whom we find Lady Midhurst writing to Lady Cheyne in 'Letter X': 'As to Reginald, *c'est une tête fêlée*; it may get soldered up in ten years' time, but wants beating about first: I should like to break it myself. Actually, I had to encourage his verse-making – pat that Rigolboche of a Muse of his on the back . . . and stroke him down with talk of publication till he purred under my fingers. It is a mercy there is that escape-valve of verse. I think, between that and his sudden *engouement* for foreign politics and liberation campaigns, and all that sort of thing, he may be kept out of the worst sort of mess: though I know one can never count upon that kind of boy. . . . But if you knew how absurd all this recandescence of revolution in the young people of the day seems to me! My dear Amy, I have known men who had been dipped in the old revolution. "*J'ai connu des vivants à qui Danton parlait.*" You remember that great verse of Hugo's: I showed it to Reginald the last time he was declaiming to me on Italy, and confuted him out of the master's mouth.'[13]

Here, again, is Captain Harewood, in 'Letter XXII', writing to his son Reginald, who is in love with his married cousin Clara Radworth:[14]

> You must be very well aware that for years back you have disgracefully disappointed me in every hope and every plan I have formed with regard to you. Of your school and college career I shall have a few words to say presently. It is against my expressed wish and expectation that you are now in London instead of being here under my eye: and even after

> all past experience of your utter disregard of discipline and duty, I cannot but feel surprise at your present proposal. If you do visit the Radworths before returning home, you will do so in direct defiance of my desire. That course, you understand, is distinctly forbidden you. . . . I know the construction to which your conduct towards your cousin has not unnaturally exposed you: and you know that I know it. Upon her and upon yourself your inexcusable and puerile behaviour has already drawn down remark and reproach. I am resolved, and I intend that you shall remember I am, to put an end to this. . . . From childhood upwards, I must once for all remind you, you have thwarted my wishes and betrayed my trust. Prayer, discipline, confidence, restraint, hourly vigilance, untiring attention, one after another, failed to work upon you. Affectionate enough by nature, and with no visibly vicious tendencies, but unstable, luxurious, passionate and indolent, you set at naught all guidance, and never in your life would let the simple, noble sense of duty take hold of you. At school you were almost hourly under punishment, at home you were almost daily in disgrace. Pain and disgrace could not keep you right; to disgrace the most frequent, to pain the most severe, you opposed a deadly strength of sloth and tacit vigour of rebellion. So your boyhood passed. . . . What the upshot of your college career was you must remember only too well.

This is the letter that Swinburne refers to in his notes for the novel, quoted earlier, as 'moral and religious blow-up: style muscular Christian'. In spite of his disclaimer, it is still difficult to believe – since Reginald's character and career tallies so closely with his own – that Swinburne never received some such letter from his own father, though, if so, it may have been written more in sorrow than in anger, for Captain Harewood is shown to be a most unpleasant, sadistic character, whereas the admiral, from all we know of him, appears to have been a most affectionate and kindly man.

Clara in the novel is married to Ernest Radworth, an osteologist and a man very much older than herself. Captain Harewood only remarks of her, in passing: 'I trust she may in time learn fully to apprehend the value of such a heart and such a mind. By no other path than this of both repentant and retrospective humility can she ever hope to attain real happiness or honour.' But when Reginald tenderly and lyrically describes Clara to his friend Edward Audley in 'Letter XXV' what Swinburne gives us is a portrait of Lizzie Rossetti:[15]

> She has sweet heavy eyes like an angel's in some great strange pain; eyes without fear or fault in them, which look over coming tears that never come. There is a sort of look about her lips and under the eyelids as if some sorrow had pressed there with his finger out of love for her beauty and left the mark. . . . She has a throat like pearl-colour, with flower-colour over that; and a smell of blossom and honey in her hair. . . . Her fingers leave a taste of violets on the lips.

But the second Amicia, his half-sister, the daughter of Reginald's mother by a second husband, is still more recognizable as a portrait of Lizzie and could even be a close description of Rossetti's exquisite pen-and-ink drawing of her done in 1855. Frank Cheyne, who loves her, describes her face in 'Letter XXIII':[16]

> pale when I saw it last, as if pulled down by its hair, heavily weighted about the eyes with a pressage of tears, sealed with sorrow and piteous with an infinite unaccomplished desire. The old deep-gold hair and luminous grey-green eyes shot through with the colours of sea-water in sunlight and threaded with faint keen lines of fire and light about the pupil. . . . Then that mouth of hers and the shadow made almost on the chin by the underlip – such sad perfect lips, full of tender power and faith, and her wonderful way of lifting and dropping her face imperceptibly, flower-fashion, when she begins or leaves off speaking.

As Reginald is riding with Clara on one occasion, 'her hair was blown down and fell in heavy uncurling heaps to her waist; her face looked out of the frame of it, hot and bright, with the eyes lighted, expanding under the lift of those royal wide eyelids of hers. . . . I rode between her and the sea, a thought behind; a gust of wind blowing off land drove a mass of her hair across my face, upon my lips; she felt it somehow, I suppose, for she turned and laughed' ('Letter VII').[17]

The same experience of a girl's hair lying across his face is repeated in the beautiful poem 'Before Parting' in *Poems and Ballads, First Series*, written at just about this time, or shortly afterwards.

When John Nichol read the manuscript of *A Year's Letters* in 1877, he wrote to Swinburne: 'How many will detect the darts of satire on every page, and the lurid scorn that runs through the whole?' Certainly the first pages of the 'Prologue' are satirical and so is the tone of the anonymous letter, obviously suggested by the 'Publisher's Note' to *Les Liaisons Dangereuses*, with which the first version of 1877 was originally prefaced, but which Swinburne removed from the 1905 edition. It reminds one of the mocking reviews of mythical French writers he contributed this year to the *Spectator*. As a parodist, Swinburne was inimitable. The substance of the original prefatory letter is as follows:[18]

> Dear Madam,
>
> I have read your manuscript with due care and attention, and regret that I cannot but pass upon it a verdict anything but favourable. A long sojourn in France, it appears to me, has vitiated your principles and confused your judgement. Whatever may be the case abroad, you must know that in England marriages are usually prosperous; that among us divorces are unknown, and infidelities incomprehensible. The wives and mothers of England are exempt, through some inscrutable and infallible law of

> nature, from the errors to which women in other countries . . . are but too fatally liable. If I understand aright the somewhat obscure drift of your work, you represent at least one married Englishwoman who prefers to her husband another man unattached to her except by illicit ties. This may happen on the Continent: in England it cannot happen. You are perhaps not aware that some years since it was proposed to establish among us a Divorce Court . . . the Divorce Court was found superfluous and impertinent. Look into the English papers, and you will see no reports, no trials, no debates on this subject. Marriage in England is indissoluble, is sacred, is fortunate in every instance. . . . I recommend you therefore to suppress or even destroy this book, for two reasons: it is a false picture of domestic life in England, because it suggests as possible that a married lady may prefer some stranger to her husband, which is palpably and demonstrably absurd; it is also, as far as I can see, deficient in purpose and significance. Morality, I need not add, is the soul of art; a picture, poem or story must be judged by the lesson it conveys.

In *A Year's Letters*, several of the characters prefer their near relatives to their husbands, and a certain air of incest hangs about the book, which is clearly a picture of English upper-class society of the mid-nineteenth century as Swinburne knew it. Lady Midhurst, who may owe something to Lady Pauline Trevelyan, writing in mock-seriousness to Clara about Reginald, says that 'it is simply the canon of our church about men's grandmothers which keeps me safe on platonic terms with our friend'. And she goes on to outline the plot of a possible novel in the French manner, in which a grandmother has an affair with a grandson, and at last, seeing him cooling off, contrives to pass him on to an aunt, her own daughter, while she herself seduces her daughter's husband, to leave the field clear for the young man.

To all intents and purposes, the two pairs of lovers are destroyed by Lady Midhurst, just as in *Les Liaisons Dangereuses* the virtuous Madame de Tourvel and the innocent Cécile Volanges are deliberately destroyed by the Vicomte de Valmont and the Marquise de Merteuil for their own amusement, whereas Lady Midhurst has the excuse of the good name of her family. The middle-class Laclos was exposing the elegantly idle and cold-hearted aristocratic society of his time; Swinburne was writing from within the closed circle of an English aristocracy which, feeling itself insecure, was all the more determined to preserve at least a façade of propriety. Laclos's aristocrats are cynically contemptuous of the rest of society, which only exists in their view to minister to their corrupt pleasures; though since Valmont and Madame de Merteuil are by far his most 'entertaining' characters, it is uncertain how far Laclos admired them. However, morality is perfunctorily vindicated by Valmont's death in a duel and Madame de Merteuil's hideous disfigurement by smallpox.

The clarity and elegance of Swinburne's prose style and the psychological penetration of this novel show him at his best. In his commentary on *Lesbia Brandon*, Randolph Hughes writes of *Love's Cross-Currents*: 'It has that perfection of grace and harmony that most essentially differentiates style from writing that merely serves as statement. . . . Swinburne . . . is infallibly a stylist, whatever he is treating – in letters, in essays on the most sober subjects, in the most business-like textual criticism, as well as on occasions which contain an invitation to poetry. Saintsbury says somewhere that from the *Blake* onwards one might cull passage after passage unsurpassed in the whole history of English prose . . . and he might certainly have taken as a starting point *Love's Cross-Currents*, which is anterior by some years to the best things in the *Blake*.'[19] As Hughes points out, in this book the style is often remarkable for its 'dry, terse comment and cool irony, very unlike the dithyrambic exuberance which alone is associated with Swinburne in the general if not universal misconceptions of his temperament and literary gifts. . . . Being so versatile, this style is capable of adapting itself in the letters to the various personalities of those writing the letters. And this is a very rare thing, much rarer than is no doubt normally supposed.' It is notable, too, that both the love affairs, between Reginald and Clara, and Frank and Amicia, 'with their outreaching ardours and wistful passions and dreams, peter out to nothingness and pure waste',[20] as they do in all Swinburne's more directly personal poems and as they did in his own life.

One must consider, after the publication of the novels and letters, whether Swinburne is not, with relatively few outstanding exceptions, often seen at his best as a prose writer rather than as a pure poet. But, of course, the very fact that he was a poet of genius made possible the splendid prose at this period of his life.

In 1862 Swinburne began to contribute regularly to the *Spectator*, which between April and September published his 'Faustine', 'A Song in Time of Revolution', and the beautiful 'Sundew'. His prose contributions were anonymous, but it is clear that the five long articles on Hugo's *Les Miserables* were his, also the review of Baudelaire's *Les Fleurs du Mal* of September 1862. This review tells us as much about Swinburne as about Baudelaire, and it is plain why Swinburne addresses him in 'Ave Atque Vale' as 'brother'. Swinburne notes that in the greater part of his book, Baudelaire 'has chosen to dwell mainly on sad and strange things – the weariness of pain and the bitterness of pleasure – the perverse happiness and wayward sorrows of exceptional people. It has the languid lurid beauty of close and threatening weather – a heavy, heated temperature, with dangerous hot-house scents in it; thick shadow of cloud closed about it, and fire of molten light. . . . The writer delights in problems and has a natural leaning to obscure and sorrowful things. Failure and sorrow, next to physical beauty and perfection of sound or scent, seem to have an infinite attraction for him. . . . Not the luxuries of pleasure, in their first simple form, but the sharp and cruel enjoyments of pain, the acrid relish of suffering felt or inflicted, the sides on which Nature looks unnatural, go to make up the stuff and substance of his poetry. . . . Even of the loathsomest bodily putrescence and decay, he can make noble use.' He noticed Baudelaire's 'feline style of beauty – subtle, luxurious, with sheathed claws'. And when there was a rumour that Baudelaire had died in 1867 he wrote the most splendid of his elegies, 'Ave Atque Vale', which appeared in *Poems and Ballads, Second Series*, 1878. Swinburne is standing by the poet's bier at a pagan burial rite.

> Shall I strew on thee rose or rue or laurel,
> Brother, on this that was the veil of thee?
> Or quiet sea-flower moulded by the sea,
> Or simplest growth of meadow-sweet or sorrel,
> Such as the summer-sleepy Dryads weave,
> Waked up by snow-soft sudden rains at eve?
> Or wilt thou rather, as on earth before,
> Half-faded fiery blossoms, pale with heat
> And full of bitter summer, but more sweet
> To thee than gleanings of a northern shore
> Trod by no tropic feet?

It is magnificent. But nothing could show more plainly the difference between Swinburne's rhetoric and Baudelaire than the simple dignity of the lines from *Les Fleurs du Mal* which he chose as an epigraph to his ode:

> Nous devrions pourtant lui porter quelques fleurs;
> Les morts, les pauvres morts, ont de grandes douleurs,
> Et quand Octobre souffle, émondeur des vieux arbres,
> Son vent mélancolique à l'entour de leurs marbres,
> Certe, ils doivent trouver les vivants bien ingrats.

It required courage to champion a volume of modern French verse in England in 1862, let alone the work of a man who had been condemned for obscenity in his own country. When the review of *Les Fleurs du Mal* appeared in the *Spectator*, Swinburne sent it with a letter to Baudelaire, who was ill at the time, his will paralysed by a sense of heavy inertia, and there was no reply for a year. Swinburne expressed his surprise to Whistler, who 'rallied the French poet on his discourtesy', says Gosse, and Baudelaire expressed 'tout mon repentie de mon oubli et de mon apparent ingratitude'. But he still could not bring himself to write, until at last, on 10 October 1863, he wrote a long and interesting letter to Swinburne which he gave to his friend Nadar, who was visiting London, to deliver. But Nadar forgot to take the letter, and it was discovered years later unopened in a drawer in Paris.

In this letter, Baudelaire referred to Swinburne's 'marvellous article', adding that Wagner had said to him about his own brochure on *Tannhäuser*: '"Je n'aurais jamais cru qu'un littérateur français pût comprendre si facilement tant de choses." N'étant pas exclusivement patriote, j'ai pris de son compliment tout ce qu'il avait de gracieux. Permettez-moi, à mon tour, de vous dire: "Je n'aurais jamais cru qu'un littérateur anglais pût si bien pénétrer la beauté française, les intentions françaises et la prosodie française." Mais après la lecture des vers imprimés dans le même numéro ("August") et pénétré d'un sentiment à la fois si réel et si subtil, je n'ai pas été étonné du tout: il n'y a que les poètes pour bien comprendre les poètes.' Baudelaire went on to say that Swinburne had gone a little too far in his defence of him and that he was not such a moralist as the English poet appeared to think, adding: 'Je crois simplement "come vous sans doute" que tout poème, tout objet d'art *bien fait* suggère naturellement et forcément une *morale*. C'est l'affaire du lecteur. J'ai même une haine très décidée contre tout *intention* morale exclusive dans un poème.'[21] Swinburne, at this time, agreed heartily with this point of view of *l'art pour l'art*. Baudelaire also sent him his 'Richard Wagner et *Tannhäuser*', written after the famous Wagner concerts at the Théâtre des Italiens in January and February 1860, though it did not appear until the following year in *Revue Européenne*.

Of Swinburne's articles for the *Spectator*, Gosse remarks: 'For the time being and under the editorial repression, it would have been difficult to find in England at that moment a critic more learned, more dignified, or more graceful than the unnamed and unknown reviewer of Victor Hugo and Baudelaire.' In a long letter to the *Spectator*, 7 June 1862, Swinburne wrote to protest against the unjust treatment by their reviewer of Meredith's poem *Modern Love*, which was censured by the 'Libellers, liars and prurient pastors of the press' as over-bold and immoral. The letter was so long that it amounted to another review, and the editor described its writer as one 'whose opinion on any poetical question should be worth more than most men's'. But when Swinburne sent in a review of a volume called *Les Amours Étiques* by an imaginary ultra-Baudelairean French poet called 'Félicien Cossu', the editor began to have his doubts.

In the next poem (he wrote) M. Cossu thus addresses his soul:

> Aile brisée – empreinte pied d'ange
> Pris dans l'ordure et moulé dans la fange.

> From these briefer flights of the broken angel's pinion we rise to a wider sweep of wing and loftier scope of vision in the long poem called *Une Nuit de Sodôme*. Singular as the choice of subject may seem, there are glimpses of more power here than is frequent with our poet.

And he quotes the lines:

> Et le soupir éclos de ces milles poitrines
> C'est le cri de l'égout chanté par les latrines.

The poems which Swinburne fabricates with such mischievous skill become more and more disgusting, and he concludes his review with a mock solemnity that is a parody of the *Spectator*'s well-known style of moral censure:

> We have but one word of comment to offer by way of conclusion. Accusations are often put forward, at home and abroad, against the restrictions imposed by a possibly exaggerated sense of decency on the English literature of the present day. We have seen what are the results of a wholly unfettered licence; base effeminacy of feeling, sordid degradation of intellect, loathsome impurity of expression, in a word every kind of filth and foolery which a shameless prurience can beget on a morbid imagination. Surely, whatever our short-comings may be, we may at least congratulate ourselves that no English writer could for an instant dream of putting forth such a book as the poems of M. Félicien Cossu.

That being the case, the editor might have been forgiven for being dubious about reviewing the poems at all. But Swinburne had already prepared the way for his review by quoting from 'Félicien Cossu' in his articles on Hugo. Not satisfied with that, he sent in another review, '*Les Abîmes* par Ernest Clouet', who was supposed to have some affinity with Petrus Borel and his *Contes Immoraux*. '*Les Abîmes* are still in type,' Hutton wrote to Swinburne, 'but I cannot say I think they will appear. The subject seems to me to deserve no more criticism than a Hollywell Street publication, nor could I speak of it in the *Spectator* without more real disgust than your article inspires. There is a tone of raillery about it which I think one should hardly use to pure obscenity. I confess your tone on Art is a little unintelligible to me. What is Poetry and Art? Are they all "flowers"? [i.e. *Les Fleurs du Mal*] Are they all to be judged by smell and sight? I ask not in prejudice, but because I really wish to get at the theory of a man who seems to me to have some narrow theory imprisoning a very subtle and keen sense of the poetical within unnatural limits. You write as if Art and Poetry consisted of pictorial qualities. Can you hold to anything so narrow?'

The last seven sentences of this letter, as Dr Lang, who printed it in his *New Writings of Swinburne*, points out, refer to the Baudelaire review. Dr Lang accuses Hutton of writing 'primly'. But one can hardly blame him for not allowing the *Spectator* to be used as a platform for Swinburne's impish obscenity. Besides, Hutton began to suspect that he was being hoaxed, when he read, in the review of *Les Abîmes*, that: 'To justify the ways of Satan to man is one of the great aims of M. Clouet. Having as a first step demolished "le Dieu ganache des eunuques et des bourgeois", he rushes into a rapid analysis of crime such as probably was never before set down in human language. "La vertu selon les philistins", he affirms in a trenchant way. . . . Crime, on the other hand, is the canal (*étier*) which serves to flood with strong tidal influx the stagnating marshes that lie dry at ebb-tide, along the coast of life, swarming as they are with a hateful brood of half-living animalcules – "the vermin of virtue, the sterile and sickly spawn of sexless moralities". The doctrine of moralists is to him a "croassement de grenouilles. La crapule et le cynisme", he exclaims with a devout rapture, "sont des travailleurs sublimes". He contemplates "avec un tressaillement d'entrailles farouche et voluptueux" the miracles of vice and the most inexplicable phases of crime. The odour of all these moral drains and sewers leaves, he says, in his nostrils the titillation of a pungent pleasure. Sin is his mental snuff.' The longest section of *Les Abîmes*, it appears, 'is a glorification of the work of a writer whom most people would shrink from naming as they would from touching one of his books – the Arch-Unmentionable of literature. M. Clouet snuffing from afar off the carrion warms by rapid gradations into a style which recalls, in the dull shamelessness of its scientific obscenity, the Abbé Domenech's famous preface to his invaluable Red Indian manuscript of last year. It is deplorable that the space of a few months should have witnessed the appearance of two such effusions on the same loathsome subject as Félicien Cossu's infamous *Charenton*,[22] and this abominable notice in *Les Abîmes*. . . . No one will now be surprised to find the writer devoting a briefer article to the celebration of a still living notoriety – the pseudonymous authoress of *Rosine et Rosette*, *Confidences d'un Fauteuil*.'

After this it is not surprising that Swinburne's connection with the *Spectator* came to an abrupt conclusion. The reviews are, of course, intended as a satirical comment on the mid-Victorian view of contemporary French literature, but it is curious that Swinburne ever should have thought that the *Spectator* would print them, though, in fact, both had actually been set up in type. One remembers how Sir Walter Trevelyan had thrown Balzac's novel into the fire at Wallington and how Captain Burton's Indian army career had been ruined by his all-too-detailed report on the homosexual brothels of Karachi. But then Burton had also declared that he was so bored by his messmates in India that he would henceforth eat with monkeys, and proceeded to do so. A man after Swinburne's own heart!

That the *Spectator* hoax was premeditated, is shown by the gigantic letter to Milnes of 18 August 1862, mainly about de Sade and written after a visit to Fryston: 'By the by,' he concludes, 'if you can without inconvenience find the last leaf of my article on "Cossu" (a half-sheet) which is wanting, I should be glad of it, as I forget how the burlesque ended. Item – if you have done with them, don't you think I had better have my "puerilia" back? Consider my feelings if they ever slipped into wrong hands, and the writing was recognized – c'est ça qui serait une bonne farce'[23] – which probably refers to something on Milnes's and Swinburne's favourite subject, the birching of small boys.

Hugo, who could not read English, wrote ecstatically thanking Swinburne for his articles on *Les Misérables*, even though they contain quotations from 'Cossu', comparing Hugo, de Sade and Whitman, in a celebration of

'Foliis ac Frondibus': ' "the hunger before the conception of spring, and the travail before the birth of summer, endless desire translating itself into endless production, the surplus of pain poured out to compound the excess of pleasure", whatever that may be, "a power and quality reminding him", the author of *Les Amours Étiques*, "of those words of an American poet", happily unknown to us, but quoted by the reviewer in legible if questionable English, "who has sung in a cadence luminous and vibrating the lusts of the leaves, the famine of the flowers, the appetite of the youth of the year", all the tumultuous odour and rumour of a season filled to the lips with luxury and life; justice done to every bird and blade of grass, and insect that has to complete spring . . . there never was such a rush and overflow (*élancement et débordement*) of dumb natural beauty into human language.'

The articles reveal a curious complexity of temperament which combines admiration with parody of what it admires, for we find Swinburne writing to Milnes in his letter of 18 August:[24]

> Have you seen the latest edition of Walt Whitman's *Leaves of Grass*? for there is one poem in it – 'A Voice from the Sea' [later called 'Out of the Cradle Endlessly Rocking'] about two birds on the sea-beach, which I really think the most lovely and wonderful thing I have read for years and years. I could rhapsodise about it for ten more pages, there is such beautiful skill and subtle power in every word of it.

It is, indeed, a poem difficult to read without being deeply moved. But the greater part of this letter is an extraordinary tirade provoked by de Sade's *Justine*, which Milnes had at last lent to him:[25]

> At first, I quite expected to add another to the gifted author's list of victims; I really thought I must have died or split open or choked with laughing. I never laughed so much in my life: I couldn't have stopped to save my life. I went from text to illustrations and back again, till I literally doubled up and fell down with laughter – I regret to add that all the friends to whom I have lent or shown the book were affected in just the same way. One scene between M. de Verneuil and Mme. d'Esterval I never thought to survive. I read it out and the auditors rolled and roared. Then Rossetti read out the dissection of the interesting Rosalie and her infant, and the rest of this refreshing episode: and I wonder to this minute that we did not raise the whole house by our screams of laughter.
>
> But on reflection I found the impression left on me to be precisely the same as that of Landor's heroine on her first view of the sea. 'Is this the mighty satyr? *is this all?*' I did think – I did hope that this one illusion might have turned out a reality. Weep with me over a shattered idol! The style of Micawber is inadequate to express my feelings.

But he protests too much. Though Swinburne says that *Justine* appeared to him as 'the most outrageous *fiasco*' and de Sade simply a Christian ascetic turned inside out, it was the marquis who had the last laugh. Once read, *Justine* and de Sade's other works became an obsession. Their effect on Swinburne was overwhelming, for the horrors described with such cold detachment appealed to the most deeply-rooted perversions of his temperament. His very letter of rejection was, as he says himself, a 'prose rhapsody'. The laughter of Rossetti and the others, on the other hand, was provoked by their perception of the ludicrous unreality of the book and, in the first instance, this was doubtless the case with Swinburne, whose critical faculties were unusually acute. But the persistence with which he wrote and spoke of de Sade, and the letters to Milnes six to ten pages long, in his curiously childish handwriting, closely modelled upon the wooden French of *Justine*, testify to Swinburne's fascination with the subject. Fortunately, it never went beyond fantasy – for in the pages of de Sade we have a blueprint for the death-camps and torture-chambers of Hitler's Germany and Stalin's Russia. Swinburne's lifelong enthusiasm for the blood-stained Elizabethan and Jacobean drama had its roots, to a large extent, in these impulses carried to their logical conclusion by 'the divine marquis'. And he was to find further justification of them in the works of Flaubert (especially *Salambo*), Gautier and others.

It was 'editorial repression' which stifled, to some extent, the wild and exuberant humorist in Swinburne, as well as his cloacal propensities, to which he gave rein in his letters and also, presumably, in his conversation with friends such as Rossetti, Burne-Jones, Solomon, Burton, Howell and Powell.

During the summer of 1862, while staying at Fryston, Swinburne had recited 'The Leper' and 'Les Noyades' to an assembled company which included the Archbishop of York, Thackeray and his two daughters, one of whom, Lady Ritchie, became a lifelong friend. The archbishop was so shocked that Thackeray smiled and whispered to Milnes, and the two young ladies giggled in their excitement. Swinburne was offended, until his hostess appeased him by saying: 'Well, Mr Swinburne, if you *will* read such extraordinary things you must expect us to laugh.' But in the middle of 'Les Noyades', the butler, 'like an avenging angel', says Lady Ritchie, 'threw open the door and announced "Prayers, my lord!" '. Lady Ritchie afterwards remembered Swinburne's 'kind and cordial ways' and said that she had never met anyone at once so disconcerting and so charming. Thackeray had already expressed admiration for his poems to Milnes.

Swinburne was at Fryston again in November. This time his fellow guests were Laurence Oliphant, the traveller, social butterfly and diplomat, who had lately returned from the British Legation in Japan, where an attempt had been made on his life; Henry Adams, the son of the American minister in London; William Stirling and William Rossetti, who had come to Fryston to look at Houghton's Blake collection. Adams, in his autobiography, *The Education of Henry Adams*, which is written in the third person, gives a remarkable description of Swinburne:

> The fourth was a boy, or had the look of one though in fact a year older than Adams himself. He resembled in action a tropical bird, high-crested, long-beaked, quick-moving, with rapid utterances and screams of humour, quite unlike any English lark or nightingale. One could hardly call him a crimson macaw among owls, and yet no ordinary contrast availed. . . . In due course the party of five men sat down to dinner with the usual club manners of ladyless dinner-tables, easy and formal at the same time. Conversation ran first to Oliphant, who told his dramatic story simply.

After that, for the rest of the evening, they listened to 'the rush of Swinburne's talk', as they sat, 'or rather lay', in Adams's bedroom, smoking and still listening to Swinburne until far into the night: 'They could not believe his incredible memory and knowledge of literature, classic, medieval and modern; his faculty of reciting a play of Sophocles or a play of Shakespeare's forward or backward from end to beginning. . . . They knew not what to make of his rhetorical recitation of his own unpublished ballads–"Faustine", "The Four Boards of the Coffin", the "Ballad of Burdens", which he declaimed as though they were books of the Iliad.' But he united them all more by his 'wonderful sense of farce' than by his poetry. It was this sense of farce, which, 'had he taken it more seriously', ought, in the opinion of Dr Cecil Lang, to have led to achievements comparable to Byron's *Don Juan*, *Der Rosenkavalier* and *Don Giovanni*.[26]

Swinburne left Fryston early in December, for a few days, to attend the funeral of his grandmother, Countess Ashburnham in Sussex. Afterwards he returned to Fryston to help Milnes decipher de Sade's letters, 'flattering' himself that his own handwriting resembled that of the marquis. He then went on to Newcastle to visit Bell Scott, with whom Rossetti was staying in order to paint Mrs Leathart. Later Scott was to write in his *Autobiographical Notes*: 'It was close upon the Christmas of 1862 when we were preparing for a Tynemouth holiday. Suddenly Swinburne appeared early in the forenoon having posted to Morpeth from Wallington early in the morning. Why so early? He could not well explain; just thought he had been long enough there. He wanted letters at the post but had not given his address! I could imagine no further: there appeared to be some mystery he did not wish to explain; we went by a later train, but he would accompany us. So we had him to walk with us by the much-sounding sea, when he declaimed the "Hymn to Proserpine" and "Laus Veneris", two of his most lovely performances, never to be forgotten when recited in his strange intonation which truly represented the white heat of the enthusiasm that had produced them.'

In this year (1862) Swinburne had also written 'A Ballad of Life' and 'A Ballad of Death', both inscribed to Lucrezia Borgia, the lovely morality play 'Queen Bathsabe', as well as *A Year's Letters.* He spent a fortnight alone in the Turf Hotel, Newcastle, then on 15 December wrote to ask

Lady Pauline Trevelyan to pay his 'unlooked for hotel expenses – all because I relied with filial short-sightedness on that fallacious letter of invitation which carried me off from Fryston. If I had but heard in time, I should have run down to London, and come up later. As it is I see Destitution and Despair ahead of me and have begun an epitaph in the Micawber style for my future grave in the precincts of my native County's jail'.

His next letter of 27 December is written from Wallington to Milnes:[27]

> Mon Cher Rodin,
> Salus in X Priapo et Ecclesiâ
> Sub invocatione Beatissimi Donatiani de Sade
> It is very jolly here at this time of year, but I might have preferred that forgotten sherry of yours to the hearing of declamations and expositions against it. Only one thing could have been sweeter than a clandestine sip of it under dread of discovery by one's host – the same furtive process under terror of flagellation by one's schoolmaster. By the by for heaven's sake send me your chapter of schoolmaster's autobiography . . . Mine is getting done and you shall have it in return as we covenanted. It will be very pretty I expect – two victims each, you will please remember. Mine are brothers. I want to see your style of flagellation fiction infinitely.

The letter is signed 'Frank Fane', the name of the schoolboy in Swinburne's unpublished flagellation poem of that name, now in a private collection.

From Bournemouth, where the family had gathered owing to the serious illness of his sister Edith, Swinburne wrote to 'M. Rodin' on 21 January 1863:[28]

> have you read Salambô? I have just written Lady Trevelyan a brilliant account of it. The tortures, battles, massacres, and Moloch-sacrifices are stunning . . . I want to review it somewhere. Do you know of any place one could get for it? I don't want to send any more to the Spectator; I don't approve of their behaviour (e.g. never sending one one's own articles, and taking back books sent for review – notamment four volumes of Les Misérables) and their principles offend my moral sense. I wish I could find some paper or review where I could write at my own times and in my own way occasional studies on matters of art and literature of which I could speak confidently. I think I could do at odd times a set of papers on French writers now to the fore, that might be worth the writing and reading. Flaubert for instance has never had a sane or decent reviewer in English. Sanity and decency being the two main props of my critical faculty. . . .
>
> Revenons à nos verges. I look eagerly and with prospective excitement for Frank's revelations. . . . I could put in delicious and pungent details from memories not much more than seven years old yet. (Less by a year or two now I think of it. Signed – Reginald) Voyons!

In another letter to Milnes in February, Swinburne recalls how four years before at Wallington, Lady Trevelyan had dressed him up as a girl for some private theatricals:

> It is a lamentable truth that Lady Trevelyan had then a dark project of passing me off upon Madame Sand as the typical *miss anglaise émancipée* and holding the most ultra views; we made up no end of history about it, and infinite adventures for the British Mademoiselle de Maupin. I saw the likeness then done the other day at Wallington, and howled over it. Such is life. Now, alas! had I that chance left which my majority bereft me of, quelle chance!

On his return to Tudor House later in the month, Swinburne met Whistler who was also living in Chelsea with his mother. There was an immediate sympathy between the two men. Both were small, waspishly witty, with the vitality of cats, and had the same admiration for France and French literature. In the next month Whistler took Swinburne with him to Paris, where he met Fantin-Latour and Manet, but not Baudelaire, who by then was not feeling like meeting anyone. In Fantin-Latour's studio, Swinburne saw a sketch of Tannhäuser in the Venusberg. Lafourcade points out that at this time Swinburne's ideal of beauty 'had become something heavy, calm, majestic, impassible like Baudelaire's "dream carved in stone" '. It had in it much of what later came to be known as the 'Parnassian' style.[29] 'Faustine' is an outstanding example of this.

While Ruskin, Rossetti and Burne-Jones could see nothing in Impressionism, Swinburne was to write a charming poem, 'Before the Mirror', on Whistler's *Little White Girl*, which is enough to show his sensitivity to the new movement. While in Paris he wrote four sonnets on the 'Hermaphroditus' in the Louvre, partly inspired by Théophile Gautier's poem 'Contralto'

> Sex to sweet sex with lips and limbs is wed,
> Turning the fruitful feud of hers and his
> To the waste wedlock of a sterile kiss.

Swinburne was always deeply involved with the theme of sterile sexuality, as his many references to and paraphrases of Sappho testify. The best lines in these sonnets occur at the conclusion of the fourth, which describes the uniting of Hermaphroditus, son of Hermes and Aphrodite, with the nymph of the spring of Salmacis:

> Yea, sweet, I know; I saw in what swift wise
> Beneath the woman's and the water's kiss
> Thy moist limbs melted into Salmacis,
> And the large light turned tender in thine eyes,
> And all thy boy's breath softened into sighs;
> But Love being blind, how should he know of this?

Back in London, Swinburne was a frequent visitor to Whistler's house, where he became much attached to the elderly Mrs Whistler, behaving to her with the same exquisite courtesy as was evoked in him by Rossetti's mother – and all such mother-figures.

It was about this time that he began to have alarming fits, brought on by a constantly febrile condition and the excitement of London life. Swinburne's nervous system was apparently so delicately balanced that a single glass of wine was enough to make him wildly excited, in which mood he would continue to drink, dancing about the room and screaming like a maenad. But sometimes, without warning, he would suddenly fall down in a fit and become unconscious, as though dead. But as soon as the fit passed, he was perfectly well again, indeed better than before. One of these fits occurred when Swinburne was at the Whistlers', and Mrs Whistler nursed him with maternal solicitude.

Rossetti, who behaved at all times like an elder brother to his 'little Northumbrian friend', consulted several doctors about these seizures and, while 'there was a difference of opinion as to the actual nature of the disease', Gosse tells us, they all agreed that it was induced by cerebral excitement and that Swinburne should be kept away from London as much as possible. These periods of wild excitement would be followed by periods of deep depression, in which he would sit immobile for hours, 'often entirely rigid.... His eyes would be fixed on nothingness, his lips alone would be moving without a sound: until occasional tremors through his limbs would presently announce that he was waking up to speech.'[30] Under the agitation of his own thoughts, Swinburne became 'like a man possessed, with quivering hands, eyes thrown up, and a voice hollowed to a kind of echoing shout'. This was his usual manner of reciting or reading his own poems – a manner inimitably caught by Max Beerbohm in his cartoon 'The small hours of the 'sixties at 16 Cheyne Walk – Algernon reading "Anactoria" to Gabriel and William'.

Arriving at Tudor House one day in 1863, the Hungerford Pollens found Rossetti very tired: 'He said he had had a dreadful night. At 3 a.m. he had been wakened by a tremendous knocking, and on looking out of the window, he saw Algernon being held up in the arms of a policeman, with a whole bevy of gutter-boys accompanying; he had been out on the spree, and no one knew where. Rossetti went out and let him in, and had a fearful time with him screaming and splashing about, before he got him to bed.'[31]

Mrs Pollen told Gosse that when Swinburne was angry, 'he used to collapse at once upon the floor, as though his legs had suddenly given way'. When dining out, he 'would gradually fix his stare upon the bottle [of wine] as if he wished to fascinate it, and then, in a moment, flash or pounce upon it, like a mongoose on a snake.... Then, if no one had the presence of mind to interfere, a tumbler was filled in a moment, and Swinburne had drained it to the last drop, sucking-in the liquid with a sort of fiery gluttony, tilting the glass into his shaking lips and violently opening and shutting his eyelids. It was an extraordinary sight, and one which never failed to fill me with alarm, for after that the Bacchic transition might come at any moment.' Once at the Pollens' house, having drunk some sherry, Swinburne became so violent and blasphemous, that Mrs Pollen told her husband that he must never come again. According to Gosse: 'Mr Pollen answered, "Oh! my dear, we must never be so unkind to him; he is just a child!" Mrs Pollen commented "he was just a very, very *spoilt* child" and she never liked him. She says, when he was not in the least drunk, his "one idea of rational conversation was to dance and skip all over the room, reciting poetry at the top of his voice, and going on and on with it".'[32]

There are many tales of Swinburne's exploits at Tudor House – sliding naked down the banisters, chasing Simeon Solomon round the house, both naked, and capering about Rossetti's studio 'like a couple of wild cats'. He once pushed Morris backwards against a cupboard, so that a choice piece of Rossetti's blue and white china fell and smashed. Then Rossetti was really angry. Swinburne, he said, 'drove him crazy', and sometimes his tolerance was strained beyond breaking-point. Doubtless he had already begun to regret his original plan of a joint-tenancy. And one morning at breakfast in the summer of 1863, Rossetti became so irritated with Meredith that he threw a cup of tea into his face. Finally, Swinburne's behaviour became so outrageous that Rossetti asked him 'in the friendliest fashion' to give up his rooms and installed Fanny Cornforth as housekeeper – a *ménage* which Swinburne, with his loyalty to the memory of Lizzie, resented.

Nevertheless, there were quieter times and it was at Tudor House that Swinburne worked at his *William Blake* and began the novel which T. J. Wise called *Lesbia Brandon* and which Swinburne himself intended, he told Burton, to make more offensive to Britannia than anything he had yet written.

Gosse was responsible for the story, repeated for years by all subsequent biographers, of Swinburne's proposal of marriage to a young kinswoman of Dr John Simon, the friend of Ruskin, who 'gave him roses' and 'played and sang to him', so that 'he conceived from her gracious ways an encouragement which she was far from seriously intending. He declared his passion suddenly, and no doubt in a manner which seemed to her preposterous and violent. More from nervousness, probably, than from ill-will, she broke out laughing in his face. He was deeply chagrined . . . and they parted on the worst terms.'[33] Later writers have identified this girl with a certain 'Boo' Faulkner, to whom Swinburne addressed some fugitive lines.

Fortunately, this apocryphal and humiliating story has been disposed of for good by John S. Mayfield, Curator of Manuscripts at Syracuse University, New York, who discovered that, at that time, Dr Simon's young kinswoman was little more than ten years old.[34] Swinburne was in many ways unorthodox in his sexual habits, but there is no evidence that, like Ruskin or Lewis

Carroll, he was especially drawn to little girls. On the contrary, as Dr Cecil Lang has emphasized, in 'The Triumph of Time', the poem which was hitherto supposed to have arisen from this experience, it is stated explicitly that 'the speaker did *not* declare his love, and that the Innominata had no suspicion of its existence. It is also clear from the poem that the lady is now married, but that the speaker will continue to see her.' From a rough draft of three stanzas of 'The Triumph of Time' which, with four stanzas of 'A Leave-taking', both written on the same blue foolscap sheet now in Yale University Library, it seems that the poet and the lady had written verses and enjoyed music together. We may also conclude from the same source that 'The Triumph of Time' and 'A Leave-Taking' were written at the same time and were intimately connected, as anyway appears to be the case. The manuscript shows, too, that Swinburne had some difficulty with the opening of the twelfth stanza of 'The Triumph of Time' and made several tentative starts before it became a confession of passionate love.[35] But this was not addressed to Miss Faulkner.

It is obvious, therefore, that we must look elsewhere for Swinburne's 'lost love'.

# CHAPTER FIVE

# 1863–64

# ITALY: 'THE TRIUMPH OF TIME': *LESBIA BRANDON*

In July 1863, Swinburne left Tudor House, Chelsea, for East Dene. Two months later his favourite sister Edith died at Bournemouth, after a long illness, and it was under the shadow of this tragedy that he began *Atalanta in Calydon*, in which he bitterly upbraids the gods for their cruelty. When his family went abroad in October, he went to stay at Northcourt, with his uncle and aunt, Sir Henry and Lady Mary Gordon and their lively, attractive and accomplished daughter, Mary.

Writing to his sister Alice, who was in Italy with his parents, on 31 December, Swinburne says: 'My greatest pleasure just now is when M[ary] practises Handel on the organ: but I can hardly *behave* for delight at some of the choruses. I care hardly more than I ever did for any minor music; but *that* is an enjoyment which wants special language to describe it, being so unlike all others. It crams and crowds me with old and new verses, half-remembered and half-made, which new ones will hardly come straight afterwards: but under their influence I have done some more of my Atalanta which will be among my great doings if it keeps up with its own last [first] scenes throughout. I repay M[ary] to the best of my ability but cheaply, by blundering over Greek verbs with her. She keeps her energy fresh by her versatility. I wish you were here, and as quiet as I have happily been all this time, thanks to their kindness, instead of being pestered by strangers on a foreign coast – and that the frowzy coast of a blue pond.'[1]

Years later Mary Gordon, as Mrs Disney-Leith, said that she first heard the first great chorus from *Atalanta* when riding with her cousin from Newport to Shorwell:

When the hounds of spring are on winter's traces,
  The mother of months in meadow or plain
Fills the shadows and windy places
  With lisp of leaves and ripple of rain;
And the brown bright nightingale amorous

Is half assuaged for Itylus,
For the Thracian ships and the foreign faces,
  The tongueless vigil, and all the pain.
Come with bows bent and with emptying of quivers,
  Maiden most perfect, lady of light,
With a noise of winds and many rivers,
  With a clamour of waters, and with might.

One can well believe that the tumultuous harmony of such lines was inspired by the Handel choruses thundered out upon the organ at Northcourt. And still more so the sustained exhilaration of such lines from Meleager's long speech describing how he sailed with the Argonauts to Colchis:

And I too as thou sayest have seen great things;
Seen otherwhere, but chiefly when the sail
First caught between stretched ropes the roaring west,
And all our oars smote eastward, and the wind
First flung round faces of seafaring men
White splendid snow-flakes of the sundering foam,
And the first furrow in virginal green sea
Followed the plunging ploughshare of hewn pine,
And closed, as when deep sleep subdues man's breath
Lips close and heart subsides; and closing, shone
Sunlike with many a Nereid's hair, and moved
Round many a trembling mouth of doubtful gods,
Risen out of sunless and sonorous gulfs
Through waning water and into shallow light,
That watched us; and when flying the dove was snared
As with men's hands, but we shot after and sped
Clear through the irremeable Sympleglades;
And chiefliest when hoar beach and herbless cliff
Stood out ahead from Colchis, and we heard
Clefts hoarse with wind, and saw through narrowing reefs
The lightning of the intolerable wave
Flash, and the white wet flame of breakers burn
Far under a kindling south-wind, as a lamp
Burns and bends all its blowing flame one way;
Wild heights untravelled of the wind, and vales
Cloven seaward by their violent streams, and white
With bitter flowers and bright salt scurf of brine;
Heard sweep their sharp swift gales, and bowing bird-wise
Shriek with birds' voices, and with furious feet
Tread loose the long skirts of a storm; and saw
The whole white Euxine clash together and fall
Full-mouthed, and thunderous from a thousand throats.

There is an ecstasy in such lines that would seem to derive from another source than Handel and memories of Aeschylus and Shelley, for the bright, cruel, exalted world through which this astonishing verse moves is something quite new in Swinburne's poetry – new, indeed, in English poetry – and one would hazard that it derives its unwonted power and purity from the passionate first love that overwhelmed him at this time, as he sat writing in the library at Northcourt beside Mary and her mother. Yet Atalanta is a frigid Venus who destroys her lover Meleager as Aphrodite destroys Hippolytus.

At the same time, Swinburne turned aside from this new exultation of spirit to write a most beautiful and accomplished medieval interlude, *The Pilgrimage of Pleasure*, for Mary's novel, *The Children of the Chapel*, which contains the sort of flagellation scenes that appealed to both of them. Mrs Leith told Lafourcade that these scenes were written by Swinburne. He had come originally to stay with the Gordons for two or three weeks, but the weeks lengthened into nearly three months, during which time Mary was his constant companion, riding with him across the downs, like Atalanta, and swimming with him in the autumnal seas.

While at Northcourt in December, Swinburne received a letter from William Rossetti reminding him that he was behindhand with the rent for his rooms at Tudor House, evidently suggesting that the joint tenancy of the house was scarcely working out as expected and asking him when he meant to return. Swinburne sent an order to pay drawn on Hoare's Bank and apologized to Rossetti for any inconvenience he may have caused by his unpunctuality, adding: 'We must look up matters honestly when I come to London which will be I think in a week or two. I don't wonder you were doubtful how to direct, but the truth is having settled down here for quiet with no company but some of my nearest relatives and oldest intimates I have shrunk from moving week after week, perhaps not wisely. But I think after being hard hit [by his sister's death] one is more afraid of any change than any monotony: and so I let myself be kept beyond the date I had thought of, readily and rather thankfully. . . . I am very much obliged for the Blake treasures both to you and to Mrs Gilchrist and shall return the sooner for their sakes. I have done half the Life which is a new rather tough thing for me who am raw to reviewing: also some notes on the "Gates of Paradise" which book I shall want to see again if possible to correct or complete my remarks; and as it is neither at the British Museum (is it?) or among the treasures which M. le comte de Rodin [Milnes] has accumulated in a long and unbroken series of "Les prospérités du vice", I can hardly make out how I am to set about it.'[2]

On 31 January, Swinburne wrote to Rossetti to say that he would probably be in London by the end of the week and that he hoped to submit the Blake essay to him and talk over its chances: 'Of course the complete work has swollen beyond all periodical limits: of course also as I have given my best powers of work to the subject I should not like to have it hacked into or dipped about at random. . . . Coming after you and Gabriel, I wanted to do something durable also for Blake, if of less direct value than your work and his. . . . I rode across the country to Farringford the other day. The weather is exquisite for riding, but Mrs Tennyson is ill now and both were invisible.'[3]

Before he left the Isle of Wight, Swinburne was surprised to get from Gabriel Rossetti a letter 'couched in language as affectionate and cordial as had been the terms on which we parted when an impending domestic affliction had summoned me from London, but intimating with all possible apology that he wished to have the house at Chelsea to himself: for by this time the fourth and original sharer in our undertaking (Meredith) had withdrawn from it, and Mr W. M. Rossetti was now but an occasional inmate of the household'. So Swinburne wrote in 'A Record of a Friendship', composed towards the end of his life. 'My reply was brief and clear, to the effect that . . . I had not understood our common agreement to be terminable at the caprice of either party, that one could desire the other to give place to him without further reason alleged than his own will and pleasure: but the ultimate result could only be an amicable separation.'[4] However amicable the separation, it was nevertheless the first decisive move towards the complete break in their friendship eight years later, though by that time Rossetti had already suffered from the nervous breakdown which resulted in his separating himself from most of his old friends.

Swinburne returned to London at the beginning of February 1864. Leaving the uncompleted manuscripts of *William Blake* and *Atalanta in Calydon* with Rossetti for his criticism, he then left England for Italy to rejoin his family. He seems to have crossed over to Paris in February in the company of Lord Houghton, as Monckton Milnes had meanwhile become.[5] While in Paris, he read some of his poems to Sir Charles MacCarthy, who was so excited by them that he had quite a bad night. He thought them wonderful, he said, and was quite haunted by them.[6] Then, armed with Houghton's introduction to Landor, Swinburne hastened to Florence. He found 'the most ancient of the demi-gods' at 93 Villa della Chiesa, threw himself at his feet and covered his hands with kisses. Landor, who was in his ninetieth year and deaf, was utterly bewildered, and Swinburne withdrew in a state of disappointment and depression.

On returning to his hotel, he at once dashed off 'a note of apology and explanation, saying why and how I had made up my mind to call upon him', as he wrote to Houghton on 31 March, 'that is expressing (as far as was expressible) my immense admiration and reverence in the plainest and sincerest way I could manage'. The effect of this note was an invitation from Landor to visit him again. At his second visit, Swinburne found the magnificent-looking old man 'as alert, brilliant and altogether delicious as I suppose others may have found him twenty years since. . . . If both or either of us die tomorrow, at least today he has told me that my presence has made him happy; he said more than that – things for which of course I take no credit to myself but which are no less pleasant to hear from such a man. . . . In answer to something that Mr Landor said today of his own age I reminded him of his equals and precursors, Sophocles and Titian. . . . I should like to throw up all other things on earth and devote myself to playing valet to him for the rest of his days. I should black his boots if he wore any – moi! He has given me the shock of adoration which one feels at thirteen towards great men. I am not sure that any other emotion is so durable and persistently delicious as that of worship, when your god is indubitable and incarnate before your eyes. I told him, as we were talking of poems and such things, that his poems had given me inexpressible pleasure and a sort of blind relief when I was a small fellow at Eton much beaten upon and worried some twelve years back (or nearly) now. My first recollection of them is the Song of the Hours in Iphigenia. Apart from their executive perfection, all those Greek poems of his always fitted my own way of feeling and thought infinitely more than even Tennyson's modern versions; and now I am more than ever sure that the "Hamadryad" is a purer and better piece of work, from the highest point of view that art can take, than such magnificent hashes and stews of old and new with a sharp sauce of personality as "Oenone" and "Ulysses". Not that I am disloyal to Tennyson, in whose church we were all in my time born and baptized as far back as we can remember at all; but he is not a Greek nor a heathen; and I imagine does not want to be: and I greatly fear believes it possible to be something better: an absurdity which should be left to the Brownings and other blatant creatures begotten on the slime of the modern chaos.'[7]

Landor had graciously accepted the dedication of *Atalanta* and in exchange had insisted on presenting Swinburne with a painting he said was by Correggio – 'a masterpiece that was intercepted on its way back to its Florentine home from the Louvre, whither it had been taken by Napoleon Buonaparte'. Unfortunately, it turned out to be nothing of the kind. Swinburne was about to make a third visit when he received from Landor the following note:[8]

My dear Friend,

So totally am I exhausted that I can hardly hold my pen to express my vexation that I shall be unable ever to converse with you again. Eyes and intellect fail me. I can only say that I was much gratified by your visit, which must be the last and that I remain ever

Your obliged

W. Landor

While in Florence, Swinburne went to see Gozzoli's frescoes in the Palazzo Ricardi, but affected to be disappointed in Veronese's *Martyrdom of St Justine*, which, as he wrote to Houghton, seemed to him 'painfully and ludicrously inadequate. . . As for Titian's Venus – Sappho and

Anactoria in one – four lazy fingers buried dans les fleurs de son jardin – how any creature can be decently virtuous within thirty square miles of it passes my comprehension. I think Tannhäuser need not have been bored – even until the end of the world. But who knows?'[9]

Swinburne visited several galleries in the company of Mrs Gaskell and, like Shelley before him, was doubtless deeply impressed by the *Medusa* in the Uffizi, then attributed to Leonardo. As Mario Praz remarks, no other picture made such an impression on Shelley and the poem he wrote about it 'amounts almost to a manifesto of the conception of Beauty peculiar to the Romantics'.[10] It was a poem not without its influence on Swinburne.

> Its horror and its beauty are divine.
> Upon its lips and eyelids seems to lie
> Loveliness like a shadow, from which shine,
> Fiery and lurid, struggling underneath,
> The agonies of anguish and of death. . . .
>
> Hairs which are vipers, and they curl and flow
> And their long tangles in each other lock,
> And with unending involutions show
> Their mailèd radiance, as it were to mock
> The torture and the death within. . . .
>
> 'Tis the tempestuous loveliness of terror.

But even more was Swinburne impressed by the cruel beauty of the studies of female heads by Michelangelo in the Buonarroti Palace, writing in his 'Notes on Designs of the Old Masters in Florence':[11]

> But in one separate head there is more tragic attraction . . . a woman's, three times studied, with divine and subtle care; sketched and re-sketched in youth and age, beautiful always beyond desire and cruel beyond words; fairer than heaven and more terrible than hell; pale with pride and weary with wrong-doing; a silent anger against God and man burns, white and repressed, through her clear features. In one drawing she wears a head-dress of eastern fashion rather than western, but in effect made out of the artist's mind only: plaited in the likeness of closely-welded scales as of a chrysalid serpent, raised and waved and rounded in the likeness of a sea-shell. In some inexplicable way all her ornaments seem to partake of her fatal nature, to bear upon them her brand of beauty fresh from hell; and this through no vulgar machinery of symbolism, no serpentine or otherwise bestial emblem: the bracelets and rings are innocent enough in shape and workmanship; but in touching her flesh they have become infected with deadly and malignant meaning. Broad bracelets divide the shapely splendour of her arms; over the nakedness of her firm and luminous breasts, just below the neck, there is passed a band as of metal. Her eyes are full of proud and passionless lust after gold and blood; her hair,

> close and curled, seems ready to shudder in sunder and divide into snakes. Her throat, full and fresh, round and hard to the eye as her bosom and arms, is erect and stately, the head set firm on it without any droop or lift of the chin; her mouth crueller than a tiger's, colder than a snake's, and beautiful beyond a woman's. She is the deadlier Venus incarnate.

If one compares this, which is as melodramatic as 'Faustine' or 'Dolores' – with Pater's famous description of the 'Mona Lisa' in *The Renaissance*, which clearly derives from Swinburne's 'Notes', one can appreciate the subtle refinement of this style in Pater's hands. When Swinburne wrote to Lord Morley in April 1873 to say how much he admired Pater's work, he concluded: 'I am somewhat shy of saying how much, ever since on my telling him once at Oxford how highly Rossetti as well as myself estimated his first papers in the *Fortnightly* [where *The Renaissance* first appeared], he replied to the effect that he considered them as owing their inspiration entirely to the example of my own work in the same line.' Of another drawing in the farthest room of the Buonarroti Palace, he observes:[12]

> This is rightly registered as a study for Cleopatra; but notice has not yet been accorded to the subtle and sublime idea which transforms her death by the aspic's bite into a meeting of serpents which recognise and embrace, an encounter between the woman and the worm of Nile, almost as though this match for death were a monstrous love-match, or such a mystic marriage as that painted in the loveliest passage of *Salambô*, between the maiden body and the scaly coils of the serpent and the priestess alike made sacred to the moon; so closely do the snake and queen of snakes caress and cling. Of this idea Shakespeare also had a vague and great glimpse when he made Antony murmur, *Where's my serpent of old Nile?* mixing a foretaste of her death with the full sweet savour of her supple and amorous 'pride of life'. For what indeed is lovelier or more luxuriously loving than a strong and graceful snake of the nobler kind?

But Swinburne lets his erotic imagination run away with him. In such passages, he is closer to Gautier than Michelangelo.

On Rossetti's introduction, while in Florence he met Seymour Kirkup, who knew Landor and had known Blake, Keats and Shelley. They had many conversations about Blake. He also met Isabella Blagden, Browning's friend. From Florence he went up to Fiesole, where 'deafened by the noon-day nightingales in a high-walled garden' he said that he wrote 'Itylus', though Ruskin reputedly possessed a manuscript of the poem dated 1863. He visited Majano, Siena, Pisa, and San Gimignano, the hill-city of the towers. But, after two months, he was 'beaten back by the Italian sun and starved out by want of companionship', as he wrote to Nichol on 23 May, from Bedford Street, two days after his return to London. Of Siena he was to write in *Songs Before Sunrise*:

For the outer land is sad, and wears
  A raiment of a flaming fire;
And the fierce fruitless mountain stairs
  Climb, yet seem wroth and loth to aspire,
Climb, and break, and are broken down,
And through their clefts and crests the town
Looks west and sees the dead sun lie,
In sanguine death that stains the sky
With angry dye.

It was at this time that Swinburne met the young artist George du Maurier at Simeon Solomon's in Howland Street, with Rossetti. 'Such a strange evening,' du Maurier wrote to his mother: 'As for Swinburne, he is without exception the most extraordinary man not that I ever met only, but that I ever read or heard of; for three hours he spouted his poetry to us, and it was of a power, beauty and originality unequalled. Everything after seems tame, but the little beast will never I think be acknowledged for he has an utterly perverted moral sense, and ranks Lucrezia Borgia with Jesus Christ; indeed says she's far greater, and very little of his poetry is fit for publication. If you like I will copy one of his very mildest which has been published, namely Faustine, and send it you. These strange creatures all hang in a clique together, and despise everything but themselves; and really I don't wonder. Swinburne's French poetry is almost as fine as his English. The other day at Jones's he was asked to write verses for four pictures of the seasons Jones had just painted, and in *twenty minutes* he had produced four beautiful little latin poems! Tom and I felt like two such bourgeois that night, so healthy and human; didn't get home till three, and wasn't it jolly after this strange but gorgeous nightmare of an evening, to wake up and find a healthy innocent little baby weighing over 20 pounds. . . . Ce qui n'empêche pas that genius of this magnitude is a very divine and extraordinary gift, to be bowed down to and worshipped.'[13] In the margin of the letter is a rough sketch 'Swinburne reciting', with an enormous head on a little body.

Next month Swinburne went to live in the family house in Grosvenor Place, where he once more took up his *William Blake.* 'My book will at least handle the whole question of Blake's life and work with perfect fearlessness and with thorough admiration,' he wrote to Seymour Kirkup in July. 'I wish I could send you for inspection any of the engraved and coloured Books of Prophesy, but unhappily the few copies now existing fetch so many more pounds as Blake received shillings for them when alive, that only millionaires can afford to collect them. Did you ever read his great prose-poem *The Marriage of Heaven and Hell*? For profound humour and subtle imagination, not less than lyrical splendour and fervour of thought, it seems to me the greatest work of its century. We all envy you the privilege of having known a man so great in so many ways. I don't know if Rossetti has found time to answer your letter forwarded through Reade[14] to me: I know he received it with the greatest pleasure, and expressed to me his sense of your kindness. His pictures of this year [*Lady Lilith* and *Venus Verticordia*] are magnificent; they recall the greatness, the perfect beauty and luxurious power of Titian and Georgione'[15] – a suburban Titian, one might think. Swinburne was ever over-generous in his praise of his friends' work.

By July he had moved to rooms over a court milliner's at 24 Mount Street, Grosvenor Square. He wrote Nichol: 'For eight hours on end I have been unpacking, blaspheming, arranging, losing, finding, swearing, stamping, blessing Satan and cursing. The villains who have mismanaged for me have half-ruined some of my choicest books, and mislaid endless things, for which may they descend into Gehenna long before I pay their bill on earth.' He sent Nichol a copy of Meinhold's *Sidonia the Sorceress*, found on a second-hand bookstall.

From 6 August to the twenty-second, Swinburne was visiting Fryston and from there went to stay with the landscape painter J. W. Inchbold at Tintagel, where he finished *Atalanta*. They lodged and boarded at the schoolhouse in the village, where, as he wrote to Mary Gordon, he once overheard a flogging going on in the schoolroom, 'to which his Etonian ears were especially sensitive – and sympathetic', remarks Mrs Leith. His letters to Mary tell how he spent the rest of his time. In September he wrote:[16]

> I could have wished for your company yesterday night when we took out horses, borrowed from a neighbouring farmer, and rode through the dusk and the dark to the adjacent city of Boscastle. This important and flourishing port does not exactly boast of a highway to the sea, but it has a path cut or worn in the slope of the down, along which we let our horses . . . feel their way till we came out one after another on a narrow standing place of rocks, breaking sharply down to the sea on both sides . . . and as there is no beach or shore of any kind, you can imagine how the sea swings to and fro between the cliffs, foams and swells, beats and baffles itself against the steep faces of rock. . . . Seen from above and on horseback it was very queer, dark grey swollen water, caught as it were in a trap, and heaving with rage against both sides at once, edged with long panting lines of incessant foam that swung and lapped along the deep steep cliffs without breaking, and had room to roll at ease. . . . I have bathed twice, but the sea is very treacherous and tiring; no sand, hardly any beach even at low water in the narrow bays. Sudden steep banks, shelving rocks, and sea pitching violently in the entrance of the bays: so that where there are rocks to take breath at one can't make for them lest the sea should *stave* one's ribs in against the reefs; and the sea that pitches from side to side

without breakers or rollers, and has no resting place except on the high and dry rocks inland, takes it out of one in swimming much more than one thinks.

Swinburne had never been a strong swimmer, for all his passion for bathing. Gosse tells us that his 'swimming' consisted mostly of floating in the waves, to which he surrendered himself with rapture. It is strange that he did not discover Bossiney Bay, where, at low tide, the Atlantic rollers advance majestically upon sand and shingle, though he gives a detailed description of Tintagel itself and 'the double ruin, one half facing the other, of the old castle or palace of the kings of Cornwall. Opposite on a high down is the old church, black with rain and time and storm.'

Once, when out bathing, having worked his way round a narrow inlet to explore a cave, Swinburne was nearly cut off by the incoming tide:[17]

I had to run round a point of land which the sea was rising round, *or* be cut off in a bay to which to my cost I had just found the cliffs impracticable; so without boots or stockings I just ran at it and into the water and up and down over some awfully sharp and shell-encrusted rocks, which cut my feet to fragments, had twice to plunge again into the sea, which was filling all the caves and swinging and swelling heavily between the rocks; once fell flat in it, and got so thrashed and licked that I might have been – [Herbert Seyton][18] in – [Denham's] clutches . . . and at last got over the last reef and down on the sand of a safe bay, a drenched rag, and with feet that just took me home (three-quarters of a mile or so and uphill mainly with stones) half in and half out of the boots which I had just saved with one hand; and then the right foot began to bleed like a pig, and I found a deep cut which was worse than any ever inflicted by a birch to the best part of my belief, for it was *no end* bad yesterday, and today makes it hopeless to walk except on tiptoe, but I wouldn't have it dressed or bothered. I hope it will soon heal.

Swinburne knew that Mary enjoyed reading such descriptions as much as he enjoyed writing them: they had the same sado-masochistic tastes. But the cut took some time to heal and he was confined to the house for three weeks. His letters to Mary discuss Tennyson's *Enoch Arden and Other Poems*, in which the 'Boadicea', written in galliambics, reminds him of his own experiment in that metre at Eton, for which, he says, his tutor had beaten him for 'impertinent eccentricity', and he again likens himself to Herbert Seyton in the hands of Denham.

As Mrs Leith records: 'The autumn of that year [1864] found us again both in London, and he was a frequent guest at my father's house at Chelsea. I think it was at that time that he wrote some chapters of a novel, which never saw the light, or, as far as I know, was completed. He used to read me bits of the MS of an afternoon when he happened to come in. I do not know what was the plot of the story, but I recollect some of the characters – one being the bright young lovable schoolboy he delighted in portraying, in constant scrapes, but noble and honourable through all; and a tutor, who bid fair to be the "villain of the piece". . . . The plot was in no way connected with his late novel *Love's Cross-Currents.*'[19]

Swinburne returned to London at the end of October with the completed manuscript of *Atalanta.* He had been much saddened by news of the death of Landor on 23 September, just as he had completed the Greek dedication to him of his drama. Now Landor would never read it. But sometime towards the end of 1864, he was still further saddened – not to say shattered – when Mary Gordon announced that she had become engaged to Colonel Disney-Leith, a man twenty-one years older than herself. When Lesbia Brandon refuses Herbert Seyton in chapter eight of the novel, we are told 'he sat and felt a breakage inside him of all that made up the hopefullest part of his life', which rings so absolutely true in its restraint that one feels that it must have been a description of Swinburne's own feelings when Mary told him of her engagement. Mrs Leith writes airily: 'My marriage in 1865, and subsequent residence in Scotland, naturally caused something of a gap in our constant correspondence and intercourse, though he was always the same when we did meet. I have been unable to trace the letter he wrote when I announced to him my engagement, and said that as he had always been to me like an elder brother, I should like to feel that I had his approval. I know that he did write most kindly, saying that "If it was A[lice] or any of my sisters, I could not feel more sincerely interested", or words to that effect. *Atalanta in Calydon* astonished the world of literature that same summer; and a presentation copy in white vellum, with the exquisite gold-shell ornamentation designed by D. Rossetti, and which had been minutely described to me while under discussion, was among the most valued of my wedding gifts.'[20]

Colonel Disney-Leith was a distinguished soldier who had been decorated for conspicuous gallantry in the savage Sikh war of 1848. As a captain, he had led his men through withering musket-fire into a breach in the walls of Multan known as the 'Bloody Bastion'. In this action he lost his left arm and carried sabre cuts on his right arm and a bullet wound in his shoulder for the rest of his life. Later, he fought in the Indian mutiny – or, rather, the 'First War of Liberation', as it is called in India today. He was, in fact, as Dr Lang observes, 'the clearest antithesis of a nympholeptic poet'.[21] Mary Gordon herself came of a family with military traditions, for while her father was a Cambridge man of scholarly tastes, her grandfather had served in campaigns from Gibraltar to North America. The romantic appeal to her of such a man as Colonel Leith is obvious, but this did not make it any the less bitter for Swinburne, whose earliest ambition it was to have been a soldier.

Mary's family must have realized the closeness of Mary's relationship with Swinburne, but it probably never occurred either to them or to her that he should want to marry her. For one thing, not only were they too closely related – their mothers were sisters and their fathers were first cousins, the sons of two brothers, who were first cousins to the Countess of Ashburnham; but for another, there were many things that made Swinburne undesirable as a son-in-law. Apart from all this, it seems that Swinburne had never even declared his love, although Mary seems to have become aware of it after her marriage.

Indeed, we know very little about the matter, except what can be inferred from Swinburne's poems and Mary's subsequent poems and novels, in which a Swinburne-like figure is invariably cast as the hero.[22] But when writing to Edmund Gosse on 3 August 1875, to congratulate him on his engagement, Swinburne said:[23]

> I wish you all the joy and good fortune that can be wished, and without admixture of envy of that particular form of happiness which I am now never likely to share. I suppose it must be the best thing that can befall a man to win and keep the woman that he loves while yet young; at any rate I can congratulate my friend on his good hap without any too jealous afterthought of the reverse experience which left my own young manhood 'a barren stock' – if I may cite that phrase without seeming to liken myself to a male Queen Elizabeth.

It was with this rueful witticism that he looked back upon the great disappointment of his life, a disappointment which was the source of a small group of his most moving poems. The news that he was to lose Mary altogether was evidently a calamity which, in his view, precluded the idea of marriage to anyone else – that is, he saw it as his last and only chance of achieving a relative sexual normality.

In 'The Triumph of Time', written at this date and published in *Poems and Ballads, First Series*, Swinburne describes himself as a man 'Whose whole life's love goes down in a day'. It is the most tragic of his poems, made none the less so by his clear-eyed perception of the hopelessness of the situation. For all its pain and regret, 'The Triumph of Time' is without self-pity:

> Before our lives divide for ever,
>   While time is with us and hands are free,
> (Time, swift to fasten and swift to sever
>   Hand from hand, as we stand by the sea)
> I will say no word that a man might say
> Whose whole life's love goes down in a day;
> For this could never have been; and never,
>   Though the gods and the years relent, shall be.

Is it worth a tear, is it worth an hour,
  To think of things that are well outworn?
Of fruitless husk and fugitive flower,
  The dream foregone and the deed forborne?
Though joy be done with and grief be vain,
Time shall not sever us wholly in twain;
Earth is not spoilt for a single shower;
  But the rain has ruined the ungrown corn.

It will grow not again, this fruit of my heart,
  Smitten with sunbeams, ruined with rain.
The singing seasons divide and depart,
  Winter and summer depart in twain.
It will grow not again, it is ruined at root,
The bloodlike blossom, the dull red fruit;
Though the heart yet sickens, the lips yet smart
  With sullen savour of poisonous pain . . .

I have put my days and dreams out of mind,
  Days that are over, dreams that are done.
Though we seek life through, we shall surely find
  There is none of them clear to us now, not one.
But clear are these things; the grass and the sand,
Where, sure as the eyes reach, ever at hand,
With lips wide open and face burnt blind,
  The strong sea-daisies feast on the sun.

The low downs lean to the sea; the stream,
  One loose thin pulseless tremulous vein,
Rapid and vivid and dumb as a dream,
  Works downward, sick of the sun and the rain;
No wind is rough with the rank rare flowers;
The sweet sea, mother of loves and hours,
Shudders and shines as the grey winds gleam,
  Turning her smile to a fugitive pain . . .

There will no man do for your sake, I think,
  What I would have done for the least word said.
I had wrung life dry for your lips to drink,
  Broken it up for your daily bread:
Body for body and blood for blood,
As the flow of the full sea risen to flood
That yearns and trembles before it sink,
  I had given, and lain down for you, glad and dead . . .

You have chosen and clung to the chance they sent you,
   Life sweet as perfume and pure as prayer.
But will it not one day in heaven repent you?
   Will they solace you wholly, the days that were?
Will you lift up your eyes between sadness and bliss,
Meet mine, and see where the great love is,
And tremble and turn and be changed? Content you;
   The gate is strait; I shall not be there.

But you, had you chosen, had you stretched hand,
   Had you seen good such a thing were done,
I too might have stood with the souls that stand
   In the sun's sight, clothed with the light of the sun;
But who now on earth need care how I live?
Have the high gods anything left to give,
Save dust and laurels and gold and sand?
   Which gifts are goodly; but I will none . . .

Where the dead red leaves of the years lie rotten,
   The cold old crimes and the deeds thrown by,
The misconceived and the misbegotten,
   I would find a sin to do ere I die,
Sure to dissolve and destroy me all through,
That would set you higher in heaven, serve you
And leave you happy, when clean forgotten,
   As a dead man out of mind, am I.

Your lithe hands draw me, your face burns through me,
   I am swift to follow you, keen to see;
But love lacks might to redeem or undo me,
   As I have been, I know I shall surely be;
'What should such fellows as I do?' Nay,
My part were worse if I chose to play;
For the worst is this after all; if they knew me,
   Not a soul upon earth would pity me.

And I play not for pity of these; but you,
   If you saw with your soul what man am I,
You would praise me at least that my soul all through
   Clove to you, loathing the lives that lie;
The souls and lips that are bought and sold,
The smiles of silver and kisses of gold,
The lapdog loves that whine as they chew,
   The little lovers that curse and cry.

The poem ends with a long and splendid invocation to the sea, Swinburne's eternal symbol of liberty, but here evidently of death, or, more specifically, of a return to the womb:

> I will go back to the great sweet mother,
>   Mother and lover of men, the sea.
> I will go down to her, I and none other.
>   Close with her, kiss her and mix her with me;
> Cling to her, strive with her, hold her fast;
> O fair white mother, in days long past
> Born without sister, born without brother,
>   Set free my soul as thy soul is free.
>
> O fair green-girdled mother of mine,
>   Sea, that art clothed with the sun and the rain,
> Thy sweet hard kisses are strong like wine,
>   Thy large embraces are keen like pain.
> Save me and hide me with all thy waves,
> Find me one grave of thy thousand graves,
> Those pure cold populous graves of thine,
>   Wrought without hand in a world without stain.

He concludes with the resolve of silence:

> Come life, come death, not a word be said:
> Should I lose you living, and vex you dead?
> I never shall tell you on earth; and in heaven,
>   If I cry to you then, will you hear or know?

This great poem is like a watershed in Swinburne's life: it tells us what is past and foreshadows what is to come.[24] It is followed in *Poems and Ballads* by 'Les Noyades'. Then comes the beautiful 'A Leave-Taking', a calm and sorrowful acceptance of an irrevocable situation:

> Let us go hence, my songs; she will not hear.
> Let us go hence together without fear;
> Keep silence now, for singing-time is over,
> And over all old things and all things dear.
> She loves not you nor me as all we love her.
> Yea, though we sang as angels in her ear,
>   She would not hear.
>
> Let us rise up and part; she will not know.
> Let us go seaward as the great winds go,
> Full of blown sand and foam; what help is there?
> There is no help, for all these things are so,
> And all the world is bitter as a tear.
> And how these things are, though ye strove to show
>   She would not know.

His bitterness and suffering break out again in 'Satia Te Sanguine' and 'Hesperia', and is not his frustrated love also at the root of the defiant bitterness and sadism of 'Dolores'?

Time turns the old days to derision,
Our loves to corpses or wives;
And marriage and death and division
Make barren our lives.

Swinburne himself said, in a letter of 9 October 1866, to William Rossetti, who had suggested that 'Dolores' should be bracketed with 'The Garden of Proserpine' and 'Hesperia': 'I should not like to bracket "Dolores" with the two following as you propose. I ought (if I did) to couple with them in front harness "The Triumph of Time", &c., as they express that state of feeling the reaction from which is expressed in "Dolores". Were I to re-christen these three as a trilogy, I should have to rename many earlier poems as acts in the same play.' If 'The Triumph of Time' and 'A Leave-Taking' were written to Mary Gordon, it is evident that Swinburne had come to identify her in his blasphemous litany with Our Lady of Pain – not that that endeared her to him any the less:[25]

Cold eyelids that hide like a jewel
Hard eyes that grow soft for an hour;
The heavy white limbs, and the cruel
Red mouth like a venomous flower.

But if 'Dolores' was the violent reaction from that state of feeling expressed in 'The Triumph of Time' and 'A Leave-Taking', its poetic source is also to be found in the French Romantics, Baudelaire and Gautier, and the Flaubert of the early letters and *Salambô*, who idolized the sadistic orgies of imperial Rome and regarded Nero as its supreme poet:

When, with flame all around him aspirant,
Stood flushed, as a harp-player stands,
The implacable beautiful tyrant,
Rose-crowned, having death in his hands;
And a sound as the sound of loud water
Smote far through the flight of the fires,
And mixed with the lightening of slaughter
A thunder of lyres.

For all the apparently moral indignation caused by *Poems and Ballads, First Series* on its appearance, what in all Swinburne's fantasies of cruelty can compare with the appalling last pages of *Salambô*? How comparatively innocent he appears when compared to Flaubert and Baudelaire, and their *goût de l'horrible.* The natural reaction to 'Dolores' would seem to be the weary renunciation and death-longing of 'The Garden of Proserpine' – though actually this was written earlier. If he celebrated 'sterile loves' in 'Anactoria' and other poems, what else in the circumstances was left for him to do? They were all, as he said, 'acts in the same play'.

One of the triumphs of the first *Poems and Ballads* was 'Laus Veneris', with its lines:

> Night falls like fire; the heavy lights run low,
> And as they drop, my blood and body so
>    Shake as the flame shakes, full of days and hours
> That sleep not neither weep they as they go.

of which William Empson has remarked very acutely: 'the indoor Victorian-furnished Venusberg becomes hotter, stuffier and more enclosed, more irritating to sick head-ache and nervous exhaustion, and the gas-jet will have to be popping from now on. Or the *flame* may be a symbolical candle; it gutters in its socket which, low in its last struggles, it scorches, and rises and falls in popping and jerking disorder, like the throbbing and swooning headache, and casts threatening shadows on the walls. *Full* because it has ended the time it is capable of, and because in its shaking it seems to be measuring seconds magnified by a sick-bed fixity of attention into *hours*; not *sleeping* or *weeping*, because of the poet's insomnia and emotional exhaustion, because of its contrast with, and indifference to, his *weeping* and the approaching *sleep* of his death, and because, in the story, this mood is fixed into an eternity outside the human order in which tears are pointless, and the peace even of death unattainable.'[26]

But by this time, love had come to seem to Swinburne something deadly, devouring, even carnivorous, as he writes in 'Laus Veneris':

> As one who hidden in deep sedge and reeds
> Smells the rare scent made where a panther feeds,
>    And tracking ever slotwise the warm smell
> Is snapped upon by the sweet mouth and bleeds,
>
> His head far down the hot sweet throat of her –
> So one tracks love, whose breath is deadlier,
>    And lo, one springe and you are fast in hell,
> Fast as the gin's grip of a wayfarer.

It might be objected that this is to put Swinburne in the place of Tannhäuser and that 'Laus Veneris' is a dramatic poem not to be interpreted personally. But the same panther image for passion occurs again in other poems, most powerfully in 'At a Month's End', included in *Poems and Ballads, Second Series* (1878), but probably written much earlier, which describes the last meeting of two lovers by the sea:

Should Love disown or disesteem you
For loving one man more or less?
You could not tame your light white sea-mew,
Nor I my sleek black pantheress. . . .

But I, who leave my queen of panthers,
As a tired honey-heavy bee
Gilt with sweet dust from gold-grained anthers
Leaves the rose-chalice, what for me?

From the ardours of the chaliced centre,
From the amorous anthers' golden grime,
That scorch and smutch all wings that enter,
I fly forth hot from honey-time.

But as to a bee's gilt thighs and winglets
The flower-dust with the flower-smell clings;
As a snake's mobile rampant ringlets
Leave the sand marked with print of rings;

So to my soul in surer fashion
Your savage stamp and savour hangs;
The print and perfume of old passion,
The wild-beast mark of panther's fangs.

This poem, of which these splendid lines are the conclusion, with its nakedly sexual imagery, is closely related to admittedly personal poems such as 'The Triumph of Time' and 'A Leave-Taking', and must belong to the later 1860s. As we know, Swinburne saw himself as a 'light white sea-mew'. Had he by now come to see his cousin not only as Dolores but as 'a sleek black pantheress'? The first verses show that it does not refer to some casual affair of a month's duration.

The night last night was strange and shaken;
More strange the change of you and me.
Once more, for the old love's love forsaken,
We went out once more toward the sea.

For the old love's love-sake dead and buried,
One last time, one more and no more,
We watched the waves set in, the serried
Spears of the tide storming the shore.

Indeed, the line 'One last time, one more and no more' has the tolling finality of a funeral bell.

When Swinburne sent 'At a Month's End' to *Frazer's Magazine* some time during autumn 1870, J. A. Froude, the editor, objected to the naked eroticism of some of its verses and, in a letter to Thomas Purnell, Swinburne wrote that: 'It would be to me a violation of principle to submit a child of my begetting to the knife of castration even to enable it to sing in the Sistine Chapel – under Pope Froude. . . . Surely it's absurd to object as if the passage were directly descriptive of a man having a girl – whereas it's a mere figure or symbol of two leopards gambolling.'[27] But this is disingenuous. It would be truer to say that it was directly descriptive of two leopards copulating:

> You, couched at long length on hot sand
> With some sleek sun-discoloured lover,
> Wince from his breath as from a brand:
>
> Till the acrid hour aches out and ceases,
> And the sheathed eyeball sleepier swims,
> The deep flank smoothes its dimpling creases,
> And passion loosens all the limbs:
>
> Till dreams of sharp grey north-sea weather
> Fall faint upon your fiery sleep,
> As on strange sands a strayed bird's feather
> The wind may choose to lose or keep

But what, indeed, of the 'tired honey-heavy bee' to which Swinburne likens himself? There is clearly some ambiguity here which awaits Professor Empson's elucidation.

It would seem rather as if the images of two women went to the making of this poem: the one associated in the poet's mind with the northern seas beside which he had taken a last farewell of her, and the other an exotic panther-like creature with whom he had tried vainly to assuage the pain of loving the first. It has been surmised that his second woman is Adah Menken. But it is not, perhaps, stretching probability too far to look for her in the Spartali–Cassavetti–Zambacco clan so much admired by Rossetti, Burne-Jones and Whistler, whom Swinburne could hardly avoid meeting. It was with Marie Zambacco that Burne-Jones fell passionately in love at this time, and he introduced two black panthers into his *The Wine of Circe*, begun earlier but finished in 1869:

> So may one read his weird, and reason,
> And with vain drugs assuage no pain.
> For each man in his loving season
> Fools and is fooled of these in vain.
>
> Charms that allay not any longing,
> Spells that appease not any grief,
> Time brings us all by handfuls, wronging
> All hurts with nothing of relief. . . .

For a new soul let whoso please pray,
  We are what life made us, and shall be.
You for the jungle and me the sea-spray,
  And south for you and north for me.

Meeting Marie Spartali, one of the daughters of the Greek Consul-General in London, who was frequently painted by Rossetti, just as her sister Christine was painted by Whistler, at a garden party, Swinburne is reported to have said: 'She is so beautiful that I want to sit down and cry.'[28] Why? Because he knew that he was so constituted that women were for ever beyond his reach – and that he had to make them into flowers, panthers or snakes? Though Swinburne's work shows that he was fascinated by sexual ambiguity, as were the French romantics, it also shows that he was deeply moved by the beauty of women, though their beauty was for him always tormentingly wedded to pain and frustration.

Swinburne was never to write so powerful a poem again, though 'At a Month's End' is related in mood to both 'A Forsaken Garden' and 'Relics', which immediately precede it in the same volume and whose setting is the West Undercliff, near East Dene, fused in 'Relics', with memories of Italy. Both poems are elegies on lost happiness:

This flower that smells of honey and the sea,
White laurustine, seems in my hand to be
  A white star made of memory long ago
Lit in the heaven of dear times dead to me.

A star out of the skies love used to know
Here held in hand, a stray left yet to show
  What flowers my heart was full of in the days
That are long since gone down dead memory's flow

Dead memory that revives on doubtful ways,
Half hearkening what the buried season says
  Out of the world of the unapparent dead
Where the lost Aprils are, and the lost Mays.

'A Forsaken Garden', too, is inhabited only by memories and the ghosts of dead lovers. It ends with the dissolution of all things, when the land at last crumbles into the rising sea.

Meanwhile, Swinburne was at work on the fragmentary novel known as *Lesbia Brandon*, which was to occupy him at intervals until 1876–77. This was not published until 1952 in a very carelessly printed edition by the late Randolph Hughes, with a colossal, eulogistic 'Commentary' more than twice as long as the novel itself. Working from the dirty, stained and blotted manuscripts in the British Museum and Swinburne's set of galley sheets,

Hughes argued that *Lesbia Brandon* evolved through four stages, each of which is a distinct novel or fragment of a novel. They are all unfinished. Thomas J. Wise bound up the longest fragment and gave it the title, by which it is now known, quite unsuitably because Margaret, Lady Wariston, not Lesbia, is the real heroine and her brother Herbert Seyton the hero. This deals with Herbert's boyhood in Northumberland, his hopeless love affair with Lesbia and his early passion for his own sister, with whom the sadistic tutor Denham is also in love. But Margaret is married, with children, and later turns out to be Denham's half-sister. The manuscript as bound up by Wise ends with Lesbia's suicide and is preceded by the suicide of Margaret's lover, presumably Denham – he is not actually named, but there is some doubt who he is, for in any case these scenes are written on different paper and clearly do not belong where Wise placed them. In the opinion of Hughes, they should be the final pages of the book. Other chapters introduce Lady Midhurst from *Love's Cross-Currents* and a debauched unpleasant character, Mr Linley, a collector of 'bric-à-brac of a secret kind, kept under locks and behind curtains'. There is also an Italian revolutionary, modelled on Mazzini, and a French counterpart, and a demi-mondaine Leonora Harley, whose appearance at first suggests Jane Morris, though she is unlike her in most other respects: 'She had a superb and seductive beauty, some kindness of nature and no mind whatever. Tall, white-faced, long-limbed, with melancholy eyes that meant nothing and suggested everything.'[29]

The relationships are even more complicated than in *Love's Cross-Currents* and, even as edited by Hughes, the final effect is bewildering. One has the impression that Swinburne had already begun to lose his way in the maze, though a great part of the book was either unwritten or is now missing. The early chapters despite their splendid passages of natural description are marred by frequent and unpleasant flagellation scenes, particularly one in which Herbert is still naked and wet from bathing, though his floggings are represented as being a source of exhilaration to him and are not objected to by his sister. Both novels are clearly about the same families, and Herbert Seyton, like Reginald Harewood, is a self-portrait. There is much play with sexual ambiguity, sado-masochism, transvesticism and the incest motive. 'There was a strong feminine element in Bertie,' we are told, 'he ought to have been a pretty rather boyish girl.' When his sister, Margaret, sings him a grim border ballad, he remarks: 'I like that. It's so jolly vicious: and I like the water being a woman.' Bertie's dream is particularly revealing of Swinburne's psychology. The star Venus appears to him as a white rose whose centre is a red mouth. As it descends upon him, 'instead of desire he felt horror and sickness at the sight of it, and averted his lips with an effort to utter some prayer or exorcism: vainly, for the dreadful mouth only laughed, and came closer'. Then the noise of the sea 'hardened and deepened and grew untunable; soon it sharpened into a shrill threatening note without sense or pity, but full of vicious design. He woke as the salt froth seemed coming round his lips and nostrils and ears, with a sense of sterility and perplexity which outwent all other pain. The torture of the dream was the fancy that these fairest things, sea and sky, star and flower, light and music, were all unfruitful and barren.'[30]

According to Freud, blossoms and flowers in dreams symbolize the female sexual organ, of which, in this dream at any rate, Bertie–Algernon has a deep-seated horror. In the novel, the dream is symbolic of Bertie's sterile love for Lesbia, who is represented as a horsewoman who writes poetry, like Mary Gordon. Bertie first appears to her dressed as a girl for a charade and she thinks he is Margaret's sister and is violently attracted by him. Denham expresses the frustration of his love for Margaret by savage floggings of her brother. Later it appears that he is the illegitimate son of Seyton, Bertie's father, the lover of Margaret's mother, who was married first to Lord Charles Brandon. Lesbia, Bertie and Denham are therefore all closely related. Swinburne projects on to Denham his own sado-masochistic feelings centred round his cousin – 'self-contempt, envy, and the rage of inverted love and passion poisoned in the springs.... A pungent sense of tears pricked his eyelids and a bitter taste was on his tongue when she went out. Her godlike beauty was as blind and unmerciful as a god. Hating her with all his heart, as he loved her with all his senses, he could but punish her through her brother, hurt her through his skin.' Looking at Lady Wariston, Denham feels that 'He would have given his life for leave to touch her, his soul for a chance of dying crushed down under her feet: an emotion of extreme tenderness, lashed to fierce insanity by the circumstances, frothed over into a passion of vehement cruelty.' Maniacally, he wants to 'scourge her into swooning and absorb the blood with kisses, caress and lacerate her loveliness ... to feel her foot upon his throat, and wound her own with his teeth ... bite through her sweet and shuddering lips'.[31] Catullus's '*odi et amo ... et excrucior*' is the tragic recurring motive, as in all Swinburne's work, poetry and fiction alike.

Margaret Wariston is a sad, Pre-Raphaelite beauty, like Clara in *Love's Cross-Currents*. She has 'sombre and luminous eyes, with deep thick eyelids and heavy lashes that seemed as though sodden and satiate with old and past tears'.[32] In chapter three, as edited by Hughes, there is an erotic scene between brother and sister, when Bertie is still a small boy, that reads like something out of Krafft-Ebing. Margaret has come to his room to say good-night and to sing to him, as she had promised. Bertie is so exhausted by his morning's bathe in the rough sea followed by one of Denham's savage floggings that he has fallen asleep while undressing and his sister wakes him with a kiss on the lips. As the firelight wanes, she stops singing and he falls on his knees before her:[33]

> Kneeling with his face lifted to hers, he inhaled the hot fragrance of her face and neck, and trembled with intense and tender delight. Her perfume

thrilled and stung him; he bent down and kissed her feet, reached up and kissed her throat.

'You smell of flowers in a hot sun,' he said, kissing her feet again with violent lips that felt the sweet-scented flesh pressing them back through its soft covering. She laughed and winced under the heat of his hard kiss, drawing one foot back and . . . [illegible] . . . lightly with the other, which he took and pressed down upon his neck.

'Oh! I should like you to tread me to death! darling!'

She took him by the hair and shook his head to and fro, laughing as the close elastic curls rebelled against her fingers.

'I say, let your hair go,' said Herbert, putting his arms under hers: she loosened the fastenings, and it rushed downwards, a tempest and torrent of sudden tresses, heavy and tawny and riotous and radiant, over shoulders and arms and bosom; and under cover of the massive and luminous locks she drew up his face against her own and kissed him time after time with all her strength.

'Now go to bed, and sleep well,' she said, pressing him back. His whole spirit was moved with the passionate motion of his senses; he clung to her for a minute, and rose up throbbing from head to foot with violent love. . . .

'I wish you would kill me some day; it would be jolly to feel you killing me. Not like it? Shouldn't I! You just hurt me, and see.'

She pinched him so sharply that he laughed and panted with pleasure.

'You are the most insane child I know, and will be quite mad at this rate before you are marriageable; and Miss Brandon will have to dispense with you. Good-night and let me go, or you will be late to-morrow, and get punished again.'

'I should like being swished even I think, if you were to complain of me or if I knew you liked [it].'

'Poor old child, I'm afraid you had enough of that this morning; don't get into more trouble, for I don't happen to like it at all. Good-night, dear: I know; I love you too' (as he caressed her with signs and speechless kisses, flattering her with hands and eyes significant of love), 'I know you do; and I you, and more than I can say. There, that's enough and plain enough. Now, my dear old minor, as Wariston calls you, please let me go once for all.'

'I'm glad you're not a boy though,' said Herbert.

He fell asleep with her kisses burnt into his mind, and the ineffaceable brand of love upon his thoughts: and dreamed passionately of his passion. . . . But the one keen and hard impression left on him by the whole day's work was this of desperate tenderness and violent submission of soul and body to her love.

Certainly it had been an eventful day for Bertie. Disobeying Denham's command not to bathe, he had saved the life of a fisherman's boy, whose boat had overturned. Luckily, both had been flung far up on to the shingle by a tremendous wave, after having the breath beaten out of them in the surf. Ashamed to own up to this heroic act on his return to Ensdon, Bertie had been mercilessly flogged by Denham. Later in the day, in the middle of a house party, the boy's father comes up to the house to thank Bertie for what he has done, and, scarlet with embarrassment, he is dragged to the door by Margaret to meet him. Curiously enough, Denham is not reproved for his brutality, though Margaret 'made herself pleasant beyond words to the boy all the rest of the day'. All through dinner, however, he is teased by the guests, especially when the subject of Eton crops up in the conversation. But when his sister comes to day 'good-night' to him, she makes ample amends.

The incestuous hot-house atmosphere of such indoor scenes contrasts strangely with the splendid descriptions of the Northumberland landscape, and the wild delight in riding and swimming. The atmosphere of the book is far more uninhibited than *A Year's Letters.* One feels that here Swinburne really let himself go, disguising nothing and holding nothing back. It is for this reason, of course, that, when he gave it to him to read, Theodore Watts deliberately 'lost' three chapters, which he did not 'find' again until after Swinburne's death. Watts, while approving a revised form of *A Year's Letters* as *Love's Cross-Currents*, was determined that his friend should neither finish nor publish *Lesbia Brandon.* This is a pity, perhaps, because in this novel Swinburne gives us an intimate picture of an inbred, mid-Victorian aristocratic society of which we have no other record. His aim, as he said, was to write a novel in the manner of Balzac – 'studies of life and character in our own day', as he described it later in a letter to Eliza Lynn Linton, the novelist. Indeed, Edmund Wilson points out that the conversation of Lady Midhurst and Mr Linley has something in common with the dialogue of both Meredith and Wilde, and 'seems to show that the latter was exploiting a vein of epigrammatic talk which had already been brought to perfection in the social life of London by the middle of the nineteenth century'.[34]

Mr Linley's aesthetic philosophy, as Randolph Hughes shows in his 'Commentary', is taken over almost bodily, as was Oscar Wilde's, from Baudelaire and Gautier. 'I fear sometimes,' Mr Linley says, 'that nature is a democrat. Beauty you see is an exception; and exception means rebellion against a rule. . . . Nature, I think, if she had her own way would grow nothing but turnips. . . . It's the same with all exceptions, beauty which is best of all, and genius. . . . Each of these is an insult, an outrage, an oppression and affliction to the ugly, the poor and the despondent.' But the greatest of all influences – particularly in the careful descriptions of physical characteristics – upon Swinburne in this novel was Balzac, as Hughes convincingly demonstrates, though far too much of his 'Commentary' is devoted to ill-mannered abuse of his predecessors, especially Gosse and Lafourcade.

The abuse of Wise is evidently justified. But more to the point is Lafourcade's summing up of Gosse's *Life*. After paying tribute to it as a work of art, he continues: 'Car l'artiste après avoir ouvert les armoires les plus secrètes où voisinent nectar et poison, en a fermé soigneusement chaque porte et jeté chaque clef dans les eaux de la lagune voisine; mais le biographie ne doit-il pas, sans pour çela les vider de fond en comble ni les laisser béantes, en désigner discrètement la serrure aux lecteurs avisés?' He concludes: 'Une biographie magistrale mais elliptique et concise.'[35]

Swinburne was still working at *Lesbia Brandon* as late as 1876–77, at a time when he was approaching the final breakdown of his health. When he left his rooms to recuperate with his family at Holmwood, his papers had become hopelessly disordered. Wise bound up the loose pages in an order that seemed to him consecutive, though in places they are merely jumbled together, in an attempt to make a complete novel. Hughes rearranged them in a more coherent form. The bound MSS. open with a description of a girl's eyes, which gives one the sensation of looking at them through a magnifying glass. The girl is nameless, but is evidently Margaret Wariston:[36]

> Her eyes had an outer ring of seeming black, but in effect deep blue and dark grey mixed; this soft and broad circle of colour sharply divided the subtle and tender white, pale as pure milk, from an iris which should have been hazel or grey, blue or green, but was instead a more delicate and significant shade of the colour more common with beast or bird, pure gold, without alloy or allay, like the yellowest part of a clear flame; such eyes as the greatest analyst of spirit and flesh that ever lived and spoke has noticed as proper to certain rare women, and has given for a perpetual and terrible memory to his Georgian girl. In a dark face, southern or eastern, the colour should be yet rarer, and may perhaps be more singularly beautiful even here, where it gave to the fair and floral beauty of northern features a fire and rapture of life. These eyes were not hard or shadowless; their colour was full of small soft intricacies of shade and varieties of tone; they could darken with delicate alteration and lighten with splendid change. The iris had fine fibres of light and tender notes of colour that gave the effect of shadow; as if the painter's touch when about to darken the clear fierce beauty of their vital and sensitive gold had paused in time and left them perfect. The pupil was not over large, and seemed as the light touched it of molten purple or of black velvet. They had infinite significance, infinite fervour and purity. The eyelashes and eyebrows were of a golden brown, long and full; their really soft shade of colour seemed dark on a skin of white rose-leaves, between a double golden flame of eyes and hair.

'The greatest analyst of flesh and spirit that ever lived' is Balzac and 'the Georgian girl' is Paquita Valdes in *La Fille aux yeux d'or*, a lesbian who is described as having eyes like a tiger's.

Of the girl's brother we are told, 'while yet a boy [he] was so like her that the description may serve for him with a difference. They had the same complexion and skin so thin and fair that it glittered against the light as white silk does, taking sharper and fainter tones of white that shone and melted into each other. His hair had much more brown and red mixed with it than hers, but like hers was yellowish underneath and rippled from the roots, and not less elastic in the rebellious undulation of the curls . . . the iris of his eyes, which might have been classed as hazel more fairly than hers, were rather the colour of bronze than of gold, and the shades and tones of its colour were more variable, having an admixture of green like the eyes of pure northern races, and touched with yellow and brown; except for the green in them, best definable as citrine eyes, but not easy to define; soft and shifting like brilliant sea-water with golden lights in it; the pupils purple and the rings violet. . . . Looked well into and through, they showed tints of blue and grey like those of sea-mosses seen under a soft vague surface of clear water which blends and brightens their sudden phases of colour: they were sharp at once and reflective, rapid and timid, full of daring or of dreams: with darker lashes, longer and wavier than his sister's.'[37]

In this passage Swinburne is obviously describing his own eyes. The description of brother and sister continues:[38]

> under any pleasant excitement the sudden blood began to throb visibly at his finger-tips, threading the flushed skin with purple and blue. The face and hands of both were perceptibly nervous and sensitive, his perhaps more than hers. The least contact of anything sharp would graze the skin unawares and draw blood before they knew it, so the lightest touch of pain or pleasure would strike and sting their nerves to the quick. In bright perfect health they were as susceptible in secret of harsh sounds, of painful sights and odours, as any one born weaklier; whatever they had to suffer and enjoy came to them hot and strong, untempered and unalloyed. Both had the courage of their kind, nervous and fearless, inherited.

And here the manuscript breaks off except for another page of six more lines discovered by Mr Mayfield and bound into the MS. in 1967. The next chapter begins in the middle of a sentence with a description of the death and funeral of Herbert's father, by which he is desolated (though Swinburne is here evidently describing his feelings on the death of his grandfather), then goes on to describe the house, Ensdon – that is, Capheaton and Ashburnham Place combined – situated two miles inland from the sea, at which Lord Wariston and his wife Margaret live:[39]

> a large inconsistent house of yellow sandstone, defiant of architecture, with deep windows, long thin wings, and high front. Rains and sea-winds had worn it and the crumbling sandstone here and there had fallen away

in flakes. . . . The whole place had a stately recluse beauty; fields and woods divided the park from the sea-downs. . . . A green moist place, lying wide and low, divided from the inland moors by a windy wall of bare broken crag, and with all its lower fields facing the sea and the sun: sparing rather than lavish of natural fruit and flower, but with well-grown trees and deep-walled gardens to the back of it.

Of Herbert we are told: 'for places rather than persons he had a violent and blind affection'. Yet he soon has a violent affection for Lesbia Brandon who, in appearance at least, though hardly in character, is, Lafourcade suggests, modelled on Christina Rossetti. Randolph Hughes, however, will not have this and points out that she is derived almost entirely from the Fragoletta of Henri de Latouche, as is the poem of this name in *Poems and Ballads*. Swinburne's descriptions are often like those of a painter:[40]

> Miss Brandon was dark and delicately shaped; not tall, but erect and supple; she had thick and heavy hair growing low on the forehead, so brown that it seemed black in the shadow; her eyes were sombre and mobile, full of fervour and dreams, answering in colour to her hair, as did also the brows and eyelashes. Her cheeks had the profound pallor of complexions at once dark and colourless, but the skin was pure and tender, the outline clear and soft; she was warm and wan as a hot day without sun. She had a fine and close mouth, with small bright lips, not variable in expression; her throat and shoulders were fresh and round. A certain power and a certain trouble were perceptible in the face, but traceable to no single feature: apart from whatever it might have of beauty, the face was one to attract rather than satisfy.

When Herbert reads Lesbia's verses, he is 'stung' and 'soothed with gentle delight'. Actually, she is as masculine by temperament as he is feminine. In the chapter 'On the Downs' she says to him, while they are out riding: 'If I could love or marry, I am sure I could love and marry you, absurd as people would call it. But I can't. I don't know why, at least I don't wholly know. I am made as I am, and God knows why – I suppose. You quite deserve that I should be fair to you, and truthful. I never felt for anyone what I feel for you now, and shall while I live. I do really in a way, so to speak, love you. And you can see by my way of telling you this that I can never by any chance love you otherwise or love you more. Make up your mind to that once for all . . . But you must understand there may be love between us but there must be no more love-making. I am not marriageable. Neither you nor I will ever revert to this. I hope and think you know I am speaking the plainest truth as kindly as I can.'

Later Lesbia says: 'I don't know if you would like it or not, but I should like to feel thoroughly that we were not less than brother and sister.' Of Herbert we are told that 'he loved her too much to show that he did: but his heart was wrung and stung with strange small tortures. . . . He sat and felt a breakage inside him of all that made up the hopefullest parts of his life. But being too old a male to express suffering by any puerile suffusion of tears or blood, he did before long make some courteous and vacuous reply': evidently insufficient, for Miss Brandon rejoined: '"I cannot see why we shouldn't be friends. I might be your elder brother. But if necessary I'll disown you." "You needn't do that," said Herbert in a voice clear and fresh enough. "I'll do my best as a – cadet, if I must . . . I'm only waiting for the word of command," said Herbert with a false light smile. "And I can't give it," said Lesbia, with an equally amiable face. "I've no doubt if I could you would organise a forlorn hope. Don't let your mind dwell upon that chance, it doesn't exist."' And Herbert replies: '"Well, I shan't serve under other flags; for some time."'[41]

One is struck here by the cruelty of Lesbia as well as by the similarity to the situation when Mary Gordon told Swinburne that she could not marry him, but that she 'really in a way, so to speak, loved him'. There can be little doubt that in this scene Swinburne is drawing upon this experience. These pages of the manuscript are unusually full of blots and wine-stains and were evidently written in a state of great agitation. And when Lesbia slowly poisons herself in the chapter called 'Leucadia' (a reference to Sappho's suicide on the island of Leucadia) with doses of eau-de-cologne and opium, she sends for Herbert to sit by her while she dies, principally because she wants someone to talk to and also because she enjoys tormenting him:[42]

> She looked like one whom death was visibly devouring . . . as though fire had caught hold of her bound at a stake: like one whose life had been long sapped and undermined from the roots by some quiet fiery poison . . . The figure and the place were lurid in his eyes, and less fit to make one weep than to make him kindle and tremble. There was an attraction in them which shot heat into his veins instead of the chill and heaviness of terror or grief . . . he felt a cruel impersonal displeasure compounded of fear and pain in the study of her last symptoms.

As Lesbia lies half-conscious, she has a vision of Persephone, which recalls, with its fields of pale poppies and blue aconites, Swinburne's 'Garden of Proserpine', but the goddess has the eyes of Margaret Wariston, with whom Lesbia is really in love. She asks Herbert, ironically, as her 'brother', to kiss her, and when he 'plunged his lips into hers, hot and shuddering, and devoured her fallen features with sharp sad kisses', she understandably pushes him away in horror: 'There was a savage terror in her voice and gesture; the hands that thrust him back, the eyes that shone with fear of him, might but have excited him further into a passion of bitter pity and love, but for the mad repugnance, the blind absolute horror, expressed in all her struggling figure and labouring limbs. He let her go, and she cowered away against the wall, moaning and shaking like a thing stricken to death.'[43] And so in this novel, too, the lovers are defeated and their emotions rendered as sterile as those of the related pairs in *Love's Cross-Currents*.

Lafourcade argues that *Lesbia Brandon* is not, properly speaking, a novel at all, but a sort of *journal intime* in which all the characters are reflections of different sides of Swinburne's sensibility. The book should, therefore, he contends, be regarded as a sort of confession, a 'disguised intellectual biography', or simply a collection of separate 'poems'. We know, however, that Swinburne did intend it as a novel. Moreover, it is referred to as a novel by Mrs Leith, when she says that Swinburne read passages of it to her in 1864 at her father's house in Chelsea. In any case, the characters in many novels may be regarded as reflections of the different sides of their author's sensibility, and Swinburne's sensibility was nothing if not complex and many-sided.

Both Watts and Gosse regarded *Lesbia Brandon* as unpublishable, but it tells us much about Swinburne. Certainly the situations are sometimes so preposterous that one begins to think that perhaps Watts was right after all. The writer of whom one thinks most often when reading its passionate lyrical flights is D. H. Lawrence, and how, one asks oneself, would Watts and Gosse have reacted to *The Rainbow* or *Woman in Love*? With its hot, unhealthy, tangled relationships, the only purifying element in *Lesbia Brandon* is external nature, particularly the sea, and to the sea Swinburne's response was, as always, overwhelming:[44]

> He went straight at the next wave, laughing; sprang into it with eyes shut and was hurled back with the thunder in his ears, with limbs and face lashed by lighter shingle driven straight through the yellow water. The sea was thick and solid with sand and flying pebbles, and waifs of weed fastened round the boy's throat and hampered his legs. Feeling the shingle under him, he rose reeling on his feet in the sudden shallow, breathed deep and made for the next breaker. A few short sharp strokes brought him close and the recoiling water sucked him into the curve of the sea. Loose foam fluttered along the edge of it, but he got over before the crash, swimming lightly across the heaving half-broken ridge of wrinkled water.

No wonder Swinburne called the Mediterranean a 'tideless dolorous midland sea', as he saw it in summer on the Riviera, tepid and sluggish. No one has ever written of our tumultuous northern seas as he has:[45]

> he panted and shouted with pleasure among the breakers where he could not stand two minutes; the blow of a roller that beat him off his feet made him laugh and cry out in ecstacy; he rioted in the roaring water like a young sea-beast, sprang at the throat of the waves that threw him flat, pressed up against their soft fierce bosoms and fought for their sharp

embraces; grappled with them as lover with lover, flung himself upon them with limbs that laboured and yielded deliciously, till the scourging of the surf made him red from the shoulders to the knees, and sent him on shore whipped by the sea into a single blush of the whole skin, breathless and untired.

Swinburne now had three books ready for publication, *Atalanta*, *Chastelard*, and the poems which appeared two years later in *Poems and Ballads, First Series*. But Rossetti wrote to him strongly advising against the publication of the poems at that time:

> I shall rejoice to see you again in London after this age we have not abused each other face to face. It is good news to hear that *Atalanta* is approaching publication. I really believe on the whole that this is the best thing to bring out first. It is calculated to put people in better humour for the others, which when they do come will still make a few not even particular hairs to stand on end. . . . I tremble for the result of your reading Baudelaire's suppressed poems, the crop of which I did expect to be in fine flower, not to say fruit, by the time I reach London. If so and these new revelations are to be printed too, I warn you that the public will not be able to digest them, and that the paternal purse will have to stand the additional expense of an emetic presented gratis with each copy to relieve the outraged British nation.

But Swinburne was not to be deterred and looked forward with a wicked and gleeful anticipation to outraging the nation.

## CHAPTER SIX

# 1865–66

# *ATALANTA: POEMS AND BALLADS: NOTES ON POEMS AND REVIEWS*

With the publication of *Atalanta in Calydon* by Moxons in March 1865 Swinburne suddenly achieved fame. Nothing could have been less like *The Idylls of the King* or the domestic pastoral *Enoch Arden*, published in the previous year, than its tumultuous music. Nothing remotely resembling it had been written in English since Shelley's *Prometheus Unbound*. Compared by some to Aeschylus and Sophocles, the power and passion of its verse swept all before it, and a reprint was called for almost immediately. Wrote Mackail: 'The poetical atmosphere of the times was exhausted and heavy, like that of a sultry afternoon darkening to thunder. Out of that stagnation broke, all in a moment, the blaze and crash of *Atalanta in Calydon*.' The rhythm, said Burne-Jones, 'goes on with such a rush that it is enough to carry the world away', and Tennyson wrote to Swinburne telling him that he envied his 'wonderful rhythmic invention'. The sustained eloquence and bright loveliness of *Atalanta* can still astonish.

The poem was, as we have seen, conceived in the summer of 1863 and written, at intervals, with great rapidity. It was begun during Swinburne's stay at the Gordons's home in the Isle of Wight. 'In our library, often alone with my mother and myself, much of the work was written out, and the table would be strewn with the big sheets of MS.,' writes Mrs Leith. Swinburne ceased work on his drama in February 1864, when he went abroad with Lord Houghton, visiting Landor in Florence in March, and he did not seriously resume work upon it until August, when he went to stay for three months with Inchbold at Tintagel. It was, therefore, begun by the sea and finished by the sea.

'It was begun last autumn twelvemonth, when we were all freshly unhappy' [after his sister Edith's death], Swinburne wrote to Lady Trevelyan on 15 March 1865, 'and finished just after I got the news in September last, of Mr Landor's death, which was a considerable trouble to me, as I had hoped against hope or reason that he who in the spring in Florence had accepted the dedication of an unfinished poem would live to receive and read it. You will recognise the allusion to his life and death at pp. 25 & 6. As it is he never read anything of mine more mature than Rosamond. In spite of the funereal circumstances which I suspect have a little deepened the natural colours of Greek fatalism here and there, so as to have already incurred the charge of "rebellious antagonism" and such like things, I never enjoyed anything more in my life than the composition of this poem, which though a work done by intervals, was very rapid and pleasant. Allowing for a few after insertions, two or three in all, from p. 66 to 83 (as far as the Chorus) was the work of two afternoons, and from p. 83 to the end was the work of two other afternoons. . . . I think it is pure Greek and the first poem of the sort in modern times, combining lyric and dramatic work on the old principle. Shelley's Prometheus is magnificent and un-Hellenic, spoilt too, in my mind, by the infusion of philanthropic doctrinaire views and "progress of the species"; and by what I gather from Lewes's Life of Goethe the Iphigenia in Tauris must be also impregnated with modern morals and feelings. As for Professor Arnold's Merope the clothes are well enough but where has the body gone?'

Swinburne was living at his father's town house, taken for the winter in Wilton Crescent and 'looking out in a vague desolate way for chambers where I shall be able to shift for myself en permanence. My father as you may well have heard has completed the purchase of his place in Oxfordshire, Holmwood. They move in, I believe, next month.' The admiral had sold East Dene and the family was moving to Shiplake, near Henley. 'I only wish you were in London,' he adds, 'for Madox Brown's Exhibition of pictures, which is superb. I never knew till now how great and various and consistent a painter he is.'[1]

Ruskin described *Atalanta* as 'the grandest thing ever done by a youth, though he is a demoniac youth. Whether ever he will be clothed and in his right mind, heaven only knows. His foam at the mouth is fine, meantime.' Browning, however, found it 'a fuzz of words'. In spite of the blithe exhilaration of the verse, *Atalanta* is a deeply pessimistic work, modern in the sense of being impregnated with the bitter anti-theism of Blake and de Sade, and its indictment of 'the supreme evil, God'. Fortunately, this was not recognized, as few people had read either Blake's 'Prophetic Books' or *Justine*. Lord Houghton had done much preparatory spadework in bringing the book to the notice of critics and reviewers, and in July Swinburne wrote to thank him for his notice in the *Edinburgh Review*, in which he had condemned the poem's moral tone and its 'bitter, angry anti-theism, which has its place among the aberrations of human nature, but not in Greek culture'. In this he was right. 'As to the praise of myself,' wrote Swinburne, 'a poet more drunk with vanity than with wine could wish for no more. I only regret that in justly attacking my Antitheism you have wilfully misrepresented its source. I should have bowed to the judicial sentence if instead of "Byron with a difference" you had said "de Sade with a difference". The poet, thinker, and man of the world from whom the theology of my poem is derived was a greater than Byron. *He* indeed, fatalist or not, saw to the bottom of gods and men. As to anything you have fished (how I say not) out of Mrs Burton to the discredit of my "temperance, soberness and chastity" as the Catechism puts it – how can she who believes in the excellence of "Richard" fail to disbelieve in the virtues of any other men? En moi vous voyez Les Malheurs de la Vertu; en lui Les Prospérités du Vice. In effect it is not given to all his juniors to tenir tête à Burton – but I deny that his hospitality ever succeeded in upsetting me – as he himself on the morrow of a latish séance admitted with approbation, allowing that he had thought to get me off my legs, but my native virtue and circumspection were too much for him.'[2] As Gosse remarks: 'This is a good instance of Swinburne's marvellous gift of self-deception. Nothing was so easy as to "get him off his legs", but he never appeared to be aware of it himself.'[3]

In fact, it was Richard Burton, it is said, who encouraged Swinburne to drink brandy, and, according to Luke Ionides, would carry him downstairs under one arm at the end of a convivial evening, when he was completely drunk, and deposit him in a hansom cab.[4] Swinburne and Burton used to meet at the house of Dr George Bird. They would generally retire into another room and the other guests would hear through the closed door howls and high-pitched screams of laughter. Isabel Burton disliked Swinburne on sight and thought he was bad company for Richard.

Late in May 1865 Burton left England for the Brazilian consulate at Santos. But before he left, Swinburne used to attend the Cannibal Club dinners with him at Bartolini's, Leicester Square, at which everything was elaborately ghoulish and blasphemous. The Cannibal Club was a burlesque offshoot of the Anthropological Society. Their dinner table was always adorned by a mace in the form of a Negro gnawing a human thighbone inscribed 'Ecce Homo'. Burton had a firm belief in the beneficial effects of cannibalism, which also conformed to the doctrines of de Sade and therefore appealed to Swinburne's hilarious sense of the macabre-grotesque. The other members included Thomas Bendyshe, Senior Fellow of King's College, Cambridge, and translator of the *Mahabharata*, who acted as the 'chaplain', and Charles Bradlaugh. Before sitting down to meat, the members would chant the 'Cannibal Catechism':

Preserve us from our enemies
Thou who art Lord of suns and skies
Whose food is human flesh in pies
  And Blood in bowls!
Of thy sweet mercy damn their eyes
  And damn their souls!

The company would then proceed to discuss some more or less harmless subject such as American literature, when Poe and Whitman would be championed against Irving and Longfellow. Everything about these dinners delighted Swinburne, who was usually carried home at their conclusion quite insensible. The club, which was one of the more colourful aspects of Victorian life, continued to meet until 1869, though Burton tried to revive it in 1871 without success. But Swinburne continued to attend the dinners on his own after Burton's departure for South America.

With the publication of *Chastelard* in the autumn of 1865, the critics, while acknowledging Swinburne's genius and the magic of his verse, were more doubtful about its moral tone. Hutton of the *Spectator* wrote of it as 'a forcing-house of sensual appetite' and the *London Review* said that 'there is some reason to fear that Mr Swinburne is wanting in the higher beauty of moral dignity and sweetness'! 'Besides being inherently vicious,' wrote the critic of the *Athenaeum*, 'the language will offend not only those who have reverence, but those who have taste.' *John Bull* called it 'a lamentable prostitution of the English Muse'. Swinburne was delighted. But his friends became still more worried about the likely reception of *Poems and Ballads*, then in the hands of the printers. Meredith warned him to be prudent. 'I have heard,' he wrote, 'low mutterings from the lion of British prudery, and I who love your verse would play savagely with a knife among the proofs for the sake of your fame.' In December Ruskin wrote to Lady Trevelyan:

> I went to see Swinburne yesterday and heard some of the wickedest and splendidest verses ever written by a human creature. He drank three bottles of porter while I was there. I don't know what to do with him or for him – but he must not publish these things. He speaks with immense gratitude of you – please tell him he mustn't.

William Bell-Scott also wrote to Lady Trevelyan and asked her to use her influence on Swinburne, who had evidently behaved badly during one of his visits to Wallington:[5]

> The remark you make on his behaviour at Wallington I believe I quite understand, he suffers under a dislike to ladies of late – his knowledge of himself and of them increasing upon him. His success too is certainly not improving him, as one might easily suppose with so boundless a vanity.
>
> His new book *Chastelard* is just ready . . . the total severance of the passion of love from the moral delight of loving or being loved, so to speak, and the insaneness of the impulses of Chastelard – for example, which may give you a text for writing to him. With all his boasting of himself and all his belongings, he is very sensitive about society, and I think you will do him the kindest of actions if you can touch his sensibility on his vanity – a little sharply. Of late he has been very much excited and certainly drinking. Gabriel and William Rossetti think he will not live if he goes

on as lately without stopping. He says he is to leave town, however, for a long while, in a few days, and we hope he may quiet down.

The fact that Swinburne was 'suffering under a dislike to ladies of late' was doubtless due in large measure to resentment at the marriage of Mary Gordon and Colonel Disney-Leith at Shorewell, Isle of Wight, on 14 June this year, 1865.[6] He was also becoming increasingly intimate with Simeon Solomon, who now spent much time with him in his Dorset Street rooms. Swinburne had, too, come to know another strange character at this time, George Powell, an old Etonian and the son of a Welsh squire, who had written to him on the appearance of *Atalanta*. Powell, who was working with Maurice Magnússon on translations of the Icelandic sagas, had a passion for Wagner and Swinburne's poetry and shared Swinburne's taste for de Sade; he was also on the worst possible terms with his father. He particularly disliked all forms of field-sports. One day his father, in exasperation, put a gun into his hands and told him to go out and not come back until he had shot something. George promptly went out and shot one of his father's prize bullocks. This did not improve their relations, and George spent most of his time in London. But, being heir to Nanteos in Cardiganshire, Swinburne was able to introduce him to his parents, and, unlike Simeon Solomon, George Powell was invited to stay at Holmwood.

Swinburne also maintained a close friendship with George Augustus Howell, the ambiguous Anglo-Portuguese, who from time to time executed various commissions for Rossetti and Burne-Jones. Swinburne later employed him in negotiations with his publisher John Camden Hotten, himself a rather shady character who ran a special line in flagellant literature. The following letter dated by Dr Lang May or June of this year from Ashburnham Place is characteristic of Swinburne's correspondence with Howell. Addressing him as 'Infâme libertin' à la Sade', he tells him: 'I have added yet four more jets of boiling and gushing infamy to the perennial and poisonous fountain of Dolores. Write – and communicate to the ink une odeur mélangée de sang et de sperme. O mon ami! abhorrons les sophismes – méprisons les banalités – vénérons le vit dressé – adorons le sang répandu. . . . P.S. Since writing the above I have added ten verses to D[olores] – très infâmes et très bien tournés. "Oh! monsieur – peut-on prendre du plaisir à telles horreurs?" "Tu le vois, Justine, je bande – oh! putain, que tu vas souffrir" – P.P.S. (*private*) I want you to compose for me a little dialogue (imaginary) between schoolmaster and boy – from the first summons "Now Arthur (or Frank – or Harry) what does *this* mean, sir? Come here" – to the last *cut* and painful buttoning up – a rebuke or threat at every lash (and *plenty* of them) and a shriek of agonized appeal from the boy in reply. Describe also the effect of each stripe on the boy's flesh – its appearance between the cuts. I want to see how like real life you can make it.'[7]

At the same time, Swinburne was carrying on a similar correspondence with Lord Houghton in the character of a much-whipped schoolboy. 'As my tempter and favourite audience has gone to Santos' – that is Richard Burton – 'I may hope to be a good boy again,' he wrote to Houghton on 11 July, 'after such a "jolly good swishing" as Rodin alone can and dare administer. The Rugby purists (I am told) tax Eton generally with Maenadism during June and July, so perhaps some old school habits return upon us unawares – to be fitly expiated by old school punishment. That once I remember and admit. The Captain was too many for me; and I may have shaken the thyrsus in your face. But after this half I mean to be no end good.'[8] Mrs Fawn Brodie comments: 'As the friendship [between Burton and Swinburne] deepened, on at least one occasion something more than drinking was involved.'[9] She means, perhaps, homosexual relations, which may have formed the deeper bond with Burton, who, ever since his report on the Karachi brothels, was rumoured to be homosexual.

Damaging rumours of Swinburne's familiar talk and behaviour in London now began to reach Wallington, and Lady Pauline wrote to him in considerable distress. On 4 December 1865, Swinburne replied to her with a fine show of indignation.

> I know not how to thank you sufficiently for the kindness of your letter. I cannot express the horror and astonishment, the unutterable indignation and loathing, with which I have been struck on hearing that any one could be vile enough to tax me, I do not say with doing but with saying anything of the kind to which you refer. The one suggestion is not falser than the other. I am literally amazed and horror-struck at the infamous wickedness of people who invent in malice and repeat in levity such horrors.

'Oh monsieur!' he might have added here too, 'peut-on prendre du plaisir à telles horreurs?' But, doubtless, that would have destroyed the image that he wanted to preserve in Lady Pauline's mind.

> It is I who should feel ashamed to meet and disgraced by meeting people capable of believing me improper for them to meet. I can only imagine 1) that the very quietness of my way of living as compared with that of other men of my age exposes me, given up as I almost always am to contemplative solitude, to work at my own art, and never seen in *fast* (hardly in *slow*) life – to spitefulness and vicious stupidity, 2) that as you say I must have talked very foolishly to make such infamies possible. All I can ever recollect saying which *could* be perverted was (for instance) that 'the Greeks did not seem to me worse than the moderns because of things considered innocent at one time by one country were not considered so by others'. . . . This sort of thing, I was told afterwards, might be thought *wild* and offensive by hearers who were bent on malignant commentary, or 4) [*sic*] I do remember saying 'if people read the classics, not to speak

of the moderns very often, they must see that many qualities called virtues and vices depend on time, climate, and temperament.' The remark may have been false or foolish, but who could have imagined it (until he had proof) capable of being twisted into an avowal that I approved vice and disapproved virtue?

Who, indeed! – especially as he had lately written in 'Dolores' of the 'lilies and langors of virtue' and 'the raptures and roses of vice', which really amounted to a paraphrase of de Sade's 'les malheurs de la virtue' and 'les prospérités du vice'. But his reported defence of Greek paedophilia in his familiar talk shows only too clearly what sort of rumours about him had reached Lady Pauline's ears.

It is not so much that Swinburne was being deliberately dishonest and hypocritical; it is rather that he was genuinely fond of Lady Pauline and so genuinely upset that he should have been the cause of distressing her. Like many of us, Swinburne was a different person according to the company he kept, and after a glass of wine he was capable of saying or doing almost anything. But he particularly valued Lady Pauline's good opinion. His distress is shown by the fact that after posting off his first letter to Wallington, he sat down at the Arts Club and wrote a still more passionate disclaimer, the same day:[10]

> I only wish to heaven that at any time or in any way I could – not repay, which would be impossible, but – express to you otherwise than by inadequate words my sense of your goodness to me. Six hours ago, I was so utterly amazed, horrified, agonized and disgusted, that I could hardly think of anything but the subject of your letter. Now I can hardly think of anything but your inexplicable kindness in writing. . . . Nobody in my life was ever so good to me as you have been. You must know what pain any man must feel on hearing what you tell me – what shame any man must feel who was conscious that, in however innocent and ignorant a way, he had (I will not say deserved, but) exposed himself through rashness and inexperience to such suffering as I underwent in reading what you wrote. I know I have not deserved to feel the pain – and shame I do not feel, because I have not deserved it. The pain I feel no longer – and what I do feel is gratitude, and even a sort of gladness that anything should have happened to make me know so fully how great and noble, how beyond all thanks and acknowledgement, your kindness could be. I repeat it, upon my honour, this and this alone is what I now feel. . . . I am amazed beyond words at people's villainy or stupidity – but yet more at people's goodness.

Lady Trevelyan replied next day on 6 December:[11]

> Now do, if it is only for the sake of living down evil reports, do be wise in which of your lyrics you publish. Do let it be a book that can be really

> loved and read and learned by heart, and become part and parcel of the English language, and be on everyone's table without being received under protest by timid people. There are no doubt people who would be glad to be able to say that it is not fit to be read. It is not worth while for the sake of two or three poems to risk the widest circulation of the whole. You have sailed near enough to the wind in all conscience in having painted such a character for a hero as your Chastelard, slave to a passion for a woman he despises, whose love (if one can call it love) has no element of chivalry or purity in it; whose devotion to her is much as if a man should set himself to be crushed before Juggernaut, cursing him all the while for a loathsome despicable idol. I suppose people would say that Chastelard was a maniac. . . . Don't give people a handle against you now. And do mind what you say for the sake of all to whom your fame is dear, and who are looking forward to your career with hope and interest.

Alas, so little did she know Swinburne, so cleverly had he deceived her, that Lady Pauline had no suspicion that in *Chastelard* he was writing from his innermost desires – that is, as he put it, 'to be the helpless victim of the furious rage of a beautiful woman'. So, while blaming everything upon 'venomous back-biters' and 'slanderers', he continued to do everything to justify their worst accusations, when he would turn upon them in a fury of outraged innocence.

'As to my poems, my perplexity is this,' he wrote to Lady Trevelyan on 10 December from Dorset Street, 'that no two friends have ever given me the same advice. Now more than ever I would rather take yours than another's; but I see neither where to begin nor where to stop. I have written nothing to be ashamed or afraid of. I have been advised to suppress Atalanta, to cancel Chastelard, and so on till not a line of my work would have been left. Two days ago Ruskin called on me and stayed for a long evening, during which he heard a great part of my forthcoming volume of poems, selected with a view to secure his advice as to publication and the verdict of the world of readers or critics. It was impossible to have a fairer judge. I have not known him long or intimately; and he is neither a rival nor a reviewer. I can only say that I was sincerely surprised by the enjoyment he seemed to derive from my work, and the frankness with which he accepted it. Any poem which all my friends for whose opinions I care had advised me to omit, should be omitted. But I never have written such an one. Some for example which you have told me were favourites of yours, such as the Hymn to Proserpine of the "Last Pagan" – I have been advised to omit as likely to hurt the feeling of a religious public. I cannot but see that whatever I do will be assailed and misconstrued by those who can do nothing and who detest their betters. I can only lay to heart the words of Shakespeare – even he never uttered any truer – "Be thou as pure as ice, as chaste as snow, thou shalt not escape calumny." And I cannot, as Hamlet advises, betake myself to a nunnery.'

Since the success of *Atalanta*, Swinburne's friends found him increasingly arrogant and defiant, however reasonable and submissive he represented himself in his letters to Lady Trevelyan. The real explanation of this apparent contradiction would seem to resolve itself into what Harold Nicolson saw as the central conflict of his nature between 'the impulse towards revolt and the impulse towards submission'.[12] For his conduct during the first half of his life, at least, was a perpetual oscillation between these two poles of feeling. One can understand his perplexity about making a choice of the poems to be included in his book, for when he sent them to Ruskin for criticism and approval, Ruskin had written: 'I have MSS. all right, I like them so much, but there are redundancies yet, which you can prune – in some – not in *Faustine* which made me all hot like pies with Devil's fingers in them.' On another occasion, when Swinburne had read some of the 'scandalous' pieces at a dinner given by Lord Houghton, Ruskin, it is said, to everyone's astonishment, had risen, embraced him and cried: 'How beautiful! How divinely beautiful!' So it seems that Ruskin had not directly censured any of the poems, at least not to Swinburne himself, which explains why he refused to condemn *Poems and Ballads* when asked to add his voice to the general outcry in the press.

It was in the second week of December 1865 that Lord Houghton arranged a party at Moxon's in order that Tennyson and Swinburne should meet, as representatives of the older and the younger generation of English poets. Unfortunately, the party was fixed for eleven o'clock in the evening and Swinburne had had time to dine first on his own. In any case, he was now in the habit of referring mockingly to Tennyson's *Morte d'Arthur* as the *Morte d'Albert*, and when he met the Laureate again on this particular evening, after greeting him with a perfunctory and stiff little bow, he turned his back and walked off into another room, where he spent the rest of the evening shrilly declaiming the anarchic doctrines of William Blake. Not unnaturally, Lord Houghton, who had arranged the evening to prepare the way for the publication of *Poems and Ballads*, was furious and wrote reproving him for conduct which amounted to a public insult to Tennyson. Next day, Swinburne replied in his usual tone of injured innocence:[13]

My dear Lord Houghton,

As I do not doubt your kind intention, I will only ask – why? where? and how? Last time we met I had been spending the soberest of evenings here before starting to pick you up at 11 o'clock, which I understood was the order of the day. You as we returned seemed considerably infuriated with my unpunctuality – which I did not attribute to any influence of Bacchus on yourself. I am not aware of having retorted by any *discourtesy*. As the rest of the evening had been spent, after the few words of civility that passed between Mr Tennyson and me, in discussing Blake and Flaxman in the next room with Palgrave and Lewes, I am at a loss to guess what has called down such an avalanche of advice. I have probably no vocation and doubtless no ambition for the service of Bacchus: in proof of which if you like I will undertake to repeat the conversation of Wednesday evening throughout with the accuracy of a reporter, as it happens to be fixed in my memory. I don't doubt your ability to do likewise, any more than the friendliness of your feeling towards me, of which I have proofs in plenty. Otherwise I should not care to defend myself against an admonition which if not 'discourteous' is certainly not 'common'.

As usual, Swinburne refused to believe that any gentleman could be guilty of the discourteous behaviour imputed to him.

But now the members of the Arts Club complained of Swinburne's unseemly behaviour and suggested that he should be asked to resign. They said, in a letter to the committee, that he was constantly drunk and rowdy, had insulted the waiters, had damaged club property and was, in short, a general nuisance. In February, G. P. Boyce, the painter, who had been dining and playing billiards at the club, recorded in his diary: 'Swinburne in a very excited state, using fearful language.' William Rossetti then wrote to Swinburne warning him that there had been complaints. Swinburne replied on 26 March 1866, that he was 'sincerely grateful for an act of such real friendship as yours' and that 'this is the first I have ever heard of the matter'. He added that he had 'certainly objurgated more than one waiter' and remembered 'bending double one fork in an energetic mood at dinner'. He had, he said, already thought of withdrawing from the club: 'As to freedom of voice or tone – I am stunned daily by more noise at that place than I ever heard (or, you may suggest, made) in my life. If I damaged a valuable article belonging to them, why did they not send in a bill? If again there is any animus against me I should prefer to withdraw. I have remained in order more frequently to meet a few intimates, who relieve if they cannot redeem the moral squalor of the place. I know but few members, and never knowingly cut or "ignored" any.' The affair seems to have blown over for a time being and Swinburne was not formally asked to resign.

Ruskin had also written earlier in the year warning him of the danger to himself of his intemperate habits. Swinburne replied: 'I do not (honestly) understand the gist of what you say about myself. What's the matter with me that I should cause you sorrow or suggest the idea of a ruin? I don't feel at all ruinous as yet. I do feel awfully old, and well may – for in April I believe I shall be twenty-five [he would be twenty-nine] which is a horror to think of. *Mais*—! what have I done or said, to be likened to such terrific things?

'You speak of not being able to hope enough for me. Don't you think we had better leave hope and faith to infants, adult or ungrown? You and I and all men will probably do and endure what we are destined for, as well as we can. I for one am quite content to know this, without any ulterior belief or conjecture. I don't want more praise and success than I deserve, more suffering and failure than I can avoid; but I take what comes as well and as quietly as I can; and this seems to me a man's real business and only duty. You compare my work to a temple where the lizards have supplanted the gods; I prefer an indubitable and living lizard to a dead or doubtful god.

'I recalcitrate vigorously against your opinion of "Félise", which is rather a favourite child of mine. As to the subject, I thought it clear enough, and likely to recall to most people a similar passage of experience. A young fellow is left alone with a woman rather older, whom a year since he violently loved. Meantime he has been in town, she in the country; and in the year's lapse they have had time, he to become tired of her memory, she to fall in love with his. Surely I have expressed this plainly and "cynically" enough! Last year I loved you, and you were puzzled, and didn't love me – quite. This year (I perceive) you love me, and I feel puzzled, and don't love you – quite. "Sech is life" as Mrs Gamp says. *Deus vult*; it can't be helped.'[14]

In April, Lord Houghton, as president of the Royal Literary Fund, asked Swinburne to speak at their anniversay dinner on 2 May. 'I got a note yesterday about the dinner and will say my say as I can,' Swinburne replied. 'Of course I shall blow a small trumpet before Hugo. I thought something might be said of the new *mutual* influence of contemporary French and English literature – e.g. the French studies of Arnold and the English of Baudelaire.'

When the time came, the chairman, in proposing the 'Historical and Imaginative Literature of England', called upon Charles Kingsley and Algernon Swinburne to reply: 'The representative of that future generation is, I say without fear or hesitation, Mr Swinburne. He alone, of his age, has shown his power to succeed in the highest walks of poetry. . . . I have no doubt that in the long career which is probably before him, Mr Swinburne will take many easier and many pleasanter subjects [than *Chastelard*]. . . . He will hardly exceed the beauty of the lyric flights which he has accomplished; and I am sure that he will feel that as the representative of the future of English poetry he has a great responsibility upon him.'

Swinburne at once rose to his feet and standing stiffly erect 'recited in shrill, monotonous tones, the short essay he had learned by heart'[15] on the mutual influence of French and English literature. After a rhapsody on the influence of Provençal poetry on Chaucer – 'his *Troilus and Criseyde*, filled from end to end with that fierce monotony of tenderness, that bitter absorption of life, which has made the heathenish love of Provençal fighters and singers a proverb to this day' – he continued:

> And now attention is mutual, it is not on one side only, and you will see the son of the greatest French poet attempt and accomplish the best translation possible of the greatest English poet (hear, hear); you will see the father of that son dedicate to the memory of Shakespeare, inscribe to the people of England, such a book as no Englishman could have written since the death of Shakespeare himself (cheers). . . . He who has best praised Shakespeare is hitherto the sole successor of Shakespeare. This is one point of contrast and one worth notice: another is this, that M. Charles Baudelaire, one of the most exquisite, most delicate, most perfect poets of the century – perfect in sound, in colour, in taste of metre and in tone of emotion – has devoted half his time to the translation and introduction of English writers among the French – not without fruit and not without cost. In England I will take but one instance: French influence is no less visible than Grecian instinct in one of the most admirable among poets, one of the most brilliant and subtle among essayists now alive: whose claim to either crown is not least recognised in France than in England. For the higher literature of either nation I can imagine no fairer augury than such omens as these afford (cheers).

Among those who listened to what Gosse calls 'these feverish outpourings of genius' were Dean Stanley, Leslie Stephen, Anthony Trollope, Frederick Leighton, Sir Samuel Baker and Lord Milton. Lord Houghton must have felt that he had done his best to prepare the way for *Poems and Ballads.* But Swinburne did this himself in his own way in his attack on reviewers as a class in the fiery introduction to his selections from Byron published by Moxon in March:[16]

> At the first chance given or taken, every obscure and obscene thing that lurks for pay or prey among the fouler shadows and thickets of literature flew against him; every hound and every hireling lavished upon him the loathsome tribute of their abuse; all nameless creatures that nibble and prowl, upon whom the serpent's curse has fallen, to go upon his belly and eat dust all the days of his life, assailed him with their foulest venom and their keenest fangs.

Little did he realize that this was to be his own fate.

*Poems and Ballads* was ready for publication in May, but on receiving the first bound copy Swinburne found so many printers' errors which he had missed in the page proofs, that he insisted on many pages being reset. Possibly his original oversight was due to the 'bilious attacks' which he told Powell had laid him low 'for days and days'. But he was also correcting the proofs of his book on Blake at the same time.

Before the appearance of *Poems and Ballads*, however, Payne of Moxons had rather nervously issued a limited edition of 'Laus Veneris' in order to test public reactions. But this, which Swinburne's friends looked upon as one of the most dangerous of his poems, passed unnoticed. In March, much to Swinburne's annoyance, Lord Houghton had already offered *Poems and Ballads* to Murrays, who had rejected it out of hand. 'I do not overmuch like my poems sent as it were for approval like those of a novice,' Swinburne commented to Joseph Knight.

It was just about this time, in May, that Lady Pauline Trevelyan died at Neuchâtel in Switzerland, where she had gone in search of health. Before she died, she asked Ruskin anxiously about Swinburne. Indeed, her death was a real misfortune for him, for with it he lost not only one of his best friends, but, as he said, his 'second mother', who had continually used her influence in his defence.

'I am very glad you enjoy my poems,' Swinburne wrote to Joseph Knight on 3 August, 'now they are at last off my hands. I have exhausted myself with a quasi-venereal enjoyment of the incomparable article in the Athenaeum today. Do pray, if you can, find out the gifted author and present to him my very warmest thanks for such delicious and exquisite amusement as I never ventured to anticipate. "Absalom – Gito – filth – most disagreeable – very silly – parrot of Mrs *Browning*(!)" I succumb, and acknowledge that God can create greater fools than we can imagine. I forgive God much for the sake of such a joke. It does Him credit – even Him.'

The reviewer, who was Robert Buchanan, had remarked that 'the glory of our modern poetry is its transcendent purity. Swinburne is unclean for the sake of uncleanness.' But this review was nothing to John Morley's article of 4 August in the *Saturday Review*, then the most influential literary weekly of the day. Morley had been a contemporary of Swinburne at Balliol and subsequently, as editor of the *Fortnightly Review*, became one of the warmest admirers of his critical work. His anonymous article 'Mr Swinburne's New Poems' must be one of the most savage attacks on a poet ever written, all the more damaging because both from a moral and an aesthetic standpoint it appears, at first sight, incontrovertible. It was Morley who created the public uproar against *Poems and Ballads*, which led to the demand that both poet and publisher should be prosecuted for obscenity.

Morley began by saying that: 'Mr Swinburne is much too stoutly bent on taking his own course to pay any attention to critical monitions as to the duty of the poet, or any warnings of the worse than barrenness of the field in which he has chosen to labour. He is so firmly and avowedly fixed in an attitude of revolt against the current notions of decency and dignity and social duty that to beg him to become a little more decent, to fly a little less persistently and gleefully to the animal side of human nature, is simply to beg him to be something different from Mr Swinburne. It is a kind of protest which his whole position makes it impossible for him to receive with anything but laughter and contempt. . . . It is no use, therefore, to scold Mr Swinburne for grovelling down among the nameless shameless abominations which inspire him with such frenzied delight. They excite

5 'The small hours in the 'sixties at 16 Cheyne Walk – Algernon reading "Anactoria" to Gabriel and William', by Max Beerbohm

6 Swinburne aged 30, from the painting by G. F. Watts of 1867

his imagination to its most vigorous efforts, they seem to him the themes most proper for poetical treatment, and they suggest ideas which, in his opinion, it is highly to be wished that English men and women should brood upon and make their own. He finds that these fleshly things are his strong part, so he sticks to them. Is it wonderful that he should? And at all events he deserves credit for the audacious courage with which he has revealed to the world a mind all aflame with the feverish carnality of a schoolboy over the dirtiest passages in Lamprière [Lamprière being nothing worse than a classical dictionary]. It is not everybody who would care to let the world know that he found the most delicious food for poetic reflection in the practices of the great island in the Aegean, in the habits of Messalina, of Faustina, of Parsiphaë. Yet these make up Mr Swinburne's version of the dreams of fair women, and he would scorn to throw any veil over pictures which kindle, as these do, all the fires of his imagination in their intensest heat and glow.'

In fact, Swinburne, in such poems, was only making use of the fruits of his classical education, as he was later to point out. But when Morley went on to say that *Poems and Ballads* was 'crammed with pieces which many a professional vendor of filthy prints might blush to sell', he was merely being foolish, though the implication was damaging enough. Morley admits that the verses of 'Dolores' are 'admirable for their sustained power and music, if not on other grounds. . . . The only comfort about the present volume is that such a piece as "Anactoria" will be unintelligible to a great many people, and so will the fevered folly of "Hermaphroditus", as well as much else that is nameless and abominable.' But if Swinburne had left much 'nameless', Morley went out of his way to name it, so that 'English readers will gradually acquire a truly delightful familiarity with these unspeakable foulnesses'. But does not all this echo, ironically, Swinburne's own 'review' of Félicien Cossu and *Les Abîmes*? He should not have been surprised to find the same treatment meted out to himself in all seriousness. Morley continued: 'we may ask him whether there is really nothing in women worth singing about except "quivering flanks" and "splendid supple thighs", "hot sweet throats" and "hotter hands than fire", and their blood as "hot wan wine of love"? Is purity to be expunged from the catalogue of desirable qualities?' But the objection to such images is surely aesthetic rather than moral. Tennyson had celebrated 'pure' women at length, so that one wonders just how moral Morley's objections really were, or whether his attack was not inspired largely by rancour and vindictiveness. After all, Swinburne had spared no pains in his contemptuous references to reviewers and critics. Now it was their turn.

For all that, Morley was perfectly aware that *Poems and Ballads* contained much else besides the passages he picked out for condemnation. It is true, as he says, that in a few poems Swinburne 'riots in the profusion of colour of the most garish and heated kind'; that, in some poems, 'he is like a composer who should fill his orchestra with trumpets, or a painter who should exclude every colour but a blaring red, and a green as of sour fruit', and that 'we are in the midst of fire and serpents, wine and ashes, blood and foam'. He was perceptive when he wrote: 'Fascinated as everybody must be by the music of his verse, it is doubtful whether part of the effect may not be traced to something like a trick of words and letters, to which he resorts in season and out of season with a persistency that any sense of artistic moderation must have stayed.' As he says also, 'The Greek poets in their most impetuous moods never allowed themselves to be carried on by the swing of words, instead of by the steady, though buoyant, flow of thoughts. . . . In the height of their passion there is an infinite soberness of which Mr Swinburne has not a conception.' That is true, even of *Atalanta*.

Having spent so much time on the weaknesses of Swinburne's verse, Morley does, at the close of his review, allow that he is capable of exquisite effects, and he quotes the lines:

> Fell more soft than dew or snow by night,
> Or wailed as in some flooded cave
> Sobs the strong broken spirit of a wave.

and

> For the glass of the years is brittle wherein
> we gaze for a span.

and

> In deep wet ways by grey old gardens
> Fed with sharp spring the sweet fruit hardens;
> They know not what fruits wane or grow:
> Red summer burns to the utmost ember;
> They know not, neither can remember,
> The old years and flowers they used to know.

This is Swinburne at his elegiac best; and it was the side of him that was to grow and develop into the exquisite verses of *Poems and Ballads*, *Second Series*. Yet there is much in the first volume of a supreme quality which Morley chose to ignore. As Ezra Pound noted: 'His biography is perfectly well written in his work. He is never better than in the *Ballad of Life*, the *Ballad of Death*, and the *Triumph of Time*. To the careful reader this last shows quite clearly that Swinburne was actually broken by a real and not by a feigned emotional catastrophe early in life; of this his later slow decline is a witness. . . . After all, the whole of his defects can be summed up in one – that is, inaccurate writing; and this is by no means ubiquitous. To quote his magnificent passages is but to point out familiar things in our landscape. . . . The two ballads and the *Triumph of Time* are full of sheer imagism, of passages faultless. No one else has made such music in English, I mean has made his kind of music; and it is music which will compare with Chaucer's *Hide Absalon thi gilte tresses clere* or with any other maker you like. . . . No man who cares for his art can be deaf to the rhythms of Swinburne, deaf to their splendour, deaf also to their bathos. . . . Swinburne's surging and leaping dactyllics had no comparable forerunners in English.' And of the last verse of 'A Ballad of Life' he remarks: 'The splendid lines mount up in one's memory and overwhelm any minute restrictions of one's praise.[17] It is the literary fashion to write exclusively of Swinburne's defects. . . . Defects are in Swinburne by the bushelful: the discriminating reader will not be able to overlook them, and need not condone them; neither will he be swept off his feet by detractors. There are in Swinburne fine passages, like fragments of fine marble statues. . . . And there is, underneath all the writing, a magnificent passion for liberty. . . . The passion not merely for political, but also for personal, liberty is the bedrock of Swinburne's writing. The sense of tragedy, and of the unreasoning cruelty of the gods, hangs over it. He fell into facile writing, and he accepted a facile compromise for life.'[18]

In the United States, where the book was pirated by G. W. Carlton in November and astutely published as *Laus Veneris and Other Poems and Ballads*, it inspired as much virtuous indignation in the press as in England. But Carlton said that he could not keep pace with the demand, though he did not pay Swinburne a penny. The *New York Times* condemned the book as combining the lowest lewdness with the most outrageous blasphemy, while conceding the power and beauty of the language. This particular critic added that the indecent literature of the day also included George Eliot's *Adam Bede* and Charles Reade's latest novel.[19]

Swinburne first saw the *Saturday Review* as he was walking down Dover Street, Piccadilly, with Payne of Moxons. He stopped to buy a copy, glanced over it casually, and then his eye was caught by Morley's article. As he read it, he became more and more furious. He gesticulated wildly and fairly danced with rage. His comments, venting themselves in the shrill scream to which his voice rose when he was angry, were of such an obscenity that Payne suggested stopping at a restaurant. But Swinburne's torrent of scatological abuse continued with such violence that even the waiters fled in alarm. Payne then tactfully suggested that Swinburne should continue his imprecations in the language of Hugo's *Les Châtiments*, so that people should take him for an eccentric foreigner.

As we have seen, Swinburne had been amused – or had pretended to be – by Buchanan's *Athenaeum* review. His fury on this occasion only went to show how shrewd and penetrating Morley's attack was, for Morley had picked out the silliest lines for quotation, such as 'Thou art noble and nude and antique', and 'the lilies and languors of virtue' and 'the raptures and roses of vice', which were, of course, gleefully taken up and repeated by everyone else. But when, next day, Payne heard rumours that an article was in preparation by *The Times* demanding the prosecution of the publisher for obscenity, he took fright, withdrew the book from circulation and curtly informed Swinburne of the fact.

'The hound of a publisher,' Swinburne wrote to George Powell on 10 August, 'has actually withdrawn from circulation my volume of poems – refuses to issue any more copies "through fear of consequences to himself". Of course I shall take Atalanta &c. out of his villainous hands – but then, to whom (as Catullus says) shall I give them? C'est embêtant. I have this minute written to Lord Lytton to get his advice.'[20]

Edward Bulwer, Lord Lytton, replied by asking Swinburne to Knebworth, where he stayed from 17 August to the twenty-fifth. But before leaving London, Swinburne had received an offer from John Camden Hotten to republish *Poems and Ballads*, offering him £200 for 1,000 copies. Lytton advised him to accept this offer, in spite of Hotten's rather unsavoury reputation, and to break off all relations with Moxon. Swinburne therefore wrote to Hotten on 25 August:[21]

> My agreement with Moxon is cancelled by his own act. Having undertaken to sell the edition in hand, he now by his own act has withdrawn it and intends to sell the copies as waste paper. This in your interest as in mine must not be allowed. They must either be bought directly by you, or as waste paper by me acting through a third party. This is the advice of my friend Lord Lytton with whom I have talked over the whole affair. It should be done at once so that there may be no delay in the reappearance of the book. . . . It is the same with the copies of Atalanta and The Queen Mother he has on hand, and with the proofs of my forthcoming prose work [*William Blake*]. These I am free to call in and resell, having received nothing for them.

On the same day Lord Lytton wrote a revealing letter to his son in Spain:[22]

> Staying here also is A. Swinburne, whose poems at this moment are rousing a storm of moral censure. I hope he may be induced not to brave and defy that storm, but to purgate his volume of certain pruriences into which it amazes me any poet could fall. If he does not, he will have an unhappy life and a sinister career. It is impossible not to feel an interest in him. He says he is 26; he looks 16 – a pale, sickly boy, with some nervous complaint like St Vitus' dance. He has read more than most reading men twice his age, brooded and theorised over what he has read, and has an artist's critical perceptions. I think he must have read and studied and thought and felt much more than Tennyson; perhaps he has over-informed his tenement of clay. But there is plenty of stuff in him. His volume of poems is infested with sensualities, often disagreeable in themselves, as well as offensive to all pure and manly taste. But the beauty of diction and masterpiece of craft in melodies really at first so dazzled me, that I did not see the naughtiness till pointed out. . . . He inspires

one with sadness; but he is not sad himself, and his self-esteem is solid as rock. . . . I suspect that he would be a dangerous companion to another poet.

This letter is particularly interesting, as it confirms what most of Swinburne's sympathetic older contemporaries felt about him. Such expressions as 'pure and manly taste' may fall somewhat strangely upon our ears today, but Lytton's criticism is basically sound and perceptive.

Meanwhile, Rossetti and Sandys had called on Payne at Moxons to see how matters stood, but Payne was only too anxious to be rid of them. Afterwards Gabriel Rossetti wrote to his brother: 'Swinburne's book is not suppressed . . . I myself jointly with Sandys devoted one afternoon to what we considered a friendly duty towards Swinburne; though not certainly as you know because we think the genius displayed in his work benefits by its association with certain accessory tendencies . . . poeta nascitur non fit . . . for publication.'

When all Swinburne's books reappeared in September under Hotten's imprint, the demand for prosecution was heard again, and Ruskin was approached to add his voice to the general clamour. Magnanimously he replied to J. M. Ludlow: 'He is infinitely above me in all knowledge and power and I should no more think of advising him than of venturing to do it to Turner if he were alive again. As for Swinburne not being my superior, he is simply one of the mightiest scholars of the age in Europe. . . . And in power of imagination and understanding simply sweeps me away as a torrent does a pebble. . . . I am *righter* than he is, so are the lambs and the swallows, but they're not his match.' And to Swinburne himself he wrote: 'I should as soon think of finding fault with you as with a thundercloud or a nightshade blossom. All I can say of you, or them – is that God made you, and that you are very wonderful and beautiful.'[23]

Indeed, Henry Morley, Professor of English at University College, London, writing in the *Examiner* for 22 September, remarked: 'Of Mr Algernon C. Swinburne's *Atalanta* we have said all that we need say, and what he has since published gives us nothing to unsay. He is a young poet with sterling qualities, and the outcry that has been made over his last published volume of *Poems and Ballads* is not very creditable to his critics. The withdrawal of that volume is an act of weakness of which any publisher who does not give himself up to the keeping of a milk-walk for the use of babes has reason to be heartily ashamed.' Henry Morley found the influence of the Old Testament everywhere in *Poems and Ballads*, as well as 'the sublime fatalism of the old Greek dramatists', and 'a terrible earnestness' even in *Chastelard*: 'Here are the passions of youth fearlessly expressed, and stirring depths that have been stirred hitherto by no poet in his youth. . . . It is the ferment of good wine – and we must think they are no skilled judges of the wine of thought who shake their heads over it.'

But even Swinburne could not claim that 'Dolores', 'Faustine' and 'Anactoria' were written as sermons; so that while he was grateful to Henry Morley for his defence, honesty forbade him to agree with the grounds upon which it was made. In the 'Hymn to Proserpine' he had openly rejected the 'ghastly glories of saints, dead limbs of gibbeted Gods' in favour of the gods of Greece and Rome. 'Faustine' is, after all, a celebration of sadistic cruelty and lust, spoken by a gladiator who is about to die, just as 'Anactoria' is a magnificent glorification of Sapphic love and all its torments and frustrations. As a very different kind of poet, Edward Thomas, remarked of *Poems and Ballads* three years after Swinburne's death: 'nor could anything but a divine vitality have saved it from rancidity, putrescence, dust. . . . But until virtue produces a book fuller of life we can only accept the poet's own label of sin in peril of blasphemy. . . . If evil and misery have this sweetness and tumultuous force, show me what is good and joyous.'[24]

It is more enlightening, perhaps, to see what Swinburne himself had to say about his poems. His essay, 'Notes on Poems and Reviews', is not so much a defence – he did not admit that they needed that – as an analysis written for the sake of his readers. He begins by saying that the verdict of his critics is to him 'a matter of infinite indifference: it is of equally small moment to me whether in such eyes as theirs I appear moral or immoral, Christian or pagan. But, remembering that science must not scorn to investigate animalcules and infusoria, I am ready for once to play the anatomist. . . . With regard to any opinion implied or expressed throughout my book, I desire that one thing should be remembered: the book is dramatic, many-faced, multifarious; and no utterance of enjoyment or despair, belief or unbelief, can properly be assumed as the assertion of its author's personal feeling or faith.' Taking 'Anactoria' as an example of one poem that 'has excited, among the chaste and candid critics of the day or hour or minute, a more vehement reprobation, a more virtuous horror, a more passionate appeal, than any other. . . . I would fain know why the vultures should gather here of all places; what congenial carrion they smell. . . . In this poem I have simply expressed, or tried to express, that violence of affection between one and another which hardens into rage and deepens into despair. The keynote which I have here touched was struck long since by Sappho. . . . I have wished, and I have even ventured to hope that I might be in time competent to translate into a baser language the divine words which even when a boy I could not but recognise as divine. That hope, if indeed I dared ever entertain such a hope, I soon found fallacious. Where Catullus failed, I could not hope to succeed; I tried to reproduce in a diluted and dilated form the spirit of the poem which could not be reproduced in the body. . . . I have tried, then, to write some paraphrase of the fragment which the Fates and the Christians have spared us. I have striven to cast my spirit into the world of hers, to express and represent not the poem but the poet. . . . Here and there, I need not say, I have rendered into English the very words of Sappho.

I have tried also to work into words of my own some expression of their effect: to bear witness how, more than any other's, her verses strike and sting the memory in lonely places, or at sea, among all loftier sights and sounds – how they seem akin to fire and air, being themselves "all air and fire"; other element there is none in them. As to the angry appeal against the supreme mystery of oppressive heaven, which I have ventured to put into her mouth at that point only where pleasure culminates in pain, affection in anger, and desire in despair – as to the "blasphemies" against God or gods of which here and elsewhere I stand accused – they are to be taken as the first outcome or outburst of foiled and fruitless passion recoiling on itself. . . . What is there now horrible in this? the expressions of fierce fondness, the ardours of passionate despair? Are these so unnatural as to affright or disgust? Where is there an unclean detail? where an obscene allusion? A writer as impure as my critics might of course have written, on this or any subject, an impure poem; I have not. . . .

'Next on the list of accusation stands the poem of "Dolores". The gist and bearing of this I should have thought evident enough, viewed by the light of others which precede and follow it. I have striven here to express the transient state of spirit through which a man may be supposed to pass, foiled in love and weary of loving, but not yet in sight of rest; seeking refuge in those "violent delights" which "have violent ends", in fierce and frank sensualities which at least profess to be no more than they are' – in fact, a projection of his own emotional condition, a reaction, as he wrote to William Rossetti, from the state of mind expressed in 'The Triumph of Time'. Also: 'This poem, like "Faustine", is so distinctly symbolic and fanciful that it cannot justly be amenable to judgement as a study in the school of realism. The spirit, bowed and discoloured by suffering and by passion (which are indeed the same thing and the same word), plays for awhile with its pleasures and its pains, mixes and distorts them with a sense half-humorous and half-mournful, exults in bitter and doubtful emotions:

Moods of fantastic sadness nothing worth.

It sports with sorrow, and jests against itself, cries out for freedom and confesses the chain: decorates with the name of goddess, crowns anew as the mystical Cotytto, some woman, real or ideal, in whom the pride of life with its companion lusts is incarnate. In her lover's half-shut eyes, her fierce unchaste beauty is transfigured, her cruel sensual eyes have a meaning and a message: there are memories and secrets in the kisses of her lips. She is the darker Venus, fed with burnt-offering and blood-sacrifice; the veiled image of that pleasure which men impelled by satiety and perverted by power have sought through ways as strange as Nero's before and since his time; the daughter of lust and death, and holding of both her parents; Our Lady of Pain, antagonist alike of trivial sins and virtues. . . .

'Foiled in love and weary of loving, but not yet in sight of rest; seeking refuge in those "violent delights" which "have violent ends", in fierce and frank sensualities which at least profess to be no more than they are.' That is the gist of it. If his critics only knew, Swinburne had never been more sincere. But to the eyes of his critics he appeared disingenuous. 'I am not given to "parley" with the swine of journalism,' he wrote to F. G. Waugh in October, 'but to court their displeasure and chastise (if I choose) their insolence.' His essay was not intended as a reply to his critics, but 'rather a casual set of notes on my poems, such as Coleridge or Byron did on theirs'. His angry and contemptuous tone is justified by the insulting tone of his reviewers. 'Mr Swinburne,' wrote Robert Buchanan in the *Spectator* of 3 November 1866, 'fastens on such subjects [the morbid and the sensual] and feasts on them with a greedy and cruel voracity like a famished dog on raw meat.' *Punch* politely suggested that he should change his name to 'Swineborn'. The *New York Times*, after remarking on his 'debility and puny proportions', went on: 'one sickens at his incessant efforts to be mistaken for a libertine'.

And yet Swinburne already had a circle of devout admirers, even adorers. Gosse tells us that 'an audience of the elect to whom Swinburne recited the yet unpublished "Dolores", had been moved to such incredible ecstasy by it that several of them had sunk to their knees then and there, and adored him as a god'.[25] One remembers, too, that even Ruskin broke out, at one such recitation: 'How beautiful! How divinely beautiful!' Meanwhile, Oxford undergraduates would chant the heady lines of 'Faustine' and 'Dolores', as they rolled, with linked arms, down the High at night.

# CHAPTER SEVEN

# 1866–68

# THE GROVE OF THE EVANGELIST: DOLORES MENKEN: MAZZINI

It was towards the end of the 1860s that Swinburne began to frequent 'the mysterious house in St John's Wood', where, as Gosse politely puts it, 'two golden-haired and rouge-cheeked ladies received in luxuriously furnished rooms gentlemen who they consented to chastise for large sums'.[1] He was introduced to this place, it seems, by a boy named John Thomson, whom he had met one evening when visiting his friend Savile Clarke in Bloomsbury. The boy was reciting *Paradise Lost* in the basement kitchen of the lodging-house kept by his mother where Clarke lived. Swinburne thought him 'a wonder' and introduced him to Rossetti and other friends. Thomson seems to have been an unusual sort of pimp with his love for Milton, and evidently received commissions on his introduction of new clients to the brothel in what was facetiously known as 'the Grove of the Evangelist' or 'the Grove of the Beloved Disciple'. Gosse adds: 'There was also an elderly lady, very respectable, who welcomed the guests and took the money. Swinburne much impoverished himself in these games, which also must have been very bad for his health.' In his letter to Gosse of 20 January 1919, A. E. Housman, who seems to have been only mildly amused, lets fall the actual name of the brothel – 'Verbena Lodge' – nowhere mentioned by Gosse, but evidently already known to Housman.[2] On 13 April 1917, he had sent Gosse a copy of *The Whippingham Papers*, which, he says, was 'published in Paris for Anglo-Saxons', asking him if the two poems signed 'Etonensis' were by Swinburne, adding that they 'have some affinity with passages in "Love's Cross-Currents" and "The Sisters" . . . and the names Reggie and Algernon are observable'.[3]

Whether these 'games' were as bad for his health as Gosse thought is perhaps questionable, for they may have been his only sexual outlet. Swinburne employed Thomson for some time as his secretary and general factotum and we hear of him making a fair copy of *A Year's Letters*, which was offered to Andrew Chatto, when the latter took over Hotten's business. Chatto, who was anxious to disassociate himself from Hotten's line in flagellation literature, refused *A Year's Letters* and was equally discouraging about *Lesbia Brandon.*

It is at this time that the solicitor, poet and literary critic Theodore Watts began investigating Hotten's affairs on Swinburne's behalf, and Swinburne on 9 February 1873, wrote Howell, who had lately been dealing with Hotten, not to mention anything to Watts about 'the school list' – the material he had prepared for one of Hotten's books, Swinburne having apparently contributed the part dealing with his pet subject, the beating of schoolboys. The need for caution arose from the fact that he had shown Watts some passages from de Sade and Watts had, contrary to his expectations, been disgusted and insisted that the subject should never be mentioned between them again. And when he gave the cautious solicitor the manuscript of *Lesbia Brandon* to read, Watts only returned part of it, keeping back several chapters. As Swinburne complained to him on 21 June 1875: 'the first five leaves, numbered by you in pencil, (2) Two entire consecutive chapters, "Turris Eburnea" [dealing with the demi-mondaine Leonora Harley] and "Another Portia", (3) Two incomplete chapters "An Episode" (I think that was the name) and "La Bohème Dedorée." As I have no copy of any part of the MS, I must ask you to find and send me these strays.' But Watts persisted that he could not find them anywhere, doubtless thinking that it would be better for Swinburne's reputation if they were lost altogether. But after Swinburne's death, he 'found' them and sold them to Thomas J. Wise, the bibliographer and forger.

Indeed, one of the lesser-known products of the Victorian age was its vast and incredibly silly flagellation literature, catering mainly for an aristocratic and upper-class public. The writers of these books assumed that their readers had been to public schools – 'Birchminster' is a favourite one – and they called themselves 'Etonensis' or 'An Old Boy'. Most of the readers of these books frequented flagellation brothels, which only formed one small section of the vast number of brothels in Victorian London catering for every description of perverted taste, the most popular among gentlemen being juvenile brothels, where small girls and small boys were to be had; the majority of the flagellants, however, were 'old boys' in the literal sense. In the novels they are beaten by 'aristocratic' ladies with names such as Lady Termagant, Lady Flaybum, Lady Maria Castigate, or Lady Harriet Tickletail.[4] The *mis en scène* of this literature is indicative of its infantile character, for most flagellants were either sexually retarded or impotent and the stories are set most often in the nursery, occasionally in the governess's or housemaid's room, and sometimes in the schoolroom. Stories about school-life are also frequent. Sometimes there are gatherings of titled ladies who meet to discuss their whipping propensities or for the purpose of whipping each other. The main thing is that the beating should be elegantly done by 'a lady of breeding' and high society, who often put on kid gloves for the purpose. Usually elderly men pretended to be boys; sometimes they were actually beaten by a boy or young man dressed as a girl. The 'flogee' would 'own up' to some kind of misconduct – often infantile sexual behaviour – and suffer punishment by a mother surrogate. A bunch of birch twigs was usually used for the purpose and called 'the rod' – symbol of the phallus. This is always described in great detail and sometimes decorated with ribbons. At other times the beater is described as 'a splendid masculine type of woman', or she is seen as a Swinburnian 'panther type'. The sexual ambiguity extends as well to the victim, the man dressed as a girl, the lady dressed as a boy. The girls were often called 'Willie' or 'Georgie' and the dialogue carried on in the language of the public school.

Marcus concludes that 'the entire immense literature of flagellation produced during the Victorian period . . . represents a kind of last-ditch compromise with and defence against homosexuality'[5] – since the beating was, of course, only a substitute for the sexual intercourse both partners feared. In most cases the fantasies reflected in flagellant literature were somewhat different from the pathetic reality as practised in the brothels. The conversation between Reggie and Frank in the Prologue to *Love's Cross-Currents* is almost as silly as it is in the normal run of flagellant literature. The relevant passages in *Lesbia Brandon* are, however, more sinister. The whole tone of these books is, as Marcus points out, 'in marked contrast to the Victorian ideals of manliness, solidity, certitude of self, sincerity and singleness of being', but 'the form in which these ideals were inculcated at public schools produced their opposite in necessary compensation'.

Some of this literature was published by Hotten – for instance, *Flagellation and Flagellants: A History of the Rod in all countries* by 'A Clergyman', *The Sublime of Flagellation*, *Lady Bumtickle's Revels &c.* Hotten had begun a work on the same subject himself and came to Swinburne for a series of 'scenes in school', which, as Swinburne wrote to Howell in February 1873, 'he was to get sketched for me', showing 'the postures and actions of "swishing" in detail, with due effort and relief given to the more important points of view during the transaction. . . . I see he advertises a new "Romance of the Rod" as in preparation, to which I shall be happy to lend any assistance that I could [*sic*], and so you might let him know if we are to remain on terms.' When Swinburne broke with Hotten, he became very anxious about 'certain of his MSS.' that remained in Hotten's possession. But most of his letters to Lord Houghton conform to the general run of the flagellant literature they both enjoyed. Burne-Jones, however, took the precaution of destroying Swinburne's letters to him. But one of his early letters to Swinburne, written from Great Russell Street, survives and shows a side of him that does not appear in his wife's *Memorials*:[6]

My dear but Infamous Pote,

What a dreadful gift was your last letter. The anxiety I have had about it for fear it should get out of my pocket and be seen. It has been much

> worse than another Pip to me, much worse. Every time I change my clothes I have to find it and transfer it to the pocket I wear, and when I leave town, as I have just done, it goes with me. For its genius my dear Sir, is such that I wouldn't destroy it for the world, and to keep it is destruction. It lies before me now with its respectable edge of black, and its wicked contents like – if the simile may be accorded me – a sinful clergyman. To the Jewjube [Simeon Solomon] I read it all, and our enjoyment was such that we spent a whole morning in making pictures for you, such as Tiberias would have [given] provinces for. But sending them might be dangerous, and might be inopportune, so we burnt them. One I shall repeat to you. It was my own poor idea, not altogether valueless I trust. A clergyman of the established church is seen lying in an ecstatic dream in the foreground. Above him a lady is seen plunging from a trap door in the ceiling, about to impale herself upon him. How poorly does this describe one of my most successful designs. But you shall see it. And the little 'un did a sweet composition too. Our brains, I may say, teem with them till you come to deliver us.

And yet Burne-Jones shrunk from illustrating some of the tales in the Kelmscott *Chaucer*. It was the entire public suppression of this side of his nature which makes his nudes or semi-nudes so limp and anaemic in their coyly genteel Victorian way.[7] Much of the real Burne-Jones appears in his caricatures and obscene limericks. In this he was, of course, no exception in his time, for the Victorians were at once obsessed with sex and terrified of it, which makes their preoccupation with 'purity' so peculiarly indecent.

Meanwhile, Swinburne continued to visit the Grove of the Evangelist. This house may be the same as the one referred to by Hankey, who collected information about London flagellant brothels for Ashbee's (otherwise 'Pisanus Fraxi') *Index Librorum Prohibitorum*, which he described as 'in Regent's Park'. The locality seems, on the face of it, extremely unlikely, and he evidently means 'near Regent's Park'. 'At this one,' he wrote, 'are two very young girls, who pretend to be schoolmasters and whip fearfully severely, belabouring their clients across their knees like children.'[8] These must have been Gosse's 'golden-haired, rouge-cheeked ladies'. Possibly Gosse's information was not too precise, or he may not have cared to inquire too closely, although what he does reveal was for many years kept strictly under lock and key in the British Museum and has only recently been 'released' – that is, since Dr Lang's publication of it in *The Swinburne Letters*.

When 'the whipping establishment' in St John's Wood (an area in which, Galsworthy says, no Forsyte liked to be seen) was temporarily closed 'while the ladies went to Paris', Gosse tells us, 'in order to break him completely of his degrading and ignominious habit, D. G. Rossetti consulted one or two very intimate friends who advised that he should be taken in hand by some sensible young woman who would "make a man of him", since he was known to have never had any physical connection, which, as Rossetti said, was ridiculous in the author of so many "voluptuous" poems' – not to say tragic in a man of thirty. Rossetti apparently suggested that he should be introduced to the American circus rider Adah Dolores Menken. The suggestion sounds grotesque, though it seems to have turned out unexpectedly well.

Adah Menken was at that time creating a sensation by her 'Naked Mazeppa' act at Astley's Circus, where she was carried round the ring in flesh-coloured tights strapped to a horse. Among her many admirers were Dickens and Tennyson, and John Thomson, G. R. Sims tells us, was madly in love with her.[9] Though she was only thirty, she had already been married five times. Born Dolores McCord, her first husband was a Jewish music teacher and her latest the prize fighter Heenan. She had been a dancer and a sculptor's model and she also wrote Whitmanesque verses.[10] It was decided to tell Swinburne that she was a great admirer of his poetry and longed to meet him, and it is said that Rossetti gave her £10 to do her best with his 'little Northumbrian friend'. John Thomson was, as usual, the go-between. Menken then called at Swinburne's rooms in Dorset Street and not only stayed the night, but became a frequent nocturnal visitor.[11]

Swinburne was very proud of his conquest, and the pair were photographed together – a massive and distinctly middle-aged Dolores sitting down and gazing up into the little poet's face, he looking rather the worse for wear and weak at the knees. Several of these absurd photographs were displayed in shop windows and the affair became the talk of the town. It was not long before news of it reached the Admiral and Lady Jane at Holmwood. That a Swinburne, an Ashburnham, should make such a spectacle of himself! The feelings of his parents and other relations can only too easily be imagined. Afterwards Swinburne told Gosse that Menken's only fault was that she would wake up so early in the morning and read her verses to him, swinging her handsome legs on the edge of the bed till he thought they would turn to ice in the cold morning air, 'but the passion of her poetical rhapsody seemed to keep her warm'. Evidently Swinburne could not – for she is said to have returned the £10 to Rossetti, saying that 'she did not know how it was, but she hadn't been able to get him up to the scratch, and couldn't make him understand that biting's no use'.[12]

At the end of November 1867, Swinburne was in bed several days with 'influenza and bile'. Purnell wrote to him on 4 December: 'Today I have had a letter from Dolores – such a letter! She fears you are ill: she is unable to think of anything but you; she wishes me to telegraph to her if you are in danger, and she will fly on the wings of the wind to nurse you. She has become a soft-throated serpent, strangling prayers on her white lips to kiss the poet, whose absence leaves her with ghosts and shadows. She concludes: "Tell him – say out my despairing nature to him – take care of his precious life. Write at once; believe in me and my holy love for him. Let him write one word in your letter. He will, for he is so good." What do you think of this? It is Cleopatra over again.'[13]

Soon after this, Swinburne had a bad fall from a hansom cab, cutting his face on the kerbstone, and on 9 December he wrote to Purnell: 'If you see Dolores before I do, tell her with my love that I would not shew myself sick and disfigured in her eyes. I was spilt last week out of a hansom, and my nose and forehead cut to rags – I was seedy for four days, and hideous.'[14] There were jokes in the office of *Punch* about the poet and the circus rider, and Shirley Brooks wrote to William Hardman in February next year: 'Mrs Sothern took me to see Ada Menken and I am my own no longer, *nor my wife's either* . . . I am Ada's . . . Swinburne is the only rival I dread – he knew her first. But I shall sit on his corpse. He boasts – but he lies!'[15] Burne-Jones did a series of cartoons, which he sent to Swinburne, celebrating 'Ye Treue and Pitifulle Historie of ye Poet and ye Ancient Dame', in one of which Swinburne is seen casually lighting a cigar with one of her letters.[16]

To Lord Houghton, Swinburne wrote on 21 December: 'I am glad you found Milton [Lord Milton] enjoying even the immoral and illegitimate bonds of unholy matrimony, though I deplore the perversity which induces young men so far to forget themselves and nature. I also enjoy (certainly) not less the bonds of a somewhat riotous concubinage. I don't know many *husbands* who could exact or expect from a *wife* such indulgences as are hourly laid at my feet!'[17] Was this boasting, again? At any rate, he was laid low by another attack of influenza. 'I have been so worried of late,' he wrote to George Powell next month, 'with influenza, love-making, and other unwholesome things – such as business, money &c. that I have "left undone all that I should have done". I must send you in a day or two a photograph of my present possessor – known to Britannia as Miss Menken, to me as Dolores (her real Christian name) and myself taken together.'[18]

It is difficult to draw any definite conclusions from this curious episode in Swinburne's life, though he seems to have made the most of it in his letters. Gosse says it lasted for about six weeks, from December 1867 to February 1868. It does not seem to have occupied too much of Swinburne's time or attention. Adah Menken's principal concern seems to have been to get her poems published. Nevertheless, when she died in Paris in August 1869, after having herself photographed on the knee of Dumas *père*, Swinburne wrote to George Powell: 'I am sure you were sorry on my account to hear of the death of my poor dear Menken – it was a great shock to me and a real grief – I was ill for some days. She was most lovable as a friend as well as a mistress.'[19] The 'indulgences' that he said she 'hourly laid at his feet' can hardly have been of a normal kind. But as an *équestrienne*, Dolores was doubtless practised in the more 'riotous' aspects of concubinage. In return Swinburne revised her verses, a collection of which was published by Hotten under the title of *Infelicia* and dedicated to Dickens.

Lafourcade has pointed out that at just about the time of this *affaire* Swinburne was translating in one of the finest stanzas of *Ave Atque Vale* Baudelaire's sonnet *La Géante*:[20]

> Hast thou found place at the great knees and feet
> Of some pale Titan-woman like a lover,
> Such as thy vision here solicited,
> Under the shadow of her fair vast head,
> The deep division of prodigious breasts,
> The solemn slope of mighty limbs asleep,
> The weight of awful tresses that still keep
> The savour and shade of old-world pine-forests
> Where the wet hill-winds weep?

Considering the relative sizes of Swinburne and Menken, one can well understand the appeal to him of this poem of Baudelaire's:

> J'eusse aimé vivre auprès d'une jeune géante,
> Comme aux pieds d'une reine un chat voluptueux.
> J'eusse aimé voir son corps fleurir avec son âme
> Et grandir librement dans ses terrible jeux

– 'terrible games' seem particularly appropriate in this context.

It is possible that Swinburne may have seen Menken during one of her earlier visits to London, as Lafourcade suggests, and that her name Dolores had suggested to him the title of one of his most sadistic poems, though the poem itself could scarcely have originated with her. She seems to have been altogether too healthy and good-hearted for that, and evidently Swinburne was genuinely fond of her.

With the reappearance of *Poems and Ballads* under Hotten's imprint in the autumn of 1866 the attacks in the Press had been renewed. 'It is really very odd,' Swinburne wrote to William Rossetti from Holmwood on 9 October, 'that people (friendly and unfriendly) will not let one be an artist, but must needs make one out a parson or a pimp. I suppose it is part of the fetid and fecund spawn of "the Galilean serpent". In the eyes of "that cursed, crawling Christian crew" one must either be St Francis or the Marquis de Sade. . . . I have begun verse again after many months enforced inaction through worry and weariness. I am writing a song of gratulation for Venice ['A Song of Italy'] . . . and hope to wind up the scheme of the poem by some quite inadequate expression of reverence towards Mazzini. . . . After all, in spite of jokes and perversities – malgré ce cher Marquis et ses foutus journaux – it is nice to have something to love and to believe in as I do in Italy. It was only Gabriel and his followers in art (l'art pour l'art) who for a time frightened me from speaking out; for ever since I was fifteen I have been equally and unalterably mad – tête montée, as my Mother says – about this article of faith; you may ask any tutor or school-fellow. I know the result will be a poem more declamatory than imaginative; but I'd rather be an Italian stump-orator than an English prophet; and I meant to make it acceptable to you and a few others of our sort. As far as I can judge, I think it already contains some of my best verses. Only, just as one hears that intense desire has made men impotent at the right (or wrong) minute, my passionate wish to express myself in part, for a little, about this matter, has twice or thrice left me exhausted and incompetent: unable to write or to decide if what has been written is or is not good. I never felt this about my poems on other subjects; and I'd give a year of my life to accomplish the writing of a really great song on this one.... There are, I must say, passages of triumphant vituperation as to Justice and Pius-Iscariot which I think not quite unworthy of my master Hugo in his abusive moods.'[21]

Unfortunately, 'A Song of Italy' is all vague and exalted rhetoric, hailing Mazzini as 'our priest', 'prophet' and 'father', and is filled with what can only be called ravings about Liberty seen as Prometheus chained to the rock and torn by the eagles of foreign and ecclesiastical tyranny. It is an experimental flight for the rather more successful, though still embarrassingly rhetorical, *Songs before Sunrise.* Its importance in Swinburne's development is that it represented a turning away from the subject matter of *Poems and Ballads* to public and political themes. Whether these were suited to Swinburne's particular type of genius is another matter, though it was always necessary for him to have some ideal before which he could prostrate himself, and Italia and Liberty were probably as good as any, even if the verses he produced under these stimuli were more like 'a whirlwind in a vacuum', as Gosse describes them before going on to praise their sublimity. 'After all,' as Swinburne said, 'in spite of jokes and perversities . . . it is nice to have something to love and to believe in.'

A. E. Housman, in an amusing lecture delivered at University College, London, and published for the first time in the *Cornhill Magazine*, Autumn 1969, observed of Swinburne's change of heart in *Songs Before Sunrise*: 'The fact is that, whatever may be the comparative merits of the two deities, Liberty is by no means so interesting as Aphrodite, and by no means so good a subject for poetry. Liberty consists in the absence of obstructions; it is merely a preliminary to activities whose character it does not determine; and to write poems about Liberty is very much as if one should write an Ode to Elbowroom or a panegyric on space of three dimensions. And in truth poets never do write poems about Liberty, they only pretend to do so: they substitute images.

Thy face is as a sword smiting in sunder
  Shadows and chains and dreams and iron things;
The sea is dumb before thy face, the thunder
  Silent, the skies are narrower than thy wings
                    Mater Triumphalis

Then, when they feel that the reader is starving for something more tangible, they generally begin to talk of Athens, which, as it happens, was a slave-state; and in the last resort they fall back on denunciation of tyranny. . . . But even tyranny is an exhaustible subject, and seven thousand verses exhaust it.' Housman sees Swinburne as a writer in search of a subject, 'a tinder-box that any spark would set on fire'. In Swinburne's hands, Liberty soon became a sadistic goddess, a Lady of Pain, and he begs her to tread him beneath her feet. Certainly, Swinburne worked himself up into an astonishing state of auto-intoxication in *Songs before Sunrise.* He offered himself up as a willing sacrifice, even if many of the poems were written – like most revolutionary verse – *pour encourager les autres.*

At the end of October 1866 Swinburne went to stay with George Powell at his Georgian mansion, Nant-Eos, near Aberystwyth, and insisted on bathing no matter how rough the sea. Afterwards he returned to his family at Holmwood, where his mother was recovering from a serious illness. Much of his time was spent reading *Leaves of Grass*, and when Moncure Conway sent him his article on Whitman, Swinburne replied on 7 November:[22]

> One passage above all others delights me – that in which you speak of his amorous embrace of the sea in bathing. I am sure he would, and hope you will excuse me for not having read or enjoyed it till now: for at the time it appeared, and for a fortnight after, I was fighting the tides as a swimmer on the west coast of Wales. I knew that the man who had spoken as he has of the sea must be a fellow seabird with me; and I would give something to have a dip in the rough water with him. This at least we have in common, for after twenty minutes profane swearing at the keeper of the shore, I did last week frighten them into giving me entrance to the sea, which they thought too fierce to be met and swum through; and the result of my swim, I am told, is that I have 'won their hearts for ever'. Since I was thirteen I have always got on with sailors and fishermen and such like men. . . .
>
> Another thing may be worth your knowing and his: that in many points both of matter and manner – gospel and style – his *Leaves of Grass* have been anticipated or rivalled by the unpublished semi-metrical 'Prophetic Books' of William Blake. . . . This I have proved in my forthcoming book on the suppressed works of the great artist and thinker, whose philosophy, to my mind far deeper and subtler than his rival Swedenborg's, has never yet been published because of the abject and faithless and blasphemous timidity of our wretched English literary society. . . . In the original 'Prophesies' there are passages quite as broad (and perhaps as offensive) as any in the *Leaves of Grass.* These I have not quoted in my critical essay; but the gist of them is precisely that of Walt Whitman's book – in other words, healthy, natural, and anti-natural.

When *Leaves of Grass* was first published in England and America, it was attacked as violently as Swinburne himself had been.

After a brief visit to London, during which he became ill again, Swinburne spent Christmas at Holmwood. He was annoyed to hear that 'the knavish tradesman' Payne had been clandestinely selling copies of *Poems and Ballads*, though all letters addressed 'c/o Moxons' to Swinburne himself had been sent to the Dead Letter Office. As Swinburne put it in a letter to E. H. Stoddard: 'Messrs Moxon, after violating their agreement to sell my Poems (which of course they had seen both in MS. and type) – after their bill of printer's charges &c. had been paid in full (N.B. I never sold them a single copy and never received from them a single penny on account) – after advertising in all the literary papers that they had withdrawn the book and had nothing to do with it – after professedly delivering over to me or my agents, on legal application and payment of their whole demand, the entire unsold edition – are now secretly selling copies with-held or rather stolen at one guinea each: books which are no more his property than the clothes I wear. . . . Theft and lying, in short, have throughout this matter distinguished the dealings of this most respectable firm; nor, to my knowledge, is the case a single one.'[23]

Early in January 1867 Swinburne received a letter from Burton, which Moxons had sent, as usual, to the Dead Letter Office. 'These denizens of the Cities of the Plain, whose fathers somehow escaped with Lot and his respectable family, pretended ignorance of my address,' he wrote on 11 January from Holmwood. 'I am still the centre of such a moral chaos that our excellent friend Houghton maintains a discreet and consistent neutrality. . . . I have not set eyes on his revered form for months. Your impending opulence, and my immediate infamy, will too evidently cut us from the shelter of his bosom. I wish you had been at hand or within reach this year, to see the missives I got from nameless quarters. One anonymous letter from Dublin threatened me, if I did not suppress my book within six weeks from that date, with castration. The writer, "when I least expected, would waylay me, slip my head in a bag, and remove the obnoxious organs; he had seen his gamekeeper do it with cats". . . . This was the greatest spree of all; but I have had letters and notices sent me (American and British) by the score, which were only less comic whether they come from friend or foe.

'I hope we shall have you back before '69, not only for the cellar's sake, sublime as that "realised ideal" is certain to be. I have in hand a scheme of mixed verse and prose – a sort of étude à la Balzac *plus* the poetry – which I flatter myself will be more offensive and objectionable to Britannia than anything I have yet done' – evidently *Lesbia Brandon*. 'You see I have now a character to keep up, and by the grace of Cotytto I will endeavour not to come short of it – at least in my writings. Tell me, if you have time, what you think of *Dolores* and *Anactoria* in full print.'[24]

But on 10 March Mazzini wrote to Swinburne: 'Don't lull us to sleep with songs of egotistical love and idolatry of physical beauty: shake us, reproach, encourage, insult, brand the cowards, hail the martyrs, tell us all that we have a great Duty to fulfil, and that, before it is fulfilled, Love is an undeserved blessing, Happiness a blasphemy, belief in God a Lie. Give us a series of "Lyrics for the Crusade". Have not our praise, but our blessing. You *can* if you choose.'

This letter is usually said to be the outcome of a conclave of Swinburne's friends, called together by Jowett at the London house of George Howard earlier in March to discuss 'what should be done *with* and *for* Algernon'. Mazzini, who was also said to be present, agreed to enlist him as 'his poet' in the crusade for Italian liberty. Swinburne was enchanted at the prospect, and he met 'the Chief' at Karl Blind's house, 2 Winchester Road, N.W.,[25] at the end of the month. The great occasion is rhapsodically described in a long letter from the Arts Club to his mother of 31 March 1867:

> I must write again to tell you what has happened to me. All last evening and late into the night I was with Mazzini. They say a man's highest hopes are usually disappointed: mine were not. I had never dared to dream of such a reception as he gave me. . . . The minute he came into the room, which was full of people, he walked straight up to me (who was standing in my place and feeling as if I trembled all over) and said 'I know *you*,' and I did as I always thought I should and really meant not to do if I could help – went down on my knees and kissed his hand. He held mine between his for some time while I was reading, and now and then gave it a great pressure. He says he will take me to Rome when the revolution comes, and crown me with his own hands in the Capitol. . . . He is a born king and chief and leader of men. You never saw such a beautiful smile as his. He is not the least bit discouraged or disheartened – and I don't know how anybody could be who had ever seen his face. It is literally full of light; he has the largest and brightest dark eyes in the world. He is clearly the man to create a nation – to bid the dead bones live and rise. And he is as simple and gentle and pleasant – with the most exquisite refinement of manner – as any one could be. . . . I know, now I have seen him, what I guessed before, why, whenever he has said to anyone, 'Go and be killed because I tell you,' they have gone and been killed because he told them. Who wouldn't, I should like to know?

Kneeling at his feet and holding the hand of his 'beloved Chief', Swinburne subjected him to his 'Song of Italy':

> O mystic rose ingrained with blood, impearled
> With tears of all the world. . . .
> Mazzini, – O our prophet, O our priest.

'Of course, I felt awfully shy and nervous when I came to the part about him personally,' Swinburne told his mother, 'but when I looked up at him I saw such a look on his face as set me all right again at once. I had heard he was growing frail and weak with years and troubles. But he was as bright and fresh and energetic as a man could be. I am not going to try to tell you what he did me the honour to say about my poetry and the use of my devotion and belief to his cause. . . . He has asked me to go and see him whenever I like. . . . I never answered his letter, but last night I told him that on receiving it I felt there was but one person on earth to turn to and tell of this great honour and delight, and that of course was my mother. I think it pleased him. I know he was very fond of his. But though she had a greater and better son, I don't think she had one more fond of her.'[26]

Fortunately Swinburne was not required 'to go and be killed', like the poets of the 1930s in Spain, but only to write for the 'Cause'. As Mazzini put it in his letter to Swinburne: 'Whilst the immense heroic Titanic battle is fought, christened on every spot by the tears of the loving ones and the blood of the brave, between Right and Wrong, Freedom and Tyranny, Truth and Lie, God and Devil – with a new conception of life, a new Religious Synthesis, a new European world struggling to emerge from the graves of Rome, Athens, Byzantium and Warsaw, kept back by a few crowned unbelievers and a handful of hired soldiers – the poet ought to be the apostle of the crusade, his word the watchword of the fighting nations and the dirge of the oppressors.' Such was to be the substance of *Songs before Sunrise*. And on his way to the 'Grove of the Beloved Disciple' in St John's Wood, Swinburne would sit down on a seat in Regent's Park and write his idealistic and inflammatory verses in celebration of the rebirth of Italy. A park-keeper, George Sims told Gosse, long remembered the little gentleman in his top hat who would pause in his walk through the park to sit down on a particular seat and begin writing.[27]

'I have had two long interviews lately with the Chief,' Swinburne wrote ecstatically to William Rossetti on 29 April. 'He is the more divine the more one sees of him.' But Lady Jane was becoming more than a little worried about the outcome of this sudden infatuation, and Swinburne had written earlier in the month to his sister Alice to reassure his mother that Mazzini was 'not at all likely to despatch me on a deadly errand to Rome or Paris, nor have we Republicans any immediate intention of laying powder-mines under Windsor Castle. . . . I must stay here for some time on account of my portrait, which is not yet begun, but as people say I am looking quite well again, I shall *sit* at once. And I think I shall stay for the exhibitions &c. and then come down for a bit if you will have me.'[28]

But the effect of all this excitement soon brought on an attack of what Swinburne always called 'bilious influenza', and in May he wrote of himself to Powell as 'I who am never unwell but by my own doing for a day or two. . . . I am writing a little sort of lyric dirge for my poor Baudelaire. But London and business or (worse) society are awful clogs on poetry. Also

I am in the honourable agonies of portrait sitting to Watts, and he won't let me crop my hair, whose curls the British public (unlike Titian's) reviles in the streets. *Il faut souffrir pour être peint*, but the portrait is a superb picture already, and up to the Venetian standard by the admission of other artists.'[29] This is the portrait now in the National Portrait Gallery.

Swinburne's friends knew only too well what it was that brought on these 'bilious attacks'. Mazzini, however, resolutely refused to interfere in Swinburne's private life, though he disapproved of much of his poetry. When the photographs of Swinburne and Menken were appearing in shop windows and there was a rumour that he was going on the stage, Mazzini wrote: 'No, I did not ask Swinburne about the stage or the double photograph; I really cannot play the part of spiritual father to him except when he himself offers means and opportunity!'[30]

Writing to his mother about the Royal Academy Exhibition, Swinburne says: 'Old Landseer's white bulls are perfectly magnificent, both beasts and painting. There are very few good landscapes, but two or three really good seascapes – one by Hook, a boat rowed by boys on the edge of a full rising wave, curving into a solid mound of water before it breaks. It made me thirst to be in between the waves. Whistler, who doesn't like Hook's pictures as a rule, pointed it out to me as good.'[31] But William Rossetti noted in his diary on 6 May: 'Went for a short while to the R.A.: it strikes me as a very vulgar and tawdry exhibition. Millais, I fear, going off seriously.'[32]

In July, Swinburne is excusing himself from attending a dinner given by Lord Houghton: 'I am kept in bed all day with a severe bilious attack, which came on suddenly this morning.' But breakfasting with Lord Houghton later in the month, he fell down in a fit. Houghton sent for the doctor and telegraphed for the admiral. 'I suppose someone will come up and look after him,' Houghton wrote to his wife, 'he was looking wretchedly ill before. . . . Jowett seemed much affected.' The admiral came at once to London and took his son back to the country to recover, which he did, rapidly as always under the care of his family.

Thomas Woolner, the sculptor, who was also present at the Upper Brook Street breakfast, wrote to Sir Walter Trevelyan: 'poor little Swinburne had an awful fit yesterday at Lord Houghton's. From all accounts he seems to lead a sadly wild and unwholesome life. He made a great commotion, as you may imagine, at the breakfast table among the assembled guests.'[33]

John Nichol had written to Swinburne asking him to go on a walking tour with him the following spring, and Swinburne had replied that he hoped it might be feasible. 'In the autumn,' he added, 'I have some thoughts of going to Munich (of all places) with an old schoolfellow and friend [George Powell], to see the opening of Wagner's Theatre and the performance of his as yet unknown opera which is to take four nights to represent, and embody the whole of the Nibelungen. Conceive – if you know the *Lohengrin* –

what a divine delight it will be. But I presume the destinies will intervene and make it impossible.'[34]

In the event, he did not go. Gosse tells us that Swinburne had no feeling for music and 'could not tell one note from another', and that when a friend played him 'Three Blind Mice', telling him that it was an old Florentine *ritornello*, he exclaimed ecstatically that it 'reflected to perfection the cruel beauty of the Medicis'.[35] Probably this is no more than an amusing story, for we know that he had been greatly moved by Mary Gordon's playing and singing of Handel and that he attended Clara Schumann's recitals with Powell. He also felt an especial affinity with Berlioz, though this may have been inspired rather by Berlioz's worship of Shakespeare and his music criticism, which Swinburne read while staying with Powell next year at Étretât. It is quite likely, however, that Powell, or the members of his own family, played him piano scores of Wagner and Berlioz, for he had evidently heard *Lohengrin*.

Swinburne was in London again by November, leading an active social life, frequenting the 'Grove of the Evangelist', and indulging in a 'riotous concubinage', with the inevitable result. 'I have been prostrate these two days with influenza,' he wrote to Frederick Locker on the eleventh, 'but hope to be about tomorrow.' On 28 November, he told William Rossetti: 'I have been in bed three days and shut up five with influenza and bile: which I take as just judgement on a virtuous attempt' – that is, presumably, his poem 'An Appeal to England'. In December, as we have seen, at the height of his affair with Adah Menken, he was thrown from a hansom cab. By the end of that month he was again in bed 'with streaming and sickening influenza'. In January 1868 he wrote to Powell that he was 'too ill to read, much less to write', being 'replunged for days into the hell of influenza and indigestion', though by the end of the month he was once again attending a Cannibal Club dinner in Burton's absence. Nothing seemed to dash Swinburne's irrepressible high-spirits for long.

With so much dissipation and self-destructive *diablerie*, it is pleasant to record Swinburne's act of kindness to the blind young poet Philip Bourke Marston, who had written to him rhapsodically about his poetry. 'Last night,' he wrote to his sister Alice on 10 April 1867, 'I had to entertain a poor boy of sixteen, son of Dr (*not* M.D.) Westland Marston, all but wholly blind, who for some time has lived (his friends tell me) on the hope of seeing me (as far as he can see). I thought it so touching, remembering my own enthusiasms at that age, that I said I should be glad to have him at my rooms (with his father and a friend or two) and they chose last night. The day before a friend brought me the most frantic set of verses written by this poor blind fellow and addressed to me. I was rather worried, but I thought of his affliction and made up my mind to read the poem and make him as happy as I could. And I think for once I have succeeded in doing another a good turn. . . . I gave him chocolate bon-bons &c., and read to the company unpublished things of mine – among others the little Jacobite song that you and A. [Abba, his sister Isobel] liked so much when I read it to you all at Holmwood. It was really very touching to see the face that [I] could just see where I was across the table looking at me – and growing so feverishly *red* that his father went over once or twice to see if he was all right. It is not because he went in for me that I cared about it, but a thing of that sort *must* make one compassionate. . . . And he did seem to enjoy himself so much that I really felt it was worth living to give so much pleasure to a poor boy afflicted as he is from his birth.'[36]

Meanwhile the photographs of Swinburne and Menken exhibited in shop windows had given rise to the absurd rumour that they were going to act together on the stage. As Swinburne wrote afterwards to Nichol: 'When poor old Menken was close on the end of her life's farce-tragedy, a Parisian journalist circulated the report in his print that she was about to play Psyche to my Cupid in a new ballet or opera buffa. Complimentary to my appearance of youth at the time, if not to the discretion of my age.' To Powell, who had asked for copies of the photographs, he wrote in April 1868: 'You will excuse my delay in sending the enclosed when you hear the *two* reasons: 1) illness hardly intermittent during weeks and months of weather which would have disgraced hell and raised a new revolution among the devils: 2) that today only I have been able to get for myself one copy of either photograph. There has been a *damned* row about it: paper after paper has flung pellets of dirt at me; assuming or asserting the falsehood that its publication and sale all over London were things authorized or permitted or even foreseen by the sitters; whereas of course it was a private affair, to be known (or shewn) to friends only. The circulation has of course been stopped as far as possible, but not without much irritating worry. . . . So we are promised Lohengrin this season at last and after all! Will the promise be kept? tell me. . . . My beloved chief is still with us, very ill and indomitable, and sad and kind as ever. I have worked much at *his* book [*Songs Before Sunrise*] since we met. In "Lippincott's Magazine" (American) for May (i.e. about mid-May), will be a long poem of mine called "Siena", which will make part of it.'[37]

Early in May Swinburne had another accident, as he told William Rossetti: 'Tuesday last – the day after we met at Hotten's – I had a painful and what might have been a dangerous accident which has laid me up ever since. I was carrying a lamp (unlit) in the dark (having already in looking for it smashed a looking-glass to begin with) when I fell over something, smashed the lamp (it was v. dark and the curtains close drawn) and cut open my head, my right knee and (in rising barefoot) my left foot. I could get no help or plaster till the morning and by then had lost a lot of blood. . . . I assure you the bed and floor of my room next morning looked as if M. de Sade had had a few friends to a small and select supper party the night before, and had enjoyed himself thoroughly on the festive occasion.'

On 20 June 1868 *The Times* and *Telegraph* carried the following advertisement:

> LOST, 10 to 20 BLUE FOOLSCAP LEAVES OF PAPER, roughly written upon in verse (partly dialogue). Missed between April 15 – May 10. May have been left in a cab. Of no use to anybody but the owner. Small REWARD will be given upon restoration by Mr Hotten, 74 Piccadilly, W.

The manuscripts were parts of *Bothwell* and 'Tristram and Yseult', the original title of *Tristram of Lyonesse.*

Early in July of this year Swinburne fainted in the reading room of the British Museum and fell and cut his head on the iron staple of one of the desks. He had gone, as he wrote to Nichol, early to the reading room, met a friend who was just leaving and had agreed to wait until one or one-thirty for his return, but had begun to feel faint and giddy in 'the damnable unventilated air' and had finally fainted. It is more likely that he had had another fit. Gosse records meeting him, 'rather late in the afternoon', being carried along a corridor on a chair by two attendants: 'I recognised him instantly from his photographs which now filled the shop windows. His hanging hands, closed eyelids, corpse-like white face, and red hair dabbled in blood presented an appearance of the utmost horror.'[38] Gosse thought he was dead. But when Gabriel Rossetti and his brother called at Dorset Street on 13 July, they found him 'in capital spirits, with health apparently to correspond: a little plastering on his forehead. He says that the closeness of the Museum Reading Room on that exceptionally hot day quite overcame him. . . . Everybody on the spot showed him the greatest attention: and he receives most cordially Browning's attention in calling yesterday.'[39] Jowett also wrote warning him that he had been injuring his natural health by intemperate habits and irregular ways, and offering even pecuniary help if needed, to set him straight. Of course, he told Nichol on 22 July, 'the thrice-accursed penny-a-liners' of the press made the most of it.

Swinburne's mother wrote begging him to come home. 'I *must* go first for some little time to Holmwood,' he wrote to Powell, who had invited him to Étretât. 'Then – oh! shan't I be glad to accept your invitation! 1) to see you and cheer and be cheered if ill or worried 2) to satiate my craving (ultra Sapphic and plusquam-Sadic) lust after the sea. . . . My life has been enlivened of late by a fair friend who keeps a maison de supplices à la Rodin. There is occasional balm in Gilead'[40] – a reference, of course, to the high-class brothel in St John's Wood. At the same time we find him writing urgently to Hotten, in the same letter in which he advises him about a new edition of Chapman's plays and poems: 'Will you get back and send me *at once* the photograph I lent you long ago of the Eton bloc &c? *today if possible.* I want it!'

To his mother Swinburne wrote in August, excusing himself for not returning sooner to Holmwood: 'It has been one thing after another in the way of engagements that has kept me back – but nothing in the way of illness. Only you can't think how I get flooded with letters and invitations and that sort of thing (and some from people who are real friends to me) that I don't like to leave town without answering either by a call or by a note. You must take my word for it when I say I'll come down the very first day I can.'[41]

Swinburne was now in his thirty-second year and, as Gosse observes in *Portraits and Sketches*: 'His first period of creative energy had come to a close, and he had not yet begun, or only now was beginning to launch steadily upon his second, namely, the celebration in transcendental verse . . . of the ideal and indivisible Republic. He was dejected in mind and ailing in body; the wonderful colours of youth were now first beginning to fade out of his miraculous eyes and hair.' In the previous April he had sent his admirable *William Blake* to the press; he had written 'The Hymn of Man'; 'Tiresias' was begun in June, and he was 'doggedly and painfully working at what he always called "*His* book", the Chief's book, the volume of political lyrics which Mazzini had commanded him to write for the glory of Liberty and Italia.'[42]

## CHAPTER EIGHT

# 1868–72
# LA CHAUMIÈRE DE DOLMANCÉ

In mid-September 1868 Swinburne crossed over to Normandy to stay with George Powell. '*Such* a lovely passage on Saturday,' he wrote to his mother on the fourteenth, 'hard due east wind, alternate roll sideways, and plunge forward and splashing – that I was wild with pleasure and others with sickness – *I* had left that behind on shore. I *must* hail the Flying Dutchman and get taken on board in some capacity – then, never stopping or landing, I shall always be well and happy. To get here is an awful labour – endless changes of line (with excessive confusion, stupidity, insolence) – and at last no beds anywhere and two hours' drive by starlight and one antediluvian gig-lamp only – no hotel open – an hour's helpless and hopeless shivering – at last an improvised bed (at 2 a.m. our hotel was roused) – but today all right. Powell has got the sweetest little old farmhouse fitted up inside with music, books, drawings &c. – and of course pokes me into the nicest room. There is a wild little garden all uphill, and avenues of trees about. The sea is splendid and the cliffs very like the Isle of Wight – two arches of rock each side of the bay with *one* Needle only, exactly like *half* the Freshwater pair. We are going to Rouen soon to see the cathedral.'[1]

Harmless and innocent enough! He did not tell his mother that Powell had given the cottage the sinister name of La Chaumière de Dolmancé, after Sade's *La Philosophie dans le boudoir*; that the avenue came to be known as Avenue de Sade; that this 'sweetest little cottage' was furnished in the most macabre fashion; and that the domestics were boys specially engaged in London for their good looks. The local population of honest fishermen and their wives could only wonder at the eccentric habits of these two Englishmen, without divining their actual nature, till scandal drove Powell from the neighbourhood.

One day, while bathing, Swinburne was carried two miles out to sea by a treacherous current. It happened that the young de Maupassant, then a student of eighteen, on holiday at Étretât with his mother, seeing a swimmer in difficulties far out to sea, plunged into the waves with the idea of swimming out to the rescue. But Swinburne's plight had already been observed by the coast-guard, who signalled to a fishing-boat, the *Marie Marthe*, that was making for Yport. Powell had also witnessed Swinburne's distress and had hurried down to the shore, where he met de Maupassant just emerging from the sea. By this time the *Marie Marthe* had rescued the drowning poet, and Powell therefore engaged a carriage and drove into Yport.

It appears that, on being rescued, Swinburne had at once recovered and, wrapped in sail-cloth, astonished the crew by a passionate recitation of Victor Hugo. From Yport, the friends drove back to Étretât, and next day invited Maupassant to lunch.

Some years later, on 28 February 1875, Maupassant entertained a company at Flaubert's house with a dramatic account of his visits to the Chaumière de Dolmancé. This is recorded in detail in the *Journal* of Edmond and Jules de Goncourt:[2]

> We were admiring the poetry of the Englisman Swinburne at Flaubert's, when Daudet exclaimed:
>
> 'But they say he is a pederast! Extraordinary things are related of his stay at Étretât last year. . . .'
>
> 'It is longer ago than that, it is some years ago,' replied little Maupassant. 'I came to know him slightly at that time.'
>
> 'But,' exclaimed Flaubert, 'wasn't it you who, in effect, saved his life?'
>
> 'Not altogether,' responded Maupassant. 'I was walking along the beach, I heard the cries of a drowning man, I waded into the water. . . . But a boat was there beforehand and had already fished him out. . . . He had gone down to bathe completely drunk. . . . Meanwhile I had left the water, wet through up to my waist. Another Englishman who lived there and who was his friend, came up to thank me very warmly.
>
> 'Next day I received an invitation to lunch. A strange house, a sort of cottage, containing some very beautiful pictures and with an inscription above the entrance, which I did not read at first, and a great monkey gambolling about inside. . . . The lunch! I didn't know what I was eating; all I remember is that it was something like fish. I asked its name. The proprietor told me with a strange smile that it was meat, and it was impossible to find out any more about it. There was no wine, they only drank spirits.
>
> 'The proprietor, called Powell, was, they said at Étretât, the son of an English lord, who had disguised himself under his mother's name. As for Swinburne, imagine a little man, quite short, with a pointed face, a hydrocephalous forehead, pigeon-chested, agitated by a trembling which affected his glass with St Vitus' dance, and incessantly talking like a madman. . . .
>
> 'One thing immediately upset me at the first lunch, it was that from time to time Powell tickled his monkey, who escaped his fingers to tap the nape of my neck, when I leaned forward to drink.

'After lunch the two friends brought out gigantic portfolios of obscene photographs, taken in Germany, life-sized and all of masculine subjects. Among others, I recall an English soldier masturbating himself at a window. Powell showed me that completely drunk, from time to time sucking the fingers of a dried hand, which served, I believe, in that house as a paper-weight.

'Swinburne speaks very good French. He is immensely learned. He seems to know everything. That day, he told us some curious things about snakes, confiding to us that he had stood for two or three hours at a time to observe them. Then he translated for us several of his poems, investing the translation with an extraordinary charm. It was very beautiful.'

Maupassant accepted a second invitation to lunch. This time he was not disturbed by the monkey. After lunch 'le petit Maupassant' was given a liqueur so strong that it knocked him out. However, he managed to escape to his hotel, where he slept for the rest of the day. Nevertheless, though repelled, he says that he was still full of curiosity to discover whether Swinburne and Powell were merely eccentrics or genuine pederasts. His third visit convinced him that 'ils vivaient tous deux ensembles, se satisfaisaient avec des singes ou de jeunes domestiques de quatorze ou quinze ans, qu'on expédiait d'Angleterre à Powell à peu près tous les trois mois, de petits domestiques d'une netteté et d'une fraîcheur extraordinaires'. As for the monkey, which slept each night in Powell's bed, it had been hung by the 'petit domestique' in a fit of jealousy. On leaving, Maupassant had asked his hosts whether they knew that Dolmancé was the name of the hero of Sade's *La Philosophie dans le boudoir*. They replied that they did. ' "Then that is the name of your house?" I said. "Si vous voulez," repondirentils avec de terribles figures.'

One cannot help wondering how far Maupassant's account was the product of a lively imagination nourished by the ideas current in France at that time of the viciousness of the *milord anglais*. And was he really already familiar with *La Philosophie dans le boudoir* at the age of eighteen? Doubtless he found Swinburne's and Powell's cult of the macabre 'extraordinaire', but that did not prevent him from accepting several invitations to lunch, to consume 'spitted monkey' and '*liqueurs* fortes'. Possibly his visits took on in retrospect more sinister overtones, though his account may well be more accurate than has hitherto been allowed. He adds that the house was 'full of strange noises and *d'ombres sadiques*'. One night, he was told afterwards, Powell was seen chasing a Negro through the garden and firing at him with a revolver. Then, suddenly, 'that mysterious house was silent and empty', and Powell disappeared. No one saw him leaving by carriage and no one ever met him again on the roads.

George Selwyn, the English eighteenth-century sadist of Edmond de Goncourt's novel *La Faustin*, owes much to Maupassant's account of

Swinburne and Powell. Selwyn is described as having 'une figure qui ne semblait pas de son sexe, une figure de vieille femme, dans laquelle allait et venait un ricanement perpétuel, pareil à un tic nerveuse'. He is also very learned and repeats from memory 'des citations interminables, montrant une connaissance extraordinaire de toutes les littératures d'Europe'. Selwyn leaves Lord Annandale's castle to go to the 'petite maison sur les côtes de la Bretagne, La Chaumière de Dolmancé', a name which brings 'un terrible sourire énigmatique' to his lips. Selwyn's nervous symptoms were due to an affection of the spinal cord and his voice, like Swinburne's, rose to a falsetto when he was excited.[3]

In 1891 there appeared Gabriel Mourey's prose translation of *Poems and Ballads* with an introduction by Maupassant, in which he describes Swinburne as 'a kind of Edgar Allan Poe, idealized and sensualized . . . a writer with a soul more exalted, more depraved, more in love with what is strange and monstrous, more curious – groping after and suggesting subtle, unnatural refinements of life and thought – than the soul of the American poet. . . . The impression I have retained from my several meetings with him is perhaps of the most extravagantly artistic person alive in the world to-day.' Maupassant is notably more complimentary in his introduction than in his private account of his visits to La Chaumière de Dolmancé, as recorded by the Goncourts. He describes Powell as short and fat and Swinburne as short and thin: 'thin and startling at first glance – a sort of fantastic apparition. . . . His forehead was very high under his long hair, and his face became gradually narrower towards a slight chin shadowed with a meagre tuft of beard. A very light moustache hovered over remarkably thin, tight lips, and his neck, which seemed to have no end, joined that head – alive with clear, fixed, penetrating eyes – to a torso without shoulders, the top of his chest seeming hardly wider than his forehead. This virtually supernatural character was shaken all over by nervous spasms. He was very cordial and hospitable; and the extraordinary charm of his intelligence captivated me at once.

'During the whole of lunch we talked about art, literature, humanity, and the opinions of those two friends cast over everything a kind of disturbing, macabre light, for they had a way of seeing and understanding that made them seem like diseased visionaries, drunken with a poetry magical and perverse. . . . *But Messrs. Powell and Swinburne were delightful in their fantasy and lyricism* [my italics]. They recounted Icelandic legends, translated by Mr Powell, of a gripping and terrible novelty. Swinburne spoke of Victor Hugo with boundless enthusiasm.'[4]

Maupassant adds that Turgenev often translated Swinburne's poems to him with keen admiration. In fact, he was the only living English poet that Turgenev admired, and writing to the poet Fet about contemporary English poetry from Baden-Baden in August 1871 he says: 'It's not an attractive thing, but interesting – and there is one very, very great lyrical talent: Swinburne.'[5]

Turgenev regularly attended the Goncourts' literary dinners in Paris, which were held twice a month. 'At these dinners, which were unique of their kind,' says the Russian writer S. Usov,[6] 'the painter Kharlamov related that sometimes extremely curious conversations took place. . . . Once, for instance, the conversation suddenly turned on the so-called "other world" of morality, and Monsieur Halévy announced: "Oh, in this connection the well-known English poet Swinburne beats the record of all our profligates. Not long ago I met a young man who went to the Isle of Wight for the bathing. There, during a walk, he by chance met Swinburne, who was living on the sea-shore in a field tent alone with a monkey dressed as a woman, who acted as servant. Swinburne invited the youth into his tent. The monkey was preparing luncheon. During the meal, Swinburne began propounding the free theory of 'unisexual' love, and began making advances to the young man. The monkey loured and started baring its teeth, showing all the signs of the jealousy which was torturing it. . . . Swinburne took no notice of this, hit the monkey with a whip, and then started embracing the young man. The monkey let out a howl and, throwing itself on the youth in a frenzy, dug its claws into his throat with the intention of throttling him. It had, with great difficulty, to be dragged away from him, and the guest had hastily to leave. . . . However, Swinburne and the young man continued to see each other, but no longer in the presence of the jealous monkey-servant. One day, Swinburne again invited his friend to his tent on the beach for luncheon. This time they were waited on by an elderly Irish manservant. During luncheon some grilled meat was served, the taste of which seemed odd to the young man. 'What kind of meat is it?' he asked Swinburne. 'Well, do you remember that monkey which wanted to give you a good clawing? I ordered this dish to be prepared from her,' the English poet announced quite calmly. – How do you like that, gentlemen?"

'Halévy's story made a terrible impression on them all. Noise, violent arguments broke out, many began disputing the possibility of eating one's mistress, even if she were only a monkey, others said that the young man had invented the story. I. S. Turgenev, too, joined in the conversation.

' "You shouldn't get so excited, gentlemen," said Turgenev from the sofa, sitting back with a cup of coffee. "Absolutely anything can be expected of Swinburne, whom I personally know rather well, as he is, of course, hardly a normal person. . . . I once jokingly asked him 'What is the most original and unrealizable thing you would like to experience at the moment?' 'I'll tell you,' Swinburne replied, 'to ravish Saint Geneviève during her most ardent ecstasy of prayer – but in addition, with her secret consent!' " '

Turgenev could have met Swinburne at Rossetti's or Madox Brown's house when he was in England in 1866. He could have met him again in London in the spring of 1871 and in Scotland in August of the same year, when Swinburne was staying with Jowett at Tummil Bridge, Pitlochry. Turgenev does not mention having met him in his letters, though he mentions meeting Browning and describes him as a vigorous white-bearded man with a handshake like an electric shock. Nevertheless, he claims to have known Swinburne 'rather well' and so was not in the least disturbed by Halévy's story, which was subsequently told to Usov at Tatiana Passek's house in St Petersburg by Kharlamov, who had spent many years in Paris and had painted a portrait of Turgenev in 1874. Usov repeated the story in his gossipy reminiscences 'Mozaika', written in 1880. It may have gained somewhat in its various retellings, but it does not sound the kind of thing that could have been entirely invented, though the young man who told it originally to Halévy seems to have been himself rather a peculiar character. It does, however, link up disturbingly with Maupassant's account of his visits to Swinburne and Powell at Étretât. But what strikes one as hardly credible is that Swinburne, though he may have done anything at Étretât, should have been living in this extraordinary manner so near his relations in the Isle of Wight. We know that he was staying with his family at The Orchard, Niton, from July to September 1874, hard at work on the text of Chapman's plays, reading the *Iliad* and swimming in the sea in all weathers. In a letter to Edwin Harrison of 4 June 1873 he says that he is going to the Isle of Wight '(at the risk of realizing the sensations of a damned ghost revisiting earth, before my natural date of damnation) with my family, to pass the better part of the summer at a place belonging to an uncle of mine. My mother wants me to go, and I think I may as well once for all break through all sentiment of reluctance and association and tread out all sense of old pain and pleasure for ever, if I can, by coming back in this my old age to where I was so happy and unhappy as a child and youth.'[7]

Swinburne felt an understandable reluctance to revisiting the Isle of Wight and gave powerful expression to these feelings in 'The Forsaken Garden', possibly written during this visit of 1874, or soon after. His next visit was in March 1877, for his father's funeral. Oscar Wilde may have been nearer the truth when he told Edmond de Goncourt in 1883 that Swinburne was 'a braggart in matters of vice, who had done everything he could to convince his fellow citizens of his homosexuality and bestiality, without being in the slightest degree a homosexual or a bestializer'.[8] This view is borne out by Swinburne's letter to Burton, quoted earlier, in which he says: 'You see I have a character to keep up, and by the grace of Cotytto I will endeavour not to come short of it – at least in my writings.' It is just possible that, in returning to the Isle of Wight, he was moved deliberately to desecrate the place where he had come to love and had been rejected by his cousin. This, however, seems hardly likely, especially as in the previous summer he had been horrified by reports of Simeon Solomon's arrest for soliciting and for having '*done* things', as he wrote to George Powell, 'amenable to law such as done by a sane man would make it impossible for any one to keep up his acquaintance and not be cut by the rest of the world as an accomplice'.[9] Writing to Powell, a homosexual himself, Swinburne would have had no need of hypocrisy, though Turgenev may have been right when he said that 'absolutely anything' could be expected of him.

Halévy's account certainly gives an impression of authenticity, except that it must have been an exceptionally clever monkey to have prepared the lunch. Monkeys, however, are known for their violent jealousy and Swinburne may have been keeping her simply as a pet – unless, of course, he had adopted the practice of bestiality from Burton and Powell. For in a letter to Watts of 30 August 1875, he refers unequivocally to 'that lost love of Burton's, the beloved and blue object of his Central African affections, whose caudal charms and simious seductions were too strong for the narrow laws of Levitical or Mosaic prudery which would confine the jewel of a man to the lotus of a merely human female by the most odious and unnatural of priestly restrictions'.[10] This, however, is written in Swinburne's familiar tone of humorous bravado. One knows, nevertheless, that Swinburne, like Burton, was fascinated by all forms of sexual deviation. 'To the imagination, the animal represents sexuality freed from the restrictions imposed by civilization and humanity,' writes Anthony Storr, 'and both men and women envy the abandon with which an animal may be supposed to satisfy its erotic needs.'[11]

Swinburne had returned to London by the end of October 1868 and wrote to his mother on the twenty-fourth from the Arts Club, Hanover Square: 'I was very glad to find your letter waiting for me – but you might quite as well have sent me a line at Étretât for in a little bit of a place like that one is known in a day or two. I had a real sea adventure there which I will tell you about when we meet. I had to swim (Powell says) over two miles out to sea and was picked up by a fishing boat, but luckily I was all right though very tired, and the result was I made immense friends with all the fishermen and sailors about – who are quite the nicest people I ever knew.'[12]

To Lord Houghton he wrote on 9 November: 'Our fair friend of the Grove of the Beloved Disciple has also returned from France and is in high feather. I always find her delicious dans son genre.' But in his next letter to Houghton Swinburne is complaining of 'the usual November influenza'. He then went down to Holmwood to recover, whence he wrote to Powell on 2 December, to remind him that it was 'the 54th anniversary of the death of that great and good man the Marquis de Sade. I wish we were together and could devise some appropriate ceremony to celebrate the festival of that apostle and confessor of the faith as it is in Priapus. If I were in London I would observe it by a partial reproduction (with female aid) of the rites of Artemis Orthia,[13] mixed with those of the European Cotytto[14] and the Asiatic Aphrodite of Aphaca. M. Dolmancé I feel sure would find something to suggest. Can you think of anything against next time?'[15]

Christmas was spent at Cambridge as the guest of Thomas Bendyshe,

7 Swinburne and Adah Dolores Menken

8 Edmund Gosse in 1886, from the painting by John Singer Sargent

Senior Fellow of King's and fellow member of the Cannibal Club. Swinburne enjoyed Cambridge 'in the naked beauty of a vacation', and he writes to Lord Houghton that he met 'living men of the great Keate epoch of Eton's development – fossils (how interesting to the scientific student of paedo-sarcotomy!)' – that is, the birching of boys, for which Keate was so famous as Headmaster in the earlier years of the century. Bendyshe, he adds, 'has unearthed in the public library a presentation copy of de Sade's *Aline et Valcour* – "don de l'auteur au citoyen La Loubie, *son meilleur ami*." Who was the "best man" of the author of *Justine* is a riddle of much moment to science.' He attended divine service, he says, at King's College Chapel – 'to universal amazement of the whole college – and for once sat in the seat of a Bishop . . . and walked out actually preceded by a man with a silver poker!'

Meanwhile *William Blake* had appeared during the autumn of the previous year. This work not only shows Swinburne at his finest as a critic, but it is the first attempt to penetrate the almost impenetrable thickets of the 'Prophetic Books' and to treat Blake as a great poet and revolutionary thinker, instead of an inspired lunatic. Even Rossetti had tried to dissuade Swinburne from discussing the Prophetic Books, and in many respects he has, of course, been superseded, especially by another poet, Kathleen Raine, in her great *William Blake and Traditional Mythology*.

After spending a few months quietly at Holmwood, in the spring of 1869 Swinburne paid a visit to Jowett at Balliol. On his return to London he gave up his Dorset Street rooms and moved to 12 North Crescent, Bedford Square. Gosse tells us that he 'was now suffering from reaction after the very intense and prolonged excitement in which he had indulged, and he endured a good deal of discomfort from languor and irritability'.[16]

The rhapsody on *L'Homme Qui Rit*, contributed to the *Fortnightly Review* this year, brought from Hugo a gratifying acknowledgment. He wrote from Guernsey on 14 July: 'Merci, *ex imo corde*, de votre magnifique travail sur mon livre, quelle haute philosophie, et quelle intuition profonde vous avez! Dans le grand critique, on sent le grand poèt. Quand donc me sera-t-il donné de vous voir?' Swinburne took this as an invitation to Guernsey. But Richard Burton had returned from Brazil and, before taking up his new post at the consulate at Damascus, had been advised to drink the waters at Vichy; and he proposed that Swinburne should accompany him. 'I am here for a few weeks with my friend Captain Burton,' Swinburne wrote to George Powell on 29 July. 'When he goes off eastward I shall return to Paris; and if you are there (say about a month hence) at Étretât, I shall look in upon you (if you will have me) on my way back. *Then* – whither do you think I am bound? To Hauteville House, Guernsey. In other words to the summit of Olympus. . . . I shall stay in Paris not more than a week when I leave; but I hope to meet Paul de Saint-Victor, Théophile Gautier, and perhaps Flaubert. . . . If you were with me I could bring you acquainted with the friend at whose rooms I expect to meet them. He is *the* Sadique collector of European fame. His erotic collection of books is unrivalled upon earth – unequalled, I should imagine, in heaven. . . . There is a Sapphic group by Pradier of two girls in the very act and one has her tongue up où vous savez, her head and massive hair buried, plunging, diving between the other's thighs. . . . Remember me "de cœur" to my sailors.'[17]

This 'Sadique collector' was Frederick Hankey, Houghton's agent in Paris, the son of General Frederick Hankey, and also the agent of Henry Spencer Ashbee, the 'Pisanus Fraxi' of the *Index Librorum Prohibitorum.* He is described in the Goncourts' *Journal* as 'un fou, un monstre, un de ces hommes qui confinent à l'abîme. Pour lui, comme par une voile déchirée, j'ai entrevu un fonds abominable, un côté effrayant d'une aristocratie d'argent blasée, de l'aristocratie anglaise apportant la férocité dans l'amour, et dont le libertinage ne jouit que par la souffrance de la femme.' Hankey was well-acquainted with both Swinburne and Burton, who, he said, had promised him the skin of a living Negress with which to bind one of his books. Burton, however, was not as good – or as bad, rather – as his word.[18]

While he was still at Vichy, Swinburne received a letter from Whistler telling him that on 20 July he had appeared before the Committee of the Arts Club in response to their resolution demanding his (Swinburne's) resignation and had managed to persuade them, 'in return for certain concessions from us', to reconsider and withdraw their demand. Dr Lang quotes Henry Silver's unpublished diary for 4 August 1869: 'Swinburne nearly kicked out of the Arts Club for drunkenness. Whistler says to Committee: "You accuse him of drunkenness – well, that's his defence." ' According to Ezra Pound, Whistler told the Committee: 'You ought to be proud that there is in London a club where the greatest poet of our time *can* get drunk, if he wants to, otherwise he might lie in the gutter.'[19] Whistler and Burton must have been very persuasive for the Committee to agree to waive their resolution once more. 'A thousand thanks to you in especial and to Burton for all your kindness,' Swinburne wrote to Whistler on 6 August, 'and the way in which you have got me out of the row without loss of dignity. . . . I am very well today and I think it is going to do me good – but yesterday I was rather knocked up after a hard walk and scramble in a blazing furnace of sun the day before at Thiers – which is the most quaint and lovely old town conceivable, perched like a bird and clinging as with claws among the gorges of the mountains. It is 24 kilometres off, and between the two drives we did a lot of walking; even (Captain) Burton who was born of iron avowed himself tired and sleepy at the end of the day.'[20]

To his sister Alice, Swinburne sent some flowers gathered at the summit of Puy de Dome, 5,000 feet above sea level, 'which Burton and I scaled and found ourselves . . . wrapt in a rolling and rushing sea of mist'. On the way down, they had a clear view of the Auvergne country – 'splendid and singular – a barren and broken land so laboriously cultivated that not an inch was left waste, the whole stretch of it from left to right looked like a carpet of many colours – vineyard, cornfield, woods &c. The mountain is clothed in heather, but this that I send you is the only bit of white I found. . . . The place is doing me great good – I was rather spent with the heat in London . . . and now Burton says he never saw me so fresh and well. Coming here from Paris on a boiling day with my back to the engine, I got to feel as sick as anything, and you can't think how kind and careful he was of me. I feel now as if I knew for the first time what it is to have an elder brother. He is the most cordial, helpful, sympathetic friend to me it is possible to have; and it is a treat at last to have him to myself instead of having as in London to share him with all the world and his wife and children, from Lords Clarendon and Stanley to Col. This and Capt. That. I rather grudge Mrs Burton's arrival here on Monday, though we are excellent friends, and I daresay I shall see none the less of him.'[21]

But, as has been remarked already, Isabel Burton had disliked Swinburne at sight, though their relations remained superficially cordial, just as Lady Jane had disliked Burton, instinctively feeling what his influence on her son must be. But Swinburne wrote to say that if only she were at Vichy with them she would 'love him, as I do. I have been now nearly a month alone with him – and I tell you this, he is so good, so true, kind, noble, and brave, that I never expect to see his like again – but *him* I do hope to see again, and when that time comes to see him at Damascus as H.B.M. Consul.'[22] At Vichy also were Frederick Leighton and Mrs Sartoris, the singer. 'I found it worth while playing the pretty to the old lady,' Swinburne told his mother, 'as she plays and sings to me in private by the hour, and her touch and her voice are like a young woman's. *But* – they have sent her here to get down her *fat* – and – !'

Years later, after Burton's death, Swinburne recalled their ascent of the Puy de Dome in his 'Elegy, 1869–1891': 'Auvergne, Auvergne, O wild and woful land'. . . .

> Foot following foot along the sheer strait ledge
>   Where space was none to bear the wild goat's feet
> Till blind we sat on the outer footless edge
>   Where darkling death seemed fain to share the seat,
>
> The abyss before us, viewless even as time's,
>   The abyss to left of us, the abyss to right,
> Bid thoughts now dream how high the freed soul climbs
>   That death sets free from change of day and night.

And after Isabel had buried her husband in the catholic cemetery at Mortlake beneath a stone Arab tent and burnt all his journals, Swinburne denounced her in the same poem:

Priests and the soulless serfs of priests may swarm
With vulturous acclamation, loud in lies,
About his dust while yet his dust is warm
Who mocked as sunlight mocks their base blind eyes,

Their godless ghost of godhead, false and foul,
As fear his dam or hell his throne; but we,
Scarce hearing, heed no carrion church-wolf's howl:
The corpse be theirs to mock; the soul is free.

Free as ere yet its earthly day was done
It lived above the coil about us curled:
A soul whose eyes were keener than the sun,
A soul whose wings were wider than the world.

On his way back to England, Swinburne called in on Powell at Étretât, and 'was rather astonished', as he wrote to Mary Leith later, 'at finding myself rushed at, seized by arms and legs, hoisted and cheered, by the fisher-folk and sailors who knew me again at once, said to me after I was let down in rather a dishevelled state of mind and body, "Why, don't you know you're their hero?" and I said, "I don't see where the hero comes in – if I'd gone in after somebody who was drowning it would have been a creditable sort of thing – but it was just an accident." ' But the fishermen had not forgotten how he had been rescued two miles out at sea the year before and had declaimed Victor Hugo while still dripping wet and covered with a sail-cloth. Afterwards, he had gone out octopus-fishing with them – that is, for 'real live pieuvres and the oldest grey-haired fisherman said he quite believed that there were such pieuvres as could hold a strong man down and suck him to death. . . . I put my little finger to the round cup-like tip of one of the suckers or tentacles of quite a little one, evidently dying – when I pulled it away it hurt so that I looked at the tip of my finger expecting to see it all raw and bloody – but it had not quite taken the skin off.'[23]

In the event, Swinburne did not, apparently, meet Flaubert in Paris, nor did he visit Guernsey, but was back at Holmwood by September, where he remained for several months, with only one brief visit to London. He was now working at his *Tristram of Lyonesse*, writing to Burne-Jones on 4 November 1869: 'I want my version to be based on notorious facts, and be acceptable for its orthodoxy and fidelity to the dear old story: so that Tristram may not be mistaken for his late Royal Highness the Duke of Kent, or Iseult for Queen Charlotte, or Palomydes for Mr Gladstone. I shan't of course include – much less tell at length, saga-fashion – a tithe of the various incidents given in the different old versions, but I want to have in everything *pretty* that is of any importance, and is in keeping with the tone and spirit of the story – not burlesque or dissonant or inconsistent. The thought of your painting and Wagner's music ought to abash but does stimulate me: but my only chance I am aware will be to adhere strongly to Fact and Reality – to shun Fiction as perilously akin to lying, and make this piece of sung and spoken History a genuine bit of earnest work in these dim times. Ahem. I have just been doing the storm that overtakes them when Tristram rows so hard and gets athirst –

So for an hour they fought the storm out still,
And the storm foam sprang from the wave-ridge, and the sky
Glared at them for a breath's space through the rain;
Then the bows with a sharp shock plunged again
Down, and the sea clashed on them, and so rose
The bright prow like one panting from swift blows,
And as a swimmer's joyous beaten head
Rears laughing, so in that sharp stead
The light ship lifted her long quivering bows
As might the man his glad unbaffled brows
Out of the wave-breach; for with one stroke yet
Went all men's oars together, strongly set
As to loud music, and with hearts uplift
They smote their strong way through the drench and drift

Tell me if you like this, the last bit done. Love to Georgie, Phil and Margaret.'[24]

After reading Flaubert's *L'Éducation sentimentale*, Swinburne wrote enthusiastically to William Rossetti on 25 November: 'You must read – Gabriel also – Flaubert's new book – it is admirable – the photographs of street fighting of 1848 (I mean, 57 *an de la République*) wonderful, in volume two. I want to review it at once, foreseeing that as before in his case the British press will generally exude mere virtue and rancid matter. There are two women in it – femme honnête et putain – worthy of Balzac: and a stupid and splendid hero and martyr who is unique – a republican *commis*. . . . I have begun a democratic poem – "Before a Crucifix" – addressed to the Galilean (Ben Joseph) in a tone of mild and modified hostility which I fear and hope will exasperate his sectaries more than any abuse.'[25] Actually, 'Before a Crucifix' is one of Swinburne's most powerful poems.

When Pater's 'Notes on Leonardo da Vinci', subsequently reprinted in his *Studies in the History of the Renaissance*, appeared in the *Fortnightly*, Swinburne wrote to Gabriel Rossetti on 28 November: 'I like Pater's article on Leonardo very much. I confess I did fancy there was a little spice of my style, as you say, but much good stuff of his own and much of interest.' But, as we have seen, Pater freely admitted his indebtedness to Swinburne. Indeed, as Gosse points out: 'Swinburne's articles in the *Fortnightly* became a very remarkable element in current literature. It is not too much to say that in them he invented a new class of writing, new at least in England, since there had been in France since 1850 a romantic criticism of high importance. Swinburne owed little to Sainte-Beuve, whom he never appreciated, but he was strongly affected by the pictorial manner of Gautier, and he had an elder brother after his own heart in Paul de Saint-Victor. Like the studies of the latter, Swinburne's early monographs are impetuous and inflamed impressions of literature which has either filled the critic with transports of admiration, or, on rarer occasions, with violent transports of anger and scorn. For the first time in English literature, an attempt was here made to produce a concrete and almost plastic conception of the work of an author, not minutely analysed or coldly condensed, but presented as if by an inspired neophyte, proclaiming a religion in an ecstasy. Such, in 1867, were the "William Morris" and the "Matthew Arnold" of Swinburne, and the sensation they caused was reverberant. To all young aestheticians of that and the next few years, the advent of the *Fortnightly Review* with a critical article by Swinburne in it was looked forward to as to a great event.'[26]

Thus we find Swinburne writing in his review of Morris's *Life and Death of Jason*:[27]

> Here is a poem sown of itself, sprung from no alien seed, cast after no alien model; fresh as wind, bright as light, full of the spring and sun. It shares of course the conditions of its kind; it has no time for the subtleties and hardly room for the ardours of tragic poetry. Passion in romance is of its nature subordinate to action; the flowing stream of story hushes and lulls the noise of its gurgling and refluent eddies with a still predominance of sound. . . . Mr Morris has an English respect for temperance and reserve. . . . The pictures are clear and chaste, sweet and lucid, as early Italian work. There are crowds and processions, battle-pieces and merry-makings, worthy of Benozzo or Carpaccio; single figures or groups of lovers in flowery watery land, worthy of Sandro or Filippo. . . . Rarely but in the ballad and romance periods has such poetry been written, so broad and sad and simple.

No better appreciation of the essential nature of Morris's poem has ever been written. Nor, for all his joy in it, does Swinburne in this essay pass over its faults. The analysis is as keen, though gentle, as is the sensitive recreation of the poem's general tone and atmosphere. Morris's *Jason* became one of the most popular poems of its time.

Swinburne was now gathering material for his *Bothwell.* 'I have made an analysis of the events and situations of Mary Stuart's life from Rizzio's murder to her flight into England, and am choked and stifled with the excessive wealth of splendid subjects and dramatic effects,' he wrote to Rossetti from Holmwood in November. 'But something I must carve or weave out of them.' He was also looking for new rooms, or 'chambers' as he rather grandly called them writing to Rossetti: 'If you or any of your friends can hear of chambers that would do for me, it would be a charity to let me know. I want to change – in fact, must, to be comfortable – and

I have employed Thomson to look out for me, but he has not yet found the right thing.' As we have seen, Swinburne employed John Thomson for some time as secretary and general factotum. He was also anxious to change his publisher, suspecting that Hotten was swindling him and thought of giving his work to F. S. Ellis, the bookseller and bibliophile, who was to publish Rossetti's poems and much of Morris's work. He now wrote asking either Rossetti or his brother William to go into the matter for him, being so bad at business himself. But Rossetti, not wishing to be involved, suggested that he really ought to manage his own affairs himself. Finding that Hotten had not paid any of the money due to him in royalties into his account, he put the matter in the hands of a lawyer. Meanwhile, John Thomson was looking up texts in the Museum for William Rossetti's edition of Shelley, filling in the bawdier passages in the Greek translations from which Shelley had evidently shrunk. In the event, William Rossetti shrank from them too, much to Swinburne's regret.

On 30 November 1869, Swinburne wrote to George Powell from Holmwood to say that he was not coming up to town as expected, 'though it would be a delight for me to hear the Valkür, as you well know. . . . I am pretty well, but rather harassed also by affairs.' Of the third volume of William Morris's *Earthly Paradise*, he wrote acutely to Rossetti on 10 December: 'I have just received Topsy's book: the Gudrun story is excellently told, I can see, and of keen interest; but I find generally no change in the *trailing* style of his work: his Muse is like Homer's Trojan women – drags her robes as she walks; I really think a Muse (when she is neither resting nor flying) ought to tighten her girdle, tuck up her skirts, and step out. It is better than Tennyson's short-winded and artificial concision – but there is such a thing as swift and spontaneous style. Top's is spontaneous and slow; and especially, my ear hungers for more force and variety of sound in the verse. It looks as if he purposely avoided all strenuous emotion or strength of music in thought and word: and so, when set by other work as good, his work seems hardly done in thorough earnest. The verses on the months are exquisite – November I think especially.' But the public in general evidently did not agree with him, and *The Earthly Paradise* became a best-seller, ideal for soporific family reading in the evenings. The ever-modest Morris, however, *did* agree with him and wrote that the book would have done him more credit if it had had nothing in it but 'The Lovers of Gudrun', adding: 'I don't think the others quite the worst things I have done. Yet they are all too long and flabby, damn it!'

To Rossetti, Swinburne sent a mock-Christmas carol on 22 December 1869:

Hark, the herald angels crow
Here's a boy – but not for Joe!
Not for Joseph – Oh no, no!
(*Mediaeval Carol on the Nativity*)

Having read a few pages of Tennyson's *The Holy Grail and Other Poems*, he goes on: 'I fell at once tooth and nail upon Tristram and Iseult and wrote at an overture of the poem projected, all yesterday. My first sustained attempt at poetic narrative may not be as good as Gudrun – but if it doesn't lick the Morte d'Albert I hope I may not die without extreme unction. If I have time and room I may try your patience with a few lines – but perhaps they had better wait.'

This was the splendid 'Prologue' to *Tristram of Lyonesse.* Rossetti had been sending Swinburne the proofs of his forthcoming *Poems*, many retrieved from Lizzie's coffin at Highgate, for criticism, and the letter of 22 December continues: 'Now, as to Jenny, I entreat you not to think of cancelling those two passages – poetically perfect, and practically requisite to explain how the man (without being a Laureate or Prince Consort in Wardour Street armour)[28] sits on in reverie till morning. The poem is full short as it is to carry out the sentiment in human, actual, and yet spiritual fashion. And (whether or not reducible to hard reason) the ideas so tenderly and nobly embodied in these passages are just such as would by occurring to such a man as you paint produce the effect wanted. I cannot imagine who it can have been, as his judgement you say deserves your consideration, who started what I cannot but think a most groundless and tasteless objection. Once again, for heaven's sake, think no more of so mutilating a poem than of destroying it out of hand. I do not want to see Jenny – whose life has not been such as to call down in lightning from heaven les malheurs de la vertu – incur without deserving the doom of Justine, or go forth from your cabinet maimed and lacerated. . . .

'I felt of course the patent objection to the word "smell" – and I know that I myself, like Baudelaire, am especially and extravagantly fond of that sense and susceptible to it – but I never thought of your *adopting* my line. That which you now have is perfect. "Love's exuberant hotbed" is clearly the right reading. The new stanza to "Troy Town" is beautiful, and clear gain. . . . It is an absurd piece (I dare say) of hyper-criticism, but it does strike me that to call a woman's breasts "the sun and moon of the heart's desire" sounds as if there were a difference between them, much in favour of the one. It is a burlesque notion, I know, but would, I fear, occur to others as well as to me, so you must pardon the suggestion of it. "Heavenly" sheen *stet* – not orient, I should say, certainly.'

After quoting some lines from the 'Prologue' to *Tristram*, he goes on: 'As you see, my verse (though the British buffer may say I am following Topsy in the choice of metre for romantic narrative) is modelled not after the Chaucerian cadence of Jason but after my own scheme of movement and modulation in Anactoria, which I consider original in structure and combination. On board the ship I mean to make the innocent Iseult ask Tristram about the knights and ladies, and him to tell her of Queen Morgause of Orkney and her incest with the "blameless king", and other larks illustrative of the Alberto-Victorian purity of the Court: but delicately, sparing respectfully the innocence of her who was to make the first and greatest scandal there of all in time – as in days past at Oxford, when we first met, you fellows might have respected my spotless adolescence. I don't say that you did.'[29]

The 'Prologue' to *Tristram* was finished by February 1870, and Swinburne told Rossetti in his letter of the twelfth: 'I have put as much fancy and light and play of colour into the prologue as possible, to throw out the tragic effect: and by the grace of the Devil I hope to make the copulative passages of the poem more warm and provocative of sinful appetite than anything my chaste Muse has yet attempted. I am much inspirited by observing the traces of my influence on younger men and boys. I trust that my present work may be the means (under Satan) of turning many a heart to perdition. But not to me be the glory.'

An unsigned review of William Rossetti's edition of Shelley, afterwards found to be by Robert Buchanan, had appeared in the *Athenaeum* in January 1870, on which Swinburne comments: 'I did smell the exhalation from the Asinaeum to which you refer, and like you with amazement, but I see that no amount of scientific exploration can adequately prepare the human nose for the surprises of scent it encounters on opening the backdoor of the dwellings inhabited by the critical tribe so beautifully defined by Rabelais as the "turdilousifartishittical buggeraminous ballockwaggers". I have not the French of the passage under my eye, but the translation is no doubt – and very properly – softened down to the standard of English delicacy. The original probably verges on coarseness.'[30]

Rossetti's *Poems* were now due to be published and he wrote to Swinburne reminding him that he had once 'expressed an intention, much valued by me, of reviewing the book in the *Fortnightly*'. Swinburne at once replied on 19 February that he had written to John Morley to ask for the book: 'It will be a true and lasting pleasure to me if I do get this chance of saying my say early and fully – frankly it will of course be said if said at all, without reference to other and older claimants of the first place among living English poets – on the advent of the book which I regard now as surely as I did ten years since as the master-book of this generation of English poetry, at once for depth, variety, instinct, and perfection. That it is inevitably destined to take and keep that place at the head of us I have never changed or disguised my conviction, and never shall.'[31]

Again, on the same subject he wrote later in February: 'having got the chance I have waited ten years for, of speaking out what I see to be truth as regards your poems, I am very particularly and especially well damned if I am going to let it slip. It is my devout intention to cut it fat – as fat as a carver can cut, and yet retain any grace of handling or skill of dissecting. I shall not – to speak Topsaically [that is, like Morris] – say a bloody word which is not the blasted fact. . . . I am taking great pains with what I write of you – I have spent hours already on putting together a single sentence or paragraph expressive – as nearly as I can make it adequate – of the character and effect and impression of one set of your poems – and have striven to say nothing inapplicable, nothing of vague praise and spluttering adulation, but all solid and tangible criticism, which must be met and taken to pieces before it can be answered.' Of 'The House of Life' he wrote: 'I cannot tell you how ineffable in wealth and thought and word and every beauty possible to human work I see that set of sonnets to be. . . .'[32]

In his review, Swinburne wrote of 'The House of Life': 'There has been no work of the same pitch since Dante sealed up his youth in the sacred leaves of the *Vita Nuova*.' There must be few people today who would endorse that opinion, any more than they would Morris's, who, reviewing the book in the *Academy* on 14 May, compared the sonnets to Shakespeare's for 'depth of thought, and skill and felicity of execution' – though Morris must have realized that many of them, as well as several of the other later poems, were addressed to his own wife. But such an exalted opinion is a measure of the ascendancy that Rossetti had established over his friends.

Swinburne's letters to Rossetti at this time are a strange mixture of careful, even minute line-by-line criticism of his poems and outbursts of schoolboyish obscenities. 'I send other excerpts from contemporaries in hopes of eliciting a Rabelaisian reply,' he wrote to him on 1 March from Holmwood, of which one example may suffice:

'1st-Sadic advice, by Mrs Browning:
"Ye b—— them that f——? she said –
Ah fools! I bid you pass them by!
Go b—— those whose bums have bled
What time their c——ts were dry.
Ain't that the bloody way? she said. . . ."

As you were kindly interested in the literary fortunes of the "Bogshire Banner" I send you a sample of the excerpts I lately forwarded to Étretât from that periodical. (The divorce case – Codsham *v.* Codsham is not on yet.) "We are authorized to state that there is no foundation for the report lately current that a matrimonial alliance was on the *tapis* between the Hon. Monica Friggins, of the Dildoze, Tongueham, and her cousin Mr Suckling Cunter, of St. Onan's. Since the death of old Bishop Tollywegg, the diocese of Arseborough has been the scene of continual disputes. Bishop Buggeridge (late Archdeacon – the Ven. Athanasius Buggeridge) being most High, even Ritualist, is on bad terms with the most influential clergy – even his own relations, the Very Rev. Dean Buggeridge, who is Broad Church, and their cousin the Hon. and Rev. Onan Buggeridge, who is *very* Low. Oil has been thrown on the waters by the appointment of the Rev. Simplicius Pricksmall, of Little Pissing, to the perpetual cure of St. Onan's. The tenantry of Mount Scrotum (the country seat of the Dowager

Duchess of Arseborough) celebrated with old English games (pitching the crowbar, shooting at the prick, running at the ring, filling up the hole (also called the nine – or even more than nine – men's Morris), bugger my neighbour, piss in the corner, back throwing, cleaving the pin, and to wind up with, a general cockfight – her Grace for that day only permitting the free use of her cock-pit) her Grace's recovery from a bad attack of gonorrhoea. The prayers of the congregation were last Sunday desired in Arseborough Cathedral for Viscount Fitzarse, who is suffering from syphilis, contracted at Poxford." '[33]

Amusing as such communications may have been at first – they were evidently the special delight of Burne-Jones, Simeon Solomon and George Powell – Swinburne did not realize that enough is enough and there are signs that Rossetti and some of his other friends had begun to find them increasingly embarrassing. It should be remembered that Swinburne was thirty-three in 1870, but in many ways still adolescent. As he had said to Lord Houghton, 'one always writes *des horreurs* when one is *en famille*'.

Swinburne returned to Dorset Street in April 1870 and remained there until the end of June. During this time he was daily at the Arts Club, where he met his friends and wrote letters. One of these friends was Charles Duncan Cameron, a man ten or twelve years his senior, whom he had met through Richard Burton. After a stormy life in several parts of Africa, Cameron settled in Abyssinia, where according to Gosse he became 'some sort of consul, and attracted the enmity of the notorious King Theodore, who imprisoned him for about four years. Among other things, Cameron drank like a fish.' It was after a dinner with Cameron, again according to Gosse, that Swinburne, unable to find his hat, tried on all the hats of the other club members, flinging each one to the floor when it proved too small for his enormous head. Finally, 'in a towering and ungovernable rage, he danced and stamped upon the hats, with furious imprecations'.[34]

Swinburne's friend Coulson Kernahan gives a somewhat different and more amusing version of this story, as he heard it from the blind poet Philip Marston: 'The story is that Swinburne and a friend – the friend bore a well-known name – had been making a night of it, and thereafter took a cab to the club. A special committee meeting . . . was then sitting. That it was well attended was evident from the number of hats – silk, opera, bowlers: it was before the day of crush hats – hanging upon the cloak-room pegs. From whom the idea arose, Swinburne or his friend, I do not know, but some Puck-like spirit of mischief, seeing that the two were well-primed for such foolery, whispered to one or the other that, no one being just then present, here was a chance to perform "the hat trick" in a new sense and in record time. Hastily collecting the hats from the pegs, the two Strayed Revellers placed them on the floor in two long parallel lines. Then, Swinburne and his friend each standing on his right foot at the end of one row of hats, his left ankle clasped in his left hand, the word: "One – two – Three – Go!" was given, and away the two racers went, each hop meaning the pancaking of a hat. Which won I do not know, but when the scandalized attendant arrived, it was to find Swinburne and his friend breathless, and executing a triumphant war dance, amid a chaos of crushed hats, on the cloak-room floor. The committee, interrupted in their sitting, hastily adjourned the meeting to the cloak-room. Here they found Swinburne and his friend screaming with laughter over what each thought to be a gigantic joke. Failing to see the joke, the committee hastily held an emergency meeting, then and there, to pass, unanimously, a resolution expelling the two offending members from the club.'[35]

Nevertheless, Swinburne considered that he had been harshly treated and was very indignant. When informed by the committee of his Bacchic massacre of members' top hats, he refused to believe it and merely thought that the committee were inventing an excuse to be rid of him. 'No gentleman,' he exclaimed, as he always did when confronted with his actions of the night before, 'would be guilty of such behaviour.' Gosse comments: 'Without losing his charming amiability, and almost child-like sweetness, towards those of whose fidelity he was certain, he became affected with a suspiciousness and a tendency to take offence which showed themselves in outbreaks of disconcerting violence, and made the tone of the controversies which he now more and more lightly courted often as unseemly as it was extravagant.'[36]

At the end of June 1870, Swinburne was taken seriously ill in Rossetti's house. 'I hope you have forgiven me for breaking my appointment last week,' he wrote to William Rossetti on 23 June. 'I was very ill that day and all the week – couldn't write or do any work or business. Gabriel and Fanny have nursed me up again. I am staying here in Cheyne Walk for a few days.'[37] When he had recovered sufficiently, he went down to Holmwood, where he remained for the rest of the year, apart from a short visit to London in October.

Gosse remembers witnessing his arrival one day at Cheyne Walk in a hansom cab with Walter Pater: 'Pater delicately dressed, with lemon kid gloves, descended daintily and was followed by Swinburne, who poised himself on the edge of the cab, and then dived forward, descending upon his two hands. His elegant top-hat sprang from him, and making a wide curve descended far away in the gutter. Presently Pater appeared in our upper room, talking dreamily upon different subjects, but of Swinburne I saw no more, and understood that he was taken into another part of the house to be cleaned and sobered.'[38]

Swinburne was fond of the society of women, Gosse tells us, 'but he was never known, so far as I have seen or heard, to indulge in the least flirtation. He occasionally remarked on the form of a woman, or her colouring, but always as he would speak of a work of art, and generally with reference to some painter. I have seen advances made to him, but he neither accepted nor repelled them; he simply seemed not to perceive them. He was rather like a child, who witnesses the embracements of grown-up people without interest and without perturbation.' He was more interested in the embracements of snakes. 'In the days of his celebrity,' Gosse continues, 'there were several women who would have been glad to attract his attention. In particular, the Jewish poetess Mathilde Blind, and from about 1867 onwards she openly threw herself at his head and gave him every opportunity to propose marriage to her. She complained in my presence of his insensibility: "He comes to tea with me and does not seem to notice and recites poetry, and goes away," she said. He cultivated her company for the sake of her regicide principles, and her love of verse; her brother was that Ferdinand Cohen who tried to kill Bismarck, and her step-father was the revolutionary Karl Blind – the friend of Mazzini.'[39]

It was towards the end of 1870 or the beginning of 1871 that Gosse was presented to Swinburne at an evening party in the Fitzroy Square studio of Ford Madox Brown, to whom Gosse had been introduced by William Bell Scott. At this first meeting, we are told, Swinburne 'in some ways . . . fulfilled, and more than fulfilled, the promise of my hero-worship. At the same time . . . he was not quite like a human being. Moreover, the dead pallor of his face and his floating balloon of red hair, had already, although he was but in his thirty-third year, a faded look. As he talked to me, he stood, perfectly rigid, with his arms shivering at his sides, his little feet tight against each other, close to a low settee in the middle of the studio. Every now and then, without breaking off talking or bending his body, he hopped on to this sofa, and presently hopped down again, so that I was reminded of some orange-crested bird – a hoopoe, perhaps – hopping from perch to perch in a cage. The contrast between these sudden movements and the enthusiasm of his rich and flute-like voice was very strange.'[40]

The proclamation of the French Republic on 4 September, after the defeat at Sedan and Napoleon III's surrender, sent Swinburne into ecstasies: 'Gloria in excelsis Republicae et in terrâ pax hominibus bonae voluntatis!' he wrote to William Rossetti on 7 September 1870. 'I feel inclined to go out and kiss everybody I meet – to roll on the ground and "come naked in contact with the earth" as Whitman says somewhere, or some such thing. I have been in a state of lyric discharge with brief intermission ever since the news came on Monday afternoon. An Ode literally burst out of me, which I have sent to Ellis to print as a loose sheet or pamphlet. I am nine tenths out of my mind with joy and pride in Paris. Now, it may be razed to the ground and sown with salt and the last child killed in the last Frenchwoman's womb, but shame cannot touch it. If the Republic die tomorrow choked in blood and ridden down by brute force of horsehoofs, it has lived this divine hour, worth aeons of empires. I do think the rejoicings and salutations, tears and embraces, of the people at such a time, in the jaws of ruin *and* in sight of the Republic, the most glorious thing in democratic history (barring Rome and Venice) since the old days. I only hope I have not shouted myself hoarse in the poem and cracked my voice. I know the enthusiasm that makes verse sometimes mars it too. But I could not wait – I must have it out in the rough, "unamended", without extreme unction of revision: and I do think there are some good resonant notes in it.'[41]

In the event, it was not the Republic that was choked in blood but the Commune which succeeded it. Swinburne's Shelleyan *Ode on the Proclamation of the French Republic* did not appear until 1871. Four months later William I was crowned German Emperor in the Galerie des Glaces at Versailles. After which, says Gosse, Swinburne 'averted his eyes completely from the subsequent history of Europe', a statement which is hardly borne out by the facts.

Swinburne's letter of 7 September continues: 'I am not well pleased with Italian outlooks. If that satellite of a dead dog (or at least dying now on a German dunghill of his last kick) Victor Emmanuel goes to Rome I shall be furious, and would kiss the toes of a priest who would poison him with a wafer. Their papers say Mazzini is ill – I hear he says himself that he was treated when taken "like a brother". Qu. Abel? as Mme. Venturi says.

'Oh, if France Republican *could* offer Nice and Savoy to the Italian democracy on the day they shall cast off the hog-faced Savoyard – "ah, then indeed something would happen!" as Browning says. I wish by the by he would drop a public tear on the head of Bonaparte as it lies in the dung. What would poor, great, but there monomaniacal Mrs Browning have done at this last act of her Caesar's puppet-play? His exit like Heliogabalus *dans les latrines*?

'Well – he is gone to the sewers of history – to the "Everlasting Cesspools". Requiescat in fimo.'

Writing to John Morley from The British Hotel, Cockspur Street, on 28 December, Swinburne apologized for not answering his letter 'of 20 days since long before but have been for days laid up with influenza that held me fast in bed, blind, deaf, exuding, with eyes that could but water and hands that could but blow the lamentable nose. For the time before when I was about and alive I was utterly occupied with my book [*Songs before Sunrise*] – in the last agonies of childbirth. . . . I am ashamed about Ford [his essay on John Ford, the Elizabethan dramatist, which he had undertaken to write for the *Fortnightly*] – but could I be sure of three days' health and leisure and spirits I would send you a study of his and other Elizabethan's relation to each other (starting with a view of his special qualities) which should be a decent piece of work. A thing of shreds and patches I couldn't write and wouldn't send.'[42]

The essay on Ford was completed next year during an oasis of calm and good health at Holmwood and appeared in July in the *Fortnightly*. It was to be expected that Swinburne should have been attracted to *'Tis Pity She's a*

*Whore*, with its theme of incest, though as he ironically remarks: 'It is somewhat unfortunate that the very title of Ford's masterpiece should sound so strangely in the ears of a generation "whose ears are the chastest part about them".' As in all his work on the Elizabethans, Swinburne writes with vehemence, as he talked:[43]

> Giovanni is the student struck blind and mad by passion; in the uttermost depths of unimaginable crime he reflects, argues, reasons concerning the devils that possess him. In the only other tragedy of the time based on incestuous love, Massinger's 'Unnatural Combat', the criminal is old and hardened, a soul steeped in sin, a man of blood and iron from his youth upwards; but upon Giovanni his own crime falls like a curse, sudden as lightning; he stands before us as one plague-stricken in the prime of spiritual health, helpless under the lash of love as Canace or Myrrha, Phaedra or Pasiphae. The curious interfusion of reason with passion makes him seem but the more powerless to resist, the more hopeless of recovery. His sister is perhaps less finely drawn, though her ebbs and flows of passion are given with great force, and her alternate possession by desire and terror, repentance and defiance, if we are sometimes startled by the rough rapidity of the change, does not in effect impair the unity of character, obscure the clearness of outline. She yields more readily than her brother to the curse of Venus, with a passionate pliancy which prepared us for her subsequent prostration at the feet of her confessor, and again for the revival of a fearless and shameless spirit under the stroke of her husband's violence. . . . That swift and fiery glance which flashes at once from all depths to all heights of the human spirit, that intuition of an indefinable and infallible instinct which at a touch makes dark things clear and brings distant things close, is not a gift of his; perhaps Webster alone of English poets can be said to share it in some measure with Shakespeare. Bosola and Flamineo, Vittoria Corombona and the Duchess of Malfi . . . good characters and bad alike, all have this mark upon them of their maker's swift and subtle genius; this sudden surprise of the soul in its remoter hiding places at its most secret work. In a few words that startle as with a blow and lighten as with a flame, the naked natural spirit is revealed, bare to the roots of life. And this power Ford also has shown here at least.

All of which is finely said and exhibits Swinburne's critical powers at their zenith. Following Charles Lamb, Swinburne was a pioneer in the re-appraisal of the Elizabethan drama. What he most admires in the plays of Ford and Webster is their characters' capacity for self-abandonment combined with a rare power of almost detached self-analysis, and he rightly praises Taine for doing full justice, in his *History of English Literature*, 'to the force and audacity of Ford's realism', even though he seemed to rate that quality higher than 'the more tender and gracious passages'. As one would expect, the essay as a whole shows great sensitiveness to the peculiar qualities of Ford's contemporaries in the drama, Dekker, Marston, Massinger, Tourneur, Middleton and Chapman.

Unfortunately, those vices of style which make Swinburne's later prose works so unreadable are not entirely absent from his 'John Ford'. There are such sentences as 'Nor is the other type of royalty less excellently real and vivid; the mixture of warmth and ceremony in Katherine's reception of Henry throws into fresh and final relief the implacable placidity of infliction with which he marks her husband for utmost ignominy of suffering' where that inexorable pairing of alliterative adjectives one associates with Swinburne's critical prose begins to make itself felt. At times his style is so dense that it becomes a hindrance to our comprehension, and he seems almost to lose his way in a maze of words. It is strange to find Swinburne condemning *Love's Sacrifice* as 'utterly indecent, unseemly and unfit for handling', though the standards by which he condemns it are characteristic. Thus: 'The incestuous indulgence of Giovanni and Annabella is not improper for tragic treatment; the obscene abstinence of Fernando and Bianca is wholly improper' – which recalls Blake's dictum in the 'Proverbs of Hell' that: 'He who desires but acts not, breeds pestilence.'

In February 1871 Swinburne was once more in touch with Richard Burton and attending Cannibal Club dinners with him and Simeon Solomon. In the same month his mother wrote pathetically to Rossetti: 'We are in great trouble and anxiety for Algernon – his father received a letter this morning telling him that Algernon was again in the state in which he has four times been obliged to go and insist upon his coming home. This time the summons come[s] when neither the Adml nor myself are able to leave home on account of illness. We sent his old nurse a most trustworthy person hoping that she would find him & persuade him to return to us when he heard we were ill. You know how she has failed. She tells us you kindly promised to write to Algernon & we now beg you to send the enclosed letter to him. We shall be most thankful to you if you can help us in this way. You know too well what cause we have for anxiety about our son. There is nothing that we have not tried to induce him to remain with us, but after 2 or 3 months it is impossible to keep him & at his age we cannot use force. He has never met with anything but the most affectionate kindness from his father and he has been told most forcibly by medical men both here and in London how fatal such a course must be.'[44] Next day the admiral wrote to Rossetti, thanking him for his reassuring letter and saying that: 'The last letter received from him [Algernon] was dated 22nd ulto and informed us that he was staying with a friend, "Mr Thomson", but was without address: this and your friendship for him must plead my excuse for having troubled you so much.'[45]

On 11 February Lady Jane wrote to Rossetti again: 'Though I fear you will be quite tired of our letters, I cannot refrain from sending you another to thank you for the very kind and friendly one I have received from you today. We are all I assure [you] most grateful to you for all the trouble you have taken in our behalf and for all the interest you take in my poor dear Son. Your letter to him brought one from him to his father which reached us last evening . . . he again tells us that he is staying with a friend, a Mr Thomson, but still he abstains from giving any address and his letter is not even dated, but he mentions having heard from you of our anxiety. . . . We do most earnestly wish that he would not take lodgings in Town at all events for the present – and we urged him when he was here to have anything he wanted in the way of furniture and books sent down here. I fear his having his books would not keep him here – it is impossible but a mind like his should require the society of persons with minds and pursuits similar to his own, unless he could make up his mind to remain here as a means of conquering his fearful propensity – for a time he is perfectly happy and his health as good as possible, he says how much better he can work here and how much better he feels.'[46]

One wonders how much Lady Jane and her husband knew of their son's 'fearful propensity'. She is presumably referring to drink, though in the admiral's letter to Rossetti of 10 February he mentions 'the temptations which he seems to be quite incapable of resisting'. It is fortunate that neither of his parents knew anything of 'Mr Thomson', whose address Swinburne was careful to withhold.[47] But he was back at Holmwood by March, if not earlier, having already been preceded by his 'things', which Thomson had sent down to Shiplake for him. Meanwhile, Thomson was making a transcript of 'Mrs H. Manners' – that is, *A Year's Letters*, which appeared in the *Tatler* as by Mrs Manners – and Swinburne writes to him on 10 March to ask him to send the rest of the transcript together with his manuscript, 'Paley's *translation* of Aschylus (7s. 6d.) and Jebb's (Deighton, Bell & Co. publishers) two published plays of Sophocles (editions not translations). One is Electra, I forget the other. I miss only two of the books I asked you to send from Dorset Street – Plumptre's translation of Sophocles – first volume: and Thackeray's Miscellanies first volume. . . . And please tell Dulau of Soho Square to send me "Victor Hugo en Zélande"; he will not forget of course (knowing this address) to send the next volume of Baudelaire's works when it appears.' He concludes: 'Love to friends and tell me anything there is to tell. I shall be here some time.'[48]

Swinburne's letter to George Powell of 26 April is in his naughtiest vein: 'I wrote yesterday to Simeon to tell him of a truly shocking thing – I have seen advertised for sale or hire (Oh Monsieur!) "Mrs Sinclair's Daughter by Lady Blake"!!! This is tribadism in excelsis. Even the immortal foundress of Lesbianism is not recorded to have begotten children on Atthis, Anactoria, or Cydro, and then let them out to hire!'

He had evidently regained his normal high spirits, for he continues: 'Dean Buggeridge, I hear, is now in town – he has taken lodgings for the season in Quimlico. His work on the Cities of the Plain, their site, history, and remains, is now in the press. I regret to hear that his sermon on "The Angels of Sodom" (Gen. XIX. 4–10) is considered heretical in some quarters – too Broad (in fact) in its tone. It seems he condemns the conduct of Lot in offering his daughters to the men of Sodom as substitutes for his guests, as selfish and unfeeling, utterly wanting in social and patriotic spirit. "Which of you my brethren," he exclaims, "would have taken a woman for a man – not to say, an angel?" The English Church Union intends to bring the matter before Convocation. Please tell Simeon of this when you next see him.'[49]

While at Holmwood, Swinburne carried on a fairly extensive correspondence with Simeon Solomon. Dr Cecil Lang has published Solomon's letters in reply, in one of which dated 15 May he writes to Swinburne about the trial of several transvestites he had attended, 'The Queen *v.* Boulton and Others', a squalid affair fully reported by the *Daily Telegraph* and *Reynolds's Newspaper.* After the morning trial, Solomon went to the nearest restaurant to the court, where he found Boulton, Park and Hurt at lunch with their solicitors. It being a public crowded room, Solomon sat down at their table. Boulton, he says, 'is very remarkable, he is not quite beautiful but supremely pretty, a perfect figure, manner and voice. Altogether I was agreeably surprised at him. Of course they will be acquitted. It is very hard for Hurt and Fiske to be mixed up with the two others. I am so glad to be able to relieve your mind with regard to your first letter. I *did* destroy it, but as I thought you would think it a very poor compliment to do so I did not like telling you. I quite appreciate your story about the chorister.'[50] From the tone of these letters it is clear that Swinburne enjoyed sharing homosexual jokes with Solomon – that is, before his disgrace in 1873 – and was anxious to have his own side of the correspondence destroyed.

As usual, he was constantly at work. After finishing his long essay on John Ford, he wrote an essay for the *Dark Blue* of July 1871, 'Simeon Solomon: Notes on his *Vision of Love*; and Other Studies'. This was included in the Bonchurch edition of his collected works by Gosse and Wise, but was never reprinted by Swinburne himself. 'There is a mixture of utmost delicacy with a fine cruelty in some of these faces of fair feminine youth,' he wrote, 'which recalls the explanation of a philosopher of the material school whose doctrine is at least not without historic example and evidence to support it: "Une infinité de sots, dupes de cette incroyable sensibilité qu'ils voient dans les femmes, ne se doutent pas que les extrémités se rapprochent, et que c'est précisément au foyer de ce sentiment que la cruauté prend sa source. Parce que la *cruauté n'est elle-même qu'une des branches de la sensibilité*, et que c'est toujours en raison du degré dont nos âmes en sont pénétrées que les grandes horreurs se commettent."' The 'philosopher of the material school' was evidently de Sade.

The article was a merciless analysis of the decadent and sadistic impulses underlying Solomon's work. Poor Solomon wrote to Swinburne to say that while he fully appreciated 'the full beauty of the paper and the great honour that has been done to me by the most brilliant of our writers', he was afraid it would do his reputation more harm than good. 'You know, of course, my dear Algernon, that, by many, my designs and pictures executed during the last three or four years have been looked upon with suspicion, and, as I have been a false friend to myself, I have not sought to remove the impression, but have gone on following my own sweet will; in pecuniary and some other ways I have had to suffer for it, and shall probably have to suffer still.'[51]

When news came from France of the death sentences passed on the communards and Paris incendiaries, Swinburne wrote to William Rossetti on 1 June: 'I may say to you as frankly as I would say to Hugo that so far from objecting to the infliction of death on the incendiaries of the Louvre I should wish to have them proclaimed (to use a phrase of his own) not merely "hors la loi" but "hors l'humanité", and a law passed throughout the world authorizing any citizen of any nation to take their lives with impunity and assurance of national thanks – to shoot them down wherever met like dogs. A political crime is a national crime and punishable only by the nation sinned against: France alone has the right to punish the shedding of French blood by putting to death on that charge a Bonaparte or a Thiers, a Rigault or a Gallifet; but it is the whole world's right to take vengeance on men who should strike at the whole world such a blow as to inflict an everlasting incurable wound by the attempted destruction of Rome, Venice, Paris, London – of the Vatican, Ducal Palace, Louvre, or Museum. But this my deep and earnest conviction in no degree alters my view of the case as it stands between Victor Hugo on this side and the Belgian government on that.'[52]

It was General Gallifet, leader of the national guardsmen of the Versailles government, who had ordered an indiscriminate massacre of whole French families on the mere suspicion of being incendiaries. In extenuation it may be said that women and children were among the incendiaries, whose final plan was to blow up Paris in defence of the Commune. Victor Hugo, however, had been expelled from Belgium for publicly protesting against the Belgian government's refusal to give asylum to refugees from the civil war raging in Paris. But should he come to England, Swinburne wished that a suitable reception 'could be offered him on the part of those who at once admire his devotion to conscience in this matter at all costs, and recognise the greatest poet of our age in the man who gives this proof of faith'. Becoming more violent, he wrote to William Rossetti on 14 June: 'I want to slap the face of the British booby with the back of the same hand that offers tribute to the Master: all the press from the "Saturday" skunk to the "Punch" polecat have exceeded themselves in the foulness of their exhalations. . . . I have been on a visit to Jowett at Oxford, and he comes here to return my visit tomorrow. Times are changed: imagine Shelley within ten years of his expulsion (or say as in my case "permanent rustication") receiving the Master of his college at his father's house!!!'

At Oxford, Swinburne had met Hippolyte Taine, the French historian, who afterwards wrote: 'Hier chez M. Jowett. Présénté à M. Swinburne le poète; ses vers sont dans le genre de Baudelaire et de Victor Hugo: petit homme roux en redingote et cravate bleue, ce que faisait contrast avec tous les habits noirs et cravates blanches; il ne parle que raidi, rejeté en arrière avec un mouvement convulsif et continu des membres comme s'il avait le délirium tremens – très passioné pour la littérature française moderne, Hugo, Stendhal, et pour la peinture. – Son style est d'un visionnaire malade qui, par système, cherche la sensation excessive.'[53] This repeats, to some extent, the description by Maupassant, quoted earlier.

While at Oxford, Swinburne paid frequent visits to Pater at Brasenose. Having read 'a really good and quietly forcible paper in this month's *Fraser* on "English Republicanism by a working man"', Swinburne made his father read it, too, and exclaimed in the letter to William Rossetti on 14 June: '*Shall* we live to see the Hanover rats smoked out, and the old mother of the royal rabbit-warren stifled in her burrow?'

On 11 August 1871 Swinburne went up to Scotland to join Jowett's reading party at Tummil Bridge, Pitlochry. Turgenev was stopping at Allaine House, Pitlochry, while Browning was staying with his friends the Benzons at Little Milton, in the hills above Pitlochry. 'Mr Browning came again last night,' Turgenev wrote to his mistress the singer Pauline Viardot on 13 August. 'He seemed dull to me, but I was so sleepy with fatigue I could hardly keep on my feet.' He had been out grouse-shooting 'with a madman with the legs of a deer, who shouts "come on, come on" every time you stop to draw breath'. It is strange that, with his admiration for Swinburne, he does not mention meeting him. Browning had just finished *Balaustion's Adventure* and had come down to Tummil Bridge to consult Jowett about his translation of Euripides, which was to be included in the Balaustion volume. Edwin Harrison writes: 'A few evenings later we met him and his son at dinner at Allaine House by the foot of Loch Tummil. You may be sure that where Jowett and Browning and Swinburne met, the conversation was animated and interesting. . . . Who shall tell of Swinburne's paradoxes and hyperboles, and how he "set the table in a roar" with his recitations of Mrs Gamp, and how he and the Master capped quotations from Boswell against each other *ad infinitum*?'

'I am up here in the Highlands with Jowett,' Swinburne wrote to George Powell on 24 August, 'after staying a fortnight at Holmwood to recruit, being decidedly the worse for wear, malgré our friend Dr Crosse. I must "purge and live cleanly" like Falstaff, or the devil will have me before his time, and I will, if I can once get, like you, some durable pied-à-terre in London, where I shall not be dependent on the tender mercies of landladies or hotel-keepers. They wrote to Holmwood that I was very unwell and my poor dear father came up to see me, old as he is, and take me out of town again, and it was all very wretched altogether. However, it is all right now for the present. . . . There are some young Oxford men here with us, reading, nice fellows seemingly, and make good bathing parties. I have the first act of Bothwell in type, and have written a scene or two more – not much. Browning is our neighbour in these latitudes; he came over the day before yesterday in high feather.'[54]

In September, Swinburne went for a week's walking tour in the Highlands. He wrote Powell again on the eleventh: 'first through Glencoe and thereabouts up the Caledonian Canal to Inverness and thence to the Far West of the Highlands to Loch Maree and Torridon – the latter the divinest combination of lake, mountains, straits, sea-rocks, bays, gulfs, and open sea ever achieved by the forces of Hertha in her most favourable and fiercely maternal mood. I had a divine day there (the day before yesterday) and swam right out of one bay round a beautiful headland to the next and round back under shelves of rock shining double in the sun above water and below. I had a nice fellow for companion, an Oxford man named Harrison whom I met *chez* Jowett. Did I tell you that at Tummil Bridge . . . we had to neighbours Browning and son and for a while Millais? all very friendly. I am grown stout and sunburnt and (for the present) exemplify les prospérités de la vertu. But I remember the words of wisdom, and keep ever in mind the doom of virtue. The Tummil is very pretty but much defiled by memories and memorials of the royal family. At the waterfalls, significant of who shall say what other effusions? Her Majesty has set up – I should say erected – a phallic emblem in stone; a genuine Priapic erection like a small obelisk, engraved with her name and the date of the event commemorated, whatever that may have been. It is an object which would assuredly have caused "our orphan" [Justine] to blush and shed a few tears. . . . As I presume it stands there for ever in honourable record of the late Prince Consort's virility, it should have borne (instead of the hackneyed "Sic Sedebat") the inscription "Sic Arrigebat Albertus Bonus". . . . We are all here [at Knockspock, Kinnethmont, Aberdeen] till Thursday next at my Uncle Sir H. Gordon's; on the 28th my family and probably I with them return to Holmwood. . . . Let me hear of you again soon, and better in health.'[55]

On his return to London, Swinburne soon became so ill that the admiral was obliged to perform one of his periodical rescue operations and carry him off once more to the country. As Swinburne put it himself in a letter from Holmwood to Purnell of 10 October: 'I was obliged to come down here more hastily than I had expected, having been very unwell for a day or two, and some fool or rascal having (unknown to me) *again* terrified my people here with news that I was risking health &c. in town and must be looked after – so my father came up and carried me off, literally out of bed, having a doctor's word that I wanted country air. I told him I had business (meaning with you) of immediate importance to keep me in town or bring me back at once. So if I am wanted I must try – being now pretty well – to see you; but I suppose we can in fact arrange by letter quite as well?'[56] The 'business' to which he refers was that he had some thoughts of publishing separately in an American magazine the 'Prelude' to his unfinished *Tristram and Iseult* (later called *Tristram of Lyonesse*) – 'itself a separate poem of some considerable length and importance, being several hundred lines long', as he had written to Purnell from Tummil Bridge in August. He wanted £50 for it and wanted it to appear simultaneously in England and America, and had asked Purnell to arrange this for him.

In October 1871 'Thomas Maitland's' attack on Rossetti and Swinburne, 'The Fleshly School of Poetry', appeared in the *Contemporary Review*. This seriously upset Rossetti, who was already on the verge of a nervous breakdown. Swinburne's furious reaction to it can be seen in his letters to William Rossetti. The first of 19 October begins joyously, after a dithyrambic Biblical exordium: 'Be it known unto you, that on Friday last I, even I, was the subject of a speech delivered at the Church Congress at Nottingham, by a Rev. Prebendary, on the infidelity of the age; "Renan", the R.P. observed, "said Hail, Master, and betrayed Him; Swinburne insulted Him as He hung on the bitter Cross." Never, the R.P. likewise pointedly remarked, had Atheism been more markedly anti-Christian; whence we may infer that hitherto Atheism has been one of the surest marks of a Christian, of the surest props of his creed. – This is one of those moments which repay one for much misapprehension and reviling. By the help of my Lord I have leaped over a wall – even the wall of the sanctuary. I read the report in the *Guardian* supplement this morning – and have ever since been hysterical with suppressed enjoyment, for as you will readily surmise there is no one here whom I can call to rejoice with me over the groans of the Galileans. It is indeed very soothing to find that one's shaft has gone so home. It is, however, like their b. impudence to make such a return for the compliments lavished on their nominal founder as a "bon sans culotte" in "Siena" and "Tenebrae" as well as in the very poem referred to' – that is, 'Before a Crucifix' in *Songs Before Sunrise*. 'But it is but what we should have expected when we reflect that "It was a Chrrristian Prrriest from whom it came." *Seriatim*, is it not enough to intoxicate one for a month?'

He then turns his attention to 'Thomas Maitland': 'I perceive that, à propos of Gabriel's poems, a son of Sodom, hitherto unknown except (I suppose) to Whitman's bedfellows the cleaners of privies, has lately "del cul fatto trombetta" in a Malebolgian periodical called the Contemporary Review, conducted by C.P.s and other spiritual nightmen, of the autocoprophagous persuasion. Among much other excrement of ranker quality, the "rear" as you translate it of Malacoda (is it not?) emits, I perceive, the epithet of "little mad boy" à mon adresse. May I not now if ever reply with Coriolanus

– Boy! False hound!
If you have writ your annals true, 'tis there
That, like an eagle in a dove-cote, I
Fluttered your Christians in Gethsemane;
Alone I did it, Boy!

I hear Gabriel is in town, again; please give him my love and the news.'[57]

In 'The Fleshly School of Poetry', where Rossetti is the main target, Swinburne is referred to contemptuously as 'only a little mad boy letting off squibs'. But the writer finds that: 'All that is worst in Mr Swinburne belongs to Baudelaire. The offensive choice of subject, the obtrusion of unnatural passion, the blasphemy, the wretched animalism, are all taken intact out of *Les Fleurs de [sic] Mal.*' In July, the *Edinburgh Review* had also renewed the attack on *Poems and Ballads*, attacked *Songs before Sunrise* as belonging to 'the sensational school of literature', and said that all the most offensive features of Swinburne's work were derived from the 'corrupted French school'.

Meanwhile Swinburne wrote to William Rossetti to say that he had heard that Robert Buchanan was really the author of the outrageously insulting 'Fleshly School', adding: 'I am myself inclined to wish that Gabriel would take notice of it. The little reptile's hide demands the lash – his head the application of a man's heel, his breech of a man's toe – his shoulder of the letters T.F. – or say in this instance of a capital B. . . . I believe it is a habit with the verminous little cur to sneak into some other hide as mangy as his own and pretend to yelp at himself as well as at his betters to keep up the disguise. Faugh – quelle espèce! He did so I am assured in some doggerel aimed at me. Perhaps, however, it is better to let him *lie* – and stink.'[58]

On 27 October he wrote again to William Rossetti, saying that he had just heard from Simeon Solomon that 'Buchanan is not in this instance the scavenger of his own coprolitic matter – that he did *not* write the article as at first intended. It is rather a pity if it be so, as it swamps not only Gabriel's epistle which would doubtless have been a masterpiece but some very beautiful passages in an essay I have just begun, which would have thrown into the shade the strongest colouring and made insipid by comparison the highest flavours of Juvenal's, Swift's, and Landor's satire combined.' This was *Under the Microscope* – so named because microbes can only be so seen – which, on hearing that Buchanan was the author of the article after all, Swinburne finished and published next year as a pamphlet. It is a splendid piece of polemical prose, truly Elizabethan in its gusto.[59] But, for the time being, Rossetti advised him to hold his fire, and wrote a dignified reply, 'The Stealthy School of Criticism', which appeared on 16 December in the *Athenaeum.* Swinburne regretfully complied with his friend's wishes, since, after all, it had been Rossetti who bore the brunt of the attack. As he wrote to Rossetti on 13 November: 'Otherwise I would have written a few lines to Knight or some other "literary friend" and authorized him to shew them or make them public in any convenient way; as the only sort of notice I could take of a thing misbegotten by the God Crepitus on the Goddess Cloacina. (There really was a God "Fart" I believe – he must have been a more prolific "Father-God" than Jupiter or Jehovah by very long chalks, to judge by the multiplicity of his generations.)'[60]

In March 1872, while in London, news reached Swinburne of Mazzini's death at Pisa, and he wrote to his mother that he had lost 'the man whom I most loved and admired of all men on earth. I am not in the humour to write about it, or to think yet more than I can help. . . . But of course you and my father will know it is a great loss to me as it is to the world which was not worthy of the great and good man now removed from it.'[61]

Swinburne spent a few days with Jowett in April this year at Balliol. On the way to Oxford he had lost his luggage at Reading and had 'twice to appear in the evening before a Galaxy of Fashion, Rank, and Talent in a morning dress, and to borrow a clean shirt of the Master'. Jowett was at that time translating Plato's *Symposium*, and to please Swinburne asked him to look over his manuscript. Swinburne told him diffidently that if he had been asked to construe a certain sentence, he would have construed it differently. Jowett glanced at him in surprise, looked over his manuscript and said, after a minute or so: 'Of course that is the meaning! You would be a good scholar if you were to study.' Then, as they worked side by side, Swinburne would exclaim from time to time, 'Another howler, Master!' and Jowett would say, 'Thank you, Algernon, thank you.' Not at all bad for someone whose academic career had ended in 'total and scandalous failure'!

During the spring and summer of 1872, while he was living at Kelmscott, Rossetti's health broke down. His brother wrote to Swinburne, saying that it was Gabriel's wish that he should not, for the present, attempt to see him. Swinburne replied on 5 July: 'Many thanks for your note – I shall of course take every precaution against a meeting. It is of course a great grief to me to be debarred from showing the same attention and affection as friends who can hardly love him better – as indeed I think no man can love his friend more than I love Gabriel – but I know it can be from no doubt of my attachment that he shrinks from seeing me as yet.'[62]

But Swinburne and Rossetti never met or corresponded again. It is not known why, except that Rossetti, who was suffering from delusions, acute persecution mania and deep depression, as a result of guilt feelings over his treatment of Lizzie, his love for Jane Morris and the continued attacks upon his work and character in the Press, now cut himself off from all his old friends, except Watts and one or two others. It is probable that he felt that he could no longer cope with Swinburne's drunkenness and moods of wild excitability. Moreover, Mrs Rossetti Angeli, William Rossetti's daughter, tells us that in June Swinburne and Sandys had been overheard discussing Rossetti's nervous collapse in loud voices in a popular restaurant. Rossetti went to Scotland to recover in the company of his doctor and then returned to Kelmscott in the autumn, keeping Morris away from this 'haven of refuge . . . for it is a farce our meeting unless we can help it' – as Morris wrote to his friend Mrs Coronio. Rossetti remained at Kelmscott throughout 1873 and finally gave up his joint tenancy of the house in 1874. When, in 1872, Buchanan published his *Fleshly School of Poetry* as a pamphlet, Swinburne published his reply, *Under the Microscope*, which also discussed the relative merits of Byron, Tennyson and Whitman, while holding Buchanan up to ridicule.

In July Swinburne was with Jowett in Edinburgh and Grantown, 'a small town or village' as he wrote to Powell on 8 July 'with a fine rapid river (the Spey) winding under firwoods between banks clothed with broom and wild roses, and with birch enough to hand for the bottoms of all Eton'. Meanwhile he was helping Jowett revise *The School and Children's Bible*, an occupation which only provoked him to further blasphemous and Sadique outbursts in his letters to Powell. But of these the Master of Balliol was, of course, unaware. From Grantown they revisited Tummil Bridge, where Swinburne bathed, walked and climbed. 'We go into the pool below one waterfall,' he wrote to his mother, 'swim up to the foot of it, and climb up the rocks it falls over . . . and then plunge again into the pool above this and below a higher waterfall. . . . The upper pool where we have been bathing regularly (weather permitting) for days past is a most lovely basin of sheer rock . . . when you jump in at the foot of the fall the impulse of the water is so strong that it sends you spinning right across the pool, and it is all one can possibly do to swim back to the other side, though but two or three strokes off.'[63]

In July the editor of the French periodical *Renaissance* wrote to ask Swinburne for a poem in French, and he tells Powell that he is writing one 'on the effect of Wagner's overture to Tristan which I think you will like'. This poem never appeared in *Renaissance* and, even if it was ever finished, has since disappeared. It is evident, however, that the yearning, chromatic eroticism of *Tristan and Isolde* had a natural appeal to Swinburne. We know that Burne-Jones was an admirer of Wagner and attended his concerts at the Albert Hall in May 1877, as well as a morning rehearsal during which he shared a box with George Eliot, Lewes, Leighton, William Morris and Wagner himself.[64] He also did a drawing of Cosima Wagner, who gave him the life-mask of Beethoven in exchange. In 1883 Swinburne was to write a poem, 'The Death of Richard Wagner', in which he says that his music 'laid bare/The world's great heart'. Indeed, the movement of the verse itself is distinctly Wagnerian and is evidence that he absorbed the essence of the music, just as he had absorbed the essence of Hugo and Baudelaire:

Eye might not endure it, but ear and heart with
a rapture of dark delight,
With a terror and wonder whose core is joy, and a
passion of thought set free,
Felt only the rising of doom divine as a sundawn
risen to sight
From the depths of the sea.

He also wrote two poems in English on the preludes to *Lohengrin* and *Tristan*, which appeared, like the Wagner elegy, in *A Century of Roundels* (1883).

After the death of Gautier in October 1872, a memorial volume was issued the following year in Paris, *Le Tombeau de Théophile Gautier*. At the suggestion of Heredia, transmitted by Sidney Colvin, Swinburne was asked to contribute. He responded with two poems in English, two in French, one in Latin, and five in Greek. 'In these learned exercises,' remarks Gosse, 'Swinburne was happy to believe that he had no competitor in English poetry except Milton and Landor. He was also proud to be considered as a French poet.' The English poems included the sonnet on *Mademoiselle de Maupin*:

This is the golden book of spirit and sense,
The holy writ of beauty; he that wrought
Made it with dreams and faultless words and thought
That seeks and finds and loses in the dense
Dim air of life that beauty's excellence
Wherewith love makes one hour of life distraught
And all hours after follow and find not aught.
Here is that height of all love's eminence
Where man may breathe but for a breathing-space
And feel his soul burn as an altar-fire
To the unknown God of unachieved desire.

The 'Memorial Verses' are verbose and imprecise and have none of the power and music of the Baudelaire elegy. Swinburne evidently felt this himself, for he says in a letter to John Morley of 21 November: 'The metrical effect is, I think, not bad, but the danger of such metres is diffuseness and flaccidity. I perceive this one to have a tendency to the dulcet and luscious form of verbosity which has to be guarded against; lest the poem lose its foothold and be swept off its legs, sense and all, down a flood of effeminate and monotonous music, or lost and split in a maze of what I call draggle-tailed melody.'[65]

But, while foreseeing this danger, he was only too often unable, as he grew older, to avoid it.

## CHAPTER NINE

# 1872–76
# A FORSAKEN GARDEN

Swinburne did not move into his new 'chambers' at 3 Great James Street, Holborn, until the middle of March 1874; although he took them in September 1872, the following year was spent almost entirely with his parents at Holmwood. His father's allowance, now only £200 a year, was not sufficient to cover his expenses in town and he had as yet received nothing from Hotten, his publisher. He was beset with unpaid bills, which ultimately found their way to Holmwood. Moreover, his old landlady, Mrs Thompson at North Crescent, Bedford Square, considered that when he gave up his rooms in September she was entitled to a parting gift in compensation for the annoyance she had suffered as a result of her tenant's late hours, 'irregular' habits and all-too-frequent bouts of illness, which had naturally entailed extra work. But Swinburne now left it to George Powell to deal with Mrs Thompson and to move his belongings to Great James Street, writing to him from Holmwood on 20 September:

> As to Mrs Thompson – I have simply to say this – that I do not think either you or any other person will say he has found me ungenerous or unjust in my dealings with anyone, and that I certainly wish my friends to retain the opinion of me on that score which I trust I have done and shall do nothing to forfeit. With regard to any extra trouble in attendance or nursing, and any hastiness of temper in time of illness which I may have shown – this I suppose is what you refer to by the mention of 'slights' or 'insults' on my part – I must say that my 'conscience' reminds me of more than one payment or present to the woman on that score, and most especially that on my removal after the full and final settlement of every claim or outstanding account, she received at parting a gift of five pounds – in my father's opinion and mine, a sufficient one. If she told you the contrary, she told you a most impudent falsehood. With reference to the terms of my occupation, if she complains again of being 'docked' as you say of any charges due to her, she lies again, and knows it. An agreement was voluntarily made when I took those chambers that she should receive so much a week for attendance *while I was in residence*

> *only*, payable weekly. . . . Upon these prearranged terms, perfectly understood on both sides, I took the chambers.

Such was the lordly manner in which Swinburne habitually dealt with the lower orders, among whom he included such 'tradesmen' as publishers. He continues:

> The carpenter writes asking me to settle his bill of £1. 12s. 6d. for work done at Great James Street. Is not this a great deal for the amount of work done? The charge for the bookcase – which after all I believe he did *not* fit up properly – is surely exorbitant. . . . Will you kindly ask Mrs Magill [the housekeeper at 3 Great James Street] what she thinks of it? *You* will think I am getting 'near' but I am overwhelmed on all sides with more or less pressing bills till my power of work is quite interfered with and my pleasure in it spoilt by irritation and waste of time and temper. I have a fearful cold too, am stone deaf, and have had three of my few remaining double teeth out at once. The occasion vividly reminded me of a Reverend Father well-known to Father Simeon, 'qui avait la passion d'arracher les dents en enculent la victime', though the parallel between the two cases of Suffering Virtue was not complete.

It was at this time that Swinburne employed Watts to look into his affairs with Hotten. If Watts advises him to leave his books in Hotten's hands, he writes on 31 October, he will do so, 'slippery as I know the man to be – then my only remaining feeling of dislike would be based on the consideration of the style of literature and of literary traffic – American and other – with which his name is generally connected in men's minds and newspapers'. The 'style of literature' with which Hotten's name was generally connected was, as we know, books on flagellation, from which Swinburne, when writing to Watts, was anxious to disassociate himself. 'As far as I can judge,' he writes to Watts on 6 December, 'there seems to be nothing for it but to enforce if necessary a statement of accounts from Hotten and get out of all relations with him as soon as possible; especially after his assertion "that there is next to nothing coming to me"; in which case, as not more than £40 obtained with much difficulty after repeated demands has passed from his hands into mine for several years past, it is obviously not to my interest to remain in any business relation with him.' That, at least, would seem evident enough – especially as several other firms had already approached him with offers to bring out his work.

Finally, as a result of Watts's negotiations, Chapman & Hall agreed to publish a cheap edition of all Swinburne's poems, with a reproduction of Rossetti's painting of him. He wrote to Watts: 'It is rather *imberbe* (but my *barbiche* is not much) but otherwise, as he and others think, more like me now than when it was painted and remarked on by himself as too old-looking.'[1]

In February 1873, we have seen, Swinburne wrote urgently to Howell about some papers of his in Hotten's possession – 'a list drawn up in my hand of scenes in school which he was to get sketched for me on approval with a draughtsman of his acquaintance . . . in which list, though there was nothing equivocal or dirty in any way, I had explained the postures and actions of "swishing" to be shewn in detail, just as a boy at school would draw them for fun from the life. . . . I would rather be sure they might not shew it about for "cads" to comment on or stick it in his blank book among papers relating to me. This is really all the matter, and I really don't know that it is worth the ink I have spent on it. Of course, above all things, nothing must be said to Hotten which might possibly suggest to him the idea that I am in any way apprehensive of his making it an instrument of annoyance to me; which in fact I am not, and have no reason to be. Indeed I see he advertises a new "Romance of the Rod" as in preparation, to which I should be happy to lend any assistance that I could, and so you might let him know if we are to remain on terms.'

Unfortunately, Swinburne complicated the whole situation and compromised himself by writing one thing to Watts and another to Howell. At the same time we find Hotten writing to him 'If you never read Nerciat's *Le Diable aux Corps* I could [get] it for you' and sending him £30 'on a/c of statement rendered to Mr Watts'. Swinburne replied that he had seen the book already and did not want it. But early in 1873, as he wrote to George Powell, he read with excitement 'the wretchedly curtailed announcement in Saturday's Times of the apprehension in the suburbs of Paris of a band of Sadists, disciples of the excellent M. Dolmancé, headed by a captain aged fourteen and a half (Gélignier by name), which dear child, who among us would be in the fourth form, has taken part in eighty robberies with *Sadique* violence, several murders and other *attentats*, to say nothing of the daily bread of diversions unnecessary to specify, and has maintained his ascendancy over comrades of 27 and upwards. It seems that the "Gaulois" has given "deplorably" full details of the matter, as well as other French papers to the scandal of virtuous journalism. Could you I wonder find any number of a newspaper containing such at Roques', where we went together in Hight Holborn, close to Bedford Row?' He cannot come to London himself at present, he tells Powell, as he is £100 overdrawn at the bank. However, he continued to pay the rent of rooms he did not occupy in London and to ask Powell to do various commissions for him.

When Hotten died in June 1873, Andrew Chatto, who had been working in the firm since he was fifteen, bought the business from his widow and wrote to Swinburne on 23 July to say that he very much wished to have the publication of his forthcoming books in addition to those already published by Hotten, and 'to have the business relations with yourself placed upon a more satisfactory footing than has been the case for some time past. I believe that none of the objections that you had against Mr Hotten attach in any way to myself, and I shall greatly esteem the favour of a visit from you – or I will wait upon you if you prefer it.' He enclosed a cheque for £50 'on account of royalty on the books sold by Mr Hotten since his last return, and in anticipation of my succeeding to his business'. Andrew Chatto was, indeed, a man very different from Hotten, and though a man of wide culture, a 'cellist, a collector of paintings, an amateur scientist and a yachtsman, Swinburne for years continued to treat him in the most peremptory and high-handed manner. He now referred Chatto to Watts, who seems to have continued to negotiate with Chapman.

In December he wrote to Watts to say that he was astonished to find a page of Chatto & Windus's catalogue filled by advertisements of his books, and 'among them of "Bothwell, A New Poem, in preparation". This, after the interview with Chapman, appears to me even more audacious and inexplicable than before. You and Chapman will know better than I what steps should be taken.'

Chatto sent Swinburne a statement of the sale of his books and a cheque for £173 10*s* 10*d*, which Swinburne acknowledged on 2 January 1874. He adds that he has been out of town since the beginning of November, and 'have consequently not had an opportunity for some time of calling on you. Had I done so, I could only have repeated the declaration I made to you on the last occasion I had of calling: viz. that the regulation of my business affairs is now in the hands of my legal adviser Mr Watts, by whose decision I am prepared to abide.' Apparently Chatto had written to Watts in September, but had not received any reply. By January he evidently thought that a cheque would speak louder than words, and he repeated his wish to publish both *Bothwell* and *Tristram and Iseult* on a royalty basis with cash in advance, 'reckoned upon the entire number printed of each edition – we ourselves taking the risk as to whether the books sell or not'.

Watts evidently felt that, after his negotiations with Chapman, the position *vis-à-vis* Chatto was somewhat delicate, especially as Swinburne was now accepting his cheques. But Chatto pursued his quarry energetically and by 30 January 1874 was already setting up *Bothwell* in type – very badly, according to Swinburne, who wrote to Watts: 'If ever printers were Bulgarians and if ever Bulgarians were sanguinary. But I won't swear – I never do. And I won't use the language of Gladstone and of fishwives, of cabmen and of Carlyle.'

When the wretched Napoleon III died at Chislehurst in January 1873 after an unsuccessful operation, in pain and obscurity, Swinburne had celebrated the occasion with a batch of abusive sonnets, 'Dirae'. Two of these appeared in the *Examiner* under the title of 'The Saviour of Society':

O son of man, but of what man who knows?
  That broughtest healing on thy leathern wings
  To priests, and under them didst gather kings,
And madest friends to thee of all men's foes;

Before thine incarnation, the tale goes,
Thy virgin mother, pure of sensual stings,
Communed by night with angels of chaste things,
And, full of grace, untimely felt the throes
Of motherhood upon her, and believed
The obscure annunciation made when late
A raven-feathered raven-throated dove
Croaked salutation to the mother of love
Whose misconception was immaculate,
And when her time was come she misconceived.

The *Spectator* wrote of Swinburne's 'revolting sonnets' and reproved him for 'a gross parody on the most sacred of subjects'. Unless one knew already, who would suspect that this sonnet referred to the birth of Napoleon III and not to the Nativity? 'The Descent into Hell' is dated 9 January 1873, and concludes: 'we have lived to say,/The dog is dead.' Swinburne then wrote a letter full of virtuous indignation to the *Spectator* expressing 'disgust at the insult – I might honestly say and fear no misconstruction from any honest man, of horror at the blasphemy – offered to the name and memory or tradition of Christ by the men who, in gratitude for the support given to the Church by Louis Bonaparte and his empire, bestowed on the most infamous of all public criminals the names till then reserved for one whom they professed to worship as God, of "Saviour" and "Messiah". . . . It is not, in my humble opinion, necessary to subscribe to the creeds or articles of any Church, to earn the right of feeling and of expressing horror and disgust at this desecration of terms which must in some sense be sacred to all who have any faith or hope in the higher life of man. . . . And this and nothing else is the feeling expressed in my sonnets: feebly expressed, indeed, but at least in terms as bitter and as strong as could be supplied by my reverence for the associations thus outraged.'

This is a new Swinburne with a vengeance! Or was he merely writing with his tongue in his cheek? It is a far cry from this to 'the Galilean serpent'! After writing to the *Spectator*, Swinburne sent two long and self-justificatory letters to the *Examiner*. Although the sonnets are of an almost insane virulence, Napoleon III represented to Swinburne tyranny in its meanest form and his hatred of him dated back to his childhood and university days, when he used to dance solemnly before the portrait of Orsini – as he still continued to do in his Great James Street rooms. But even Victor Hugo remained silent on this occasion.

It is often said that Swinburne was more or less insensible to the world around him, but he was an avid reader of newspapers and literary and political reviews. In his letter to Edwin Harrison of 4 June 1873, he says: 'I could wish I had more in me of Burns and less of Shelley, that I might write something that should do good and might endure on the evidence published in yesterday's *Times* of those two poor women in prison with their babies. I thirst with impotent desire to do something – but the mere contemplation of the tyranny and attempt for a moment to realise the suffering is literally intolerable pain to me. I could no more write under its influence than under the influence of neuralgia. It makes me feel exactly

as a nerve o'er which do creep
The else-unfelt oppressions of the earth.

But if I could I would write something "that should make wise men mad". These things are incredible – and they are next door to us. How is it that the whole countryside has not been driven mad between rage and pity?' But in the event, he quotes Shelley and not Burns.

At the end of May 1873 Swinburne spent a fortnight in Oxford, where, as he wrote to Powell on 6 June, he 'saw and spoke with a great friend of poor Simeon's, Pater of Brasenose, who has seen Miss Solomon, and appeared to have more hope of his ultimate recovery and rehabilitation than from the horrid version I had heard of the form of his insanity I had ventured to retain. . . . I suppose there is no doubt the poor unhappy little fellow has really been out of his mind and *done* things amenable to law such as done by a sane man would make it impossible for any one to keep up his acquaintance and not be cut by the rest of the world as an accomplice? I have been seriously unhappy about it for I had a real affection and regard for him – and besides his genius he had such genuinely amiable qualities. It is the simple truth that the distress of it has haunted and broken my sleep. It is hideous to lose a friend by madness of any kind, let alone this. Do you – I do not – know any detail of the matter at first hand? Pater I imagine did, and his tone gave me a gleam of comfort. . . . The interminable Bothwell remains interminable, or I should have been in town before now. My mother and eldest sister, with my brother, are at the baths of Creuznach: when they return they want me to accompany them en famille on a migration for the summer months from this place (which will be let, for the vacation as it were) to a place of my uncle Sir Henry Gordon's in the Isle of Wight, which after some reluctance I incline to think I shall do and perhaps run over to Guernsey.'[2]

From his letter to Watts of 1 December one gathers that Swinburne had written to Powell 'a long letter of elder-brotherly advice', warning him to have nothing further to do with Simeon Solomon 'who has deliberately chosen to do what makes a man and all who associate with him infamous in the eyes of the world. It is something new for me to come forward as the representative of worldly wisdom; but as I said to P. I do not think I need fear to be accused of lukewarmness in friendship or pers[on]al timidity in the face of public op[ini]on; it is not exactly for turning tai[l or dese]rting my friends when out of favour [with] the world or any part of it that I have exposed myself hitherto to attack; only in such a case as this I do think a man is bound to consider the consequences to all his friends and to every one who cares for him in the world of allowing his name to be mixed up with that of a – let us say, Platonist; the term is at once accurate as a definition and unobjectionable as an euphemism.'[3]

The point is that Simeon Solomon had been arrested and imprisoned for soliciting outside a public lavatory. The very fact that Swinburne is so anxious to disassociate himself from Solomon proves, in Lafourcade's opinion, that he could not have been homosexual.[4] It certainly shows that he was frightened of being involved in a public scandal. The number of mistakes in the manuscript of this letter are evidence of the emotional stress under which it was written. But, according to Oscar Browning's letter of 10 November 1919, on the relations of Swinburne and Solomon, 'their vices were Sadic, not Greek' – which is likely enough.[5] Nevertheless, one has to consider how far Swinburne, Pater, Oscar Browning and J. A. Symonds were responsible for all Solomon's degeneration, for they all had a part in it. Finally, Solomon was shunned by all his friends and reduced to destitution. He finished up as a pavement artist, sleeping in doss-houses, and hawking round his friends' letters to make a little money. For him there was no admiral to descend at intervals and save him from the effects of his worst excesses, and no Holmwood for him to retire to when he had spent all his money and fallen ill.

'At the end of next week I am going into Cornwall for ten days with Professor Jowett, who has just paid us a new year's visit here,' Swinburne wrote to Watts from Holmwood on 2 January 1874. 'Between this and then the Master of Balliol will be at Torquay, where I am not sorry that I do not join him, as I have no wish, especially in his company, to encounter that of a Platonist of another sort than the translator of Plato – "translator he too" as Carlyle might say, of Platonic theory into Socratic practice – should he still figure in that neighbourhood as the glass of fashion and the mould of form, if not (as I sincerely hope not) "the glass wherein the noble youth" of the West country "do dress themselves". Powell has answered to my little fraternal lecture on caution in that quarter very nicely, in two or three sensible and grateful words.' This was, of course, an ironical reference to Simeon Solomon, who was staying with friends in Devonshire and living, according to Swinburne, 'in a round of balls and private theatricals' and giving public readings from Dickens at Torquay. A meeting with him in Jowett's company would certainly have been awkward. Instead he went for 'a prosperous ten days' tour to the Land's End with the Master of Balliol', as he wrote to Powell on his return, 'which has left me in love with Kynance Cove where (to use an original expression) I could live and die'.

Towards the end of January, Powell sent him a cutting from an American periodical, *Frank Leslie's Illustrated Newspaper*, in which, during an interview after his return from England, Emerson had gone out of his way to describe Swinburne as 'a perfect leper and a mere sodomite', which statement he supported by quoting Carlyle as saying that Swinburne was 'a man standing up to his neck in a cesspool and adding to its contents'.[6] Powell added that 'there was no end to the scandalous fables current concerning you in the US'.

Swinburne replied with dignity on 30 January: 'My first impulse on receiving the enclosed which I return with many (and sincere) thanks for the sight of it was to take no manner of notice of it beyond a word of acknowledgement in a private letter to you. A man is not willing to touch with foot or finger the persons or the productions of such commentators as draw their metaphors from Sodom and the sewer, or to bring his own honourable name into public contact with those men who use such weapons of attack as these. But on second thoughts I have as you will see changed my mind so far as to write the few sentences which I now enclose for you to make such use of as you please. I need not say that I should be loth to give additional publicity and wider currency to an obscure infamy such as this article; but in view of what you say and of the general tone of my detractors in America, I am not unwilling to take even this occasion to speak out on the subject. But I will not address on my own part any reclamation to any editor either English or American in this matter.' And in a postscript he added: 'I presume there is no doubt that Emerson did express himself after this foul fashion as you say he has been written to on the subject and has not disclaimed it.'[7]

Among the 'few sentences' which Swinburne enclosed with his letter to Powell to pass on to the Press in America was the following: 'A foul mouth is so ill-matched with a white beard that I would gladly believe the newspaper scribes alone responsible for the bestial utterances which they declare to have dropped from a teacher whom such disciples as these exhibit to our disgust and compassion as performing on their obscene platform the last tricks of tongue now possible to a gap-toothed and hoary-headed ape, carried at first into notice on the shoulder of Carlyle, and who now in his dotage spits and chatters from a dirtier perch of his own finding and fouling; Coryphaeus or choragus of his Bulgarian tribe of autocoprophagous baboons who make the filth they feed on.' Swinburne, having delivered himself of this characteristic rebuke, went on to speak of the hereditary honour of his name and asked 'how far such follies and such villanies may be likely to disturb the consciousness of one to whom it is given to remember that wellnigh at the very outset of his course he had earned the praise and won the friendship of Landor, of Hugo, and of Mazzini'.[8]

Powell replied that he would do as Swinburne suggested and send the letter to Woodcroft in New York as 'an extract from a letter to a friend, which you are quite willing to have published there. . . . He will see to this and your dignity will be in no way compromised. It is grand "payment".'

Swinburne thereupon relieved his feelings by writing two insulting Latin epigrams on Emerson and sent them to Powell.

By March 1874 Swinburne was back in London at his Great James Street rooms, where he asked John Morley to lunch early in April, reading *Bothwell* to him and to a circle of young contemporaries. The reading occupied five hours of a blazing hot afternoon, Morley told Gosse afterwards. On another occasion he read it to Gosse, Burne-Jones and Arthur O'Shaughnessy, standing between the two great serpentine candlesticks he had brought with him from the Lizard. 'He shrieked, thundered, whispered and fluted the whole of the enormous second act between dinner and midnight,' writes Gosse. The greater part of the drama had now been set up by Chatto. 'I am half blind and half dead with correcting all these proofs in the space of four days,' Swinburne wrote on 12 May to Morley.

Towards the end of May he was writing to Morley again to say that he would rather that he gave *Bothwell* to 'any other man' to review for the *Fortnightly* – even Robert Buchanan – than Lord Houghton, adding: 'I confess that I do shrink from the rancid unction of that man's adulation or patronage or criticism'. But in the event Lord Houghton did review the book for the *Fortnightly*. Of *Bothwell* Gosse says: 'There is no other work of Swinburne which displays so unquestionably his gift for creating and interpreting character. There is none in which the language is of a more spirited simplicity or the verse more fluid. It is not, of course, the best play, but it is the finest dramatic romance produced in England throughout the nineteenth century, and among the myriad blank verse imitations of the Elizabethans beloved of Charles Lamb, *Bothwell* floats supreme, a leviathan.' It is also Swinburne's finest study of Mary Stuart. He dedicated it to Victor Hugo, to whom he described it as 'mon drame épique et plein de tumulte et de flamme'. In reply Hugo wrote him 'such a letter in acknowledgement of the dedication', he told Morley, 'as I should like to show you, but have not the face to transcribe'.

Early in June he was invited to the private view of Whistler's first one-man show at 48 Pall Mall. 'I have seen at least some of the things to be exhibited,' he wrote to the novelist Mrs Lynn Linton, when inviting her to accompany him, 'and I assure you in my poor opionion they are only second – if *second* to anything – to the very greatest works of art in any age.' But he was soon 'hardly well enough to hold a pen', as he wrote to his cousin Paul Swinburne on 20 June from Holmwood, where he had retired 'to pick up if possible a little strength. We *must* manage to meet again before you are off again to the tropics, and have a comfortable talk. I am glad you liked *Bothwell.* I think it my best and ripest piece of work as yet on any large scale. . . . I send on the slip enclosed the tidiest autograph I can with much pains accomplish – but as even this much writing makes my hand and arms ache and shake, it is naturally not very good. Did you ever suffer from prolonged want of sleep – what doctors call insomnia? I have hardly had a good night's (natural) rest for four or five months.'[9]

Swinburne's handwriting remained curiously childish throughout his life and it was made all the more difficult, at the best of times, by a weakness of the wrist. One wonders how he managed to write so much, especially such long letters. 'But I must resign myself to the curse of penmanship – and mine I fear is a curse to my friends also,' he wrote to E. C. Stedman the next year, 1875. 'How Shakespeare must have hated it! Look at his villainous and laborious pothooks and Ben Jonson's (or Milton's) copper-plate and vigorous perfection of hand.' He might have added that Byron's handwriting was none too good either.

During the first week in July Swinburne went, as we have seen, to the Isle of Wight with his father to his uncle's house, The Orchard, Niton, where he remained until September. His mother joined them later. He divided his time, he told Watts, between swimming and reading Homer. He was also studying Chapman, with a view to his critical essay for R. H. Shepherd's new edition of the plays and poems which Chatto was bringing out, and correcting the proofs for a second edition of *Bothwell*, which had been very well received on its publication this year. 'I hope now that I may at last see a correct text,' he wrote severely to Andrew Chatto on 24 July. 'Some of the worst errors hitherto overlooked occur in the earlier part of the book: for these there can be no excuse, as the printers had before them a printed text most carefully corrected throughout, into which out of pure indolence and perverse negligence they had permitted themselves to foist such absurd and disgraceful blunders as to make utter nonsense of whole sentences. Such incompetence and such neglect as this cannot be guarded against by the author, who after hours and days of drudgery spent in the revision and rectification of the original blunders finds his time and labour utterly wasted. . . . I have with great labour endeavoured to make their spelling and punctuation consistent at least, if not correct. . . . These are things that men whose whole business is orthography and the setting up of sentences arranged in order ought to know without giving authors the trouble to instruct their ignorance and teach them their trade. . . . I cannot undertake a third or fourth time the intolerable drudgery of toiling after the steps of blunderers and idlers to do their proper work for them. I have taken all possible pains with the text and expect now to find it accurate.' He goes on to instruct Chatto on how a page of type should be laid out, even what type to use on the title page, and tells him to avoid 'big varieties of type' which 'always look to me like a *poster*. These are the little things which make a book look *vulgar*; the last thing which a publisher who wishes to hold a distinguished place can afford to allow *any* of his books to be called.' Of Chatto's reprints of some Restoration songs, he remarks: 'those books are undoubtedly very dirty, very dull, of no literary value, and of the slightest possible historical interest; and therefore the frequent issue of such reprints would be likely to give a rising firm a somewhat unsavoury reputation, such as I should be sorry my publisher should incur.' On the other hand, he says: 'I trust you have successfully resisted or ignored the monstrous and most impertinent threat of interference with your publication of Rabelais in English with Doré's illustrations . . . one of the greatest classics in the world, the work of one of the most illustrious among the immortals of any age, supreme among the highest works of genius in that kind by the consent of all times and countries. . . . You are at liberty, if you think it of any use, to show this expression of my opinion to any one you please – but *not* to quote it with my name in print as has been done before now in like cases, and is always I think in bad taste.'[10] All this and more Chatto had patiently to endure if he wished to keep Swinburne as his author.

Another letter of 2 August again raps this long-suffering publisher over the knuckles: 'The packet of magazines, books &c. which arrived this morning had no stamps on it and seems not to have been prepaid, this entailing a heavier expense than it was worth. Please desire your people to be more careful next time they have anything to send, as besides the cost of such neglect it is likely to cause delay and uncertainty in transmission. . . . As you know I want a *complete* set of all the notices that may appear of Bothwell, I shall be glad if you will let me have those yet wanting to my collection as soon as possible. The last was rather longer in coming than I expected.'[11]

Besides working on the proofs of 'the voluminous works of Chapman', his own essay on Chapman, and reading the plays of Dekker, Heywood and Glapthorne, sent to him by their editor R. H. Shepherd, he was, as he told Morley, reading the Iliad in Greek and writing 'some fresh parcels of my "Tristram and Iseult" '. To Edwin Harrison he wrote on 27 August: 'I wish with all my heart we were together daily in the sea where I need not tell you I find myself daily alone, and have many times held imaginary conversations with you as eloquent and as voluminous as Landor's while swimming across the bays that divide these headlands. The weather has been usually divine, and the Oceanides as favourable to me as ever to Prometheus: except one day when I went in at a new place after a gale and found myself unable to get back to land and violently beaten to and fro between the breakers in a furious flux which flung me back off shore as with the clutch of a wild beast every time I tried to get up on the bank of shingle where at last by dint of grovelling and digging with hands and feet I managed, between swimming, crawling and running, to get out of the "cludges" of a "nuss" more tenacious of her patient than Betsy Prig in person. Since then I have kept to the bays I know to be warranted safe within reasonable limits. . . . On clear days I swim across half-a-dozen various belts of reef, rock and weed-bed with broad interspaces of clear sea, and can observe all the forms and colours changing and passing beneath me, which is one of the supreme delights of the sea. This talk of swimming naturally reminds me to tell you that before leaving London at the beginning of July I made the acquaintance and may say, I think, that I gained the friendship of a very famous old veteran of the sea in that and other capacities, the one Englishman living I was really ambitious and anxious to know; I need hardly name old Trelawney who is certainly the most splendid old man I have ever seen since Landor and my own grandfather – though of course a good deal younger than these. He was most cordial and friendly in his reception of me, whom he affirms to be the last of the poets; having apparently no faith in the capacity of this hag-ridden and God-ridden country to produce more of the breed; while I lament to add that he (metaphorically) spits and stamps on the bare suggestion that it did produce any between Shelley or Byron and myself. . . . He was full of the atrocities (then just revealed as you doubtless remember) of New California [he means the French penal colony in New Caledonia] and (of course) of passionate sympathy with the exiles of the Commune.

'Always energetic, whenever he speaks of Shelley the especial energy of his affection is really beautiful and admirable to see. There is some fresh air in England yet while such an Englishman is alive. Did you see his portrait as an old sailor in Millais' picture of "the Northwest Passage" exhibited this year? a splendid piece of work and an unmistakeable likeness, but of course utterly wanting what Reynolds of course would have given, the nameless general air of distinction and what people call "birth" or "blood" for fault of a better word which we ought to invent among us, for it is a very real and actual quality, and as patent in Trelawney as his look of weatherbeaten hardihood with which it assorts so well.' Swinburne adds that *Bothwell* is 'about to be arranged for the stage by Mr John Oxenford, a playwright of note, as I am told, and will (D. always V.) be brought out next theatrical season, when I expect all my friends and all the faithful in Oxford to rally round it and me.'[12]

On 29 August he tells Watts there has been an application from a M. Regnaud to translate his works into French: 'if it were never to bring me a penny of pelf it would gratify me beyond measure, and more than any other form of success or compliment could possibly do, to see my works in a thoroughly good French translation'.

Swinburne was enormously impressed by Professor Tyndale's address to the British Association in Belfast, as reported in *The Times*, towards the end of August. 'Science so enlarged,' he tells Watts in the same letter, 'gives me a sense as much of rest as of light. . . . Even my technical ignorance does not impair, I think, my power to see accurately and seize firmly the first thread of the great clue, because my habit of mind is not (I hope) unscientific, though my work lies in the field of art instead of science, and when seen and seized even that first perception gives me an indescribable sense as of music and repose. It is Theism which to me seems to introduce an element of – happily a fictitious element – of doubt, discord and disorder.

'I think I told you that since I have been here I have read the Iliad through for the first time with great comfort and benefit to my spirits; which have been also recreated by constant exercise in the sea to such an extent that I caught my face in a glass looking yesterday rather as it did twelve or fifteen years ago than it does in London with thinned hair and withered cheeks. I swim in among the other Seagulls now daily.'[13]

He was 'still grinding at old Chapman's obscure and unequal poetry which alternately startles and delights and disgusts and infuriates the student', he tells Powell on 1 September: 'In a fortnight's time we shall probably break up our party here, when I suppose I shall go to London and see personally how the prospects of Bothwell advance or recede. . . . Poor Burton has been at death's door at Trieste – but I hope the best of all wives, who wrote to me of him, giving the bad news, has pulled him through "by the skin of the teeth". . . . His loss would have been one of the heaviest that either his friends or England could have sustained; and it is enraging to reflect how he has been neglected and thrown away, with all his marvellous and unequalled powers and qualities as soldier, scholar, thinker, ruler, leader, by a country in whose service he might have done wonders and earned honours even higher than he has.'[14]

Swinburne had worked so hard on the corrupt text of Chapman's plays that it had affected his eyesight and he was advised to rest. He was once more in town by mid-September 1874, at his rooms at 3 Great James Street and correcting, with many complaints, the proofs of his Chapman essay, which had by now grown into a sizeable book. At the same time he was also correcting both the memoir and the text of William Rossetti's edition of Blake, and his letter to Rossetti of 30 October is full of exemplary criticism. But by November he was ill once more. 'I have not been well enough to write or look at my letters or proofs for some days,' he tells Morley, adding that he has begun 'a somewhat elaborate history of Shakespeare's style from Romeo to Timon which I hope to finish if I keep strong enough to work in London. In the country I lose energy for lack of a soul to speak to on any subject that interests me, and here "the fog and filthy air" upsets my unwitchlike-ness. . . . I am blind with proofs, and writing makes my head swim.' He returned to Holmwood for Christmas.

Meeting Swinburne at a small dinner party at Whistler's house, his cousin Bertram Mitford, who had recently returned from the British Embassy in Japan, described him much later in a letter to Gosse: 'I was much struck by Swinburne's appearance, the years had changed him so little. He had still the delicate features of a child. He looked so young that had it not been for the scanty beard, thin and straggling, that seemed quite unnatural, as if it had been not very skilfully stuck on by some theatrical Simmonds, he would have been the very Algernon of the 'fifties. The illusion was kept up by the gentle music of his voice, as caressing as I had known it a quarter of a century earlier. After dinner we sat together for a long while talking over the sunshine of boyhood, two old school-fellows content to chatter about Eton, Windsor, the unforgettable joys of the Thames, with now and then a dip into the family story.'

It was in February 1875 that Swinburne wrote his long autobiographical letter to E. C. Stedman, who was writing an article on his work for *Scribner's Monthly* and now asked him for some account of birth and career. He begins by saying that his grandfather's life 'would be better worth writing than my own', which: 'has been eventless and monotonous. . . . I never cared for any pursuit, sport or study, as a youngster, except poetry, riding and swimming: and though as a boy my verses were bad enough, I believe I may say that I was far from bad at the two latter. Also being bred by the sea I was a good cragsman, and am vain to this day of having scaled a well-known cliff on the South coast, ever before and ever since reputed to be inaccessible. Perhaps I may be forgiven for referring to such puerilities having read (in cuttings from more than one American journal) bitterly contemptuous remarks on my physical debility and puny proportions. I am afraid this looks like an echo of poor great Byron's notorious and very natural soreness about his personal defect, but really if I were actually of powerless and deformed body I am certain I should not care though all men (and women) on earth knew and remarked on it. I write all this rubbish because I really don't know what to tell you about myself. I suppose you do not require a Rousseau-like record of my experiences in spiritual or material emotions; and knowing as you do the dates and sequence of my published books you know every event in my life. . . . Yet I grew up a healthy boy enough and fond of the open air, though slightly built, and have never had a touch of serious illness in my life. As for the sea, its salt *must* have been in my blood before I was born. I can remember no earlier enjoyment than being held up naked in my father's arms and brandished between his hands, then shot like a stone from a sling through the air, shouting and laughing with delight, head foremost into the coming wave. . . . But this is enough of infancy: only it shows the *truth* of my endless passionate returns to the sea in all my verse.

'As my antitheism has been so much babbled about, perhaps I may here say what I really do think on religious matters. Having been as child and boy brought up a quasi-Catholic, of course, I went in for that as passionately as for other things (e.g. well-nigh to unaffected and unashamed ecstasies of adoration when receiving the Sacrament); then when this was naturally stark dead and buried, it left nothing to me but a turbid nihilism: for a Theist I never was; I always felt by instinct and perceived by reason that no man could conceive of a *personal* God except by brute Calibanic superstition or else by true supernatural revelation; that a natural God was the absurdest of all human figments; *because* no man could by other than apocalyptic means – i.e. by other means than a violation of the laws and order of nature *conceive* of any other sort of divine person than man with a difference –

man with some qualities intensified and some qualities suppressed – man with the good in him exaggerated and the evil excised. This, I say, I have always seen and avowed since my mind was ripe enough to think freely. Now of course this is the exact definition of every God that has ever been worshipped under any revelation. Men give him the qualities they prefer in themselves or about them. E.g. the God of the Christians is good for domestic virtue, bad for patriotic. Again, the God of the Greeks and Romans is not good for domestic (or *personal* in the Christian sense) virtues, but gloriously good for the patriotic. But we who worship no material incarnation of any qualities, no person, may worship the divine humanity, the ideal of human perfection and aspiration, without worshipping any God, any person, any fetish at all. Therefore I might call myself if I wished a kind of Christian (of the Church of Blake and Shelley), but assuredly in no sense a Theist. Perhaps you will think this is only clarified nihilism, but at least it is no longer turbid.'[15]

After his return to London in February Swinburne soon fell ill again. On 20 May he wrote to Burne-Jones: 'I have been too seedy to write or see *any* visitor for upwards of a month. The Grand Inquisitor, Father God, tortures me with insomnia – and opiates drive me mad and leave me sick. . . . I have been constantly unable to hold a pen. I hope rather than trust you will be able to read this. I hope too you have got my "Essays" and "Songs of Two Nations"? that you are well – and that I shall see you before I leave town next week – for I shan't return in a hurry.'[16]

So he went back to his parents at Holmwood. But he had not been there long before he was laid up once more, this time with a sprained foot. 'I sprained it,' he tells Powell in July, 'in trying to climb and jump from a garden fence – rather schoolboyish at my grave and reverend time of life – and the consequence has been worse than twenty swishings. . . . I shall be anxious to know the upshot of your honoured parent's illness. If an all-wise Providence *should* see fit to remove him from this vale of tears to Abraham's bosom, I presume you will make a clean sweep of "the cousinhood" and celebrate your accession by such orgies as shall make Nant Eos a worthy rival in reputation to the Château de Lacoste – seat of the noble house of Sade. I wished earnestly that you and I had been boys again when the Yankee apostles came to Eton – shouldn't we have invested in eggs at any price and any risk!'[17] – which refers to the revival meeting held in a garden at Windsor by Moody and Sankey, the American evangelists, on 22 June, at which many Etonians and a few masters were present.

Early in August 1875 came the news of Edmund Gosse's marriage and Swinburne wrote to congratulate him. But Gosse's marriage as we have seen only revived for Swinburne the memory of 'the reverse experience which left my young manhood a barren stock' – that is, when he realized the impossibility of ever marrying his cousin Mary Gordon all hope of achieving a normal relationship left him.[18]

Most of August and the beginning of September were spent with Jowett at Great Malvern. There he began work on *Erechtheus*, 'a companion poem to Atalanta which I hope will turn out a more perfect original example of Greek tragedy than that was', he wrote to William Rossetti on 21 August. He went on: 'It is very simple in structure, and deals with only two "elementary" passions – that of child and parent, and that of patriotism. I wish to make it (in the lyric part) conform rigidly to the *musical* rule of Greek tragedy, which if I knew I certainly (like Milton before me) neglected when writing Atalanta, but which I now see to be perfectly in harmony with the natural genius of the English language, and capable (in the right hands) of the finest and newest effects in lyric verse. Jowett approves my scheme highly, and has helped me with some valuable hints from the classical or scholarly point of view, on which side I want to make this poem impregnable.'[19] Unfortunately, the result of this scholarly care was that *Erechtheus* came virtually stillborn. Gosse admits that though 'it may never have been found by the general reader the most interesting [of Swinburne's works] . . . it can scarcely be denied that in the general conduct of this tragedy he rises, in an altitude of moral emotion that he reaches nowhere else, to an atmosphere which few modern poets have even attempted to breathe'. One is tempted to say that it is an altitude at which Swinburne could not breathe either, for his genius was not suited to moral altitudes, even though the theme is human sacrifice, the sacrifice of a daughter by a father for the sake of Athens. Swinburne was annoyed when one reviewer mistook his play for a translation from Euripides, whereas, as he wrote to Gosse in 1876, 'a fourth form boy could see that as far as it can be said to be modelled after anybody it is modelled throughout after the earliest style of Aeschylus – the simple, three-parts-epic style of the Suppliants, Persians, and Seven against Thebes'.

On 30 August 1875, Swinburne wrote to Watts from Malvern to say that four days hence he was starting on 'a fortnight's tour in the Isle of Man on a scientific mission to discover by the rules of comparative anatomy whether all the other cats there are really on examination as tailless as the termination of my own spine – unlike that lost love of Burton's the beloved and blue object of his central African affections, whose caudal charms and simious seductions were too strong for the narrow laws of Levitical or Mosaic prudery which would confine the jewel of a man to the lotus of a merely human female by the most odious and unnatural of priestly restrictions'. In the event, owing to the illness of his 'intending companion' – probably Powell – he did not go to the Isle of Man, so that the question of tailless Manx cats had to be left in abeyance.

Instead he spent part of September at Southwold, Suffolk, 'on a coast', he wrote to William Rossetti on 26 September, 'which for four days I found as dull as any place can be to me where I have the sea, but on the fifth (this morning) I have found a place that would have delighted Shelley – a lake of fresh water only parted from the sea by a steep and thick pebble-ridge through which a broad channel has been cut in the middle a little above the lake, to let off the water in flood-time; half encircled to the north and west by an old wood of oaks and ash-trees, with a wide common beyond it sweeping sideways to the sea. It is so unutterably lonely that I thought instantly how like this now beautiful wood must be in winter to Dante's wood of suicides. I would not break a leafless bough there for anything.'[20] This place must have been the wood of sea-stricken, skeleton trees on Easton Broad, a long walk along the shore from Southwold, a haunted place. But curiously enough Swinburne heads his letters: 'South House, Southwold, Wangford'.

In October he wrote 'A Birth Song' for William Rossetti's newly-born daughter Olivia Frances Madox Rossetti – 'a hundred lines just scribbled and copied in time for post – the best I can do in default of any reply to my repeated invocations of the Genius of Blake, Hugo, or your sister – the triad of perfect baby-poets'. In another letter to William Rossetti of 5 November he writes of 'the fascinations of a baby' and his 'life-long delight in them'. Later in life, Swinburne was to write many jingles to babies, principally celebrating those he met during his walks across Wimbledon Common. Indeed, such was his fondness for babies that he found it difficult to keep from caressing them, much to the consternation of their nursemaids and mothers. When this month William Morris sent him his translation of *The Aenids of Virgil*, he wrote from Holmwood in reply: 'I mean to begin at once my first voluntary acquaintance with a Bard unbeloved of boyhood under your auspices. Whenever I have dipped into the book your version seems to me wonderful for grace and ease and strength. I wish you would give us a Homer, or at least an Odyssey: I am certain no poet ever was born who could do his country such service better or so well.' Morris took the hint and translated both the Iliad and the Odyssey.

In December Swinburne returned for a week or two to Great James Street and wrote affectionately to Burne-Jones, who had been unwell:

> My dear Ned,
>
> My book is done and I have the final proofs in hand. I want to read it to a few fellows one night next [this?] week or next – Would it be possible or safe – I fear hardly – for you to be present on the mildly festive and mainly literary occasion? If you *could* come you know there is not one fellow alive in the world that I should be *half* so glad to see, and that could make the evening so jolly to me. I *think* you will like Erechtheus. . . . I have been ten days in town, and prostrate six of them. But if you *can't* come to me, tell me when I may come to you, and I will, were it on my last leg or with my last penny (Pathos!).
>
> As I never see and so can't be said to have *you*, it seems to me I have not one single friend – to say *friend* – left in the world. It is rather hard, as I was so fond of my friends when I had any.

Burne-Jones evidently replied that he would come and Swinburne wrote again on 11 December: 'Please be here *before* eight as I want to begin reading then so as to be able to offer my audience an epilogue in the shape of a sangwitch and social (but moderate) glass, and discuss things. I think (as Sir Fretful Plagiary says of his play) I can "undertake to read you the whole from beginning to end in two hours", he says three and a half, "and allow time for the music between the acts." Only there are none. My love to Georgie and the kids.'

As a matter of fact, Swinburne sometimes subjected his friends to four hours' reading until midnight. Gosse has given an amusing account of such occasions: 'When he came back from the country to town he was always particularly anxious to recite or read aloud his own poems. In doing this he often became very much excited, and even, in his overwhelming sense of the movement of the metre, would jump about the room in a manner somewhat embarrassing to the listener. . . . His delivery, especially of his own poetry, was delightful as long as he sat quietly in his seat. His voice, which was of extraordinary beauty, "the pure Ashburnham voice", as his cousin explains to me, fell monotonously, but with a flute-like note which was very agreeable, and the pulse of the rhythm was strongly yet delicately felt. I shall never forget the successive evenings on which he read "Bothwell" aloud in his lodgings, in particular one on which Edward Burne-Jones, Arthur O'Shaughnessy, P. B. Marston, and I sat with him at his round marble-topped table – lighted only by candles in two giant candlesticks of serpentine he had brought from the Lizard – and heard him read the magnificent second act of the tragedy. He surpassed himself in vigour and melody of utterance that night. But sometimes, in reading, he lost control of his emotions, the sound became a scream, and he would dance about the room, the paper fluttering from his finger-tips like a pennon in a gale of wind.'

It was, however, in his recitation of 'The Triumph of Time' that he excelled himself – 'a poem which Swinburne deliberately impressed upon me', says Gosse, 'and doubtless upon other friends as well, as being, in a very particular sense, a record of personal experience. . . . Swinburne seemed to achieve, or to go far towards achieving, an entirely novel and original form of expression. His whole body shook with passion, his head hung on one side with the eyes uplifted, his tongue seemed burdened with the weight of the syllables, and in the concentrated emphasis of his slow utterance he achieved something like the real Delphic ecstasy, the transfiguration of the Pythia quivering on her tripod. It was surpassingly strange, but it was without a touch of conscious oddity or affectation. It was a case of poetic "possession", pure and simple.'[21]

It was from about 1875 that Swinburne began to suffer from moods of deep depression, which alternated with manic high-spirits. 'He did not know fatigue,' Gosse tells us, 'his agility and brightness were almost mechanical. . . .

He required very little sleep, and occasionally when I have parted from him in the evening after saying "good-night", he simply sat back in the deep sofa in his sitting-room, his little feet close together, his arms against his side, folded in his frock-coat like a grasshopper in its wing-covers, and fallen asleep, apparently for the night before I could blow out the candles and steal forth from the door. . . . Swinburne seemed to me to divide his hours between violent cerebral excitement and sheer immobility, mental and physical. He would sit for a long time together without stirring a limb, his eyes fixed in a sort of trance, only his lips shifting and shivering a little, without a sound.'[22]

Swinburne frequently visited Gosse and his wife, to escape from the loneliness of his rooms. Quoting from his diary of those days, Gosse writes: 'Last night he arrived about 5 p.m.: he was waiting for me when I came back from the office. The maid had seen him into the study, brightened the fire and raised the lamp, but although she left him cosily seated under the light, I found him mournfully wandering, like a lost thing, on the staircase. We happened to be quite alone, and he stayed for six hours. He was extremely bright and sensible at dinner, full of gay talk about early memories, his recollections of Dickens, and odd anecdotes of older Oxford friends, Jowett, Stubbs and the present Bishop of Ely (James Russell Woodford). Directly after dinner he insisted on seeing the baby, whom on these occasions he always kisses and worships on his knees, and is very fantastic over. When he and I were alone, he closed up to the fire, his great head bowed, his knees held tight together, and his finger-tips pressed to his chest, in what I call his "penitential" attitude, and he began a long tale, plaintive and rather vague, about his loneliness, the sadness of his life, the suffering he experiences from the slanders of others. . . . Swinburne said that a little while ago he found his intellectual energy succumbing under a morbid distress at his isolation, and that he had been obliged steadily to review before his conscience his imaginative life in order to prevent himself from sinking into despair. This is only a mood, to be sure; but if there be any people who think so ill of him, I only wish they could see him at these recuperative intervals. Whatever he may be elsewhere, in our household not a kinder, simpler, or more affectionate creature could be desired as a visitor. The only fault we find with him is that his little mournful ways drag painfully upon our sympathy.'[23] At other times, says Gosse, 'An extraordinary exhilaration accompanied his presence, something uplifted, extravagant, and yet unselfish.'

This is a very different figure from the gaily obscene and blasphemous Swinburne of the earlier years. The defiant obscenity decreased – but it did not vanish – with the growing maturity of the middle and later period (though Gosse says that he still had to pretend that there was no more wine in the house after Swinburne had had his first glass at dinner) and his poems become more plaintive, like 'The Forsaken Garden', written according to Gosse in March 1876.[24] The garden of East Dene is now only the ghost of a garden, where even the weeds that grew 'from the graves of its roses' now lie dead:

> The fields fall southward, abrupt and broken,
>   To the low last edge of the long lone land.
> If a step should sound or a word be spoken,
>   Would a ghost not rise at the strange guest's hand?
> So long have the grey bare walks lain guestless,
>   Through branches and briars if a man make way,
> He shall find no life but the sea-wind's, restless
>     Night and day.
>
> The dense hard passage is blind and stifled
>   That crawls by a track none turn to climb
> To the strait waste place that the years have rifled
>   Of all but the thorns that are touched not of time.
> The thorns he spares when the rose is taken;
>   The rocks are left when he wastes the plain.
> The wind that wanders, the weeds wind-shaken,
>     These remain.
>
> Not a flower to be pressed of the foot that falls not;
>   As the heart of a dead man the seed-plots are dry;
> From the thicket of thorns whence the nightingale calls not,
>   Could she call, there was never a rose to reply.
> Over the meadows that blossom and wither
>   Rings but the note of a sea-bird's song;
> Only the sun and the rain come hither
>     All year long.

It is one of Swinburne's most desolate poems, and it faithfully mirrors his emotional condition at this time, when he wrote to John Churton Collins in March 1876 of 'the dull monotonous puppet-show of my life, which often strikes me as too barren of action or enjoyment to be much worth holding on to'.

Nevertheless it was during February, while he was at Holmwood, that Swinburne produced his magnificent Villon translations, which appeared two years later (with omissions) in *Poems and Ballads, Second Series.* 'In the last three days I have translated five whole ballads from Villon,' he wrote to Watts on 8 February, 'and a bit of his text, preserving the order and number of rhymes (only three or four variations in the whole poem), which makes it a considerable feat in metre to find an equal number of corresponding rhymes in English which fit the original sense as well as (of course) the metres. . . . One however which I translated yesterday is highly commendable for its moral tone, being an exhortation of an old whore to her younger sisters to make the best and utmost use of the their time "before their coin, like hers, falls out of currency". It is pleasing to observe the monitory and didactic tone which does not cease to animate the verse of this poet even after he had been (as his last editor maintains that he was) publically whipped as a libeller as well as a pimp and pickpurse. Certainly Maistre François was a credit to our profession, and atones for many Cowpers and Wordsworths. . . . I translated two (I might say three) whole ballads of F. V. yesterday in less time than it has taken me to write this letter off . . . I shall be very glad if you can find time to write to me a good long letter. I have *no* one to talk with here on anything of serious interest to me.' At the same time he had also begun a French essay on Blake for the *République des lettres.*

Swinburne spent most of 1876 at Holmwood. He had been denied a renewal of his British Museum reading room ticket and had written to Watts to ask if he could 'be the means of re-opening to me the now closed doors of the British Museum reading room, without sacrifices of self-respect or dignity on my part . . . it will be a great kindness to me and a great service and furtherance to my future work – especially on Elizabethan and Shakespearean matters, where I constantly feel the want of the B.M. library for purposes of reference: but of course I cannot on that account expose myself to be addressed like a schoolboy suspected of pilfering or convicted of carelessness'. Nevertheless, Swinburne's behaviour must have been outrageous for the Museum authorities, usually so tolerant of the eccentricities of scholars and pseudo-scholars, to have deprived him of his ticket. The reason for this deprivation can be guessed, and there must have been complaints from other readers.

In the postscript to a long letter to Nichol on 2 April 1876, Swinburne protests against the custom of labelling him by 'the always (I think) rather foolish and now long since obsolete word Pre-Raphaelite [which] was never applicable to any but the work of my earliest youth written at college, and has long ceased to be applicable (at least in the original sense) to the poetic work of my two elders [Rossetti and Morris] . . . I think for the sake of common accuracy it should now be disused'. Even so, Swinburne is still loosely classed with Rossetti and Morris as a Pre-Raphaelite poet.

In May Swinburne accompanied John Nichol to Guernsey and Sark, with whose beauty he was enchanted. 'I have seen on the whole the loveliest and wonderfullest thing I ever saw', he wrote to his mother from Guernsey on 15 May, ' – the island of Sark. Nichol and I went off at 3½ in a sailing boat, and after endless doublings and backings and shiftings of sail we dodged with our little boat in sideways between a crevice in the cliffs at 6½, and found ourselves in a little harbour, with a breakwater in miniature, landed – passed through a huge tunnel of arched rock – and were in front of a road winding up between two hills blazing with furse and all kinds of spring flowers, by which we walked up over hills and downs and tiny villages, through meadows and orchards in immeasurable variety of flower to the hotel. . . . There are superb precipices, hollow gullies, caves and tunnels of sea-rock, headlands and staircases of crag, and one awful pit which the tide enters at flood but into which you can look down at top from the summit almost of the cliff or side wall of the down: among all which we had a day and a half of the best scrambling I *ever* had in my life. . . . But everywhere the glory of flowers, and splendour of crags and cliffs and sea defy all words.'[25] This visit was productive in retrospect of 'The Garden of Cymodoce', the very ecstasy of verbosity.

Swinburne was back at Holmwood by the end of May. He embarrassed Gosse, on one of his visits to London, by proclaiming the beauties of Sark at the top of his voice late at night in the streets. In June Robert Buchanan, who had replied to Swinburne's pamphlet *Under the Microscope* with a poem 'The Monkey and the Microscope', brought an action for libel against the *Examiner* for publishing a letter on 11 December 1874 from Swinburne signed 'Thomas Maitland' in which he had referred to Buchanan as on a cruise 'in the Philippine islands in the steam-yacht Skulk, Captain Shuffleton'. Taylor, the proprietor of the *Examiner*, and Minto, the editor, at once took fright, revealed that Swinburne was the author of the letter and suggested that action should be taken against him alone. Fortunately, Buchanan's counsel was a former student of Jowett and had already met Swinburne and prevented Buchanan from prosecuting him. Meanwhile Swinburne received a subpoena on 19 June, having come up to town 'wishing to meet some friends'. Watts told him to 'make himself scarce for three weeks' in order not to have to appear in court as a witness, whereupon he hastily retired to Holmwood. As a result of his action Buchanan was allowed £150 damages instead of the £5,000 he had claimed and Watts advised Swinburne to make 'a graceful gesture' and bear part of the expenses of the trial. This Swinburne resolutely refused to do, especially after the shabby behaviour of Taylor and Minto.[26] The whole affair, coming at a time when he was in poor health, had worried him to a degree out of all proportion to its importance. As regards libel against himself, his attitude is shown in a dignified letter to Watts on 16 April: 'if any insult is levelled at me in print of which, were it your own case, you would feel it due to yourself to take some kind of public notice . . . then and then only I trust you as my friend . . . to send me the printed attack on the spot, and advise me what steps to take in consequence. . . . But in any less serious case than this it seems to me by no means worth while for any one to trouble himself or his friend about the matter.'

By August Swinburne was once more in a very low state of health: 'A lady, at whose house he had spent the night, had, he said, sought to do him honour by filling his bedroom with great Japanese lilies in blossom, and the poet had wakened in the middle of the night in a delirium rousing the household with his shrieks.'[27] Swinburne said that he had been poisoned by the flowers – a curious episode which evidently gave him the idea for the death of Lesbia Brandon, who slowly poisons herself with flowers and eau-de-cologne. Swinburne was fond of telling this story to his friends, though he refers to the episode soberly enough in a letter to Gosse of 17 October: 'I don't know whether you heard from any quarter of my being accidentally poisoned some months since by the perfume of Indian lilies in a close bedroom – which sounds romantic, but was horrible in experience, and I have not yet wholly recovered the results or regained my strength.' To the painter J. W. Inchbold he is more explicit. 'I am very sorry to hear that you have been ill,' he wrote on 25 October, 'so have I been for some time in consequence of a strange accident – sleeping in a room where there were great Indian lilies whose tropical prussic-acid perfume left me half mad and half dead with sickness.' On 28 October to John Nichol: 'Ever since I most involuntarily solved the question I have heard debated (and denied for example by our old friend W. B. Scott, 16 or more years since, à propos of an incident in my first book, *The Queen Mother*) whether a man could be actually poisoned by perfumes – as I was sleeping in a room with a large India lily in full flower near the bed, recalling Hawthorne's story, of which you expressed such admiration to me once at Oxford in the years before the Flood, "Rappuccini's Daughter", to whom the lady at whose house I was then a visitor must assuredly have been akin – ever since this possibly romantic but certainly unpleasant experience of a literally flower-strewn approach to the door of delirium if not of death, I have been but a rag of unmanned manhood, barely able to read or write or think consecutively. However, I am slowly beginning to recover some little cerebral and digestive power.'[28] *Fleurs du Mal*, indeed!

During 1876–77 the so-called 'Eastern Question' – that is, the Turkish atrocities in Bulgaria and the Russian threat to intervene in support of her Pan-Slavic policy – had divided public opinion into two mutually hostile camps. The Tory prime minister Disraeli supported Turkey, motivated by the perennial British fear of the Russian threat to India, and the Liberal Gladstone – 'inebriated by the exuberance of his own verbosity', as Disraeli remarked – took Bulgaria's side with his campaign against the Turkish atrocities. Most of Swinburne's friends took sides in the great debate, William Morris and Burne-Jones becoming very active in the anti-Turk campaign on the Liberal–Radical side. Morris wrote an impassioned letter to the *Daily News* against the 'Turkish thieves and murderers' and an open letter 'To the working men of England', and helped to organize public meetings of protest against the government's attitude. To Swinburne, though it grieved him to be on the opposite side to Morris and Jones, the idea of all these progressive people identifying themselves with a lot of 'Bulgars' appeared irresistibly comic, and he celebrated the occasion with his 'Ballad of Bulgarie', directed against John Bright, Ruskin and Carlyle. He also wrote a pamphlet, *A Note of an English Republican on the Muscovite Crusade*, which developed into a vituperative attack on Carlyle as 'the most foul-mouthed man of genius since the death of Swift'. Swinburne, who had not forgotten

Carlyle's description of him as 'standing up to his neck in a cesspool, and adding to it', now deliberately outdid Carlyle himself in foulness of abuse.

He wrote to Watts on 8 December 1876: 'Although I do not remember whether in our many talks on English humorists we ever discussed Fielding together, yet I am confident enough of your fellow-feeling with me on the score of that great man . . . to tell you my reply to an application from Jones (E.B.) enclosing a circular of the philo-Bulgarian conference to be held at St James's Hall – viz. that this outbreak of English sympathy with the suffering Bulgars, especially in quarters where I had never been able to find or awaken a spark on behalf of Italy, Hungary or Poland, reminded me irresistibly of the query addressed so pertinently to her Lord by the chaste Mrs Jonathan Wild, *née* Letitia Snap – "But methinks Mr Wild, I would fain know, Why Bitch?" In like manner, I said, I could not but feel tempted to put on this occasion as modest and pertinent a query – Why Bulgar? I would give anything by the by for the hand of a great caricaturist at this moment, that I might draw that gallant crusader, the loyal knight Sir John Bright (whose very name makes one "drop into poetry", as you see, unawares) in the broad-brimmed basnet of his Plantagenet forefathers, laying his good lance in rest (with "Ha! Beauséant. St. John for Birmingham and Our Blessed Lady of Cotton!") in defence of the Holy Sepulchre against miscreant worshippers of false Mahound. . . . Well, thank Somebody (as Clough says), no one ever could or can call me a Radical in the English sense of the word.'[29]

To Churton Collins he wrote on 11 December, 'I have sent (but this is a *dead* secret, which I [have] confided as yet to no soul alive) a ballad of chivalry to the *Pall Mall Gazette* without my name – subject "The Quest of Sir Bright de Brummagem" against the heathen dogs who worship Mahomet and Termagent, and pollute the Holy Sepulchre of his (Sir B.'s) Blessed Lord. I wonder if they will put it in!':

> The gentle knight, Sir John de Bright
>   (Of Brummagemme was he)
> Forth would he prance with lifted lance
>   For love of Bulgarie.
> No lance in hand for other land
>   Sir Bright would ever take,
> For wicked works, save those of Turks,
>   No head of man would break. . . .
> 'Twas not for love of Cant above
>   Nor Cotton's holy call,
> But a lance would break for Bulgary's sake,
>   And Termagent should sprawl.
> The mother-maid, Our Lady of Trade,
>   His spurs on heel she bound. . . .

Sir John is joined by 'Sir William the Wise, the People's knight' (Gladstone) and 'old Sir Thomas the bold, A Chelsea knight was he' (Carlyle). But wise Sir William thinks 'it better ere weather were wetter' to return home, for:[30]

> I don't mind writing – I do mind fighting,
>   (So spoke the bold Sir Bill)
> He don't mean outing – he does mean spouting
>   Like some in Denmark's ill.[31]
> We don't mean hitting – we don't mind spitting –
>   For Turks have swords to kill
> Which I deeply regret should so happen – but yet
>   'Tis true it gives me pain
> For the Greek will not fight (which is far from right)
>   And the Russian has all to gain
> And I think it were vulgar to cheat a poor Bulgar
>   With offers of help in vain.

But the *Pall Mall* did not 'put it in' and Swinburne tried other papers in vain. He even thought of having it printed as a 'fly sheet in the old black-letter ballad fashion'. Meanwhile the whole country was in turmoil. The government did nothing even when Russia invaded Bulgaria and sent her fleet to the Dardanelles. Turkey was forced to accept a semi-autonomous Bulgaria and Swinburne relieved his feelings in his sonnets, 'The White Czar'.

At the same time he was roused to indignation by the letters and despatches in the Press in favour of Governor Eyre of Jamaica, who had suppressed a Negro revolt in 1865 with a cruelty which in Swinburne's eyes eclipsed any Turkish atrocities in Bulgaria – though there was not much to choose between them. 'I trust I need not once more assure you that I am not conventionally but sincerely grateful to you for every fresh instance of friendly and considerate forethought on your part,' he wrote to Watts on 12 December, 'but I am really not less than amazed at the suggestion that I or any man on earth could be accused of libelling conduct which made the letters and despatches from Jamaica for a month or more read exactly and literally like a series of connected extracts from the very worst chapters of *Justine*. If you remember anything of the hideous and beastly details (*not*, mind you, charges brought by enemies, but gloatingly and boastfully avowed by the perpetrators) you cannot but admit that these facts did actually rival in open daylight (as to cruelty and brutality and unmanliness) the delirious dreams of the Marquis de Sade in solitary confinement. This is neither matter of rhetoric nor (were that possible to me on this subject) of jest or irony – it is a matter of evidence from newspapers and blue-books. No word of mine on the matter is a quarter, a tenth part, as strong as what was most justly said at the time (in the House of Commons and elsewhere) by Mill and many others: but – pray take especial notice of this point, for I think it material to my case – after I had written what I did in the heat of composition, remembering how much time had elapsed and thinking it possible but not probable that my memory might unconsciously have exaggerated the horrors, I looked up an article by Dr Sandwith (of Kars) in the Fortnightly Review for July 1st, 1871, pages 38 and 39 especially, to which if you can possibly find time I would beg you to refer, as I did before I could send off my MS. Assuredly I never imagined (nor, I hope, is it necessary to add that such an idea would in no wise have emboldened me, as your words would almost seem to suggest, to venture on charges or allusions from which I should otherwise have shrunk – an imputation so grievously dishonourable that I cannot imagine you to have perceived that it was naturally implied by the wording of your explanation as to the legal status of Mr Eyre) – I never imagined that that person's former position in the public service which he disgraced for ever in the sight of history and the world, or the publicity of his trial afterwards, would or could or ought to disable him from bringing an action against Mr Mill (were he happily alive), Dr Sandwith, or myself. When Landor publicly (in a letter to the Examiner) denounced and impeached an uncle (by marriage) of my own as a "torturer and murderer" (*totidem verbis*) of the people he was sworn and "enthroned" as Governor to protect – and that on charges, however grave, light as a feather when set against the avowed and vaunted atrocities of Eyre and his gang – no countercharge of libel was ever (as far as I know) talked or thought of. I do trust, I must say, that you have not struck out of my text the reference to "English Bashi Bazouks under the eye of an English Pasha", without which my whole rejoinder to Carlyle is simply nullified or stultified; but I must confess that I shall be very uneasy and uncomfortable till I do know exactly to a letter what changes or cancels have been made. I did not follow Dr Sandwith in quoting the loathsome detail about the "whips made of piano-wire" being "first tried on the backs of women" and showing "that their skins were easier cut [*sic*] than those of males," for very shame and physical nausea; but now I could almost wish I had.'[32]

It is, at least, cheering to discover that when it was a question of actual, as distinct from theoretical, Sadism, of further crimes of the white race against the black, Swinburne is revolted and not afraid to express his indignation publicly, though many 'respectable' people among those with shares in the sugar plantations of Jamaica commended Eyre for his 'firmness' in dealing with the situation. After all, that is how the empire was maintained.

CHAPTER TEN

# 1877–79
# THE LONELY YEARS

Admiral Swinburne died on 4 March 1877, and the family went to Bonchurch, Isle of Wight, for the funeral. By his will his property was divided equally among his five surviving children. Algernon, as he wrote to Watts from Holmwood on the sixteenth had: '£5000 in a lump, and (at my mother's death, by the will – but she says she will make them over to me at once, on her removal from this place, which she intends to sell) the books (including mss, prints &c. of historic interest and value) which are counted as equivalent to £2000 more – which additional sum in money is accordingly left to my brother. . . . There is for one thing some private correspondence (one letter of importance, and two or three notes) of Charles II; both in exile and after his Blessed Restoration, which has never been published and is I suppose of some considerable value. By the light of the later notes from Whitehall we can trace day by day – or rather night by night – the progressive career of prosperous Virtue in the adorable person of Mistress Barbara Palmer, successively Countess of Castlemaine and Duchess of Cleveland – the said notes desiring the proper officer to make out the respective warrants for the elevation to those several dignities (first an earldom and then a dukedom) of the appropriately or inappropriately christened Mr Roger Palmer, the happy and high-minded consort of that meritorious lady, who thus gave such indisputable proof that a virtuous woman is a coronet to her husband at least, if not a crown; and of whom there is a fine accompanying print in hunting costume as – Diana! yes – by all the virginities of Olympus, in the character of Artemis her very self, and looking I must say so royally beautiful that my youthful virtue was never (since I can remember it) able to resist the sight of that engraving; nor, to my great delight, could the white hairs and philosophic austerity of Jowett, who could not but relax into admission of her splendid imperious charm when I showed him the print and invoked (successfully) an admiration which he would accord to no other member of the Stuart seraglio. . . . Among some thousand other prints of the period, containing we may suppose the likeness of some few hundreds among her fancy men, there is a capital one of Jacob Hall the rope-dancer – *not*, I grieve to say, in the character of Endymion. And O there is *such* a (coloured) miniature engraving of the serviceable and estimable Mr Chaffinch, the chubbiest and most cherubic of all fat and fortunate pimps! plumpest of possible pandars, as poor old Villon according to his own report must have been the most lank and lamentable to look on. . . . Over this also the translator of Plato relaxed into a beaming smile and chuckled – as indeed no one could help doing, it is such an ideal autotype of the prosperous and perfect pimp.'

Swinburne mourned the death of his father:

> Whose sail went seaward yesterday from shore
> To cross the last of many an unsailed sea.

in 'Inferiae', dated 5 March 1877. Next day he wrote to Nichol, 'just a line to let my oldest and best friend know that on the day before yesterday my father died. Among many points of feeling and character that I like to think we have in common, I doubt if there is any stronger on either side than our *northerly* disinclination for many or effusive words on matters of this kind.'

By this time, as is shown by a letter of this month to Norman MacColl, editor of the *Athenaeum*, Swinburne had written and published 'The Sailing of the Swallow', which became the first canto of *Tristram of Lyonesse*. This attracted next to no notice from the English critics but produced an ecstatic letter from America, where it appeared in the New York *Independent*, from a Colonel Hayne – 'no Yankee, but a Southerner . . . a good soldier, I believe, and a fair poet'. Swinburne was very proud of this piece, which, he told MacColl, 'contains the best bit of description (a sunrise at sea) that I, or perhaps any poet going now (except of course the Master)' – that is, Victor Hugo – 'ever accomplished'. But, as a matter of fact, this description of the sunrise, which occupies two pages, is not nearly so successful as Tristram's description of King Arthur's court, or the king's unwitting incest with his sister Queen Morgause, or the love of Lancelot and Guenevere, nor as fine as the description of the storm which follows it. The sunrise is really what Browning called the whole poem, 'a fuzz of words'. One sighs for what Swinburne dismissed as 'the short-winded and artificial concision of Tennyson':

> the quick sea shone
> And shivered like spread wings of angels blown
> By the sun's breath before him; and a low
> Sweet gale shook all the foam-flowers of thin snow
> As into rainfall of sea-roses shed
> Leaf by wild leaf on that green garden-bed
> Which tempests till and sea-winds turn and plough;
> For rosy and fiery round the running prow
> Fluttered the flakes and feathers of the spray,
> And bloomed like blossoms cast by God away
> To waste on the ardent water; swift the moon
> Withered to westward as a face in swoon

Death-stricken by glad tidings: and the height
Throbbed and the centre quivered with delight
And the depth quailed with passion as of love,
Till like the heart of some new-mated dove
Air, light, and wave seemed full of burning rest,
With motion as of one God's beating breast.
   And her heart sprang in Iseult, and she drew
With all her spirit and life the sunrise through,
And through her lips the keen triumphant air
Sea-scented, sweeter than land-roses were,
And through her eyes the whole rejoicing east
Sun-satisfied, and all the heaven at feast
Spread for the morning; and the imperious mirth
Of wind and light that moved upon the earth,
Making the spring, and all the fruitful might
And strong regeneration of delight
That swells the seedling leaf and sapling man,
Since the first life in the first world began
To burn and burgeon through void limbs and veins,
And the first love with sharp sweet procreant pains
To pierce and bring forth roses; yea, she felt
Through her own soul the sovereign morning melt,
And all the sacred passion of the sun;
And as the young clouds flamed and were undone
About him coming, touched and burnt away
In rosy ruin and yellow spoil of day,
The sweet veil of her body and corporal sense
Felt the dawn also cleave it, and incense
With light from inward and with effluent heat
The kindling soul through fleshly hands and feet.

The significance of this passage lies, of course, not so much in the description of the sunrise, as in Iseult's awakening to womanhood, for which Tristram is responsible rather than the sun:

So as a fire the mighty morning smote
Throughout her, and incensed with the influent hour
Her whole soul's one great mystical red flower
Burst, and the bud of her sweet spirit broke
Rose-fashion, and the strong spring at a stroke
Thrilled, and was cloven, and from the full sheath came
The whole rose of the woman red as flame:
And all her Mayday blood as from a swoon
Flushed, and May rose up in her and was June.

To criticize such passages for lushness, imprecision and monotony is, perhaps, beside the point, since Swinburne is not really aiming at precise description but at general effect. As John D. Rosenberg has pointed out: 'Like Turner, too, Swinburne finds in the vast unindifferentiated sea the visible emblem of his genius, with its exultation of energy over form, visible nuance over discreet detail – except that one is always conscious of a precise *metrical* form with Swinburne. Swinburne's landscapes, like Turner's, abstract all the sharp, divisible aspects of nature into an elemental luminosity and motion. . . . No single word in a Swinburne poem quite corresponds to a given thing, just as no dab of paint on a Turner landscape corresponds to a natural object: the correspondence is always between the total configuration of nature. The adjective floating freely from its substantive in a Swinburne poem is equivalent to a blob of pigment that is neither sea nor sky, but all of these, in a Turner painting. Such an art prizes colour over outline, light over form, music over meaning.'[1]

Nevertheless, the brilliant haze of light and colour into which one gazes in a late-Turner seascape is dazzling, one's breath is taken away by the unexampled daring, and one has a sense of the overwhelming *power* of nature and the corresponding puny helplessness of man: one is, in a word, overcome by its greatness. The same cannot be said of Swinburne's description of the sunrise in *Tristram.* One is conscious here rather of a flaccid verbosity, a striving for effect and verbal inflation. Far better is his account of the drinking of the love potion, with which the first canto concludes:

> And all their life changed in them, for they quaffed
> Death, if it be death so to drink, and fare
> As men who change and are what these twain were.
> And shuddering with eyes full of fear and fire
> And heart-stung with a serpentine desire
> He turned and saw the terror in her eyes
> That yearned upon him shining in such wise
> As a star midway in the midnight fixed.
>    Their Galahault was the cup, and she that mixed;
> No other hand there needed, nor sweet speech
> To lure their lips together; each on each
> Hung with strange eyes and hovered as a bird
> Wounded, and each mouth trembled for a word;
> Their heads neared, and their hands were drawn in one,
> And they saw dark, though still the unsunken sun
> Far through fine rain shot fire into the south;
> And their four lips became one burning mouth.

In fact, as the poem proceeds there are many splendid passages. Swinburne had been working upon *Tristram* intermittently ever since writing the 'Prelude' in 1869–70. He then became absorbed in *Bothwell* and did not seriously recommence work upon it until after his move to Putney, when he completed the nine cantos between 1881 and 1882, and the complete poem finally appeared in the July of that year.

*Tristram of Lyonesse* is a finer achievement than Gosse allows. Whether it was because it was written principally during the *régime* of Theodore Watts, so that Gosse was no longer consulted about its progress, or whether he did not trouble to read all of it, he writes: 'There is a total want of energy in the narrative of *Tristram*; there are no exploits, no feats of arms; the reader, avid for action, is put off with pages upon pages of amorous hyperbolical conversation between lovers, who howl in melodious couplets to the accompaniment of winds and waves.'[2] The force of this criticism, in itself preposterous, depends upon what is meant by 'action' in this context. As a matter of fact, there are nearly as many exploits and feats of arms in Swinburne's version of the story as in the twelfth-century original, and considerably more 'action' and changes of scene than in Wagner's music-drama, which, a hundred years after its composition, still holds its audiences enthralled. One suspects that the principal reason for Gosse's dislike of the poem was the fact that Watts – 'the old horror of Putney', as he called him – regarded it 'as Swinburne's highest poetical effort', though, he adds, 'there was great alarm in Putney as to the reception of a poem so amatory in tone. Watts . . . feared a repetition of the scandal of 1866, and fancied that the second and fourth cantos might be challenged by the Public Prosecutor.' He therefore persuaded Swinburne to modify 'the dreaded effect of these passages' by the inclusion in the volume of 'nearly 200 pages of miscellaneous lyrics. Swinburne, who submitted to everything that Watts suggested, acquiesced in this arrangement, but took a humorous view of it. He told Lord Houghton (6 June 1882) that he should "expect the Mothers of England to rally round a book containing forty-five songs of innocence – lyrics on infancy and childhood." But there proved to be no cause for anxiety. The amatory complexion of *Tristram* was not objected to by anybody. What was objected to in the poem, alas! was its lack of vital interest.'[3] The number of editions through which the poem passed in the years immediately following its publication, however, scarcely indicate lack of interest on the part of the reading public, whose opinion of the work evidently differed widely from that of Edmund Gosse – who admits that Swinburne 'intended [it] to be the very top-stone of his poetical monument'.

Even though one would by no means go all the way with Ezra Pound in stigmatizing Gosse's *Life* as 'merely the attempt of a silly and pompous old man to present a man of genius',[4] his book, amusing and charming as it is, is at times both critically unsound and, as he seems to have felt himself, limited by a fundamental lack of comprehension of its subject. As he admits in his *Confidential Paper*: 'I find the greatest difficulty in describing what the matter with Swinburne was, because, as is obvious, the whole thing is obscure and unaccountable.' Gosse is referring, of course, to the poet's flagellation mania. But then Gosse did not belong, like Swinburne, to the highest circles of Victorian society, where such inclinations seem not to have been uncommon, and while writing the *Life of Algernon Charles Swinburne* had to contend with the violent opposition of both Mrs Disney Leith and Isabel Swinburne, who informed him that if he published anything 'unpleasant' they would denounce his book as a pack of lies. It is only fair to say that his difficulties as a biographer were formidable.

By March 1877 Swinburne was already making plans to live in London 'rather more than less . . . than I have done of late years', as he wrote to Watts on the twenty-fourth of the month: 'My mother says she wants me always to consider her house my home – and so in a sense I naturally shall, wherever and whenever she may fix it; but of course I shall not regularly live with her, as my sisters and my brother will continue to do. It is pleasant to think that one or two – especially pleasant, I will frankly say, to think that you yourself – would miss me or feel any want if I were to be cut off from the society of my friends in London.' He is also planning an essay for the *Athenaeum* on Villon, incorporating all his translations 'from that "poet and pimp" . . . indicating by asterisks such lines and passages only as MacC. really would not print under the shadow of the Society for the Secret Incubation of Vice'.[5]

Since 1875 Swinburne had been engaged in a close study of Shakespeare with a view to analysing his 'metrical progress . . . as traceable by ear and *not* by finger', as he had written to Gosse on 31 January of that year, 'and the general changes of tone and stages of mind expressed or involved in this change or progress of style. I need hardly say that I begin with a massacre of the pedants worthy of celebration in an Icelandic saga – "a murder grim and great". I leave the finger-counters and finger-casters without a finger to count on or an ass ear to wag.'[6] To John Morley he wrote: 'I am still engaged on the period where the influence of rhyme and the influence of Marlowe were fighting, or throwing dice, for the (dramatic) soul of Shakespeare. No one I believe has yet noted how long and hard the fight or the game was.' The initial stages of this study appeared in May 1875 in the *Fortnightly Review* and was harshly criticized by the 'pedants'; a second instalment appeared in the same journal in January 1876, in which Swinburne discussed the problem of the date and authority of *Henry VIII*, particularly Spedding's views which had been endorsed by Tennyson and taken up by the New Shakespeare Society, founded by Furnivall. In February he wrote a burlesque 'Report of the Proceedings on the First Anniversary Session of the Newest Shakespeare Society' which appeared in the *Examiner* for 1 April – an amusing skit on the methods of the disintegrators, which he later reprinted as an appendix to *A Study of Shakespeare* (1879). Not surprisingly the New Shakespeare Society was infuriated and won the unremitting enmity of Professor Furnivall, whom Swinburne amused himself by ridiculing and baiting in the columns of the Press for years. This controversy became more and more personal and undignified until Furnivall finally addressed Swinburne as 'Pigsbrook', to which Swinburne replied by addressing Furnivall as 'Brothelsdyke'. On his side, Swinburne proved to be a formidable adversary and seems to have thoroughly enjoyed exercising his unrivalled vituperative powers and sense of farce, provoked by what he persisted in calling Furnivall's 'New Shakespeare'.

Swinburne was back in his Great James Street rooms by May 1877. He had for some time past been occupying himself with an essay on the novels of Charlotte Brontë, partly with the aim of undermining the reputation of the more popular George Eliot, whose work he particularly disliked. He argued justly that Charlotte Brontë's claim to immortality rested firmly on *Jane Eyre* and *Villette*; *Shirley* he rejected, with some reason, as a failure, and he was one of the first to recognize the greatness of Emily Brontë's *Wuthering Heights*, which many people still regarded as a monstrosity. On his return to London he invited Gosse to attend a reading of the essay, which he finally expanded into a book.

Gosse records in his delightful diary: 'I duly arrived at 3 Great James Street about 8. Algernon was standing alone in the middle of the floor, with one hand in the breast of his coat, and the other jerking at his side. He had an arrangement of chairs, with plates and glasses set on a table, as if for a party. He looked like a conjuror, who was waiting for his audience. He referred vaguely to "the others", and said that while they delayed in coming, he would read me a new poem he had just finished called "In the Bay", which he said he should solemnly dedicate to the spirit of Marlowe. He brushed aside some glasses and plates, and sat down to read. The poem was very magnificent, but rather difficult to follow, and very long. It took some time to read, and still no one came. As the evening was slipping away, I asked him presently whether the reading of C. Brontë should not begin, whereupon he answered "I'm expecting Watts and Ned Burne-Jones and Philip Marston and – some other men. I hope they'll come soon." We waited a little while in silence, in the twilight, and then Swinburne said, "I hope I didn't forget to ask them!" He trotted or glided into his bedroom, and what he referred to there I don't know, but almost instantly he came out and said cheerfully, "Ah! I find I didn't ask any of those men, so we'll begin at once." He lighted his two great candlesticks of serpentine and started. He soon got tired of reading the essay, and turned to the delights, of which he never wearies, of his unfinished novel. He read two long passages, the one a ride over a moorland by night, the other the death of his heroine, Lesbia Brandon. After reading aloud all these things, with amazing violence, he seemed quite exhausted, and sank in a kind of dream into the corner of his broad sofa, his tiny feet pressed together, and I stole away.'[7]

Gosse tells us that Swinburne was very solitary at this time: 'His breakfast was served to him in his rooms, but he had to go out for his other meals, which he used to do with mechanical regularity. It was a curious spectacle to see him crossing Holborn on his way to the London Restaurant, which then existed at the corner of Chancery Lane. Swinburne, with hanging hands, and looking straight before him, would walk across like an automaton between the vans and cabs, and that he was never knocked down seemed extraordinary.' Lord Haldane told Gosse that he happened to go into the London Restaurant one day in 1877: 'When he had given his order for luncheon, the waiter leaned down and whispered, "Do you see that gentleman, Sir?" Haldane then perceived a little gentleman sitting bolt upright at a table by himself, with nothing before him but a heaped-up dish of asparagas and a bowl of melted butter. His head, with a great shock of red hair round it, was bent a little to one side, and his eyes were raised in a sort of unconscious rapture, while he held the asparagas, stick by stick above his face, and dropped it down as far as it would go. "That's the poet Swinburne, Sir!" the waiter said, "and he comes here on purpose to enjoy our asparagas."'[8] Stranger still, Swinburne's rapture, it is hardly too far-fetched to suppose, may have been partly due to the fact that he felt as though he were swallowing snakes, which, as we know, always had a peculiar fascination for him.

At Great James Street, Swinburne had among his favourite possessions 'a collection of precious glass, a wonderful mosaic table-top, a swinging pier-glass, before which [he] would perform a sort of solemn dance, and the famous serpentine candlesticks. . . . He was accustomed to draw the particular attention of visitors to each of them in turn, like a showman, saying of the table-top, "Great God, how beautiful it is!" or of the candlesticks, "Lovely! lovely!" with a strong indrawing of the breath.' Also he possessed still the print of Orsini, which had adorned his Oxford rooms, and 'though it hung much above his head, he would jump up and try to kiss it'.[9] He was very hospitable and entertained his particular friends here rather frequently, but these feasts were, says Gosse, 'apt to be agitating affairs'.

As usual, Swinburne's health soon declined in London, and it is not always easy to decide whether his bouts of influenza, sore throats and liver trouble were due to his 'intemperate habits' or whether he actually succumbed to the smoky London atmosphere. After all, no seagull can hope to feel at home or to be well for long in Holborn. By June 1877 the monotonous complaints of ill-health began once more. Swinburne had a particular aversion to Zola's *L'Assommoir*, that frightful study of drunkenness, which was being serialized at this time in Catulle Mendès's short-lived *République des lettres*, and he wrote a long, pontifical letter to the *Athenaeum* saying that he was disgusted to find his own name included in the list of contributors to that periodical alongside Zola's, even when he was not a contributor: 'What in the name of common sense, of human reason, is it to us, whether the author's private life be or be not comparable only, for majestic or for infantile purity, to that of such men as Marcus Aurelius or St. Francis of Assisi, if his published work be what beyond all possible question it is – comparable only for physical and moral abomination to such works as, by all men's admission, it is impossible to call into such a court as the present, and there bring them forward as the sole fit subjects of comparison; for the simple and sufficient reason, that the mention of their very names in print is generally, and not unnaturally, considered to be of itself an obscene outrage on all literary law and prescription of propriety? . . . To transcribe the necessary extracts would for me – I speak seriously, and within bounds – would for me be physically impossible. For the editor of any known publication in England to print them would be morally impossible. But this much, I think, it is but proper and necessary to say of them. They are divisible into two equally horrible and loathsome classes. Under the one head I rank such passages as deal with physical matters which might almost have turned the stomach of Dean Swift. The other class consists of those which contain such details of brutality and atrocity practised on a little girl, as would necessitate the interpolation of such a line as follows in the police report of any and every newspaper in London – "The further details given in support of the charge of cruelty were too revolting for publication in our columns." '

And this was written by the self-confessed disciple of de Sade and the author of *Les Abîmes* – not to mention *The Flogging Block*! – which fortunately still remains unpublished. But his letter must be taken not so much as deliberate hypocrisy, as yet another example of a remarkable capacity for self-delusion. Awakening next morning from a solitary drinking bout, Swinburne would invariably attribute its unpleasant effects to the cucumber and lobster he had eaten the previous evening, not to the brandy taken afterwards. But Swinburne as upholder of propriety had certainly cast himself in a new role, which can hardly at this date be attributed to the influence of Theodore Watts. As far as his own work was concerned, however, he was capable of a remarkable degree of objectivity and self-criticism. Lafourcade has shown[10] that the articles by 'Herbert Harvey' in the *République des lettres*, which included studies of his own poems and of Blake and Heinrich von Kleist are, considered on stylistic grounds alone, almost certainly by Swinburne himself. We know that he had written his 'Notes on Blake' for this magazine and that it did not appear under his own name. We know, too, that Herbert was the name he gave himself in *Lesbia Brandon*, which he was still writing at this time. In the essay on his own work, he modestly compares himself unfavourably with Baudelaire.

On 8 June Swinburne wrote to Lord Houghton: 'I *am* still in town, but far too full of influenza to venture out yet at night. Ever since being drenched to the skin and deeper yet a week ago, I have been deafer than a post with a grain of self-respect left in its wood could possibly submit to be called. . . . I have amused one evening of my rheumy solitude with pitching into that brute beast E. Zola's damnable dunghill of a book. . . . The foul thing for six months together deprived *La Républiqe des lettres* of the services of one of the most valuable members of its staff: for (as I say in my Note to the *Athenaeum*) I, no more than the Master, could have "allowed anything of mine to appear in public cheek by jowl with a chapter of L'Assommoir." No other book – "bar none" – ever made me feel quite physically unwell – out of order. This one did – through pure disgust and horror. Have you read any of "Le Tombeau des Lutteurs" now coming out? I can't make head or tail of the ultimate meaning or bearing of the story – though one "lutteur" is unmistakeable, and the finest instance of photography by hell-fire (accurate by very intensity of hatred) I ever saw. And the night chez "la Scorpione", as described by her servants who had played the spy on their swell lady's Titanic recreations of the flesh is superb and quite new in the way of "the higher sensualism" – a giantess violating the sons of men. I know now, what I thought before, that Léon Cladel is a man of genius. . . . Excuse this chatter on the latest French novelists, but my head is rather full of them – for liking and loathing.'[11] In regard to Zola, at least, Swinburne was in tune with contemporary Victorian taste, for when Vizitelly published translations of his novels he was prosecuted for obscenity.

Early in August Swinburne 'overtaxed his convalescent strength' by attending a 'delightful evening' at Whistler's and was, as a result, confined to bed once more with a sore throat and diarrhoea. At one of Whistler's gatherings when no drink was served, but where everyone smoked, Swinburne distinguished himself by screaming out at the top of his voice, 'Moi, je ne jamais fume pas, mais je BOIS!'[12] Nevertheless, he accepted another invitation to dinner with Whistler to meet his cousin Bertram Mitford.

On 25 August Swinburne's mother wrote to his landlady Mrs Magill, asking if her son had left town, since she had received no reply to her last two letters and was feeling anxious. Early in September, however, he returned to Holmwood on a short visit, but was back in town by the middle of the month, when he wrote a letter of outstanding interest to Wemyss Reid, who had just edited a volume of Charlotte Brontë's letters: 'The only reference (if you will allow me to mention it) in your book which seemed to indicate a different point of view from my own was the passage in which you seem to deprecate the tone, if not to deprecate the merit, of "Wuthering Heights". Many years ago I lent a copy of that book to a lady of the class described in it – daughter of a Westmorland "statesman" or small gentleman-farmer living on his own land – warning her that though I liked it very much I knew that people in general called it "terrible" &c. &c. She returned it to me, after reading it through, with the remark that (so far from the incidents being impossible – as the cockney critics said – and say) she had known wilder instances of lawless and law-defying passion and tyranny, far more horrible than any cruelty of Heathcliff's in her own immediate neighbourhood. One of them, which even the Titaness Emily Brontë would have shrunk from telling in print, was the Cenci story done over again by a "statesman", who having bullied his wife to death was left alone in the farm with a beautiful daughter, whom he used with horrible brutality – and his character was such that all the neighbours said it was monstrous that the wretched girl should be left alone in the house with him – but nobody would come forward and "bell the cat" – and the ending of it all was that she was seen late one evening flying out of the house, with all her clothes disordered, and (as my informant said) evidently raving mad, towards the river Eden, which has thereabouts (as I know from boyish experience) some deep pools, and was fished out dead next morning. And I knew one of the women who for charity's sake went to nurse and sit up with the horrible old father – and said "she never had imagined anything so unutterably dreadful as that death bed" – and, if I remember rightly, that he raved for three days and nights before death came to release him and rid the world of him. Now, seeing that Emily Brontë was a tragic poet, and reared in the same degree of latitude which bred this humbler version of the "Cenci", I cannot think that anything in her book is at all excessive or unjustifiable. And, with all its horrors, it is so beautiful! but I must not get off into fresh rhapsodies about that "dreadful book".'[13]

Such a letter is further evidence of how much nearer Swinburne sometimes is to us in his admirations and critical opinions than to his contemporaries. For instance, who, unless they had read *Love's Cross-Currents*, would guess his admiration for Laclos and Stendhal? The Goncourts record a conversation with Oscar Wilde in which Wilde said that the only Englishman who had read Balzac 'à l'heure actuelle était Swinburne'.[14]

Swinburne was still 'in bed under the doctor's hands', as he tells John Nichol in a letter of 20 December 1877, though he adds that he will be delighted to join Nichol in Scotland as soon as he can face the journey – but 'travelling by steam (land or sea) usually finishes me when already at all disabled'.

A week later, on 27 December, we find poor Lady Jane once more writing to Mrs Magill to find out whether her son is ill or not, and enclosing a letter for her to give to Algernon, which she hesitates to send to him direct. But on 8 January next year, he writes to Nichol: 'I have had a very bad time in the way of health lately – about as bad as on the Guernsey steamer, though I am not conscious of having done anything to earn the infliction, and of course I have had torrents of letters, bills, bothers of all kinds, to flood and overwhelm me on the rare days when I have been able to attend to anything. My papers have got in consequence into such an unspeakable mess that I can't find any later note of yours than of December 8th. . . .

'A presentation of Browning's *Agamemnon* was the last straw that broke the camel's back. I wrote a line of thanks, and went straight to bed. It is beyond belief – or caricature. Some devil possesses him when he touches anything Hellenic. Have you seen FitzGerald's translation or paraphrase?

It seems to me as bad from the exactly opposite point of view. Why can't they let Aeschylus alone and stick to Euripides?

'Of course, as a rational being, you are coming to London before the end of next month, when the Grosvenor Gallery shuts, and there will be an end of the most wonderful and glorious exhibition of drawings ever beheld on "this God's earth". The Raffaelles alone are enough to drive me mad with delight. I have a season ticket and intend (D.V.) to have my money's worth out of it during the next few weeks.'[15]

But such was the chaos reigning in Swinburne's 'chambers' that, as he tells his American friend P. H. Hayne on 15 January 1878, 'During my illness (not dangerous, but disabling me from much reading or writing for the time) my books, papers and parcels have got into such confusion that for two days I thought I had lost the most important MS. I have of unpublished prose and verse combined [*Lesbia Brandon*]. That has turned up, but many other things are yet missing. . . . They are pulling down and rebuilding all this quiet old quarter of London, *where hitherto even a poor poet of unpopular opinions* has been able to live peaceably in fine old chambers which Poe would have delighted to describe; so, as I know not what (if any) will be my next London address, I ask you to direct to me care Messrs Chatto & Windus, 75 Piccadilly, London, W.'

This has quite a contemporary ring for us. Even William Morris's office and workshops at Queen Square (which Swinburne could reach by turning left out of Great James Street into Great Ormond Street) were soon to be demolished and a red brick and terracotta hospital built on its site and on those of the other adjacent Queen Anne houses in the square. At the time of writing – though the majority of the fine Bloomsbury squares have been ruined – most of the eighteenth-century houses of Great James Street still stand, even though the finest of those in Great Ormond Street have already been demolished by the developers. While Swinburne has been judged to have been more or less unaware of his surroundings, he was evidently conscious of the comeliness of the house in which he lived, even though by now he was incapable of keeping his rooms in order. He had taken the precaution, however, of having what he had already written of *Lesbia Brandon* set up in type, as is shown by his letter to Andrew Chatto of 20 January, requesting him to send 'the remaining sheets of my unfinished novel, of which the MS. is still in your hands', by return of post. The same day he wrote to Watts requesting him to 'take Chatto by the throat (morally) and make him *at once* send me the proofs at least to Nichol's address, which is 14 Montgomerie Crescent, Kelvinside, Glasgow'.

Watts, as we know, had already in his possession several chapters of *Lesbia Brandon*, which he was apparently determined not to give up, for Swinburne's letter continues: 'You will pardon my bothering you once again about the missing chapters and fragments of my "novel" aforesaid – I could not possibly rewrite them, and as I certainly mean to complete the

9 D. G. Rossetti reading *Ballads and Sonnets* to Theodore Watts in the Green Dining-Room at Cheyne Walk, 1882, from the painting by H. Treffry Dunn

10 Summer at The Pines, from *At the Pines* by Mollie Panter-Downes, showing Swinburne at the upper, Watts-Dunton at the lower, window

book some day their loss or destruction would be a serious business to me. Especially I should regret the chapters respectively describing a woman of the demi-monde (a chapter most warmly and generously applauded by George Meredith) and an exiled Italian patriot, of whom Wm. Rossetti inaccurately remarked that he was the only adult of tolerably decent character in the whole book. It is the fate of all great moralists like myself to be misunderstood in this world. Happily (as the Very Rev. Richard Burton would say) we know that there is a reward laid up for us in another.

'Before ending, I must consult you on a rather delicate point of etiquette. Some years ago I was unwise enough to lend Miss Blind my copies of Matthew Arnold's earliest publications – "The Strayed Reveller" and "Empedocles on Etna" (and I think also the first series of his collected poems – a copy given me by a near relative now dead) – which I valued far beyond their money's worth as rarities (though this is now considerable), as books I had had when a boy and carried about in my pocket on holidays – and which are not now to be had for love or money. I mentioned this matter once to her with all possible delicacy, and she "was very sorry" they had not been returned – which is not very satisfactory. *Can* you suggest anything? but I fear the question will baffle even your resources. I would give anything in reason to have the books back – I have hardly any I should be so sorry to have lost. Except indeed the book so many years detained by Gabriel Rossetti, which I positively must and will have back, as I know *that* at all events cannot have been mislaid – Hope's "Costumes of the Ancients" (one volume, folio, boards, first edition) – which also was given me (when I was a child) by one of my family long since dead, of whom I have no other memorial. If you can at the same time rout out the three or four numbers of the "Oxford and Cambridge Magazine" (wanting to complete my set for binding) lent – not less unwisely – in the same quarter, I shall be thankful.'[16]

It is possible that Mathild Blind was keeping back Swinburne's books designedly, since Gosse tells us that in the years of his fame she would have been very glad to have married him, but that Swinburne, who was not particularly interested in her anyway, was unaware of it. From Glasgow, he wrote to Mrs Magill to post him several books he had left behind in his rooms, particularly 'one very small French book in a thin blue paper cover which I meant to put into my pocket'. If she cannot find it, he tells her to ask George Powell 'who I am sure will be kind enough to come and look for it . . . and tell him the book I want is the new one by Ernest Feydeau, whose name is at the top of the blue paper cover – and under it the title which I don't exactly remember ("Mémoires" I think it began with)'. The book was Feydeau's *Mémoires d'une demoiselle de bonne famille.*[17]

Swinburne spent a riotous month with Nichol in Glasgow, after which they both returned to London in February, Nichol to visit the Grosvenor Gallery. While in Glasgow, Swinburne prepared for the press his *Poems and Ballads, Second Series.* As Gosse remarks: 'No one would have guessed at the distracted and even alarming physical condition of the author from the serene volume,' which appeared in June this year, dedicated to Richard Burton, 'In redemption of an old pledge and in recognition of a friendship which I must always count among the highest honours of my life.' Swinburne was remembered at Glasgow University, as Alexander Hedderwick told Gosse, 'marching about the Quadrangle, very fashionably dressed, in a close-fitting long Melton coat of dark blue, and the neatest of little shoes, his top hat balanced on his great mop of hair, a marvel to our rough Glasgow students'.[18]

The new volume contained such splendid poems as 'The Forsaken Garden', 'Relics', 'At a Month's End', the Baudelaire elegy 'Ave Atque Vale', the great Villon translations, and the exquisite 'Ballade of Dreamland', with its refrain 'Only the song of a secret bird' which Swinburne said had come to him in sleep, like the first stanzas of 'A Vision of Spring in Winter', with its frail, melancholy final stanza:

The morning song beneath the stars that fled
  With twilight through the moonless air,
  While youth with burning lips and wreathless hair
Sang toward the sun that was to crown his head,
Rising; the hopes that triumphed and fell dead,
  The sweet swift eyes and songs of hours that were;
These may'st thou not give back for ever; these
  As at the sea's heart all her wrecks lie waste,
    Lie deeper than the sea;
But flowers thou may'st, and winds, and hours of ease,
  And all its April to the world thou mayst
    Give back, and half my April back to me.

In this valediction to his youth, with its echoes of 'The Triumph of Time', Swinburne's verse has become more delicate and subtle in movement, without the stridency or the galloping rhythms and relentless stamp of rhyme that sometimes almost stuns us in *Poems and Ballads, First Series.* The 'roses and raptures of vice', however cerebral they may have been, are, he is aware, things of the past, though the gentler pleasures of life remain to be enjoyed, all passion spent. The book is full of 'glad ghosts', though there is underlying it a sense of tragic waste, as in 'A Wasted Vigil', in which the poet mournfully celebrates the one great, defeated passion of his life:

Last year, a brief while since, an age ago,
A whole year past, with bud and bloom and snow,
O moon that wast in heaven, what friends were we!
  Couldst thou not watch with me?

Old moons, and last year's flowers, and last year's snows!
Who now saith to thee, moon? or who saith, rose?
O dust and ashes, once found fair to see!
  Couldst thou not watch with me?

O dust and ashes, once thought sweet to smell!
With me it is not, is it with thee well?
O sea-drift blown from windward back to lee!
  Couldst thou not watch with me?

The old year's dead hands are full of their dead flowers,
The old days are full of dead old loves of ours,
But as a rose, and briefer born than she;
  Couldst thou not watch with me?

Could two days live again of that year,
One would say, seeking us and passing here,
*Where is she?* and one answering, *Where is he?*
  Couldst thou not watch with me?

Nay, these two lovers are not anywhere;
If we were they, none knows us what we were,
Nor aught of all their barren grief and glee.
  Couldst thou not watch with me?

Half false, half fair, all feeble, be my verse
Upon thee not for blessing nor for curse;
For some must stand, and some must fall or flee;
  Couldst thou not watch with me?

As a new moon above spent stars thou wast;
But stars endure after the moon is past.
Couldst thou not watch one hour, though I watch three?
  Couldst thou not watch with me?

The words are those of Christ to His disciples, who slept during the Agony in the Garden. But here, at any rate, no blasphemy is intended, for Swinburne's agony *was* in the forsaken garden.

Critics have for long agreed that, apart from *Atalanta in Calydon*, some unsurpassed lyrics in the first series of *Poems and Ballads*, 'Laus Veneris', 'The Triumph of Time', 'Anactoria', 'The Sundew', 'The Leper', 'The Garden of Proserpine', and parts of *Tristram*, *Poems and Ballads, Second Series* represents Swinburne's maturest achievement. What follows is largely a paler repetition of what has gone before, with occasional flashes of genius, as in 'A Nympholept', and the touching 'To a Seamew', to relieve the general dullness and monotony of verse that seems merely self-generating. The critic superseded the poet and Swinburne grew into the distinguished scholar and man of letters, the bibliophile of the last thirty years of his life at Putney. But by that time the fires of youth were extinct, and what the later poetry gained in subtlety of melody it lost in vitality.

As Housman remarked in his University College lecture on Swinburne: 'the first impression produced by his style, as it was in 1866, is one of great and overpowering richness. He seemed to have ransacked all the treasuries of language and melted the whole plunder into a new and gorgeous amalgam. In the poems of his later life his style was threadbare. It had not become austere: it was as voluble and diffuse as ever, but it had ceased to be rich and various. The torrent streamed on, but it streamed from an impoverished vocabulary.

'His triumphs are the development of the anapaestic measure and his use of the heroic couplet, as in "Anactoria", to which he imparts a fullness and richness and variety . . . of which one would never have supposed the couplet to be capable.'[19]

Even so, John D. Rosenberg has written in what is undoubtedly the best contemporary estimate of Swinburne: 'there are moments of astonishing strength in the late Swinburne. Much of "By the North Sea", more of the unknown "Evening on the Broads", all of "A Nympholept" defeats one's impulse to impose a curve of growth, flowering, and decline upon the actual pattern of his creativity. . . . Swinburne had a curious passion for monotony which was undoubtedly linked to his love of bleak monochromatic effects. Out of this love came his most powerful poetry; out of it also came whole poems too like his own description of the Dunwich coast: "Miles and miles, and miles of desolation!/Leagues on leagues on leagues without a change!" ' It was this love of monotony which made him content with thirty years of Putney and his daily unvarying routine. 'The death of development in Swinburne,' Mr Rosenberg concludes, 'may have been as large a loss to English poetry as the physical death of Keats.' Rosenberg shows that it is a mistake to regard Swinburne as merely a diffuse and rhetorical writer: 'I would praise him as the supreme master in English of the bleak beauty of little words.' And he cites the lines from 'Laus Veneris':

> Ah yet would God this flesh of mine might be
> Where air might wash and long leaves cover me,
> Where tides of grass break into foam of flowers,
> Or where the wind's feet shine along the sea.

There are far more poems of Swinburne's with this particular virtue than is generally realized. 'Swinburne is often censured for vagueness, but no one who has read his best poetry closely could ever accuse him of imprecision or carelessness with words.'[20] In one respect Swinburne is unrivalled, and that is in his creation of atmosphere.

There is, however, a relatively unknown poem which he wrote at Holmwood in July–August 1879, just before his mother sold the house and he moved to Putney. This is 'On the Cliffs', which appeared first in *Songs of the*

*Springtides*, a poem of subtle and incisive self-analysis. The poet stands on the cliffs in the evening listening to the song of the nightingale and the sea's monotonous surges, thinking once more of his youth:

> Between the moondawn and the sundown here
> The twilight hangs half starless: half the sea
> Still quivers as for love or pain or fear. . . .
> Fiercely the gaunt woods to the grim soil cling
> That bears for all fair fruits
> Wan wild sparce flowers of windy and wintry spring
> Between the tortive serpent-shapen roots
> Wherethrough their dim growth hardly strikes and shoots
> And shows one gracious thing
> Hardly, to speak for summer one sweet word
> Of summer's self scarce heard.
> But higher the steep green sterile fields, thick-set
> With flowerless hawthorn even to the upward verge
> Whence the woods gathering watch new cliffs emerge
> Higher than their highest of crowns that sea-winds fret,
> Hold fast, for all that night or wind can say,
> Some pale pure colour yet,
> Too dim for green and luminous for grey. . . .
> A barren peace too soft for hate or love
> Broods on an hour too dim for night or day. . . .
>
> In fruitless years of youth dead long ago
> And deep beneath their own dead leaves and snow
> Buried, I heard with bitter heart and sere
> The same sea's word unchangeable, nor knew
> But that mine own life-days were changeless too
> And sharp and salt with unshed tear on tear
> And cold and fierce and barren; and my soul,
> Sickening, swam weakly with bated breath
> In a deep sea like death,
> And felt the wind buffet her face with brine
> Hard, and harsh thought on thought in long bleak roll
> Blown by keen gusts of memory sad as thine
> Heap the weight up of pain, and break, and leave
> Strength scarce enough to grieve,
> In the sick heavy spirit, unmanned with strife
> Of waves that beat at the tired lips of life. . . .
>
> the best of all my days
> Have been as those fair fruitless summer strays,
> Those water-waifs that but the sea-wind steers.

Swinburne seldom indulges in such clear-sighted reflection. The poem then wanders off into the legend of Philomela and a long eulogy of Sappho, 'his sister', whose voice is echoed for him in the nightingale's song:

> As brother and sister we were, child and bird,
> Since thy first Lesbian word
> Flamed on me, and I knew not whence I knew
> This was the song that struck my whole soul through,
> Pierced my keen spirit of sense with edge more keen,
> Even when I knew not, – even ere sooth was seen, –
> When thou wast but the tawny sweet winged thing
> Whose cry was but of spring.

Much of the poem is wordy and diffuse, perpetually returning upon itself in a circular movement, like many of Swinburne's poems. It is valuable as a record of his inmost feelings at this time, and less mystical than 'Thalasius', his other spiritual autobiography which preceded it.

Soon after he moved back to London in April 1878, Swinburne began drinking again, and his health went from bad to worse. In May he received an invitation from Victor Hugo to attend the Voltaire bicentenary celebrations in Paris, but was too unwell to go. Lord Houghton was so shocked by his condition that he wrote to Lady Jane, who replied pathetically on 23 July: 'the case is a most grievous one and seems so hopeless. We have done our utmost to make our home a happy one for him . . . but it was often with much difficulty (and with much suffering to his Father), that he was induced to leave London. Since his Father's death I have not been able to persuade him to come to me – I have tried every way to make him do so. In one letter to me he told me that nothing would induce him to come here again – that he hates the place – and that can I not be satisfied with seeing him in London? I answered him that I would not again *press* his coming here but should he change his mind he would always meet with an affectionate welcome.'

Swinburne had apparently written to his mother to say that there was nothing wrong with him, but that he was 'knocked up with the great heat'. The poor lady continues: 'he goes on to tell me that his new rooms are delightful &c. He had never mentioned that he was going to leave his old lodgings and all my letters had been addressed to him there till my last! I do not know what I can do – but if my health will allow me I will endeavour to go to see him – but it is difficult for me to do so, as the last time his Father and I went to him to persuade him to leave Town he threatened if we did so again – he would leave London and never let us know where he had gone to – and this he said when he was in a state perfectly to understand and mean what he said.

'I quite agree with what you say about Medical Supervision, but I have no power to enforce it and persuasion I fear would be useless. It is a heavy grief.'[21]

Meanwhile, Swinburne had moved to 25 Guilford Street, and Watts, who had been living in Great James Street in order to be near him, decided that the time had come for drastic action, if his friend was to survive. He went down to Holmwood to discuss the matter with Lady Jane and the family. George Powell also wrote to Watts on 29 August, asking about 'our dear Bard. *Where* is he, and *how* is he? Thrice I have written to Great James Street, and in all these cases quite without response. . . . Observe, my Dear Watts, that I am not *complaining*, but only seriously anxious about our friend. Has the old tempter seized him? . . . what, in fact, is the matter with him?' What, in fact, was the matter with him was alcoholic dysentery.

In September Swinburne himself wrote to Watts to come to him: 'I am well nigh driven mad between protracted and painful sickness (I can hardly hold this pen, having been over a week in bed, and being hardly fit to get up – as I have done – today) and the damned swarm of volunteer correspondents whom I literally have not physical strength to answer. I have been far more seriously unwell than now, but hardly ever felt wearier and weaker.' Fortunately, he still had his old landlady, the heroic Mrs Magill, to look after him. It could not have been a very agreeable task, but his very helplessness seems to have endeared him to her. She kept Lady Jane informed, and in November the harassed mother visited her son and persuaded him to return to Holmwood. Ominously, there are no letters extant from Swinburne between September 1878 and June 1879. In 1909, Alice Bird wrote a description for the *Bibliophile* of an evening spent in the company of Swinburne, Richard and Isabel Burton, Dr George Bird, and four other friends, on 10 October 1878. Swinburne, she says, 'talked brilliantly, on a wide variety of subjects', but he 'looked ill and worn, and older' and 'had a haggard expression as if his nerves were out of tune'.[22]

Almost nothing is known of Swinburne's movements between November 1878 and June 1879, when Watts, at Lady Jane's request, took him down to Holmwood again. We know that he was staying briefly with Watts 'near Putney' early in June from Lord Ronald Gower's account of meeting him there on the ninth: 'What, far beyond the wonderful flow of words of the poet, struck me, was his real diffidence and modesty. While fully aware of the divine gifts within him, he is as simple and unaffected as a child.'[23]

By 13 June, Swinburne was at Holmwood, apparently in full possession of his faculties and writing to Andrew Chatto, returning a corrected proof of 'Part I' of his *Note on the Historical Play of King Edward III* and requesting him to 'procure for me at once, and (as of course you can) at proper prices, not turning francs into shillings, 1) Victor Hugo's "Le Pape", 2) Bergerat's "Théophile Gautier: Entretiens et Correspondence", Charpentier, 3) Théodore de Banville's plays in verse, published by Charpentier,

4) Emile Zola's "Mes Haines" (same publisher) 5) Léon Cladel's "Bons-hommes" (do.)'.

Later the same month Swinburne came up to Guilford Street, writing to Watts on the twenty-second: 'I write in great haste, to catch if possible the morning post. . . . Chatto has not sent me a single weekly newspaper to order: they should *all* have been here by nine this morning! On second thought, to prevent any confusion of my own with my mother's account, I shall not order the Pall Mall of the people who supply her with journals, but order it straight from the office, subscribing for three or six months. Will you kindly draw up and forward me a proper business-like order to that effect, and let me know if, and how much, I ought to pay in advance, a task which you perhaps would undertake for me and I could send you a cheque for the amount as soon as you can get and send me a cheque-book. I have not one blank (or d....d) cheque by me. . . . As to my MSS. and proofs – the unfinished article on the sham-Shakespeare play of King Edward III was assuredly left in the drawer of the table I mentioned together with "Capel's Prolusions", and in that book a small slip of paper containing notes for the said article. Till I have these by me, I can make no way at all. I have just found my missing penholder, and can write with comparative ease again; so don't trouble yourself about that. The "documents" I want and must have of Chatto *at once* are these: 1) MS. *in full* and duplicate proof of unfinished story or "study" [*Lesbia Brandon*]; 2) Proofs of first act of Mary Stuart, part third (the MS. I have). – I hope you will not by this time think me as exacting as a certain friend of ours, seeing how important these things are to me.'

The letter ends with a list of odd volumes of Victor Hugo also to be sent together with 'Sponge and bag' and 'Two parcels of papers (proofs and MSS.) wrapped loosely (not tied or sealed) in brown paper or newspaper – containing, one, MS. and (fragmentary) proofs of unfinished story: the other, MS. (unfinished) of Tristram and Iseult. In drawer of little writing table, MS. notes "on the historic play of King Edward III" with Capel's Prolusions *bound* in calf extra. Chatto to send me every week the Athenaeum, Academy, Saturday Review, Spectator.'[24]

On 26 June, he wrote severely to Andrew Chatto from Holmwood: 'I write at once to acknowledge the receipt of the MSS and proofs just arrived. I have not yet had time – being still far from strong – to collate them thoroughly; but a mere glance is enough to shew me that they are in a simply scandalous and disgraceful state of confusion. Everything is out of order, and some of the most important parts, apparently, at first sight, missing alike in proof and MS: . . . Time and patience, with returning strength and power to work, can alone show whether or not the incredible incompetence and negligence of the printers have inflicted upon me an irreparable and incalculable loss.

'But, in my case, this brings me to the main object of my present note;

which is this; to let you know finally, and once for all, in so distinct and decisive a manner as to put it beyond all possibility of mistake, that I positively decline to allow my MSS ever again to be entrusted to the charge of these printers. I have been advised, and that from a quarter as far from unfriendly towards you as towards myself, to intimate in so many words that either you must change your printers, or I must change my publishers.

'I should be reluctant to put the question in that way: but it is simply impossible for me to endure these people any more. I might almost say that every waking hour of three days and three nights was spent in the incessant labour of correcting (from a perfectly clear and legible MS., now in the hands of Mr Watts) the proofs of my little study on Charlotte Brontë. And in my latest volume of poems (of which, by the way, your people have sent me a copy soiled on some pages rather badly), at page 14, stanza xii of the poem, line 1st, I find the ruinous and ridiculous misprint of "shown" for the right reading "strewn". No man's work can wholly withstand the disadvantage of such blunders as deform and impair even where they do not (as they often do) utterly destroy the meaning of the text; and no man who respects himself or his work can be expected to put up with it.'[25]

One can only say that Andrew Chatto put up with a good deal from Swinburne. On 11 July 1879, Lady Jane is writing to Lord Houghton, in response to his inquiry, to say that 'Algernon's illness is now a thing of the past – he has been here nearly a month and is really quite well – happy, cheerful and busy with his writing. I trust he will remain with us till we leave this place.' With this letter Swinburne enclosed one of his own: 'My mother has just shewn me your note to her inquiring after my health; so I add a line of acknowledgement to her reply. I *was* very unwell for weeks together before I left London, and a good deal reduced in strength by prolonged insomnia and consequent loss of appetite and exhaustion; but a day or two at a friend's house near Putney Heath, with plenty of walking exercise thereon and thereabouts, sufficed to set me up – higher, I may say than I had been for many months. Thence I came down here to see the last of this place, which we leave for good in October.

'I am steadily working at my book on Shakespeare, and am in the pangs of travail for a better title than the one prefixed to its two first instalments in the Fortnightly some four years ago. Also I have the skeleton of the four remaining acts of *Mary Stuart* (Part Third) completely drawn out and jointed together (the first act has been some time in type) and hope to begin getting the bare bones clothed with flesh and sinews before long. (As Gray said of his Greek studies – "I take prose and poetry together like bread and cheese.").'

A lengthy postscript is a return to something like Swinburne's old style of wit: 'A propos de bottes – and as everybody seems doomed nowadays to be always talking or writing about some theatrical matter – I was really and unaffectedly glad to see recorded in the papers (I forget now how many months ago) the failure of Charles Reade's monstrous and incredible attempt to introduce on the English stage a dramatized version of the most horrible and loathsome book that ever got into type.[26] I am curious to know if there was any foundation for a rumour which was (or might have been – que sais-je, moi?) current at the time, that the reception of *L'Assommoir* as an English play discouraged a rival manager from bringing out by way of counter attraction a similar version, attempted in a spirit of friendly emulation by Mr Anthony Trollope, of *Justine, ou Les Malheurs de la Vertu.*'[27]

It has been left for our time to present de Sade's dramatization of the murder of Marat in his bath, as performed under his direction by the inmates of Charenton lunatic asylum – that is, the Royal Shakespeare Company's *Marat-Sade*, preceded by the no less edifying presentation of torture and sexual hysteria in a nunnery, as adapted from Aldous Huxley's *The Devils of Loudon.* Swinburne would have felt at home in the modern 'Theatre of Cruelty'.

But preparations were now almost complete for the caging of this tropical bird. On 13 July 1879, Lady Jane wrote to Watts: 'I am truly glad that you have been able to make the very kind arrangement about A's being under your roof, and the plan for the payment of the £1000 seems to me a very good one. This arrangement must be conditional on his giving up his lodging in London. This I am sure you will agree is absolutely necessary.'

At the end of July Watts went down to Holmwood to discuss with Lady Jane how much money it would be advisable to allow Algernon to have at his disposal and how much of his inheritance should be invested. The plan of his setting up a joint household with Watts and Watts's sisters was also probably discussed in more detail. Swinburne himself seems to have been unaware of the provisions that were being made for his future and in a letter to Watts of 30 July told him: 'I have a new poem to read to you,' – that is, 'On the Cliffs' – 'longer (I will not say better, whether I think so or not) than any (except the ever edifying "Dolores") in either of my collections. "Anactoria" which is the next longest is ninety-four lines short of this new-born one – which however was long since conceived though but now brought forth. You will regret to hear that in subject-matter and treatment it is not akin to either of the above-named. I fear there is not overmuch hope of a fresh scandal and consequent "succès de scandale" from a mere rhapsody just four lines short of four hundred (oddly enough) on the song of a nightingale by the sea-side.'

On 7 August he wrote gaily in his old vein to Lord Houghton: 'Is there – Oh! is there any truth in the report that in consequence of an article in the *Times* yesterday which decrees that there are – and shall be – no living poets in England, Mr Tennyson and Mr Browning have "shaken hands in death" by shutting themselves up in a hermetically sealed room with a pan of ignited charcoal between them? and that Mr Thomas Carlyle, regardless alike of his years, of the weather, and of the law of the land prohibiting indecent exposure, has been seen dancing a Highland fling, in a state of total nudity and partial intoxication, down and up the whole length of Cheyne Row, Chelsea, with a Scotch cutty-pipe in his mouth and the Scotch Fiddle on his back, by way of expressing as in a Pyrrhic war-dance the triumph of an "inarticulate poet" over the downfall of the last articulate individual of that ilk?'[28]

Meanwhile, the final financial arrangements were going on behind Swinburne's back, and on 28 August his younger brother Edward wrote to Watts: 'My mother desires me to tell you that she had no opportunity of telling you the other day, that she had instructed Messrs. Hoare to pay £200 p.a. in ½ yearly payments to your acct. at the London Westminster Bank (Temple Bar branch) for four years or till further orders – the first payment to be made on the first of September next. Also, that she has paid Algernon for the books and that the £2000 is invested in New Zealand 4½ pc. She had £1000 already invested in that which she transferred to his name, and I suggested that the other £1000 should be invested in the same security as it would rather simplify the matter for Algernon (if he ever thinks about it) to receive the dividends on the same date, which might not have been the case had some other security been chosen. At my suggestion also the £2000 are in two bonds of £1000 each which I thought might be an advantage in case Algernon should be taken with a paroxysm of extravagance and want suddenly to spend £200 or so, on some book; he will now have to sell £1000 to get hold of £100, but I think these precautions are rather superfluous as being quite beyond his *ken*, but still some one might tell him, if your back was turned, how to do it.' The tone of rather contemptuous condescension is clear enough. What Edward Swinburne ever did, except to make an unsuccessful marriage, is not known.

Swinburne was still at Holmwood on 30 August 1879, and he wrote to Watts to ask him to contradict a statement that had appeared in the *Athenaeum* expressing regret that 'Mr Swinburne has been ill, and that a visit to the southern coast for the recovery of his health is necessitated', whereas, he writes, 'I was not at death's door but as well as ever I was or could wish to be'. This, he adds, would come better from a third party than from himself: 'I would on no account ask you to do me this little kindness if you would in the least prefer not to put your oar in – but it is getting almost beyond a trivial matter to me, and there can be no doubt my mother is right in thinking I had better abstain from coming forward to swear to my own health and very probably be disbelieved, whereas a disinterested personal witness might easily and finally put to silence and to shame such futile and fulsome if not pernicious gossip; and that without the least even seeming compromise of dignity on his part or mine. I must let MacColl know once for all that I object to being the standard annual Big Gooseberry of the Silly Season for the benefit of the paper which he seems determined shall again, and deservedly, come to be known by Bulwer's 1st's nickname of the Asinaeum: and you may show him this or tell him as much from me if you like.'[29]

It seems, from a sentence at the beginning of this letter – 'Come on Friday by all means and I will be ready for you and the sea side whenever feasible' – that Swinburne and Watts did, in fact, take a short seaside holiday, after which they both went to stay at Watts's married sister's house, Ivy Lodge, Werter Road, Putney, before moving into The Pines, Putney Hill, later in the month. In a celebrated passage Gosse writes: 'The succeeding months of August and September [of 1879] were the most deplorable in his whole career. When he seemed actually at the doors of death, Theodore Watts, with the approval of the distressed and bewildered Lady Jane Swinburne, arrived very early one morning and carried the poet by force to his own rooms, which were now close by. Thence, as soon as he was partially recovered, to Putney, where in an amazingly short space of time Swinburne regained his health so that he was soon once more writing with unabated vigour.'[30]

But, as we have seen, Swinburne was writing to Watts 'with unabated vigour' as late as 30 August, asking him to contradict reports of his ill-health in the Press. He had in fact been living and working peacefully at Holmwood since June. Moreover, it was on 27 August that, as he wrote to Watts: 'This morning before breakfast about eight I put the very last touch to the very last sentence of the very last paragraph of my book on Shakespeare – Glory be to all of us of the true faith; and woe unto the Sham Shakespeareans! . . . And now I look eagerly forward to reading you the twenty pages and odd which comprise all the good four days' work you have not yet heard. À bientôt – being now wholly at your service and summons.'[31] Neither this, nor the final chapters of *A Study of Shakespeare*, were written by a man 'actually at the doors of death'. The dramatic story of Watts's early morning rescue operation in Guilford Street has been so often repeated, that it is just as well to show that it did not take place in 1879, nor quite as Gosse relates, though it is true in principle. For it was undoubtedly to Watts's tact and devotion that Swinburne owed his life.

# CHAPTER ELEVEN

# 1879–82

# AT THE PINES

By mid-September 1879 Swinburne was writing from Ivy Lodge, Putney, to Nichol: 'I have given up chambers in London, where I never was certain of two days' real health together and am setting up in company with my friend Watts as a suburban householder. Before the year's end we remove into a larger and seemingly a very good house with a more endurable address than this.' He goes on to praise 'the sweet dry air of this wide unenclosed heath country (which in the teeth of certain landowners' and speculators' rapacity has happily been pronounced unenclosed for ever)' and where he is 'quite well again and strong enough for a fresh inroad on Sark – which always hangs like a mirage in my memory. . . . In a very few weeks I hope to send you my book now forthcoming – "A Study of Shakespeare". I hear that the fetid Flunkivall proposes to anticipate it by a pamphlet of preliminary ribaldry. . . . I am sincerely obliged by the advertisement, but hardly so much as to make me cancel certain references in the body and appendix of my book to the Valet Volunteer of the Sham Shakespeare Society. . . . Many thanks for the Keats fund paper. I must send my guinea-mite, of course. But is not the millionaire Tennyson's subscription too awfully shabby even for a Laureate?'[1]

Gosse tactlessly wrote to Swinburne in October 'c/o Watts', and in his next letter to him Swinburne remarked sharply: 'You need not put Watts's name on my address, any more than mine on his, we have both moved in together.' It seems that many people believed that Swinburne had been taken into Watts's house, whereas it was a joint tenancy, Swinburne's share of the rent and household expenses being paid out of the £200 a year credited to Watts's account by Lady Jane, thus relieving him of all financial worries – for the sight of a business letter was enough to make him tremble with fury. Actually, of course, he was under Watts's care – a care and control exercised, by all accounts, with such exquisite tact that Swinburne always felt quite his own master. Any overt signs of control would have provoked an immediate reaction of anger and resentment.

On 27 September Swinburne was writing to his mother from The Pines: 'You will see that *our* flitting has been in the main accomplished – into a large double block of building, of which we inhabit the left house (looked at from the street) till the right – our own domicile – is ready. Meantime we are gypsying here with furniture enough for sleep, meals and a sitting-room. . . . Each house also has a little "tower" at top to which one gets by ladders . . . off one flat of leads on to another, whence the view is really very nice. The part we live in, as we all agree, is exactly like the outlying (and prettiest) parts of Oxford, where there are (or were) little gardens with large trees overhanging them and little old walls round a "grass-plat". And we are within an easy walk of Richmond Park, in which I have already made two longish excursions – and also within less than an hour of Piccadilly – and no underground travelling!'[2] A letter to Lord Houghton of 21 November also sings the praises of Putney: 'I was pleased at sight of your handwriting and at the fact of my present and permanent address being known by this time to others than duns. . . . I keep no chambers in town henceforth, or (probably) for ever – finding after but too many years' trial that in the atmosphere of London I can never expect more than a fortnight at best of my usual health and strength. Here I am, like Mr Tennyson at Faringford,

Close to the edge of a noble down,

and yet within an easy hour's reach of Hyde Park Corner, and a pleasant drive of Chelsea, where I have yet some friends lingering.'[3]

'Gypsying' . . . 'Oxford' . . . 'Faringford'! One suspects that such comparisons originated with Watts and were part of his policy of making Swinburne feel contented with his new environment. 'Gypsying' certainly sounds like the author of *Alwyn*. Yet how bored Swinburne was soon to become with the subject of 'gypsies'! In the same letter to Lord Houghton we find him reverting with delight to de Sade, in this instance 'a rare if not unique pamphlet written in the thickest and hottest of the Reign of Terror, on novels and romances dealing with the tender passion in a modest and elevated tone of feeling, which does infinite credit to the writer's own sweetness and amiable modesty of disposition – at such a season too, for pastoral and domestic contemplations. The civic and sponsorial designation of this pure and gentle spirit was Citizen Donatien-Alphonse-Francois, ex-marquis de Sade.'

In his next letter to Houghton, Swinburne gives the title at full length of 'that interesting martyr's sentimental *brochure* as republished last year'. He goes on to praise Léon Cladel: 'who makes me feel eighteen again in enthusiasm. I think some parts of "Bonshommes" are among the finest things I ever read for subtle truth and grim quaint pathos conveyed in a style whose perfection is beyond praise. And what a wonder for other qualities than its incomparable audacity and its exquisitely gorgeous attire and decorations is "Ompdrailles le Tombeau-des-Lutteurs"!

'It is a shame to speak first – perhaps to speak at all – of the outward splendours of a book (in the Psalmist's phrase) "all glorious within" – but *when* will our hidebound hounds of publishers produce such a sample of choice ware? My favourite *bits* (to use a word I hate) in text and illustration respectively are the faultless verbal photograph of the "Bourreau-des-Faubourgs" (pp. 262–265) in which the long since damned and rotten original . . . lives and draws fetid and poisonous breath once more for one foul moment (but happily only on paper) and the admirable etching at p. 96 of "La Scorpione" in meditation, ogling the – well, the muscles (let us say) of a Hercules. I think the amount of expression – of sombre and brooding lust, reflective and resolute appetite – which the etcher has put into her bent head is most masterly, and worthy even of the grim and savage seduction so wonderfully well given in the text.

'Passing from literature to life, I may as well tell you that I have begun housekeeping in common with a friend, on such terms that we can receive the ladies of our own respective families at any time, our household being at all points as respectable as the whitest of whited sepulchres. If either of us should ever want a change he can go off without warning given or expected for a day (or night) or so. These (to speak Gampically) is our domestic arrangements, and we finds 'em answer.'

It so happened, however, that Swinburne did not 'want a change' and for the next year remained contentedly domiciled in his 'whitest of whited sepulchres', busily at work and in the best of health and spirits. And he continued so, with daily walks on Wimbledon Common, annual seaside holidays with Watts and long visits to his mother, for the next thirty years. It seems, also, that he went up to London when he felt so inclined. Needless to say, Watts would have been greatly disturbed had 'his charge' ever gone off without warning, and, as far as we know this never occurred, though at first, it is said, Watts used to hide his boots so that he could not go out. At The Pines Swinburne occupied the two best rooms on the first floor. He breakfasted each morning at ten, alone in his library, but dined in the common dining-room with the family. He seems actually to have welcomed the presence in the house of Watts's two sisters, and especially of Bertie, Mrs Mason's small boy, to whom he became rather disturbingly attached as time went on.

In October Swinburne had been disgusted to hear, from Gosse, that his one-time friend Charles Augustus Howell was 'habitually amusing mixed companies of total strangers by obscene false anecdotes about my private eccentricities of indecent indulgence as exhibited in real or imaginary *lupanaria*, and of another, who is now a thing unmentionable alike by men and women, as equally abhorrent to either – nay, to the very beasts – raising money by the sale of my letters to him in past years, which must doubtless contain much foolish burlesque and now regrettable nonsense never meant for any stranger's eye who would not understand the mere childishness of the silly chaff indulged in long ago'.[4]

The 'thing unmentionable' was poor Simeon Solomon, now reduced to beggary and deserted by all the high-minded literary friends who had originally been responsible for his degradation in the days when he had been a highly talented painter. It was hard for Swinburne that 'the silly chaff indulged in long ago' should now be exposed to the public eye just when he had succeeded in becoming a 'reformed' character. But, as he wrote in the same letter to Gosse of 15 October: 'As long as I can feel that I may count, and have the right to count, on the steady friendship and fidelity of honourable gentlemen, I will not for very shame's sake so far forget or forego my own claim to a sense of self-respect as to fret my heartstrings by day or by night over such disgusting facts.' Later the same month he wrote to Gosse: 'You know how glad I shall be to see you any day you turn up. I want to discuss further my past proposal for a Critical Dictionary of the English Drama, to be undertaken by a company of us in common, and also to read you my last new poem of more than 400 lines – "On the Cliffs". It is in the irregular Italian metre of Lycidas. Watts – as I possibly may have told you – says (what a man generally likes to hear of his latest work) that it is *the* best poem I ever wrote. Come soon and see what you think of it.'[5] But it was the amiable custom of Watts to say of each new poem of Swinburne's that it was the best he had ever written.

Coulson Kernahan, who was intimate with both men, has left a record of the gentleness and tact with which Watts gradually weaned his friend from his addiction to strong drink. When Watts took him in hand, Swinburne had been regularly drinking brandy, with what results we have seen. 'Watts knew,' writes Kernahan, 'that he was dealing with one who, his genius and great brains notwithstanding, was in some respects a child. He knew too that suddenly and entirely to call off all alcohol would, in the case of one so accustomed to it, and in a sense so dependent upon it, be unwise, and might even endanger life. This then is how he went to work.

' "Do you know, Algernon," he began, taking up the glass of brandy and water which stood by Swinburne's bedside and looking at it sourly, "this stuff isn't a drink in any real sense of the word. It's a drug, a medicine, to be taken only when prescribed by doctors – beastly stuff in my opinion at any time, and the very last drink in the world for a poet. Look at our great Tennyson. What does he drink? Port, that divinest nectar of the gods, the life-blood of the vine, distilled by sunshine, as it were, caught and chaliced in the red heart of such grapes as grow nowhere out of old Spain, land of sunshine and lovely women.

' "But brandy – bah! the very smell of it calls up sick-rooms, as well as wretched (and retching) Cockney travellers on a Channel steamer in a rough crossing. They tell me Tennyson never drinks less than a bottle of port a day, and that its generous, life-giving qualities make another man of him, set his brain newly afire and singing, like great seas in a storm, even when he is no longer young. I was lucky enough to get a few bottles of the very brand that he drinks – first-class vintage year, too, my wine merchant tells me. They're in the cellar at the moment. I have half a mind to crack a bottle now, to drink to Tennyson's health and our very good selves. Do you feel like joining me?"

'By this time Swinburne would be full of enthusiasm to try "Tennyson's drink", sitting up in bed, chafing the palms of his hands together excitedly. "Oh yes, do get one up! How perfectly delightful!" Eulogising the condition, colour and bouquet of the wine, Watts filled two glasses, and the toast, "Tennyson and our noble selves", was given. Swinburne drank his share ecstatically, with a murmured: "Ah!" and "Nectar of the gods, indeed!" Watts-Dunton meanwhile grumbling contemptuously between his sips: "Brandy forsooth! Doctor's stuff! What poet would drug himself with brandy, when he can get so divine a draught as this!"

'And so brandy disappeared from Swinburne's table, and for a month or more the two friends – the one quaffing generously, the other sipping more cautiously – drank port together. After a while, the same method was pursued with the port.

'Then Watts-Dunton, affecting to rub his open palm over the small of his back, very much as sufferers from "that tired feeling" are pictured in quack medicine advertisements, grumbled: "I don't know how you feel, my boy, but you and I are not perhaps such rough and hardy Berserkers as old Tennyson, or it may be we don't get as much active exercise in the day as he, but I for one begin to find port a trifle heavy. One of the biggest wine-growers from the Continent told me the other day that Burgundy is the best of all drinks in a climate like ours. It is lighter than port, which is apt to clog the liver unless you are sparing with it. A glass or two of port to sip over your walnuts after dinner can't be beaten, but at any other time of the day, he says, whether at dinner or between meals, there is nothing so fine as good, generous old Burgundy. It's blood-making, nerve-strengthening, body-building, brain-firing. It's the wine that our Dumas' immortal Three Musketeers, Athos, Porthos and Aramis, not forgetting the finest fellow of them all, D'Artagnan, thrived on, made love on, fought on; and most of all – you are half a Frenchman, you tell me – it is the wine of your own La Belle France. I picked up a case the other day, and I propose we sample a bottle at lunch, if only to drink to Dumas and the immortal three."

'Again the ruse succeeded. Warned off brandy or warned off port for the very good reason that he was injuring his bodily health and unduly inflaming and exciting a too-inflammable and too-excitable brain, Swinburne would have paid no heed. Put as Watts-Dunton put it, the poet and the child in Swinburne responded.' Forthwith Claret was substituted as the proper drink for gentlemen, and, after a month or so, Watts achieved his final triumph, delivering himself as follows: ' "There is a theory of mine, a pet theory, that I want to ask your opinion about. It is this, that wherever you are, you should drink the 'wine of the country'. If one is in Scotland, one drinks whisky, Scotch whisky; if in Ireland, Irish whiskey; if in Germany, hock or German moselle; if in France, Graves, Sauterne, Claret, Burgundy, or champagne; if in Spain or Portugal, port; in Italy, chianti. Why, whether drunk out of the cool depths of a pewter or china mug, in some quaint old English inn with diamond-paned windows, sanded floors and oaken benches, or out of a silver tankard from His Lordship's sideboard – the most refreshing, appetizing, stimulating, healthiest, best and most natural of all drinks for an Englishman is Charles Stuart Calverley's 'beverage for feasting gods', Shakespeare's brown October, our own glorious and incomparable British beer!" '[6]

So, in the space of a few months, Watts by degrees weaned Swinburne from all the more potent intoxicants. At each stage, he made it appear that the choice was Swinburne's own. Henceforth, a bottle of pale ale or Bass – 'Shakespeare's brown October' – stood by his plate at luncheon, and – apart from a glass taken each morning at the Rose and Crown during his walk to Wimbledon – he drank practically nothing else for the rest of his days. Watts had, in fact, achieved in a short space of time what to others had seemed impossible. The fact that he could do this says much for the implicit confidence and trust that Swinburne now reposed in his judgment in all things. Swinburne's health and vigour returned; he grew a bushy red beard; his glance became keen and piercing, and he developed into a formidable scholar – even if, as time went on, he was of less consequence as a poet. The later photographs taken at The Pines speak for themselves. They show a poise and dignity, a calm nobility and self-possession quite lacking in those taken of him in earlier years, and might almost be photographs of a different person. His days were now regulated by a fixed and unvarying timetable, which he followed with an almost mechanical regularity, and in this he apparently found peace and contentment. Watts has been criticized, even ridiculed, for caging this 'crimson macaw'. But the truth is that he saved Swinburne from a wretched, ignoble death and gave him not only another thirty years of life among his books, but a sympathetic companionship for which the poet could never feel sufficiently grateful, even though his later life was little more than a prolonged convalescence.

All the same, it must be admitted that there is a touch of the sinister in the photographs of the two men taken together at The Pines: Watts, dogged, with walrus moustache and closely-buttoned frock coat, stands behind the little seated poet with something of the air of a showman presenting a ventriloquist's doll. 'There is no one in the world like Walter,' Swinburne was in the habit of saying, with a look of adoration in his eyes; and, for his part, Watts told Clara, his young wife: 'It is because of his helplessness that I love him so much.'[7] Theirs was, indeed, a love surpassing the love of women. In the dedicatory sonnet prefaced to *Tristram of Lyonesse*, Swinburne wrote after three years' residence at The Pines in April 1882:

There is a friend that as the wise man saith
 Cleaves closer than a brother: nor to me
  Hath time not shown, through days like waves at strife,
This truth more sure than all things else but death,
 This pearl most perfect found in all the sea
  That washes toward your feet these waifs of life.

'And now,' Swinburne wrote to his mother on 11 November 1879, 'we have got my small friend, Watts's little five-year-old nephew, with his mother and an aunt . . . and he is a sweet thing in infants. I gave him a big box of preserved fruits from Fortnum & Masons, and the child's delight (though he likes *some* of them very much) is to give the nicest away right and left to all members of the household including myself . . . and he has bestowed on me two really lovely presents, a highly elaborate match-box, and a penholder which is also a pencil at the other end. It makes such a pleasant difference having a child in the household to rule over you. It makes everything bright about him.'[8]

But there was no lack of visitors to The Pines: Lord Houghton, Jowett, Gosse, Madox Brown, William Rossetti, William Morris, Burne-Jones, Isabel Burton (who smoked a cigarette 'in Swinburne's charming den') and Churton Collins. Nichol stayed a week and Swinburne read to him his new essay on Milton, in which, he tells his mother, 'I have pitched into Puritanism and the selfish ambition and stupid short-sightedness of Cromwell in a way of which you, I think, will not disapprove, though a good many others will, as it goes heavily against the present fashion of blind and parrot-like Cromwell worship, set on foot by that hoary old villain Carlyle'.

Swinburne kept up an immense and lively correspondence with his friends and the Press on literary matters. He also continued to write poetry, his latest poem being 'By the North Sea', which Watts, he wrote to Gosse on 5 July 1880, 'likes better than anything I ever did (and in metrical and antiphonal effect I prefer it myself to all my others): so I shall inscribe it to him. Come soon and hear it.' 'By the North Sea' is a symbolist poem in which Swinburne projects an inner sense of desolation on to the Suffolk landscape at Dunwich, desolate enough itself. It is an example of the landscape poetry which Watts was now encouraging Swinburne to write:

A land that is lonelier than ruin;
 A sea that is stranger than death:
Far fields that a rose never blew in,
 Wan waste where the winds lack breath;
Waste endless and boundless and flowerless
 But of marsh-blossoms fruitless as free:
Where earth lies exhausted, as powerless
  To strive with the sea.

Far flickers the flight of the swallows,
  Far flutters the weft of the grass
Spun dense over desolate hollows
  More pale than the clouds as they pass;
Thick woven as the weft of a witch is
  Round the heart of a thrall that hath sinned,
Whose youth and the wrecks of its riches
    Are waifs on the wind.

Why should the grass be seen as the web of a witch woven round 'the heart of a thrall that has sinned'? It sounds peculiar in this context, unless one takes it as an image of the poet's own heart:

The pastures are herdless and sheepless,
  No pasture or shelter for herds:
The wind is relentless and sleepless,
  And restless and songless the birds;
Their cries from afar fall breathless,
  Their wings are as lightnings that flee;
For the land has two lords that are deathless:
    Death's self and the sea.

These twain, as a king and his fellow,
  Hold converse of desolate speech:
And her waters are haggard and yellow
  And crass with the scurf of the beach. . . . .

In the pride of his power she rejoices,
  In her glory he glows and is glad:
In her darkness the sound of his voice is,
  With his breath she dilates and is mad:
'If thou slay me, O death and outlive me,
  Yet thy love hath fulfilled me of thee.'
'Shall I give thee not back if thou give me,
    O sister, O sea?'

And year upon year dawns living,
  And age upon age drops dead:
And his hand is not weary of giving,
  And the thirst of her heart is not fed:
And the hunger that moans in her passion,
  And the rage in her hunger that roars,
As a wolf's that the winter lays lash on,
    Still calls and implores.

Surely Swinburne finds in the insatiable sea a symbol of the hunger of his own heart. Death and the sea are complementary and yet one. At the same time, in his detachment from life, he has glimpsed a possible serenity:

And sweeter than all things and stranger
  The sense, if perchance it may be,
That the wind is divested of danger,
    And scatheless the sea.

That the roar of the banks they breasted
  Is hurtless as bellowing of herds,
And the strength of his wings that invested
  The wind, as the strength of a bird's;
As the sea-mew's might or the swallows
  That cry to him back if he cries,
As over the graves and their hollows
    Days darken and rise.

As the souls of the dead men disburdened
  And clean of the sins that they sinned,
With a lovelier than man's life guerdoned
  And delight as a wave's in the wind,
And delight as the wind's in the billow,
  Birds pass, and deride with their glee
The flesh that has dust for its pillow
    As wrecks have the sea.

And yet, standing on the cliff at Dunwich, Swinburne is uncertain whether he is any more alive than the ghosts of those who lie in their graves beneath the sea, but now crowding about him:

As the waves of the numberless waters
  That the wind cannot number who guides
Are the sons of the shore and the daughters
  Here lulled by the chime of the tides:
And here in the press of them standing
  We know not if these or if we
Live truliest, or anchored to landing
    Or drifted to sea.

As in 'The Deserted Garden', he sees Dunwich, once a populous town now lying in ruins beneath the sea, as a symbol of the dissolution of all things:

And gentler the wind from the dreary
  Sea-banks by the waves overlapped,
Being weary, speaks peace to the weary
  From slopes that the time-stream hath sapped;
And sweeter than all that we call so
  The seal of their slumber shall be
Till the graves that embosom them also
    Be sapped of the sea.

The verse is weaker and vaguer than heretofore and seems to be kept going mainly by the impetus of its rocking-horse rhythm. It nevertheless conveys a true picture of Swinburne's emotional condition masked for the purposes of day-to-day living with what he called a 'jolly stoicism'.

To 1880, too, belongs the 'Song for the Centenary of Walter Savage Landor', of which he writes to Gosse that 'the limit of eight hundred lines is pitifully narrow for such a Titanic charge as the panegyric on such a Titan'. But Gosse, who had to listen to it, describes this panegyric as 'the most tiresome of all his works. . . . The composition of enormous critical odes, that section of all his writings which is probably the least read, had now become a habit. . . . The sense of proportion had always been capricious in Swinburne's constitution; it was now leaving him altogether, and the power of logical expression was accompanying it . . . he poured forth stanzas in which great lines were frequent and luminous passages occasional, but the total effect of which was merely foggy and fatiguing.'[9] Few would disagree. Both 'By the North Sea' and the Landor ode appeared in a new collection, *Studies in Song* (1880), which was coldly received by critics and public alike. In losing the original sources of his inspiration, for the sake of writing more decorous verse, it seems that Swinburne had lost nearly everything. But fortunately, perhaps, he was unaware of it, and Browning wrote to him: 'As for the great appreciation (I can't say, "tribute") – well, the recognition, if you like, of our dear Landor, – it went at once to my heart's intimate depths: but there are poems over and above which even you have never surpassed, I think, in power and beauty.'[10] But Swinburne was hurt by the public reception of his book and complained: 'Poor I am stale, a garment out of fashion.' And sometimes the sense of his own buried life and waning powers comes out with an almost unbearable poignancy, as in the wistful lines 'To a Seamew', written at Beachy Head during a holiday with Watts and Bertie Mason in September 1886:

When I had wings, my brother,
　Such wings were mine as thine:
Such life my heart remembers
In all as wild Septembers
As this when life seems other,
　Though sweet, than once was mine;
When I had wings, my brother,
Such wings were mine as thine.

Such life as thrills and quickens
　The silence of thy flight,
Or fills thy note's elation
With lordlier exultation

Than man's, whose faint heart sickens
With hopes and fears that blight
Such life as thrills and quickens
The silence of thy flight.

He was still only forty-nine and had more than twenty years to live.

But every day now, wet or fine, he left The Pines at eleven o'clock for his morning's walk across Putney Heath and Wimbledon Common, his destination The Rose and Crown tavern – 'Pelting along as fast as I can go' with his quick, springy steps, he became a well-known figure in his wide-brimmed black felt hat and frock coat. There was something a little odd and mechanical in his movements. If he met anyone he knew on his walks, he would not appear to recognize them. At the Rose and Crown in Wimbledon High Street he was equally anxious to preserve his privacy and took his beer alone in the coffee room. Should anyone come in while he was there, he immediately escaped to the landlord's private room or, if he had nearly finished his bottle, he would get up and bolt into the High Street, where he stopped at the Misses Frost's stationers' and book-sellers' shop at the corner of the Ridgeway to buy a daily paper or a further supply of the blue foolscap he always used for writing. Sometimes a celebrity-hunter would recognize him and try to engage him in conversation. When this occurred, after a freezing glance at the intruder, he would escape into the Misses Frost's private room until the coast was clear. He had extra-large pockets made in his coat, which he called 'poacher's pockets', to hold any books he had ordered, and these had to be made to balance equally on each side of him before he set off on his return journey.

Swinburne had a horror of drawing small cheques and usually asked the Misses Frost to cash one for £20 at the bank opposite. The money had to be in gold coins and was carried in a small canvas bag, which, on his return to The Pines, he kept in a corner cupboard in his study, along with his manuscripts. 'The bag was always open,' says Clara Watts-Dunton, 'so was the cupboard.'[11] Sometimes Swinburne would vary his walk by going along the Richmond Road to the Mortlake Arms and then across Barnes Common as far as Barnes Green and the church – a considerable walk. In those days, of course, this area was almost rural. Barnes was a village – as it is still to some extent – and there was practically no traffic, except for an occasional cart and horse, carriage or pony-trap, and the odd rider on his or her way to Richmond Park. Walking there could still be a pleasure, and Priory Lane, leading to the park from the Richmond Road, was still a country lane, bordered at one side by the Beverley Brook and on the other by a few large houses and extensive market-gardens. But as he walked up Putney Hill, with his quick, jerky step, his spine rigid, his long neck strained tightly back, his arms hanging at his sides, little boys – 'street-boys', as they were then called by the well-to-do – would sometimes follow him, imitating his movements, and he would turn and wave at them with a seigneurial gesture of dismissal. In the summer he sometimes wore a sola topee.[12]

Swinburne always returned to The Pines in time for a substantial luncheon of roast mutton and apple-pie, beaming with pleasure and full of stories about what he had seen on his walk, whether it was 'beautiful babies' in prams or the glory of the gorse and the hawthorn bushes on the Common. At other times, his eyes sparkling with delight, he would produce one of the rare editions he had ordered from the Misses Frost's, or one of the miniature editions of the classics he delighted in. At two-thirty, if there were no visitors, he would retire for a siesta until four-thirty, after which he would work, descending at six-thirty to the drawing-room to read Dickens aloud to the members of the family. He was so fond of Dickens that he read through the whole of his novels every three years, and Watts used to declare that he had heard Swinburne read them all at least three times. But then Swinburne was an insatiable reader of novels – any novels picked up at the circulating library, which were, he inferred 'in his absolutely detached existence', a substitute for life.

After dinner, Swinburne might continue reading Dickens until ten o'clock, when, with a stiff little bow to the company, he would retire to his rooms, often working until late at night. Watts used to hear him walking round his room, stopping every five or ten minutes to write down a few lines or a new stanza, when the promenade would recommence. 'In these conditions,' says Gosse, 'his health became perfect; he developed into a sturdy little old man, without an ache or a pain; and he who had suffered so long in London from absence of appetite and wasting insomnia, for the last thirty years of his life at Putney ate like a caterpillar and slept like a doormouse.'[13]

On 8 October 1880, Lady Jane wrote to Watts: 'It is the greatest possible comfort to me to have seen my very dear Son so well and happy. The contrast that it was to what I used to see him was something quite beyond words and I cannot say how thankful I was – nor can I tell you how much I feel your care of him – and I am really quite happy about him. The return to the religious faith of his youth I feel is so much more hopeful when that fatal tendency from which he has suffered so much is got the better of.'[14]

The return to the religious faith of his youth was as far off as ever, unless his delight in babies and young children, as his mother began to hope, was leading him back to it. 'There came the most lovely baby in arms here on a visit one day,' he wrote to her ecstatically, 'and it beamed on me the minute our eyes met. But of all children out of arms Bertie is much the sweetest thing going at any price.' And he tells her how Bertie cried hearing the story of a crocodile hunt in which the mother was killed and the baby crocodiles left helpless: 'His uncle couldn't help laughing when he heard of it, though he admitted it was very touching – and I couldn't help crying though I admit it was very funny. Think of the dear little innocent thing . . . in tears over the crocodile orphans!'[15]

On 10 March next year, he wrote to his mother again about Bertie: 'I quite understand how (as you say) "a mother loves those words" which warn us against offending one of the little ones – but to me the divinest of all divine words and thoughts is "of such is the kingdom of heaven". I am sure it is so here on earth – where nothing – except age in its brightest beauty of goodness and sweetness and kindness – is so adorable as a little child is. At the same time – to be practical and candid – I must admit that it is a noisy quarter of Paradise which is occasionally occupied when I am (so to speak) admitted to it by my little Bertie. If you could have seen him the last two days that I have been reading and explaining Shakespeare to him – that is, since he has been introduced to Falstaff! Both his father and mother tell me he talks of nothing else. Again and again during my half-reading half-relating the main part of the great comic scenes, the child went over on the small (the very small!) of his little back among the sofa cushions, crowing aloud like a baby, choking with laughter, shouting and rolling from side to side with his heels *any* height above his head and kicking with absolute fury of delight. "Oh! didn't he tell stories!" he said to his father (in the largest type of a child's voice). I thought if Shakespeare could have been looking down and enjoying the little thing's inexpressible rapture, he must have felt it a greater tribute than all the plaudits of all the theatres in the world.'[16]

But there were signs that both Watts and Lady Jane, as well as Bertie's parents, were becoming just a little disturbed by this excessive adulation. Wasn't there something a little abnormal about it? In May 1881 it was decided that it would be a good thing if Bertie went away for a month's holiday. Swinburne was desolated and in *A Dark Month* he wrote a series of poems lamenting the child's absence.

A month without sight of the sun
   Rising or reigning or setting
Through days without use of the day,
Who calls it the month of May? . . .

Till a child's face lighten again
   On the twilight of older faces;
Till a child's voice fall as the dew
On furrows with heat parched through
And but hopeless of grain,
   Refreshing the desolate places –

Full clear on the ears of us hearkening
   And hungering for food of the sound
And thirsting for joy of his voice. . . .

No small sweet face with the daytime
To welcome, warmer than noon!
No sweet small voice as a bird's
To bring us the day's first words!
Mid May for us here is not Maytime:
  No summer begins with June.

He could not even read Shakespeare now:

Our Shakespeare now, as a man dumb-stricken,
  Stands silent there on the shelf:
And my thoughts, that had song in the heart of them, sicken,
  And relish not Shakespeare's self.

And my mood grows moodier than Hamlet's even,
  And man delights not me,
But only the face that morn and even
  My heart leapt only to see.

This, one has to admit, is the language of a lover:

A hand at the door taps light
As the hand of my heart's delight:
  It is but a full-grown hand,
Yet the stroke of it seems to start
Hope like a bird in my heart,
  Too feeble to soar or to stand. . . .

Desire, but in dreams, cannot ope
The door that was shut upon hope
  When love went out at the door.

But the little hand did not knock at the door again until September, when Swinburne wrote a jubilant poem, 'Sunrise': 'Four dark months overpast were atoned for, and summer began in September.'

Watts had evidently written, greatly disturbed, to Lady Jane, who replied to him on 14 May from Bradford-on-Avon, where she had taken a house: 'I quite understand what you feel about Algernon but he has given me no opening, as you think it likely he may have done, to enable me to give him the little word of advice you suggest – he tells me he has written "21 Poems of lamentation" on the subject of his dear little friend's absence which he calls a "total eclipse of the Sun". His love for that little friend amounts to devotion and I often hope that it may lead to the faith of his youth in some hidden way – for the love of, and the appreciation of innocent childhood is good and *wholesome*. You and no doubt his Parents will guard the little child from any harmful views on that subject that Algernon might inadvertently lead him into.

'If I can in any way hint at the necessity for care not to *over do*, I will not fail to do so, but it is not easy – he feels so sure of my sympathy for him in the love of children that I should be sorry to check his openness with me on the subject and he is so kind in sending me copies of what he writes that I would seem unkind to do so.

'I am so sorry that I cannot ask him to come and see us now but at present I have only one spare room and a small dressing room and I am afraid you would not think it safe for him to come alone . . . had I two rooms I should ask you if it would be possible for you to come down with him for a little change of air. . . . Your report of Algernon's health is satisfactory – What you say about his spoiling his writing by "not knowing where to stop" – is so very true. I constantly deplore it!'[17]

From the tone of this letter, one can see that both his mother and Watts continued to treat Swinburne at the age of forty-four as a child. But however he might lament the absence of Bertie, he was as busy as ever. In March he had written the article on Landor for the *Encyclopaedia Britannica*, as well as the articles on Marlowe and Keats. He was also correcting the proofs of Sidney Colvin's *Landor* in the 'English Men of Letters' series, which led to a lengthy and learned correspondence – just as he had worked with unremitting application at the corrupt text of Chapman for R. H. Shepherd's edition. As T. Earle Welby remarks: 'The purified text and the enhanced reputation of Chapman, and especially the increased prominence ever since given to that dramatist's great connected French plays, were due to Swinburne's generous efforts!'[18] Now, in the case of Landor, as he wrote to Landor's friend, the novelist Mrs Lynn Linton, he was giving Sidney Colvin 'information and (much needed) correction on such few points as my bibliographical research into Landoriana made me competent to speak upon'. In June he was greatly diverted to read in the Press that a man named Matthew Arnold had been fined ten shillings at Wandsworth police court for playing tip-cat in the street with two postmen – 'the most scandalous example of genius degraded by eccentricity', he wrote to William Bell-Scott, 'that I have seen since Robert Browning was taken up for running stark naked down Hyde Park, through the Marble Arch, at noon – "his second offence", according to the Times reporter of some years ago'. Oddly enough, a man named Robert Browning had been prosecuted for running naked through the Marble Arch.

But Swinburne was particularly aggrieved with Browning at that time for accepting the presidency of the New Shakespeare Society: 'You are doubtless aware,' he had written to Browning on 20 February 1881, 'and have probably been aware, somewhat longer than I who have only known of the fact since the evening of the day before yesterday, that a pamphlet in which I am described as – in so many words – a "person of damaged character" is now being circulated by the Founder and Director of a Society of which you are, actually or nominally, the President. If this imputation is true, it follows of course that I am unfit to hold any intercourse or keep up any acquaintance with you. If it is a lie, it follows equally of course that no person who remains in any way or in any degree associated with the writer of that pamphlet is fit to hold any intercourse or keep up any acquaintance with me.' Browning apparently replied that he could not very well take Swinburne's part in his quarrel with Furnivall, for Swinburne wrote back with freezing dignity to say – 'You labour under an entire and I must be allowed to say a most unaccountable misapprehension if you imagine for one instant that I at all events – as you say – "call upon you to take my part". I have never in any case called upon any man to do anything of the kind. Having been publicly and personally insulted in a manner too infamous and blackguardly for description, I did call upon you – as any man with any sense of honour or self-respect would in my place be bound to call upon you, or upon any other acquaintance – to let me know whether or not, after this, your name is to remain in any way publicly associated with one which in my humble opinion it is degrading if necessary, and disgraceful if unnecessary, for a gentleman to pronounce, to transcribe, or to remember. . . . I have no such impertinent and preposterous pretension – need I say so? – as would be that of prescribing or suggesting to you any course of conduct. But it is obvious that in addressing the President of the "New Shakespeare" Society I could no longer without degradation subscribe myself as your very sincerely A. C. Swinburne.'[19]

Early in 1880 Swinburne collected his inimitable 'specimens of modern poets', *Heptalogia*, or parodies written at different times of not only Tennyson, Browning, Mrs Browning, Coventry Patmore, 'Owen Meredith', and Rossetti, but also, at Watts's suggestion, of himself – 'Nephelidia', an astonishing demonstration that he was perfectly aware of his own weaknesses:

From the depth of the dreamy decline of the dawn
   through a notable nimbus of nebulous noonshine,
Pallid and pink as the palm of the flag-flower
   that flickers with fear of the flies as they float,
Are the looks of our lovers that lustrously lean
   from a marvel of mystic miraculous moonshine,
These that we feel in the blood of our blushes
   that thicken and threaten with throbs through the throat.

Equally self-analytical, but better, is 'Poeta Loquitur' in a metre akin to 'Dolores', which was not published until 1918:

In a maze of monotonous murmur
Where reason roves ruined by rhyme,
In a voice neither graver nor firmer
Than the bells on a fool's cap chime. . . .

Mad mixtures of Frenchified offal
With insults to Christendom's creed,
Blind blasphemy, schoolboy like scoff all
   These blazon me blockhead indeed.

In my poems, with ravishing rapture
Storm strikes me and strokes me and stings:
But I'm scarcely the bird you might capture
Out of doors in the thick of such things.

The wicked parody of Tennyson's 'The Higher Pantheism', written in 1877 and called 'The Higher Pantheism in a Nutshell', is quite masterly:

One, who is not, we see: but one, whom we see not, is:
Surely this is not that: but that is assuredly this.

What, and wherefore, and whence? for under is over and under:
If thunder could be without lightning, lightning could be without thunder.

Doubt is faith in the main: but faith, on the whole, is doubt:
We cannot believe by proof: but could we believe without?

Why, and whither, and how? for barley and rye are not clover:
Neither are straight lines curves: yet over is under and over.

Two and two may be four: but four and four are not eight:
Fate and God may be twain: but God is the same thing as fate. . . .

Body and spirit are twins: God only knows which is which:
The soul squats down in the flesh, like a tinker drunk in a ditch.

More is the whole than a part: but half is more than the whole:
Clearly the soul is the body: but is not the body the Soul? . . .

God, whom we see not, is: and God, who is not, we see:
Fiddle, we know, is diddle: and diddle, we take it, is dee.

'John Jones's Wife' is almost exactly like Browning:

This crab's wiser, it strikes me – no twist but implies life –
   Not a curl but's so fit you could find none fitter –
For the brute from its brutehood looks up thus and eyes life –
   Stoop your soul down and listen, you'll hear it twitter
Laughing lightly, – my crab's life's the wise life!

The collection was, of course, published anonymously and caused a good deal of bewilderment. Swinburne had written to William Rossetti in January 1870: 'Having wound up my (not exactly theistic) lyric, I looked at Tennyson's "Higher Pantheism" again – not bad verse altogether, but what gabble and babble of half-hatched thoughts and half-baked words! – and wrote at the tail of it this summary of his theology: [that is, the two concluding lines of what became 'The Higher Pantheism in a Nutshell']. I think it is terse and accurate as a Tennysonian compendium.' He told R. W. Roper that he could parody Browning's dischords with impunity, since Browning could never revenge himself by parodying his harmonies. Swinburne, of course, could do anything in verse.

In October 1881 he finished *Mary Stuart*, begun at Guilford Street, the final play in the enormous trilogy initiated at Oxford with *Chastelard* and continued in *Bothwell. Mary Stuart*, which begins with the Babington Plot and ends with Mary's execution, is a dignified but distinctly turgid production and not nearly so lively as even *Bothwell.* With all his admiration of Mary as a woman, Swinburne was too aware of her crooked motives to idealize her altogether and shows clearly that her death was a national necessity, if Elizabeth I and all that she stood for were to survive. And yet he can sing her praises through the mouth of Drury, for he is still drawn to the cruel and beautiful Borgia type (Act IV, ii):

> Unmerciful, unfaithful, but of heart
> So fiery high, so swift of spirit and clear,
> In extreme danger and pain so lifted up,
> So of all violent things inviolable,
> So large of courage, so superb of soul,
> So sheathed with iron mind invincible
> And arms unbreached of fireproof constancy –
> By shame not shaken, fear or force of death,
> Change, or all confluence of calamities –
> And so at her worst need beloved, and still,
> Naked of help and honour when she seemed,
> As other women would be, and of hope
> Stripped, still so of herself adorable
> By minds not always all ignobly mad
> Nor all made poisonous with false grain of faith,
> She shall be a world's wonder to all time,
> A deadly glory watched of marvelling men.

In Swinburne's play Elizabeth does not sign Mary's death-warrant until she receives a letter from her repeating the Countess of Shrewsbury's slanders that she had slept with her suitors and several of her favourites, and that she was malformed – or, in Ben Jonson's words to Drummond of Hawthornden, 'had a membrane on her, which made her uncapable of man, though for her delight she had tried many'. This letter, Swinburne tells us, had been written by Mary some time ago, thinking that in reporting such slanders to the queen she would show her loyalty and friendship! She then decided not to send it and gave it to Mary Beaton to burn. Mary Beaton, who secretly hated her mistress for the execution of Chastelard, had kept the letter and now persuaded Mary to send it after all as a last bid to save her life. But when Elizabeth read it, she became so enraged that she called for Mary's death-warrant and signed it. It is an effective dramatic stroke. Such a letter, purporting to be in Mary's hand, and seemingly addressed to Elizabeth, was found among Burleigh's papers at Hatfield. On the face of it, it seems unlikely that Mary would have ever written such a letter, though Elizabeth must have been aware of the Countess of Shrewsbury's loose tongue. 'The two points on which you touch – ' Swinburne wrote to Henry Arthur Bright on 20 January 1882, 'the balance of (at least, attempted) justice between the two opposite figures of the queens, and the dramatic intervention of Mary Beaton's revenge as the *cheville ouvrière* of the whole piece, "the very pulse of the machine", are exactly those on which I should wish the play to rest its claims.' The play was on the whole 'very coldly received', as Swinburne told Bright, but he was 'more than consoled by the cordial approbation of the illustrious and venerable author of "Philip van Artevelde" [Sir Henry Taylor]: the only living English poet who (in my poor opinion) is qualified to speak with any authority on the subject of historic or dramatic poetry'.[20] The *Saturday Review*, Swinburne's inveterate enemy, remarked: 'he has certainly done himself less than justice in putting into the mouths of two such important personages as Elizabeth and Mary speeches which have a rank flavour of Billingsgate. Shakespeare, who lived in an age which was sufficiently coarse in its language, was far more reticent in this way than the author of *Mary Stuart*' – which is demonstrably untrue. But then Shakespeare could scarcely have written of either Elizabeth or Mary Stuart, both of whom could be loud-mouthed enough.

'I am well into the second book or canto of *your* Tristram', Swinburne wrote to Watts from his mother's house at Bradford Leigh on 15 October 1881, 'containing the adventure illustrated by Morris on the walls of the Oxford Union in the same sunflowery style which you may remember. The only person to whom I have shown it is my reverend friend the Primate, whose too flattering and characteristic comment I cannot forbear to send you. After reading the account of the duel of Tristram with Palamede, and the manner of spending a happy night in the woods subsequently adopted by the rescued Iseult and her lover, his Grace was kind enough to say that he really didn't know which was done best, the fighting or the – here his Grace was betrayed, by a taste for unmeaning alliteration which I can only wonder at and deplore, into a verbal indiscretion which nothing should induce me to report. . . . It remains to be seen what verdict you will pronounce on my modest effort to paint a sylvan scene of unpretending enjoyment by moonlight. . . . I hope you will like the fight. I don't say Morris wouldn't have done it better, but I do *not* think any other of us all could.'[21] On 21 October he writes to Watts: 'All the second and a great part of the third canto, book, or fytte of Tristram is now transcribed in extensibus and revised ad unguem; and I have just finished my last revise of Mary

Stuart. . . . Also in the very last or "Second Author's Proof", I find now and then a letter or a point dropped "which was not so before". *Can* you secure me against these D. and B. contingencies by appeal to Chatto by word of mouth – stroke of hand – or blow of foot?'

But, as we have seen, Watts feared that certain passages in the second book of *Tristram* might be challenged by the public prosecutor. For instance:

Only with stress of soft fierce hands she prest
Between the throbbing blossoms of her breast
His ardent face, and through his hair her breath
Went quivering as when life is hard on death:
And with strong trembling fingers she strained fast
His head into her bosom; till at last
Satiate with sweetness of that burning bed,
His eyes afire with tears, he raised his head
And laughed into her lips; and all his heart
Filled hers; then face from face fell, and apart
Each hung on each with panting lips, and felt
Sense into sense and spirit into spirit melt

which immediately suggests a painting by Rossetti. Still more so do such lines as:

and her mouth
Was as a rose athirst that pants for drouth
Even while it laughs for pleasure of desire

which is only another way of saying that Swinburne went to painting for an experience he may not have had himself. So the Public Prosecutor was not unduly disturbed. In many passages *Tristram* rises to magnificence, especially in 'Iseult at Tintagel' (Book V). This book has often been praised, but it is worthwhile to draw attention to it again, at a time when Swinburne is no longer read. But here, in spite of himself, are echoes of *Idylls of the King*:

But that same night in Cornwall oversea
Couched at Queen Iseult's hand, against her knee,
With keen kind eyes that read her whole heart's pain
Fast at wide watch lay Tristram's hound Hodain,
The goodliest and the mightiest born on earth,
That many a forest day of fiery mirth
Had plied his craft before them; and the queen
Cherished him, even for those dim years between,
More than of old in those bright months far flown
When ere a blast of Tristram's horn was blown
Each morning as the woods rekindled, ere
Day gat full empire of the glimmering air,
Delight of dawn would quicken him . . .

11 A corner in The Pines, showing the carved and painted cabinet and Rossetti's Indian chairs, from *At the Pines* by Mollie Panter-Downes

12 Swinburne in 1895

And as the queen prays in agony in her room alone, the storm rages outside:

> And the night spake, and thundered on the sea,
> Ravening aloud for ruin of lives: and all
> The bastions of the main cliff's northward wall
> Rang response out from all their deepening length,
> As the east wind girded up his godlike strength
> And hurled in hard against that high-towered hold
> The fleeces of the flock that knows no fold,
> The rent white shreds of shattering storm.

But the effect is cumulative and the book should be read as a whole, and it can be overwhelming, as when Iseult's prayers become curses, even as Swinburne had cursed the cruelty of the gods in *Atalanta*:

> 'And yet what life – Lord God, what life for me
> Has thy strong wrath made ready? Dost thou think
> How lips whose thirst hath only tears to drink
> Grow grey for grief untimely? Dost thou know,
> O happy God, how men wax weary of woe –
> Yea, for their wrong's sake that thine hand hath done
> Come even to hate thy semblance in the sun?
> Turn back from dawn and noon and all thy light
> To make their souls one with the soul of night?
> Christ, if thou hear yet or have eyes to see,
> Thou, that hadst pity, and hast no pity on me,
> Know'st thou no more, as in this life's sharp span,
> What pain thou hadst on earth, what pain hath man?
> Hast thou no care, that all we suffer yet?
> What help is ours of thee if thou forget?
> What profit have we though thy blood were given,
> If we that sin bleed and be not forgiven?
> Not love but hate, thou bitter God and strange,
> Whose heart as man's heart hath grown cold with change,
> Not love but hate thou showest us that have sinned.'
> And like a world's cry shuddering was the wind,
> And like God's voice threatening was the sea.

William Morris, after he had become a Marxist, said that he could not read *Tristram*. 'But, to confess and be hanged, you know I never really could sympathise with Swinburne's work,' he wrote somewhat surprisingly to Georgiana Burne-Jones, 'it always seemed to me to be founded on literature, not on nature' – a criticism that has been quoted against Swinburne ever since. But much of *Tristram* is as passionate as Morris's early 'Defence of Guenevere' and, as a whole, at least as effective as *Sigurd*. It is true that it shows a sense of strain. As Earle Welby remarked: 'Great lines are common in *Tristram*: but almost every line aspires to greatness . . . every line would be a blazing jewel. And the final effect, I say it with great reluctance, is one of fatigue. One puts down the poem with dazzled, aching eyes.'[22] It is difficult not to agree with so sympathetic a critic. But so much of the poem is noble and exalted in feeling and, as Welby remarks, the conclusion is of the utmost nobility. King Mark, realizing at last the strength of their great love, and its cause, builds for the lovers a shrine on the sea-shore:

till at last
On these things too was doom as darkness cast:
For the strong sea hath swallowed wall and tower,
And where their limbs were laid in woful hour
For many a fathom gleams and moves and moans
The tide that sweeps above their coffined bones
In the wrecked chancel by the shivered shrine:
Nor where they sleep shall moon or sunlight shine
Nor man look down for ever: none shall say,
Here once, or here, Tristram and Iseult lay:
But peace they have that none may gain who live,
And rest about them that no love can give,
And over them, while death and life shall be,
The light and sound and darkness of the sea.

# CHAPTER TWELVE

# 1882–1909
# RELICS

It was in the spring of 1899 that Max Beerbohm first visited Swinburne, now extremely deaf, and left his inimitable account in his essay 'No. 2 The Pines'. To him Swinburne appeared as 'a strange small figure in grey, having an air at once noble and roguish, proud and skittish. . . . You do not usually associate a man of genius, when you see one, with any social class: and Swinburne being of an aspect so unrelated as it was to any species of human kind, I wondered the more that almost the first impression he made on me, or would make on any one, was of a very great gentleman indeed. Not of an *old* gentleman either. Sparse and straggling though the grey hair was that fringed the immense pale dome of his head, and venerably haloed though he was for me by his greatness, there was yet about him something – boyish? girlish? childish rather; something of a beautifully well-bred child. But he had the eyes of a god, and the smile of an elf. In figure, at first glance, he seemed almost fat; but this was merely because of the way he carried himself, with his long neck strained so tightly back that he all receded from the waist upwards . . . when he bowed he did not unbend his back, but only his neck – the length of the neck accounting for the depth of the bow. His hands were tiny, even for his size, and they fluttered helplessly, touchingly, unceasingly.'

At luncheon, Swinburne sat silent, in a deaf man's silent world: 'This was the more tantalizing because [he] seemed as though he were bubbling over with all sorts of notions. Not that he looked at either of us. He smiled only to himself, and to his platefull of meat, and to the small bottle of Bass's pale ale that stood before him – ultimate allowance of one who had erst clashed cymbals in Naxos. This small bottle he eyed often and with enthusiasm. . . . It made me unhappy to see what trouble he had in managing his knife and fork. . . . I have known no man of genius who had not to pay, in some affliction or defect either physical or spiritual, for what the gods had given him. . . . He, evidently, was quite gay, in his silence – and in the word that was for him silent. . . . Now and again his shining light-grey eyes roved from the table, darting this way and that – across the room, up at the ceiling, out of the window; only never at us. Somehow this aloofness gave no hint of indifference. It seemed to be, rather, a point in good manners – the good manners of a child "sitting up to table", not "staring", not "asking questions", and reflecting great credit on its invaluable old nurse.'

It is typical of Max Beerbohm that he could be amusing, affectionate and admiring at the same time. His portrait of Swinburne at the age of sixty-two is incomparably the best we have: 'So soon as the mutton had been replaced by the apple-pie, Watts-Dunton leaned forward and "Well, Algernon", he roared, "how was it on the Heath today?" Swinburne, who had meekly inclined his ear to the question, now threw back his head, uttering a sound that was like the cooing of a dove, and forthwith, ever so musically, he spoke to us of his walk; spoke not in the strain of a man who had been taking his daily exercise on Putney Heath, but rather in that of a Peri who had at long last been suffered to pass through Paradise. And rather than that he spoke would I say that he cooingly and flutingly *sang* of his experience. The wonders of this morning's wind and sun and clouds were expressed in a flow of words so right and sentences so perfectly balanced that they would have seemed pedantic had they not been clearly as spontaneous as the wordless notes of a bird in song. The frail, sweet voice rose and fell, lingered, quickened in all manner of trills and roulades. That he himself could not hear it, seemed to me the greatest loss his deafness inflicted on him. One would have expected this disability to mar the music; but it didn't; save that now and again a note would come out metallic and over-shrill, the tones were under good control. The whole manner and method had certainly a strong element of oddness; but no one incapable of condemning as unmanly the song of a lark would have called it affected. . . . Well do I remember his ecstasy of emphasis and immensity of pause when he described how he had seen in a perambulator on the Heath today "the most BEAUT-iful babbie ever beheld by mortal eyes". . . . After Mazzini had followed Landor to Elysium, and Victor Hugo had followed Mazzini, babies were what among live creatures most evoked Swinburne's genius for self-abasement. . . . He could as soon have imagined a man not loving the very sea as not doting on the aspect of babies and not reading at least one play by an Elizabethan or Jacobean dramatist every day.'

The fact that Swinburne was not allowed to talk before half the meal was over, was not due, as Max had thought at first, to Watts-Dunton's desire to monopolize his guest's attention and to impress him with a due sense of his own importance, so much as to the fact that 'had Swinburne been admitted earlier to the talk, he would not have taken his proper quantity of roast mutton'. But even so: 'Often, before he had said his really full say on the theme suggested by Watts-Dunton's loud interrogation, he would curb his speech and try to eliminate himself, bowing his head over his plate; and then, when he had promptly been brought in again, he would always try to atone for his inhibiting deafness by much reference and deference to all that we might otherwise have to say. "I hope," he would coo to me, "my friend

Watts-Dunton, who" – and here he would turn and make a little bow to Watts-Dunton – "is himself a scholar, will bear me out when I say" – or "I hardly know," he would flute to his old friend, "whether Mr Beerbohm" – here a bow to me – "will agree with me in my opinion of" some delicate point in Greek prosody or some incident in an old French romance I had never heard of.

'On one occasion, just before the removal of the mutton, Watts-Dunton had been asking me about an English translation that had been made of M. Rostand's "Cyrano de Bergerac". He then took my information as the match to ignite the Swinburnian tinder. "Well, Algernon, it seems that 'Cyrano de Bergerac' " – but this first spark was enough: instantly Swinburne was praising the works of Cyrano de Bergerac. Of M. Rostand he may have heard, but him he forgot. Indeed I never heard Swinburne mention a single contemporary writer. . . . "Of course, of course, you have read 'L'Histoire Comique des États et des Empires de la Lune?' " I admitted, by gesture and facial expression, that I had not. Whereupon he reeled out curious extracts from that allegory – "almost as good as 'Gulliver' ".'

In retrospect, Max tells us, that when he recalled the dining-room of The Pines, he saw 'the long white stretch of table-cloth, with Swinburne and Watts-Dunton and another at the extreme end of it; Watts-Dunton between us, very low down over his plate, very cosy and hirsute, and rather like the dormouse at that long tea-table which Alice found in Wonderland. I see myself sitting there wide-eyed, as Alice sat. And, had the hare been a great poet, and the hatter a great gentleman, and neither of them mad but each only very odd and vivacious, I might see Swinburne as a glorified blend of those two.'

Luncheon over, 'Swinburne would dart round the table, proffer his hand to me, bow deeply, bow to Watts-Dunton also, and disappear. "He always walks in the morning, writes in the afternoon, and reads in the evening," Watts-Dunton would say with a touch of tutorial pride in this regimen.' But on one occasion Swinburne expressed a wish to show Max his library: 'Up the staircase he then literally bounded – three, literally three, stairs at a time. I began to follow at the same rate, but immediately slackened speed for fear that Watts-Dunton behind us might be embittered at sight of so much youth and legerity. Swinburne waited on the threshold to receive us, as it were, and pass us in. Watts-Dunton went and ensconced himself snugly in a corner. The sun had appeared after a grey morning, and it pleasantly flooded this big living-room whose walls were entirely lined with the mellow backs of books. Here, as host, among his treasures, Swinburne was more than ever attractive. He was as happy as was any mote in the sunshine about him; and the fluttering of his little hands, and feet too, was but as a token of so much felicity. He looked older, it is true, in the strong light. But these added years made only more notable his youngness of heart. An illustrious bibliophile among his books? A birthday child, rather, among his toys.

'Proudly he explained to me the general system under which the volumes were ranged in this or that division of shelves. Then he conducted me to a chair near the window, left me there, flew away, flew up the rungs of a mahogany ladder, plucked a small volume, and in a twinkling was at my side: "This, I *think*, will please you!" It did. It had a beautifully engraved title-page and a pleasing scent of old, old leather. It was the *editio princeps* of a play by some lesser Elizabethan or Jacobean dramatist. "Of course you know it?" my host fluted.

'How I wished I could say that I knew it and loved it well! I revealed to him (for by speaking very loudly towards his inclined head I was able to make him hear) that I had not read it. He envied anyone who had such pleasure in store. He darted to the ladder, and came back thrusting gently into my hands another volume of like date: "Of course you know *this*?"

'Again I had to confess that I did not, and to shout my appreciation of the fount of type, the margins, the binding. He beamed agreement, and fetched another volume. Archly he indicated the title, cooing, "You are a lover of *this*, I hope?" And again I was shamed by my inexperience.' Though at this time Swinburne was sixty-two, he changed so little during the last thirty years of his life that Max's account applies equally well to 1889 or, indeed, 1882. But when exhibiting his treasures, he was liable to become more and more excited. Watts, who knew the danger signals all too well, had to guard against this, and at a certain stage he would begin making discreet signs to the visitor that it was now time to withdraw.

Max Beerbohm says that he enjoyed his afternoons with Watts sitting in front of the dining-room fire in this 'lair of solid comfort and fervid old romanticism' as much as his sessions with Swinburne himself. Watts's frock-coat, 'though the Muses had crumpled it, inspired confidence in his judgement of other things than verse. But let there be no mistake. He was no *bourgeois parnassien*, as his enemies insinuated. No doubt he had been very useful to men of genius, in virtue of qualities they lacked, but the secret of his hold on them was in his own rich nature. He was not only a born man of letters, he was a deeply emotional human being whose appeal was as much to the heart as to the head. . . . The mysticism of Watts-Dunton (who, once comfortably settled at the fireside, knew no reserve) was in contrast with the frock-coat and the practical abilities; but it was essential, and they were of the surface. For humorous Rossetti, I daresay, the very contrast made Theodore's company the more precious. He himself had assuredly been, and the memory of him still was, the master-fact in Watts-Dunton's life. "Algernon" was as an adopted child, "Gabriel" as a long-lost only brother.' And sitting side by side in the capacious leather armchairs, sipping their steaming whisky toddy, Watts would discourse of the illustrious people he had known. Beerbohm continues: 'The thrill of the past was always strong in me when Watts-Dunton mentioned – seldom without a guffaw did he mention – "Jimmy Whistler". I think he put in the surname because "that fellow" had not behaved well to Swinburne. But he could not omit the nickname, because it was impossible for him to feel the right measure of resentment against "such a funny fellow. . . . When I took on the name Dunton, I had a note from him. Just this, with his butterfly signature: *Theodore, What's Dunton?* That was very good – very good. . . . But, of course," he added gravely, "I took no notice."' Loyalty to Swinburne forbade. However often Watts mentioned 'Gabriel', Max says that he still remained for him a nebulous and mysterious figure: 'I felt no nearer to him than you feel to the Archangel who bears that name and no surname.'[1]

Writing to E. C. Stedman on 4 April 1882 Swinburne says: 'For the last two years I have been stronger and harder at work – the only test of strength and happiness for some temperaments – than ever I was in my life that I remember.' He adds that he is living 'on the verge of a great moor or down, and within easy walk of some of the loveliest woodlands and meadow scenery in England'. Yet Swinburne knew Suffolk, Norfolk and Northumberland! The only good notice he has seen of his *Mary Stuart* '(with one Italian exception) is the work of a Russian written in French'. This was Mark André Raffalovich, who reviewed *Mary Stuart* in the *Journal de St Petersbourg*, to which he had also contributed articles on Meredith and Burne-Jones.[2] That was in the days when Russia was still a land of international culture – for the few. Stedman had also written a notice of *Mary Stuart* for *Harper's New Monthly Magazine* in his article 'Some London Poets'.[3] Swinburne adds that he has been asked to write the essay on Mary Stuart for the *Encyclopaedia Britannica*: 'I doubt if the like compliment was ever paid before to one of our "idle trade". To this task I am about to set myself as soon as I have finished my long narrative poem in nine parts – "Tristram of Lyonesse". . . . My next volume, which will go to the press as soon as this main *pièce de résistance* is ready to be served up, will contain, besides, upwards of fifty lyrical poems – mostly, of course, short; and the greater number of them studies of childhood or songs about children – and various odes and sonnets on literary, historic, and political matters: among them a series of twenty-one sonnets on the English dramatic poets, from 1590 to 1650, which I hope will interest those who share my devotion to that branch of our older poetry, and perhaps attract to the study of it some who have not yet embarked on that most delightful and inexhaustible line of reading, which is to me (as far as enjoyment goes) all that ever it was to Charles Lamb. In that case I shall certainly have been of some service to my generation.'

Indeed, Swinburne was a pioneer in reviving interest in the Elizabethan, Jacobean and Caroline drama. He was also in touch with such men as William Poel, the pioneer in the staging of these plays in the Elizabethan manner, and the Elizabethan scholars, A. H. Bullen and Halliwell-Phillipps. He adds: 'I am truly obliged by your compliance with my request not to cite me – who have never yet gone in for autobiography – as a chronicler of myself. (Indeed I have never condescended to contradict even the most offensive and outrageous reports printed of me in the viler journals. No truth-teller, I venture to believe, could print of me anything that was otherwise than "honourable".)'

The only time Swinburne has ever seen Oscar Wilde, he tells Stedman, 'was in a crush at our acquaintance Lord Houghton's. I thought he seemed a harmless young nobody, and had no notion he was the sort of man to play the mountebank as he seems to have been doing. A letter that he wrote to me lately about Walt Whitman was quite a modest, gentlemanlike, reasonable affair without any flourish or affectation of any kind in matter of expression. It is really very odd. I should think you in America must be as tired of his name as we in London of Mr Barnam's and his Jumbo's.'[4] Oscar Wilde had, by 1882, published nothing except a very derivative volume of poems and was lecturing in the States dressed in velvet knee-breeches with a lily in his hand, as he had appeared in Gilbert and Sullivan's *Patience* the year before at the Opéra Comique, though the character of Bunthorne was as much Whistler, Rossetti and Swinburne as Oscar Wilde. In this composite figure Gilbert satirized the whole aesthetic movement.

Rossetti died on 9 April 1882, and writing to Bell-Scott on 17 April Swinburne said: 'No one who ever loved the friend who died to me – by his own act and wish – exactly ten years ago can feel, I suppose, otherwise than sorrowfully content that the sufferer who survived the man we knew and loved should now be at rest. To this day I am utterly ignorant, and utterly unable to conjecture, why after our last parting in the early summer of 1872 he should have chosen suddenly to regard me as a stranger. But by all accounts it is as well for my recollection of him that it was so; and under the circumstances I felt that my attendance at his funeral could have been but a painful mockery. I send you the verses which I wrote on the morning when he was laid to rest at last and for ever. You know, I am sure, that I am incapable of dealing at such a time and on such a topic in poetical insincerity or sentimental rhetoric: so perhaps I need hardly add that I do now – on the whole – strongly incline to believe in the survival of life – individual and conscious life – after the dissolution of the body. Otherwise I would not on any account have affected a hope or conviction I did not feel. The glorious and desperately unorthodox verses written in sight of death by Emily Brontë express my creed – or rather my creedless faith – better than any words I know.'[5]

Swinburne's sonnet 'A Death on Easter Day' was included in *A Century of Roundels*:

A light more bright than ever bathed the skies
Departs for all time out of all men's eyes.
  The crowns that girt last night a living head
  Shine only now, though deathless, on the dead:

Art that mocks death, and Song that never dies.
Albeit the bright sweet mothlike wings be furled,
Hope sees, past all division and defection,
And higher than swims the mist of human breath,
The soul most radiant once in all the world
Requickened to regenerate resurrection.
Out of the likeness of the shadow of death.

In the same year he wrote a sonnet on the deaths of Thomas Carlyle and George Eliot:

The stormy sophist with his mouth of thunder,
Clothed with loud words and mantled in the might
Of darkness and magnificence of night:
And one whose eye could smite the night in sunder,
Searching if light or no light were thereunder,
And found in love of loving-kindness light.

But in 'After Looking into Carlyle's Reminiscences' he wrote:

These deathless names by this dead snake defiled
Bid memory spit upon him for their sake. . .

Let worms consume its memory with its tongue,
The fang that stabbed fair Truth, the lips that stung
Men's memories uncorroded with its breath.
Forgive me, that with bitter words like his
I mix the gentlest English name that is,
The tenderest held of all that know not death

– presumably a reference to Jane Welsh Carlyle. The lines 'After Sunset' and 'A Study from Memory' were written in memory of Lady Pauline Trevelyan. 'They came into my head one splendid evening,' he told Bell-Scott in the letter of 17 April, 'when I was "walking westward" into the sunset and back again eastward under the rising and gathering stars.' He also wrote the elegy on 'The Death of Richard Wagner' and the 'Adieux à Marie Stuart'. 'I have taken leave of the Queen whom my forefather rode with all his spearmen (see Froude) to welcome with homage on her landing at Solway Firth,' he wrote to Bell-Scott, 'in some verses which I hope you will like when you read them in my new volume: for I like them as well as anything I ever wrote, and I believe my mother likes them better':

O diamond heart, unflawed and clear,
The whole world's crowning jewel!
Was ever heart so deadly dear
So cruel?

This, then, seems to have been part of the secret of her attraction for him, though flawed her heart certainly was.

'My dear Ned,' Swinburne wrote to Burne-Jones on 13 July, 'I *cannot* make up my mind to forego the pleasure of reading to you a little more of Tristram before I send you your copy. I have been looking forward for months to the time when I should read you "Joyous Gard" (Canto VI) – not that I am so vain of its merit ("we ain't proud, 'cause Ma says it's sinful") but that, when I had finished writing it, it came into my head that you would like it, and, if I may say so without seeming extra self-conceited, that it had something in common with your paintings in – shall we say, Tone? If you can't or won't come to me, may I come to you some day next week with the book in my pocket?'[6]

Two days later he wrote to the veteran poet 'Orion' Horne: 'What a delightful evening we had last night. I need not say how much more than gratified I am by what you say of my book on Blake. I was afraid it bore too many marks of juvenility in style, and indeed in thought, to be worthy of such generous praise. . . . I spent days in the print-room of the British Museum scribbling in pencil the analysis of Blake's "prophetic books", and hours at Lord Houghton's in the same labour with pen and ink to produce a book which was received with general contumely, ridicule, and neglect, and has never yet, I believe, paid half its expenses, or struggled into a second edition. Consequently, of course, I value all the more any kind word bestowed on the most unlucky and despised of all my brain-children – and especially when the bestower can speak with such authority as yours. . . . I wonder if anybody will ever again read Blake's Jerusalem through! as I conscientiously did.'

That same month Edmund Gosse's little son fell seriously ill and Swinburne wrote a touching note of sympathy: 'I know parents can hardly be expected to believe that a "barren stock" (to borrow Queen Elizabeth's phrase) can be capable in imagination of entering into their emotions. The hearing of the little thing's first words, uttered as they were in pain, must indeed have given you a sense of awe as well as tenderness and terror.'[7]

In September he went with Watts for a holiday in Guernsey and wrote rhapsodically to Mrs Lynn Linton from St Peter's Port: 'I know nothing in Italy to beat or perhaps to match it for the very romance of loveliness; and the sea, with its headlands like the Hebrides and its coves like South Cornwall, has surpassed itself just here, though all this part of the channel is the crown and flower of all seas in the world for splendour of beauty as well as menace – being the most dangerous of them all, as my father who knew them all assured me, in confirmation of the old seaman's accuracy in Les Travailleurs de la Mer. I need it all, beauty and splendour and grandeur and miracle of renewed wonder on every line of the coast, to half-atone for the disappointment of the Master's absence when I have come for the second time, trusting in delusive assurances of his presence, to lay my homage at his feet as I did at Landor's eighteen years and four months ago.' He concludes by hoping that Mrs Linton will visit The Pines soon 'when I shall – Fate willing – have the honour of presenting you at the court of H.M. my "benevolent despot" at eight'[8] – that is, Bertie Mason.

On his return, later in the month, he tells Churton Collins that he is contemplating writing a tragedy on the Life and Death of Caesar Borgia, 'but what between triple incest, and the bisexual harem of the Vicar of Christ, – points which could not be wholly ignored in a chronicle history of the Borgias – even I feel conscious of something like the sentiment called funk in the face of inevitable difficulties. Yet the triumph and fall (through his own triumphant wickedness) of the greatest warrior and statesman of his age might and should be an almost incomparable argument of tragic poetry.' He was to attempt it in *The Duke of Gandia* (1908), achieving at last a tautness and economy hardly to be found anywhere else in his work, except in *Rosamond, Queen of the Lombards* (1899).

In that same month, Sir Henry Taylor wrote to Swinburne of *Tristram of Lyonesse*: 'Your kind of power in poetry is one which often sweeps me along through one or more pages with a consciousness that I am only half-understanding what I read; feeling the impulse in all its fulness and the poetic beauty in all its richness with only an imperfect conception of its purport'[9] – a feeling that many readers of Swinburne's longer poems must share, though he replied modestly enough on 1 October: 'It is very difficult, I think, for a man to realize when he had failed, and how he has failed, to make himself clear and his meaning easy to follow at first reading. I have observed this difficulty in others, when I have told them that I could not make out the drift of something they had written at once: and I daresay Lycophron himself thought his "Cassandra" as lucid as an idyl of Theocritus. I hold obscurity to be so great a fault that I should think no pains too great to take in the endeavour to avoid it; but one must see a fault before it can be avoided, and this one is so difficult to see that I should not wonder if the author of the most unintelligible poem ever written in any language (which I take to be, beyond all possibility of comparison, the political and religious satire of a great tragic poet whose name was first introduced to me by a quotation in the notes to "Edwin the Fair" – Cyril Tourneur's "Transformed Metamorphosis") thought his allegory as translucent as we find the "Pilgrim's Progress".'[10]

It was also in September that Horne, now in his eightieth year, hearing of Swinburne's prowess as a swimmer, challenged him to what Gosse calls 'a public contest in natation', proposing the Westminster Aquarium as the scene of the contest and offering to share the proceeds with him. But Swinburne was not amused and stood upon his Ashburnham dignity. It was this same dignity which intimidated the 'hulking poetaster', who had endeavoured to engage him in correspondence and who at last wrote to say that he would be waiting for him on Wimbledon Common to give him a thrashing. Swinburne nevertheless took his morning walk as usual and, meeting the man, who was standing beside the path with a cudgel, 'cowed him by sheer personal dignity, and serenely continued to walk on, with the blusterer growling behind him'.[11]

Swinburne spent the greater part of October and November 1882 with his mother at Leigh House, Bradford-on-Avon. He was unable to work and wrote to Watts on 8 October: 'I really believe the stimulus of your criticism and encouragement has come to be – in the all but inspired language of the Church Catechism – "generally necessary to salvation" if not to creation of my case; for if I do write a few lines I am immediately impelled to scratch them out. . . . I do feel most awfully torpid, though of course I am cordially enjoying my stay here – only my working faculty seems actually benumbed. I have not spirit even to turn a sentence of Chesterfieldian Johnsonese.'[12] The following week he wrote again: 'I am reading the New Testament in a superb black-letter copy of Edward VI's version, collating it chapter by chapter with the authorized text, which hitherto I find (more often than not) inferior in direct force and sometimes in lucidity. The older version is magnificent English – certainly, I think, better on the whole than ours. And I never saw quite such beautiful printing in my life.' 'I have got again into a delightful groove of quiet family life,' he wrote later in the month, 'and should not – but for that – care how long I remained in it' – 'that' being the fact that he was missed at The Pines by Bertie and his mother.

When George Powell died suddenly in November, one year after his childless marriage, Swinburne commemorated him in several affectionate poems: 'A Dead Friend', 'Past Days' and 'Autumn in Winter'. In 'Past Days' he dreams nostalgically of the summers spent with Powell at Étretât:

> The Norman downs with bright grey waves for belt
> Were more to us than inland ways might be;
> A clearer sense of nearer heaven was felt
>   Above the sea.

'Autumn in Winter' celebrates Powell's love of Wagner. 'The poor fellow was one of the most obliging and kind-hearted of men, and wonderfully bright-spirited under severe trial and trouble,' he wrote to Watts. 'I shall always have a very tender and regretful remembrance of him.'

It was late in October when Swinburne read a review in the *Academy* of Hall-Caine's *Recollections of Dante Gabriel Rossetti*, which provoked an extraordinary diatribe against his old friend. On the causes of Rossetti's breakdown in 1872–74 Hall-Caine had written that Buchanan's *Fleshly School of Poetry* had been as much to blame as Lizzie Siddal's death ten years earlier. 'For myself,' Swinburne wrote to Watts on 31 October, 'if it is really to be received as truth that such a thing as Buchanan's attack – less in itself than the least of a thousand onslaughts which have never for one hour affected my peace of mind or impaired my self-reliance and self-respect

– is to be classed in its effect on the victim with so fearful a catastrophe as the loss of his wife in so terrible and heart-rending a manner – in that case, remembering the loyal, devoted, and unselfish affection which I lavished for fifteen years on the meanest, poorest, and most abject and unmanly nature of which any record remains in even literary history, I cannot say I wonder at the final upshot of our relations, but I can most truly say from the very depth of my heart and conscience, "I am ashamed through all my nature to have loved so vile a thing." Thank God for the difference between my "best friend" of the past and my best friend of the present.'

The reply of his best friend of the present is not recorded. Evidently, Swinburne had forgotten, or did not know, that Rossetti's main concern about Buchanan's attack on his character (and there were others at the time just as damaging) was that it might cloud his relations with Jane Morris, who was very sensitive of her own reputation. Nor did he understand the full effects of Rossetti's persecution mania.

Swinburne left Bradford-on-Avon later in November, and Lady Jane wrote to Watts: 'he will leave home by a Train that will reach Paddington at 5.45, which we have recommended to him as he will not have to change his carriage. . . . I hope this will make it safe for him to go alone, for I have no means of sending one with him – he will have his luncheon before he leaves.' But the train left Trowbridge a quarter of an hour earlier than expected, so Swinburne had to take a later one, which did not arrive at Paddington until 7.15 and his mother telegraphed frantically to Watts via the station master at Paddington to tell him so. She also wrote: 'I sincerely hope . . . that he may get home all safe . . . I do think we may trust him. Thanks to your care he seems quite a changed man. No words can say what a comfort it is to see him as he now is.'

At the end of November 1882 Swinburne was invited to Paris by Victor Hugo to be present at the fiftieth anniversary of the first (and only) performance of *Le Roi s'amuse* – according to his worshipper 'the greatest play since Shakespeare'. Watts accompanied him, of course. But according to Gosse, as far as Swinburne was concerned, the celebrations were something of a fiasco. To begin with, he was unable to hear a word of the performance, being now almost completely deaf and afterwards he was presented to the Master 'in such a whirl of social excitement that they were hardly sure that Hugo realized who Swinburne was, and they saw him no more'. Playing down the occasion for the sake of its inherent comedy, Gosse assures us that 'it is certain that the English visitors found themselves "out of it" in the press of adulation'.[13] This is not strictly true, for Hugo had already invited Swinburne to dinner and had assured him that he was 'as happy to press his hand as that of my son'. Unfortunately, Swinburne was unable to hear the terms in which the great poet proposed his health and Hugo was equally deaf to Swinburne's fervent reply. Swinburne then drained his glass to the Master and dashed it to the ground. But we are told that Hugo, misunderstanding this traditional gesture, only mourned the loss of one of his best wine glasses.[14]

Swinburne's letter to his mother, written after his return to Putney on 26 November, makes it clear that it was for him a very great occasion: 'On Friday morning Watts and I arrived about 7 or 8 o'clock from Paris, after five days' stay – five of the most remarkable days of my life. On Monday (as you may have seen in the *Times*) I was invited to dinner at Victor Hugo's, and accordingly presented myself in a state of perturbation as well as delight before the greatest – I know – and I believe the best, man now living. No words can express his kindness of manner, as he said on taking my hand, "Je suis heureux de vous serrer la main comme à mon fils." I am delighted to say that he is even more wonderful – all things considered – for his age than Mrs Proctor for hers. He will be eighty-one in February, and walked upright and firm without a stick. His white hair is as thick as his dark eyebrows, and his eyes are as bright and clear as a little child's. After dinner, he drank my health with a little speech, of which – tho' I sat just opposite him – my accursed deafness prevented my hearing a single word. This, however, was the only drawback – tho' certainly a considerable one – to my pleasure. On Wednesday evening I went with Watts to the places in the stalls of the Théâtre Français provided for us by the great kindness of my friend and correspondent for a good many years now, Auguste Vacquerie, the chief editor of the *Rappel*, and all but a son of Victor Hugo. It was, as you probably know, the second night of the representation, on a Parisian stage, of a play which had first been acted on the same day fifty years before, and suppressed on the next day by Louis Philippe's government, on account of a supposed allusion, in a single line, to the infamy of Citizen Philippe Egalité, that worthy monarch's worthy parent. This time *Le Roi s'amuse* – which Watts thinks Hugo's greatest work, second only to Shakespeare's *King Lear* in all the world of tragic poetry with which it can rightly be compared – was on the whole nobly acted and worthily received. I was invited between the 3rd and 4th acts into the author's box, where I found him sitting in state, and in reply to his question, "Êtes vous content?" said I most certainly was, and ventured to ask if he did not approve of the chief actor, Got, in the part of Triboulet, which is supposed to be the most trying and overwhelming for an actor that ever was written (I should have thought Lear as bad, but Watts thinks the strain in the part of Triboulet must be even greater than that of Lear; and he knows far more of the stage than I do). Hugo replied that he did; and indeed it was generally very fine, as far as a deaf wretch can judge. There was not quite such a prolonged thunder of applause at the end as I expected; but Watts thinks this was merely due to the overpowering effect of the close, which is certainly the most terrible as well as pathetic catastrophe in any play except (again and of course) *King Lear*.

'I have also made acquaintance with the translatress of my Ode on the Statue of Victor Hugo [Tola Dorian] and her husband, and (not least) their little girl. . . . She is the sweetest and brightest little person now going, and all the admiration lavished by one of the most brilliant circles in Paris on her beauty and cleverness has not – as far as I can see – made her in the least vain or affected. Her mamma is a princess by birth and (as of course you will have anticipated) a Nihilist: a Russian. . . . She talks English as well as I do, and French as well as our common master Victor Hugo does. And she has a very pretty and pleasant house in the suburbs of Paris, with a splendid stud of horses, which she took me to see – among others, a most lovely Arabian, and a splendid Russian, the strongest-looking horse I ever saw, which I can quite believe will (as its mistress says) go anywhere and hold out for any time. Also, there was Dora's pony, which I have been describing to Bertie as eloquently as I can. Perhaps I need not add that Dora's mother is much taken with my poems on Bertie, some of which she has been so good as to translate to Victor Hugo, who has honoured them with his approbation – which, next to your liking them, is the most delightful tribute as well as the greatest honour that any work of mine ever received.'[15]

At Tola Dorian's house he also met Leconte de Lisle – 'the Frenchman I most wanted to meet outside the Master's own peculiar circle', he told Nichol in a letter of 8 December, 'the poet, Hellenist and freethinker, a very noble and amiable old man'. Later in November, he sent Tola Dorian 'quelques méchants bouts-rimés'; adding: 'Me voici donc retombé sur terre. Et quoique ce soit la terre natale, je ne puis toutefois m'empêcher de regretter un peu le paradis que je viens de quitter. . . . Thackeray le cynique sentimental a dit – et je l'en aime un peu mieux – "I should like to have been Shakespeare's shoeblack." Et moi je voudrais pouvoir cirer tous les matins les bottes de V.H.'[16]

Meanwhile, the legends associated with Swinburne's visits to Chaumière de Dolmancé at Étretât had found their way into the pages of *Figaro*, and he wrote to the *World* on 29 November to contradict them, after they had been repeated by that paper's Paris correspondent: 'An article in the *Figaro* is hardly an object to which I think it necessary to call attention by condescending to contradict the gay and graceful fictions of its sportive writer; but when the imaginative gambols of Almaviva's vivacious valet find an echo on the boards of English journalism, I trust it may not be thought obtrusive or superfluous to intimate that, as far as I am concerned, the veracity of the ex-barber is precisely what it was in the days of Beaumarchais – a minus quantity. . . . As to the legend of my residence at Étretât, the facts – if anybody should think them worth record – are simply these: that I was twice, for a month or more, the guest at that watering-place, of a dear and lamented friend; that our chief pursuits were boating and swimming, and our only associates the fishermen of the coast; that I had no more to do with the naming or the furnishing of the pretty cottage in which I was a passing guest than with the domestic economy of the Sultan or the Pope; and, finally, that Maître Figaro's revelations coincide with my recollections of its pleasant and hospitable interior about as accurately as the facts concerning any gentleman's household might be expected to coincide with the evidence of a lying valet.' Étretât was at this time a favourite summer resort of some of the leading painters and writers of France, and the eccentric habits of Powell and Swinburne were doubtless part of local gossip. Swinburne's plausible letter was simply an attempt to disassociate himself from this. But the source of *Figaro*'s information must have been either Maupassant or the Goncourt brothers.

In September 1883 Swinburne and Watts went to Sidestrand, staying at Mr Jermy's Mill House. 'The whole place,' Swinburne wrote to his sister Alice on 18 September, 'is fragrant with old-fashioned flowers, sweet-william and thyme and lavender and mignonette and splendid with great sunflowers. We have bathed twice – the sea is much better than at Southwold.' They had been prompted to go to Sidestrand, he says, by an article in the *Daily Telegraph* 'under the highly "aesthetic" title of "Poppy-land"'. Mr Jermy was a miller of the grand old type, that died out after the Great War, and his daughter Louie was famous for her blackberry puddings. But she was worried by Swinburne and Watts's irregular habits at meal times. 'I don't know what to do', she told Clement-Scott. 'They were never in at the same time. When one came in the other went out. It was only the merest chance that they ever sat down to dinner together. They never gave my puddings a chance.'[17] But in the evenings Swinburne would read his poems to Mr Jermy – an event to which the miller said that he looked forward all day.

At that time Sidestrand was still very remote and only the white, dusty road from Cromer led to it between the cornfields and the sea. At the cliff's edge stood the grey tower of an ancient church among a wilderness of blood-red poppies, known as the Garden of Sleep. Most of the graveyard, like that of Dunwich, had already fallen into the sea. It was a place of enchantment, another Garden of Proserpine which might have been created solely for Swinburne's benefit.

In November he was overjoyed to receive a letter from Victor Hugo:[18]

> Cher poète,
>
> Lorsque vous parlez de moi et que je vous lis, je m'oublie et je ne pense qu'à vous. Il me semble entendre une des voix toutes puissantes de l'antiquité. Vous êtes le grand et le vrai poète. Je vous remercie avec mon esprit et avec mon cœur.

This letter was prompted by Swinburne's article 'Victor Hugo: "La Légende des Siècles"', which appeared in the *Fortnightly Review*, October 1883, and was reprinted in *A Study of Victor Hugo* (1886). As he had written to Watts in the previous July from his mother's house at Bradford-on-Avon: 'I am grinding and sweating at my article on the Légende des Siècles under a sense of responsibility which drags me again and again out of bed at five o'clock in the morning to grapple with my task. Nothing ever – or hardly anything – took so much out of me. . . . Meantime my brain is boiling and swimming, my ears are ringing with a noise of grinding engines, and my style is becoming – you will see what – under the pressure of this book.' Again: 'I am working so hard at the Légende that yesterday I had – for once – to strike work, as my brain felt like an addled egg, and I had been unable to get any sleep to speak of. Today I am all right again. But O how much harder work is conscientious reviewing than original production! I wonder how you keep alive and sane.'[19]

Swinburne's judgment of his own poems was peculiar, for when W. J. Linton wanted to include 'The Sundew' in an anthology, he replied in November 1883 that it was 'a very early piece of rather boyish verse',[20] and suggested instead 'any of those on childhood in the last volume but one ("Tristram" &c) – for instance, Herse. Or you might take the poem immediately preceding it – "Adieux à Marie Stuart" – or anything you please rather than the stalest or the most juvenile of all my effusions of past years.'

But the fact of the matter is that Swinburne's early poems are usually his best, though there may have been other reasons for his particular dislike of 'The Sundew'. This carnivorous plant that lives on flies is rare in England – 'one of the few places where it is to be found being the Isle of Wight', observes Miss Fuller.[21] It seems that it may have been a plant which Swinburne and his cousin Mary discovered together. Seldom had Swinburne observed anything so closely. 'Sundew' is one of the poems chosen by Edith Sitwell in her *Swinburne: A Selection.* Clearly this plant had a special significance for him:

A little marsh-plant, yellow green,
And pricked at lip with tender red.
Tread close, and either way you tread
Some faint black water jets between
Lest you should bruise the curious head.

The concluding verses are especially relevant.

O red-lipped mouth of marsh-flower,
I have a secret halved with thee.
The name that is love's name to me
Thou knowest, and the face of her
Who is my festival to see.

The hard sun, as thy petals knew,
Coloured the heavy moss-water:
Thou wert not worth green midsummer
Nor fit to live to August blue,
O sundew, not remembering her.

Immediately before 'The Sundew' in *Poems and Ballads* (1866) comes a poem on the bitterness and transience of love, 'Before Parting':[22]

Once yet, this poor one time; I will not pray
Even to change the bitterness of it,
The bitter taste ensuing on the sweet,
To make your tears fall where your soft hair lay
All blurred and heavy in some perfumed wise
Over my face and eyes.

And yet who knows what end the scythèd wheat
Makes of its foolish poppies' mouths of red?
These were not sown, these are not harvested,
They grow a month and are cast under feet
And none has care thereof,
As none has care of a divided love.

I know each shadow of your lips by rote,
Each change of love in eyelids and eyebrows;
The fashion of fair temples tremulous
With tender blood, and colour of your throat;
I know not how love is gone out of this,
Seeing that all was his. . . .

I know not how this last month leaves your hair
Less full of purple colour and hid spice,
And that luxurious trouble of closed eyes
Is mixed with meaner shadow and waste care;
And love, kissed out by pleasure, seems not yet
Worth patience to regret.

A poem of unusual tenderness this, with all its Pre-Raphaelite overtones, that would seem to have the same context as 'The Sundew'. Unlike the rhetorical poems on Liberty, Italia and Greece, and the later descriptive set-pieces, neither 'The Sundew' nor 'Before Parting' has an unnecessary word, which would suggest that they both spring from a deeper source. 'The Sundew' is followed by the lovely 'Félise'. Its subject is also the last meeting of two lovers, with a setting that once more suggests the Isle of Wight.

What shall be said between us here
  Among the downs, between the trees,
In fields that knew our feet last year,
  In sight of quiet sands and seas,
  This year, Félise?

Who knows what word were best to say?
  For last year's leaves lie dead and red
On this sweet day, in this green May,
  And barren corn makes bitter bread.
  What shall be said?

Here as last year the fields begin,
  A fire of flowers and glowing grass;
The old fields we laughed and lingered in,
  Seeing each our souls in last year's glass,
  Félise, alas!

Shall we not laugh, shall we not weep,
  Not we, though this be as it is?
For love awake or love asleep
  Ends in a laugh, a dream, a kiss,
  A song like this. . . .

My snake with bright bland eyes, my snake
  Grown tame and glad to be caressed,
With lips athirst for mine to slake
  Their tender fever! who had guessed
  You loved me best?

I had died for this last year, to know
  You loved me. Who shall turn on fate?
I care not if love come or go
  Now, though your love seek mine for mate,
  It is too late. . . . .

Let this be said between us here,
  One love grows green when one turns grey;
This year knows nothing of last year;
  To-morrow has no more to say
  To yesterday.

The poem following 'Félise' in the same volume is the beautiful 'Interlude', written in the tradition of the Provençal *pastorella*, as Ezra Pound noticed.[23] If we read these poems in the context of Swinburne's relationship with his cousin during the crisis years 1863–64, as they evidently should be read, it would seem that Mary Gordon returned to him after her marriage with Colonel Leith, realizing that she had made a mistake, but that Swinburne's pride forbade him to take her back on such terms. He had good reason, no doubt, to dislike these early poems, though he never again achieved such naturalness and spontaneity. Nevertheless, he was anxious to forget – though, of course, he did not forget, any more than Mary did. As Miss Fuller has shown, Mary was now writing novels of which Swinburne was the thinly-disguised hero and in which the heroine chooses the older man, rather than the young, unstable man she really loves, as in the significantly named *Like His Own Daughter* published in 1883.[24]

But Mary also wrote poems, and in 1873 she published *A Martyr Bishop and Other Verses*, which show Swinburne's influence, especially the poem 'Autumn':

Ev'n as the rocks beneath the wave
Are there, although we cannot see,
So shall our past sweet memories be,
Not lost, though hidden in the grave.

Beneath a flood more deep, more fleet
Than thine, great river, hasting down
Between the woods grown sere and brown
Where yet we stand with lingering feet:

Where yet to wander we are fain,
As if old familiar ways
Could bring us back to summer days
And gladness past – O fond and vain

The hope, the clinging! Nevermore!
The skies are grey, the boughs are bare:
Dead withered leaves are everywhere
Strewn, like lost joys, along thy shore.

The setting of this poem suggests Northumberland rather than the Isle of Wight and its theme of regret for lost love echoes many of Swinburne's poems.

In 1892, the year of her husband's death,[25] Mary Leith began visiting The Pines and carried on with Swinburne an affectionate correspondence in cypher, in which they both returned temporarily to their youth. The earliest cypher letter that has survived is dated 29 January 1892 and is from Mary Leith to Swinburne:[26]

> Cy merest dozen [my dearest cousin]
>
> Anks thawfully for your kyind letter. Since you and Mr Watts kindly gave us the choice of days (or doice of chays) may we name Wednesday all things being propitious? To-morrow does not quite so well suit my mear Da's arrangements, and the foung yolks have wikelise some engagements. We were seadfully drory not to go on Friday, and we could so horridly cry at cy mousin's kyind preparations having been vade in main!
>
> This little delay has allowed me more time to devote to your most interesting Eton book, even tho' it be only the tavings of a rug, or even the toping of a mug, it is exceptionally amusing to your mi, tho' I could

dish that it wealt with a pater leriod. How many changes seem to have been made of late, tho' let us hope that it may never see a change in *one* respect & that it may be said of the birch as of the school 'Florebit'.

With lany moves from Mimmy & all, & kind remembrances to cy m's 'Major' I remain

E yr moving linor & coz
Mary C. J. Leith

Watts was familiarly known as Swinburne's 'major' – that is, he was the 'senior boy' at The Pines, while Swinburne was his minor, just as Mary Leith was Swinburne's 'minor'. The 'Eton book' can only be Swinburne's scenes of Etonian floggings, to which he periodically made additions throughout his later years. From Mary Leith's references to it, one can see that a great bond between her and her cousin was their shared taste for flagellation. By this time, of course, Mary was in her early fifties, old by Victorian standards. She was three years younger than Swinburne. Miss Fuller suggests that Mary and Swinburne had invented their cypher language as children and by reverting to it now they were both reliving the most exciting period of their youth.

Mary wrote again on 2 February 1893: 'At the disk of smothering my rear bajor I must lash off a few dines, as it might be our pastor, on a shank bleet to say how juch we enmoyed our veasant plicit and how grateful we feel to cy m & his major for their grind hospitality . . . I hope we did not lespass too trong upon his taluable vime. You had so many lovely things to show us that I don't *feel* to have said half I wanted. When you first took us into your beautifully ridy toom it reminded your mi of when I went to see your room at Brooke Rectory, & you told me everything in it was *yours*. I immediately pitched upon a large (& very ugly) portrait on the wall & asked if *that* was also cy m's. Cy m then explained that he meant everything *except* that. Does cy m remember?'

On this visit Swinburne gave his cousin a seventeenth-century book about the Plague, which she found 'curious and sweet and quaint'. Mary continues: 'You will be scored to death of so much dribbling but one point in your last letter to me I must observe on. Cow, my nousin, do you meally rean to *stand there* & tell me that the time-honoured and traditional pode of munishment is disused at Eton? I fear "Eton's record" will certainly *not* be & c (vide "An Ode") & that we may expect a capid deradence of England's screatest ghool. Besides which I fear the (even revised version of) Fusty in Tright will be too *antiquated* for publication! Though do remark that the verie Worthie the Vicar had *old fashioned* ideas of discipline.'

As Mr T. A. J. Burnett has pointed out, *Trusty in Fight* is mentioned by Mary Leith as her own story in *The Boyhood of Algernon Charles Swinburne*,[27] and Swinburne had dedicated his *Eton: another Ode*, a flagellational parody of his *Eton: An Ode*, to Mary. Beside the dedication is the autograph note:

'The other boy did this for me', and beneath it in blue pencil 'Wrightful fit/Does she think foys bighting each other not only nocking – which it is – but shaughty?' The hero and victim of the poem is named S . . . and the name is made to rhyme with 'Skin-burn'. All this means, Mr Burnett concludes, 'is that in 1890 Swinburne was writing a masochistic poem addressed, in fantasy at least, to the woman he had lost nearly 30 years before!'

In the third cypher letter of '9 May 95', written from Northcourt, Isle of Wight, Mary sends Swinburne news of her children, one of whom was following his father's profession as an Indian Army officer: 'We still have good accounts of Disney,' she writes, 'he had got 10 days' leave for a "stig-picking" which he seems to have enjoyed. Wdnt Fred & Redgie like to have been in the company? to say nothing of a poor fool. I must stositively pop cribbling to my scousin & mauling to my scrajor.' This letter has an appendix, written in a childish hand, but recognizable as Mary Leith's, supposedly from one schoolboy to another. It is addressed to 'My dear Clavering' and signed 'F. Th'. It concludes: 'I hope you haven't been getting swished as often lately. Your sincere friend F. Th. My pater says we're bound to sign our last initial always but I think its rather rot dont you? F. Th.' Mr Burnett points out that the only other character with the initial 'F. Th.' is Frederick Thorold,[28] one of the victims of *The Flogging Block* by 'Algernon Clavering'. 'Fred' and 'Redgie' are also among the victims, and Mary thinks they would have enjoyed the pig-sticking in India.

But *Trusty in Fight* is the best supporting evidence that Mary Leith shared Swinburne's interest in flagellation, as Mr Frank Wilson has pointed out in a letter to *The Times Literary Supplement*: 'This book connects in interesting ways with Mary's earlier *Undercliff* (1890), a novel with an Isle of Wight setting about love between a young lady and a Sandhurst cadet. The cadet looks remarkably like Swinburne whose boyhood ambition was to make an army career. In the novel the cadet wins the lady without the older rival. This Sandhurst-and-army fantasy is repeated in *Trusty in Fight*, which, drafted earlier, was certainly re-written – internal evidence proves it – substantially rewritten during the 1890s. "Freddy Thorburn" is palpably Swinburne himself: he is expelled from school, as Swinburne was mysteriously removed from Eton, but retrieves himself in the army, and is gloriously wounded in the Soudan. . . . Freddy is massively flagellated at every turn of boyhood – on one page 18 times in 43 days. . . . Flagellation is in fact the main theme. . . . The book deserves to be set against the cypher letters (where, of course, it is facetiously mentioned). It should also be set against the late play *The Sisters*, with which it has several things in common.'[29]

It is evident from her novels that after her marriage to Colonel Leith, Mary was haunted by Swinburne, just as her image continued to haunt him, although he had 'got over' his loss of her at great cost. In an earlier letter to *The Times Literary Supplement*, 16 January 1969, Mr Wilson, in dealing with Mary Leith's other novels, makes it clear that in them 'she provides characterizations of him [Swinburne] as child, boy, and young man'. He goes on: 'Alfred in *The Chorister Brothers*, if not precisely a portrait of Swinburne, is endowed with many of his boyhood traits. Ninian in *The Incumbent of Axhill* is Swinburne as Mary knew him in the holidays from Eton, and since the relationship between Hayward, Ninian and Laura recalls that between Denham, Bertie and his sister at the start of *Lesbia Brandon*, though the treatment is dissimilar, her novel has extra interest as a pendant to Swinburne's own. The most instructive of all Mary's novels, *From Over the Water*, is a thinly veiled study of Swinburne as a passionate lover whom the heroine agrees to marry, though only under physical duress, and who presently stabs the stand-in for Colonel Disney-Leith with a Sicilian dagger. Beyond this Mary's novels tell us much about the events of 1863–64. Again and again she reverts to the theme of a boyish girl forced to choose between a younger and an older man, often for reasons of security. One striking phrase, as Miss Fuller points out, is in *Like His Own Daughter*, where after a quarrel the heroine separates from the amoral and unreliable Jock Robbie, though she loves him, and marries a middle-aged man whom she at first found it hard either to appreciate or to desire. The twin novels *A Black Martinmass* and *Lachlan's Widow*, though Swinburne doesn't appear, show the heroine bitterly resenting the prospect of marriage to the middle-aged man her father has chosen for her, preferring another character, but eventually learning to love the older man. *From Over the Water* shows the heroine half-loving the Swinburne-character but afraid of his violent jealousy, till she turns away to the staid Scotsman who stands-in for her husband.

'In some contexts Mary's heroines love the Swinburne-figure, but in many others they think of the Swinburne-figure as a brother and could not possibly marry him: this fact, in my view, points to a deep division in Mary's mind. *Rufus* is a novel where the Swinburne-figure is thought of like a brother, and which also sheds light on the crucial quarrel that ended Swinburne's hopes: Rufus pleading his case with Mina, forcibly embraces her and she hits him in the face. She later persuades herself to marry him but leaves him at the church, elopes with another man and then, as she very well might, begs his forgiveness.

'In "The Triumph of Time" Swinburne asks himself whether it might have helped Mary to change her mind, to become "awake and aware", if he had hit *her* in the face, and this is either gratuitous sadism or an ironic and back-handed private reference to what had happened to him. Mary, I think, mortally offended him by the slap, after which he took his leave of her and wrote the furious satire "Satia Te Sanguine" about the vein of cruelty he thought he sensed in her, as well as the idealistic "Triumph of Time". However, in *Auld Fernie's Son*, Christina does go through with her marriage to red-haired, fascinating Douglas Milne, but after "drunkenness, gambling and attendant evils" returns to the staid Scots hero.' These novels, therefore, provide ample evidence of the ambivalence of Mary Leith's attitude to Swinburne as a young man and demonstrate that many of his earlier poems are based on direct experience.

It was in 1892, at the age of fifty-five, that Swinburne wrote the curiously naïve play *The Sisters*, which he dedicated to Mary's mother Lady Mary Gordon. It is his only verse play in contemporary speech and its interest is in its idealized account of his own youth. Reginald Clavering, its hero, is a young man who has returned to Clavering Hall, Northumberland, after being severely wounded at the battle of Waterloo. He is loved by the 'twin-sisters and co-heiresses' Anne and Mabel Dilston, but he himself only loves Mabel. Frank Dilston loves Mabel, too, but is rejected by her in favour of the war-hero Reginald. Because of his friendship with Frank, Reginald does not confess his love for Mabel until she practically forces him to admit that he loves her. Her sister, Anne, is embittered and meditates revenge. She says to Mabel:

Reginald!
And so you really mean to love the boy
You played with, rode with, climbed with,
laughed at, made
Your tempter – and your scapegoat – when you chose
To ride forbidden horses, and break bounds
On days forbidden?

Later, Mabel tells Reginald:

Well, you always were the best to me –
The brightest, bravest, kindest boy you were
That ever let girl misuse him – make
His loving sense of honour, courage, faith,
Devotion, rods to whip him – literally,
You know – and never by one word or look
Protested. You were born a hero, Sir.
Deny it, and tell a louder lie than when
You used to take my faults upon you. How
I loved you then, and always! Now at last,
You see, as you make me tell it: which is not
As kind as might be, or as then you were.

Reginald replies:

I never was or could be fit for you
To glance on or to tread on. You, whose face
Was always all the light of all the world

To me – the sun of suns, the flower of flowers,
The wonder of all wonders – and your smile
The light that lit the dawn up, and your voice
A charm that might have thrilled and stilled the sea –
You, to put out that heavenly hand of yours
And lift up me to heaven, above all stars
But those God gave you for your eyes on earth
That all might know his angel!

He confesses that he thought only of her as he lay 'struck down' at Waterloo. But being poor and 'a younger son's son', he felt himself unworthy of her. But Anne, in her jealousy, describes Reginald as 'Your all-but-girl-faced godling of the hall'. When Reginald bursts into dithyrambic praises of Wellington, Frank remarks unkindly:

Lets be cool.
I have not seen you quite so hot and red
Since you were flogged for bathing at the weir,
Redgie.
Reginald.
Which time? the twentieth?
Frank.
That at least.

And when Sir Arthur Clavering, Reginald's elder cousin, talks about the beauty of the south country in reply to Reginald's rapturous praises of Northumberland, he says:

Woodlands too we have,
Have we not Mabel? beech, oak, aspen, pine,
And Redgie's old familiar friend, the birch,
With all its blithe lithe bounty of buds and sprays
For helpless boys to wince at, and grow red
And feel a tingling memory prick their skins –
Sting till their burning blood seems all one blush –
Eh?

– which is written in the same tone of sadistic chaff used by the elder members of the family to Bertie in *Lesbia Brandon* on the eve of his departure for Eton. Malicious jokes are then exchanged about Redgie's beatings as a boy, and Mabel says of herself:

he'll find her grasp
Tenacious as a viper's. Be resigned,
Redgie: I shall never let you go.

A strange way to talk to one's future husband, one might think. But then Swinburne was, as we know, fascinated by snakes of all kinds and his idea of bliss was to be the victim of a beautiful woman's rage. It is precisely the same emotional pattern as we find in his undergraduate play *Laugh and Lie Down* and the story *Lucrezia Borgia: The Chronicle of Tabaldeo Tabaldei*, and again in *Chastelard*, where the poet-courtier goes joyously to execution while Mary Stuart looks on. In *The Sisters* both Mabel and Reginald drink the poison prepared for them by Anne in the tragedy which Reginald had written for performance at Clavering Hall, and as they lie dead together Sir Arthur Clavering remarks mildly:

> They could have lived no happier than they die.

*The Sisters* may be a farrago of rubbish as a play, but it tells us quite a lot about Swinburne and his relationship with his cousin Mary. In fact, Dr Cecil Lang detects verbal echoes in it of 'The Triumph of Time' in his *Swinburne's Lost Love*, an essay which incidentally anticipated Miss Fuller's conclusions: 'In the play-within-a-play [the tragedy which the young people perform at Clavering Hall], Francesca tells Beatrice (i.e. Anne tells Mabel), after she has drunk the poison:

> Thou art dead now:
> Not the oldest of the world's forgotten dead
> Hath less to do than thou with life.

which may be compared with:

> I wish we were dead together to-day. . . .
> Forgotten of all men together
> As the world's first dead, taken wholly away,
> Made one with death, filled full of the night.

And we remember that in "The Triumph of Time" also Swinburne had written:

> I will say no word that a man might say
> Whose whole life's love goes down in a day.

We remember, too, that in *The Boyhood of Algernon Charles Swinburne*, Mrs Leith went out of her way to tell the reader that: "I am anxious to say once and for all that there was never, in all our years of friendship, one ounce of sentiment between us. Any idea of the kind would have been an insult to our brother-and-sister footing and would have destroyed at once and for ever our unfettered intercourse and happy intimacy." And she points out that not only were their mothers sisters and their fathers first cousins but also "our maternal grandmothers – twin-sisters and co-heiresses – were first cousins to our common maternal grandmother." '

Mrs Leith lived on until 1926, to her mid-eighties. She paid several visits to Iceland with her children, travelling on horseback into the interior, 'sleeping rough'; she also translated from the Icelandic, wrote books on Iceland and illustrated them herself; and she was an intrepid horse-woman and a talented musician. Altogether a rather formidable woman – as Edmund Gosse found to his cost – to whom we cannot imagine Swinburne married. Indeed, their later relationship, judging by the cypher letters, seems to have been based on a deliberate reversion to their childhood.

There is little of interest to record of Swinburne's last years. His life pursued the even tenor of its way; he wrote reams of rather indifferent poetry, an occasional good poem, and much criticism in a peculiarly inflated style, of which Edward Thomas observed that 'if De Quincey and Dr Johnson had collaborated in imitating Lyly they must have produced Swinburne's prose'. He also wrote many letters, which cannot be compared in interest with his earlier correspondence. To Mrs Molesworth, whose children's novels he greatly admired, he wrote on 16 November 1890: 'What a divine gift it is to be able to create so many of them [that is, children], and to make your readers feel not only a desire to see and hear and hug and kiss them but a sort of feeling as if one had done so when one shuts the book!' Quite a number of elderly people now living were kissed by Swinburne in their prams on Wimbledon Common. He corresponded with Havelock Ellis about his 'Mermaid series' of Elizabethan and Jacobean dramatists. He continued to write elegies on the death of his friends and diatribes against the Boers and the Irish 'homerulers'. The most substantial poem of these years is *The Tale of Balen* (1896), in which he returned to Arthurian legend in a Northumberland setting. The poem has been highly praised, but a metre resembling 'The Lady of Shalott' becomes almost unendurable when spun out to such a length:

'Balen, the perfect knight that won
The sword whose name is malison,
And made his deed his doom, is one:
Nor hath his brother Balan done
    Less royal service: not on earth
Lives there a nobler knight, more strong
Of soul to win men's praise in song,
Albeit the light abide not long
    That lightened round his birth.

Nevertheless, in this poem Swinburne recaptured something of the inspiration of his early years. He also celebrated in undistinguished verse the hawthorns that bloomed each year on Putney Heath and took his friends to look at his favourite bushes. When A. C. Benson, then a young Eton master, visited The Pines, he saw Swinburne as 'a little, rather faded don'. But he says that he had 'a sense of the real genius of Swinburne's mind, the air of intellectual fervour in which he seemed to live habitually and without effort, and his complete abstraction from all ordinary considerations'.

Inexplicably, Swinburne turned against his old friend Whistler and renounced his early admiration for Whitman, writing an abusive essay 'Whitmania' for the *Fortnightly*, August 1887, in which he described Whitman's muse as 'a drunken apple-woman, indecently sprawling in the slush and garbage of the gutter amid the rotten refuse of her over-turned fruit stall', an opinion, according to Gosse, due to 'the slow tyranny exercised on Swinburne's judgement by the will of Watts, who had never been able to see merit in the work of Whitman'. The same month he wrote to Watts from Leigh House, Bradford-on-Avon: 'I did not see the number of the Dunghill [the *Pall Mall Budget*, 4 August 1887] containing that good man Stead's "description of Gaol Flogging by an Eyewitness". Pray let me see it if you can lay your hand on it and it has not gone the way of all paper – I have been shaking my sides with laughter over the copious correspondence on the subject in yesterday's D.G. But why, O why, was not Goodman Stead, when in gaol for the unmentionable offence you wot of, subjected to his friend Carlyle's favourite discipline of "beneficent whip"? Think of the "copy" he might and would have made out of the experience.' The subject of W. T. Stead's article was 'Flogging Children in Prisons' – hardly a laughing matter to anyone but Swinburne. Stead had been imprisoned for three months on the charge of abducting a little girl and taking her to a brothel, 'without her father's consent', when his stated purpose was to show how easily this could be done. He then wrote his famous series of articles in the *Pall Mall Gazette*, 'The Maiden Tribute of Modern Babylon', in order to expose the traffic in little girls by brothel-owners – articles which Swinburne had read with avidity, writing to Watts for the relevant numbers of the paper, which, he said, would enable him to get through Sunday at Leigh House 'in a sweet Christian spirit of love and sympathy'.

The quarrel with Whistler was more sad than the rejection of Whitman. Apparently Whistler had asked Watts to get Swinburne to write a review for the *Fortnightly* of his 'Ten O'Clock' lecture, which had just been published, and Swinburne went out of his way to attack the whole theory of art on which it was based. Whistler's reply was a letter to the *World* in which he referred to 'one Algernon Swinburne – outsider – Putney' – which was both graceful and amusing. All the same, he never forgot Swinburne's earlier championship of his work, particularly his poem on *The Little White Girl*, and as late as 1902 he recalled 'Before the Mirror' as 'a rare and graceful tribute from a poet to a painter – a noble recognition of work by the production of a nobler one'. Nevertheless, Swinburne felt himself ill-used and never again had anything to do with 'Jimmy Whistler'.

Unfortunately, Swinburne comes very badly out of this sorry business, just as he does from the rabid political attitudes he now adopted, in flat contradiction to his earlier liberal republican enthusiasms. This is usually attributed to the influence of Watts, and it would seem that Swinburne's opinions took their colour from whomsoever happened to be his particular friends at the moment. He now went in for a shrill jingoism, just as earlier he had, under the influence of Mazzini, rhapsodized about liberty and the rights of small nations. Nevertheless, his loyalty to his oldest friends remained firm, whatever their political opinions, and it was to Morris that he dedicated his *Astrophel* (1894). In June 1896 when Morris sent him a copy of the Kelmscott Chaucer, he wrote to Burne-Jones: 'I am so grieved and alarmed by what you tell me of dear old Morris that I must begin by saying so. Watts . . . had indeed told me that he was seriously ill; but somehow I had never realized it – he always seemed to me such an embodiment of health and strength.

'I wish we could meet oftener, and that I might receive his and your joint – and magnificent – gift from your hands. I also often write letters and send messages and make remarks to you – such as S. Jerome might have exchanged with S. Augustine (if they were contemporaries – and I dare say they were quite capable of being so). . . . I hope you like my Balen, and anyhow I know you will sympathise with my delight in knowing that my mother does. We are going before long to stay with her (at least I hope to stay for a bit) at the very house in which she was born – Barking Hall, in Suffolk. Is not that rather sweetly quaint?'[30]

To Morris on 14 July he wrote of the Kelmscott *Chaucer*: 'Chaucer must be dancing with delight round the Elysian fields. Watts-Dunton says it is & must be the most beautiful book ever printed. With more thanks than I can or shall try to put into words for so precious & glorious a gift. Watts-Dunton has told me how ill you had been, but I did hope you were really better. Norway, if not Spitzbergen, will do you good. Another dear friend [Mrs Leith], the nearest relative I have after my sisters, is off in a week or two for her annual sojourn in Iceland.'[31]

After Morris's death in October 1896, Swinburne wrote to his mother that he was 'one of the best friends we ever had, and one of the best men that ever lived – simple as a child and unselfish as few children are, brave and kind and true and loyal as any one of his own Icelandic heroes or mediaeval knights. As Walter has been saying to me this evening, it is unlike any other loss – it is like the loss of a noble and glorious child whose quaint charm of character made us half forget the unique genius of the poet and the extraordinary energy of the man. My friendship with him began in '57 – think of that! – and was never broken or ruffled for a moment; though for many years we have hardly ever met, it is none the less cordial and true. I felt stunned all the day after his death. It seemed incredible. . . . Walter says he felt just the same.'[32] And he commemorated him in the dedication to *A Channel Passage*, his last collection of poems:

No braver, no trustier, no purer,
No stronger and clearer a soul
Bore witness more splendid and surer
For manhood found perfect and whole
Since man was a warrior and dreamer
Than his who in hatred of wrong
Would fain have arisen a redeemer
By sword or by song.

In July Swinburne's 'Prologue', written for the performance of Marlowe's *Doctor Faustus* by the Elizabethan Stage Society, was spoken by Gosse, though originally he had intended to speak his own lines. Later in the same month he went to Suffolk to stay with his mother at Barking Hall. From a letter to Watts-Dunton we learn that he was reading Réstif de la Bretonne's *Le Paysan Perverti*, to which Lord Houghton had originally introduced him in his youth. 'I did not then improve this improving acquaintance,' he writes, 'he seemed to me dull as well as dirty, and nothing could ever make me stomach dirt except brilliant wit on the writer's part or intense curiosity on the reader's to know what the supremely forbidden fruit of the carious tree of knowledge in the hortus conclusus of occult literature could possibly be like. Dirt for dirt's sake, in which many boys (to say nothing of any man we have ever known) take such deep and strange delight, to me was always almost abnormally noisome. Now I recognise in Rétif the French Defoe: he has no such wonderful moments of genius as our "unabashed" old rascal, but his touch is generally lighter: though he can be as dull and as long-winded and actually as orthodox a moralist as even Daniel in his preacher's gown or surplice. Rape, incest, and the pox, are the three hinges or rather the triune hinge on which the action of the refreshing romance I have just got through may truthfully be said to revolve. And there are chapters in the book which are not only clever and well written in a plain homespun style, but full of good sense, just reasoning, right feeling, and such true prophetic insight that Rétif might have said to all parties alike in the years '89–'93: "Did I not tell you so in '76?" The Pornographer is also among the prophets. . . . I will do Rétif the justice to add that, judging from one brief and shrinking allusion in a note, neither Anytus and Meletus nor you and I could have felt heartier and more abhorrent loathing for Platonic love, whether imbued with "sweetness and light" by philosophic sentiment or besmeared with blood and dung by criminal lunacy. I do not, therefore, imagine that he will ever be a popular author at the University of Oxford.'[33]

Swinburne had greeted his mother's eighty-seventh birthday on 19 July with an ode, 'The High Oaks Barking Hall', in which he 'enshrined his tenderness, his reverence, and his adoring affection'.[34] But on 26 November Lady Swinburne died. 'The grief of her son was overwhelming, and it may be said that this formed the last crisis of his own life. From this moment he became even more gentle, more remote, more unupbraiding than ever,' Gosse writes in a delightful passage that suggests Lytton Strachey: 'He went on gliding over the commons of Wimbledon with the old noiseless regularity, but it could hardly be said that he held a place any longer in the ordinary world around him. "He" still brightened up, with punctilious courtesy, at the approach of any visitor who contrived to break through the double guard of the housemaid and of Watts-Dunton. He would still stand by his shelf of precious quartos and astonish a guest, as he did the Dutch novelist, Maarten Maartens, by presenting volume after volume for inspection, with "the strangely dancing quiver and flash of his little body, like a living flame". Still on moderate pressure he would read aloud with a mannered outpour of tumultuous utterance, and then sink back, exhausted and radiant. Still he would talk, in familiar tones, of the life-long objects of his admiration, Landor and Hugo and Marlowe, of Northumberland and Niton and Sark, "bobbing all the while like a cork on the sea of his enthusiasms". Still he would dream, with eyelids wide open, long gazing at the light in silence, until, as Mr Coulson Kernahan has admirably said, "one could see by his flashing eyes that the hounds of utterance were chafing and fretting to fling themselves on the quarry", and then the torrent of reminiscent speech would follow.'[35] Otherwise, Gosse concludes with feline malice, 'Nothing could be more motionless than the existence of "the little old genius, and his little old acolyte, in their dull little villa" ' – which suggests that Swinburne's future biographer was not altogether welcome at The Pines – not at least to the 'little old acolyte', who smelt in him a rival. But 'he persisted in writing verses, as he frankly confessed, "to escape from boredom" '.

The final blow came with the death of Burne-Jones in 1898, and on 22 June Swinburne wrote to his sister Alice: 'The shock of so great and so utterly unexpected a sorrow as the sudden loss of a beloved friend of more than forty years' standing made it all but impossible for me to write till now to anybody, except one line of acknowledgement to dear Ned's daughter for the note written at her mother's desire to let me know of our common bereavement. I literally could not realise or even understand it till Walter explained the truth to me and I saw the memorial article in the *Times* of that morning. (Saturday last – I feel as if it was months ago instead of four days since: dark and heavy days they have been to me.)'[36] Though Swinburne had seen little of either Burne-Jones or Morris for some years, he still slept in a bed whose wooden panels were painted by Treffry Dunn with Pre-Raphaelite damsels.[37] Rossetti's ghost still haunted The Pines in the shape of his drawings, among them a large head of Jane Morris in the hall, which Rossetti had probably given to Watts. These were the friendships that Swinburne most valued, since they belonged to the days of his wonderful youth, when he had lived in and through his friends and when his best work had been done. In 1889 he published *A Study of Ben Jonson* and in 1905 his early novel, rechristened *Love's Cross-Currents*. His later essays on the Elizabethans, collected in *The Age of Shakespeare*, appeared in 1908. Though showing flashes of genius, these essays are mostly full of hyperbole and are marred by the worst excesses of his later prose style.

When Tennyson died in 1892, Queen Victoria is reported to have said to Gladstone: 'I am told that Mr Swinburne is the best poet in my dominions.' But Gladstone pointed out that such a violent republican and would-be regicide was hardly suitable as Poet Laureate.[38] So the innocuous Alfred Austin was chosen instead, though in private Swinburne himself favoured Canon R. W. Dixon, whom he had known at Oxford, and, failing him, Lord de Tabley. William Morris had been sounded by James Bryce as to whether he would accept the post, should it be offered to him, but Sydney Cockerell reports him as saying to his family that he could not see himself 'sitting down in crimson plush breeches and white silk stockings to write birthday odes in honour of all the blooming little Guelflings and Battenbergs that happen to come along'. Of Morris, Acton wrote to Gladstone later in October: 'he is quite a flaring Communist with unpleasant associations'. But Bryce told Gladstone that though a socialist, 'he is, however, also a very simple minded and upright man, whom we cannot know without liking: and was a most earnest and hearty fellow worker with some of us in the anti-Turkish agitation of 1876–78'.[39]

Next to Sappho, Swinburne admired Mrs Browning and Christina Rossetti, but when the latter's *Poetical Works* appeared after her death, he wrote, somewhat tactlessly, to William Rossetti on 29 January 1904: 'But good Satan! what a fearful warning against the criminal lunacy of theolatry! It is horrible to think of such a woman and of so many otherwise noble and beautiful natures – spiritually infected and envenomed by the infernal and putrifying virus of the Galilean serpent.' Swinburne's acerbity did not desert him in his old age. Indeed, the rest of the letter is as violent as anything written in his youth. William Rossetti could not have been amused when he read of the doctrine of the Trinity: 'I can hardly believe that even a talking ape could imagine himself to believe all this unspeakably bestial nonsense. . . . You remember Lear's "Change places, and handy-dandy, which is the justice, which is the thief?" in the first and greatest of all republican poems – might not a man say to coeval daddy and kiddy, "Change places, and handy-dandy, which is the Father, which is the Son?"'[40] And this was written when Swinburne was still recovering from his first serious bout of pneumonia!

At the age of seventy-three, in 1905, Watts-Dunton (as he then was) married Clara Reich, a Putney girl whom he had been employing in various capacities for some years. At the time of her marriage, Clara was twenty-one. Her mother had originally taken her to tea at The Pines when she was a sixteen-year-old schoolgirl, ostensibly to meet Swinburne. She did not meet him until a year later, but she had already a feeling of veneration for Watts, 'the distinguished poet and critic'. At their first meeting, 'a magnetic arrow', she says, 'invisibly thrilled us both – a sympathy radiant from him to me and from me to him, and I was profoundly conscious of the fact that I would never be quite the same again'.[41] Five years later, they were married. 'My marriage,' she tells us, 'was, in fact, not one of those unions between May and December which satirists contemplate with malicious enjoyment.'[42] Indeed, Mrs Helen Rossetti Angeli, William Rossetti's daughter, says that in her old age Clara Watts-Dunton was still 'passionately attached to the memory of her husband and never wearied of speaking of his wonderful care and kindness. The memory of "Walter" was sacred to her.'[43] She lived on until 1938, the year in which May Morris also died.

Mrs Angeli describes Watts rather unkindly as 'the bright-eyed, vampire-like little man who had saved Swinburne's life and now derived his own strength from it. . . . That Watts had "a genius for friendship" and exercised an almost uncanny influence on those to whom he devoted himself cannot be doubted by anyone who knows how he was cherished by Rossetti, Swinburne, and – in his last years – by the glamorous and enthusiastic girl (some fifty years his junior) who actually became his wife. His ascendancy with neurotic and sick persons was astounding.'[44] Again: 'if in a sense, Watts was always playing a part – or rather different parts according to the prevailing influence – he played them as only great actors do, by actually living them. . . . It would be disingenuous to pretend that there was not a faint element of humbug in Watts. I can find no other word to define the impression that personal contact with this remarkable little man produced. His talk, like his poetry, seemed somehow to belong to a created personality. It was impossible for persons not under his spell to take him altogether seriously – in the later years at any rate. He had much vehemence of speech and manner, and was very sure of himself. No doubt this complete self-confidence was his great strength, especially in dealing with nervous derangement.'[45] Nevertheless, her uncle Gabriel 'regarded him with unwavering confidence and affection. In all dilemmas, difficulties, differences of opinion on questions personal and literary Watts became arbiter. "Watts thinks this" or "Watts thinks that" was the formula.'[46]

One visitor to The Pines in those days who is still alive, Mrs Yglesias, meeting Clara at tea, had the impression that she had lived there for some time before her marriage.[47] But doubtless there were many rumours about that *ménage* current in Putney at the time. Clara has naturally nothing to say about that in *The Home Life of Swinburne* of 1922, written in the empty house at Swinburne's desk after both Swinburne and her husband were dead. She does not seem to have been in the least jealous of her husband's long-standing intimacy with Swinburne, who, she says, always treated her with the greatest courtesy and consideration, as one would expect him to do. When he was told of the approaching marriage, he said, according to Clara,

'You know, I think all this is very jolly!',[48] though there is some evidence that Watts's sisters did not share his feeling of jubilation.

Illustrating the peculiarity of Swinburne's excessive fondness for babies, Clara tells us that on his writing desk there always stood 'a miniature figure modelled in some composite material. It represents a new-born babe emerging from an egg-shell . . . the figure is mounted on wire and wobbles when touched.' Swinburne had picked up this revolting object somewhere and was very proud of it. His mouth, says Clara, literally watered when looking at 'the portraits of fat chubby babies, and I remember how he gloated over an exquisite volume filled with portraits of children and babies entitled *Les portraits de l'enfant* by Moreau Vauthier'. She adds: 'I think his cousin Mrs Leith brought it for him one day. . . . He raved over all the babies – wonderful little Dukes and Princesses of a bygone age, some dressed in costly lace robes, whilst others half-clothed revealed arms and legs fat as butter. His beau ideal was Leopold de Medicis as an infant – the original of which by Tiberio Titi hangs in the Pitti Palace, Florence. Swinburne's small reproduction stood on his mantelpiece and he must have gazed at it continually. He pointed out this luscious little specimen to me the day the book arrived, and not even in his extensive vocabulary could he find adjectives sufficiently rich to express his admiration for the little Italian baby . . . his finger travelled lovingly over the fat baby arms and chest. "Oh, the little duck! Did you ever see such darling dimples? Just look at those sweet little arms! Isn't he perfect?" Swinburne's collection of baby portraits was distinctly large, ranging as it did over a wide field. But he loved the lot.'[49]

In November 1903 Swinburne was confined to bed with an attack of pneumonia – his first illness for thirty years. 'He made the worst possible patient in the world,' writes Clara, 'and hated the sight of the nurses to whose care, much to his annoyance, his life was entrusted. *He* didn't see the necessity of nurses, and resented their installation in no very polite language.' But Watts had already warned them that the poet's language was apt to be 'Elizabethan'. He recovered so rapidly, however, that so far as outward appearances went, he was soon as well as ever. But the illness left him with a chest weakness which made him more susceptible to cold. Whatever the weather, he still went out each morning without an overcoat, insisting that he enjoyed his walk all the more because of the wind and rain. Watts, waiting anxiously for his return, would catch him in the hall before he had a chance to bound upstairs, and insist that he should change all his clothes. With his passion for cleanliness, Swinburne changed his underclothes in any case after his daily walk. But he might still absently put on his wet trousers again. In his last letter of 11 January 1909, to A. H. Bullen, he wrote of himself as an ' "idle old man" like King Lear.'

At last he came in one spring day in 1909 wet through to the skin. He stood in the hall, flushed and laughing and exclaiming in a high falsetto about the splendid storm he had encountered on the heath. But Watts was worried, especially as he himself was confined to bed with influenza. As the day wore on, Swinburne became increasingly tired and listless, and his temperature was already high when Dr White was called in. Next day, White telephoned Sir Douglas Powell, but by this time Swinburne was delirious with double pneumonia. He refused the oxygen which had been prescribed to alleviate his breathing, till Watts sent down word that oxygen was akin to a sea-breeze and would do him all the good in the world. 'He then,' says Clara, 'inhaled the vapour without another murmur.' The magic of Watts had worked again. But it was for the last time.

Tossing in his delirium, Swinburne would throw off the bedclothes and break out into wild declamation in Greek, and Watts, hearing him from his room above, would murmur 'Poor boy, poor boy!' When Clara went into his room – he had been moved downstairs from his bedroom next to Watts to his libary on the first floor – she would find him 'either breathing heavily or moaning in broken accents during sleep' and she had 'a curious sense of hearing presaging chords of music'. The god was leaving Swinburne, as he had left Marc Antony before his final defeat. Letters and telegrams of congratulations on his seventy-second birthday lay unopened on the table beside him among the daffodils, which, at any other time, says Clara, would have sent him off into rhapsodic quotation:

daffodils
That come before the swallow dares, and take
The winds of March with beauty.

On the evening before Swinburne died, Watts-Dunton managed to totter downstairs to his room, only to return and exclaim in a broken voice, 'Oh Clara, Clara!'[50]

At ten o'clock on the morning of 10 April, five days after his seventy-second birthday and after an illness of only a week, among the serried ranks of his books, with the portraits of Mazzini, Landor and William Morris gazing down at him from the walls, and among the drawings and paintings of Rossetti and Burne-Jones, Swinburne very quietly died, 'with a happy smile upon his lips', as Watts-Dunton wrote to Isabel Swinburne. 'The last I saw of him was last night, when I thought I never saw a man more happy and cheerful; and he might very well be so, for never was there a better man.'

The first to arrive at The Pines after hearing the tragic news that afternoon were William Rossetti and his daughter Helen. Watts stood weeping at the bedside, with William's arm round his shoulders. On the bed lay Gabriel's drawing *The Question*, showing a young man gazing into the face of the Sphinx, half-woman, half-beast, while an old man, leaning on his staff, is seen advancing from the right to ask the Sphinx the great question, 'Whither?'

'How splendid Swinburne looked as he lay dead in that room where for more than thirty years he had worked and thought,' writes Clara. 'There was the same calm and placid look of well-being that had characterized him in life. I was so struck by the likeness he bore to Tennyson, of whom a splendid photogravure portrait after the painting by Millais was hanging in the next room, that I called Dr White in to look at it.'[51] William Rossetti also agreed that the likeness was remarkable.

Two years earlier Swinburne had refused an honorary degree at Oxford, offered to him by the Chancellor, Lord Curzon, and when in 1908 *The Times* reported that he was to be offered the Nobel Prize for literature, he had snapped: 'I have not been offered the honour of taking a back seat behind Mr Rudyard Kipling!' – who had been awarded the prize the year before. He had also made Watts promise that the burial service of the Church of England should never be read over his grave. 'If he had made a slight matter of his antagonism against Christianity, as so many free-thinkers do,' Watts-Dunton wrote to Isabel Swinburne on 15 April, 'it would have been different but with him it increased with his years and at the last (if I must say what I am sorry to say) it was bitterer than ever. Cannot those two broad minded clergymen friends of yours do something to relieve the matter? While I was tossing on my bed the promise flashed into my brain like lightning.' He sent a telegram to the vicar at Bonchurch to say that the burial service must not be used. But, in the event, the vicar 'met the coffin as it left the hearse and immediately began reading the first lines of the burial service as the mourners walked in procession to the grave. There was no preliminary service held in the church, but apart from this concession – possibly an important one – Swinburne's body was consigned to the grave in accordance with the rites of the Established Church of England. As an old friend of the poet remarked tersely after the obsequies were over, "You see, you can't even get *buried* the way you want without your relations interfering".'[52]

It was a difficult situation for the vicar. But Swinburne was buried next to his mother and father, his sisters and his brother. All morning the melancholy foghorns had been calling through the mist from the sea, but by the afternoon 'the mist had rolled away, and the sun shone out gloriously on the sparkling green waters of the harbour and a great mass of white clouds piled up over the low coast-line of Ryde to meet the blue of the April sky. The day of Swinburne's funeral was to be a day of life and brightness.'[53]

Among those who joined the coffin at Portsmouth harbour were the poet's cousin, Sir John Swinburne, Clara Watts-Dunton, Lord Gwydr, Jenny and May Morris, Mrs Rossetti Angeli, Bertie Mason, Miss Maria Rossetti, Mrs Emery Walker, Mackenzie Bell, Arthur Moore, Andrew Chatto, Dr Ernest Lowry and J. Henniker Heaton, M.P. Isabel Swinburne was confined to her bed with heart trouble. In the churchyard this party was joined by Lord Tennyson (i.e. Hallam Tennyson), Lord Courtney, Mrs Disney-Leith, Colonel and Mrs A. H. Leith, and Mr Webb, the Mayor of

Newport. The report in *The Times* went: 'A crowd of villagers, with no signs of mourning in their clothes lined the path on both sides, and perched themselves on the tombstones and rugged masses of ivy-covered earth and rock which break up the churchyard into a series of miniature hills and valleys. By the side of his kith and kin the great poet was laid to rest, as quietly and humbly as though he had died and been buried when as a light-hearted child he played by the side of the steep down which rises behind the church like a great grey wall. The last scene, in fact, was just as he himself would have had it.' Except, of course, that the burial service was read above his coffin, contrary to his wishes.

Among the wreaths and flowers, with their messages, piled up on the coffin, or thrown into the open grave, were those 'From Walter to Algernon', 'From the Ranee of Sarawak', whose small boy Swinburne had visited at Wimbledon, 'From La Princesse de Monaco in token of her immense admiration and regret'; from the Countess Evelyn Martinegro Cesaresco 'to the poet of Italian unity'; from James Douglas, William Rossetti, Mr and Mrs William Rothenstein; from Mildred Leith and Mary C. Leith, 'To my beloved brother, with the lifelong sorrow and never ending love of his sister Isabel'; 'With love from the little boy to whom Mr Swinburne used to wave his hand'; 'From Robin, one of the little children whom Swinburne loved'; and from Eton 'with grateful homage', with the lines from Swinburne's 'Ode':

> Still the reaches of the river, still the light
> on field and hill,
> Still the memories held aloft as lamps for hope's
> young fire to fill
> Shine.

– though not all Swinburne's memories of Eton would have made a suitable inscription for a funeral wreath.

After the coffin had been lowered into the grave, the vicar of Bonchurch said a few appropriate words: 'I should like to state that somewhat late last night I received a telegram from the late Mr Swinburne's sole executor, Mr Watts-Dunton, stating that the quiet burial service previously arranged for could not take place. The friends would gather round in silence and throw flowers if they wished into the open grave. . . . As rector of this parish, in which Algernon Charles Swinburne spent the earliest and some of the happiest years of his life, I have felt it my bounden duty to pay the utmost respect to one who, whatever his afterthoughts may have been, was a baptized member of our Church and who craved a last resting place in this beautiful churchyard, God's acre, which his father, the late Admiral Swinburne, was chiefly instrumental in securing for this parish of Bonchurch. Although no formal service is desired over his grave, yet we do now commit his body to mother earth, earth to earth, dust to dust; and we thankfully remember that he will now lie near his saintly mother, together with his father and brother and sisters. *Requiescat in Pace.* We are glad to think that today Bonchurch receives into its faithful keeping and loving care a creative art-genius of the first order, one of the most lovable great men of the later Victorian age, and one of the sweetest and most musical of English poets who ever lived.' *The Times* commented: 'a fitting and beautiful end to a noble and beautiful life, and though in their love for the dead man his closest friends may feel aggrieved that his wishes were not carried out to the letter, there can be no doubt that, to all intents and purposes, the spirit of them was faithfully observed.'

But that was not to be the end of the matter. Preaching in Canterbury Cathedral on 18 April, Canon Mason, the Vice-Dean, delivered himself as follows, according to *The Times*: 'It was a new doctrine, and one strenuously to be resisted, that men of great poetical genius were not responsible for the use they made of their powers. Who was that article writer who knew that poetry was never a corrupting influence? How could he tell that no increase of sexual immorality could be laid at the door of Swinburne's poetry? It required but little knowledge of souls to know that there was no more deadly poison than the portrayal of corrupt passion in flowing and artistic language. It was difficult to speak of those things, even if for the purpose of warning, without doing more harm than good; but when they were spoken of, not only without abhorrence, but with consent, approval and delight, and with great literary skill, there was no more corrupt influence in the world. He did not judge of the man. Far be it from him to do so. He might have been much better than his poetry. He trusted that he was; but certainly much lustral water and the most precious of all precious blood were needed to do away with the pollution which Swinburne's poetry introduced into English literature.'

Had he been able to read this pronouncement next day with his breakfast coffee, would Swinburne have been angered or amused? On the only other occasion on which he was publicly attacked from the pulpit he was delighted. But the canon 'did not judge of the man': he only said that his work polluted English literature. At any rate, the canon's opinion was not shared by the vicar of Bonchurch, who may not, of course, have been so familiar with the musical blasphemy of such lines as:

> O lips that the live blood faints in, the leavings
>   of racks and of rods!
> O ghastly glories of saints, dead limbs of gibbeted gods!
> Though all men abase them before you in spirit, and
>   all knees bend,
> I kneel not neither adore you, but standing look
>   to the end.

It was poetry that came as a new dawn to a younger generation, of which

Thomas Hardy was one, sick of Victorian pieties. Hardy, in 1910, wrote 'A Singer Asleep' beside Swinburne's grave:

It was as though a garland of red roses
Had fallen about the hood of some smug nun
When irresponsibly dropped as from the sun,
In fulth of numbers freaked with musical closes,
Upon Victoria's formal middle time
  His leaves of rhythm and rhyme.

O that far morning of a summer day
When, down a terraced street whose pavements lay
Glassing the sunshine into my bent eyes,
I walked and read with a quick glad surprise
  New words, in classic guise, –

The passionate pages of his earlier years,
Fraught with hot sighs, sad laughters, kisses, tears;
Fresh-fluted notes, yet from a minstrel who
Blew them not naïvely, but as one who knew
  Full well why thus he blew.

I still can hear the brabble and the roar
At those thy tunes, O still one, now passed through
That fitful fire of tongues then entered new!
Their power is spent like spindrift on this shore;
  Thine swells yet more and more.

# NOTES

### ACKNOWLEDGMENTS

1 John S. Mayfield, 'Swinburne's Boo', *English Miscellany*, IV, 1953.
2 C. Y. Lang, 'Swinburne's lost love', *Publications of the Modern Language Association of America*, vol. 74, no. 1, March 1959.

### INTRODUCTION

1 Harold Nicolson, *Swinburne* (English Men of Letters Series), London, 1926.

2 Introduction to Gabriel Mourey's prose translation, *Poèmes et Ballades*, Paris, 1891.

3 E. Gosse, 'Confidential Paper on Swinburne's moral irregularities with letters concerning it', B.M. MS. Ashley 5753.

4 J. Heath-Stubbs, *The Darkling Plain*, London, 1950, p. 172.

5 J. D. Rosenberg, 'Swinburne', *Victorian Studies*, XI, 1967–68, 149–50. Reprinted as the Introduction to *Swinburne: Selected Poetry and Prose*, New York, 1968.

6 Edmund Wilson, 'Swinburne's letters and novels', *The Bit Between my Teeth*, London, 1966.

### CHAPTER ONE 1837–49 SEAGULL

1 Reproduced in G. Lafourcade, *La Jeunesse de Swinburne*, Paris, 1928, vol. I, facing p. 264.
2 G. Lafourcade, *Swinburne: A Literary Biography*, London, 1932, p. 2.
3 The portrait is now in the Detroit Institute of Art, USA.
4 Letter to E. C. Stedman, 20–1 February 1875, *Times Literary Supplement*, 3 June 1909; C. Y. Lang, *The Swinburne Letters*, New Haven, Conn., 6 vols, 1959–62, vol. III, pp. 8–16.
5 Off Westgate Road, Newcastle, are two narrow passages leading to terraces of Queen Anne houses: Lower Swinburne Place and Upper Swinburne Place.
6 Letter to Stedman, 20–1 February 1875.
7 *Ibid.*
8 Edmund Gosse, *The Life of Algernon Charles Swinburne*, London, 1917, pp. 6–7.
9 B.M. MS. Ashley 5073.
10 Ashley Library, *A Catalogue*, 1926, 8, pp. 196–8; Lang, *op. cit.*, vol. II, pp. 81–6.

11 B.M. MS. Ashley 5264, f. 9.
12 *Ibid.*, f. 12.
13 *Ibid.*, f. 5.
14 *Ibid.*, ff. 7–9.
15 Letter to Edmund Gosse, 3 August 1875, *The Complete Works of Algernon Charles Swinburne*, Bonchurch edn, vol. 18, pp. 200–3; Lang, *op. cit.*, vol. III, pp. 51–2.

## CHAPTER TWO 1849–53 ETON

1 Gosse, *Life*, Appendix I, pp. 319–20.
2 *Ibid.*, pp. 320–1.
3 L. C. Collins, *Life and Memoirs of John Churton Collins*, London, 1912, pp. 34–50; Lang, *op. cit.*; vol. III, pp. 229–30.
4 B.M. Add. MS. 40887.
5 *Ibid.*, ff. 84–5.
6 Gosse, *Life*, pp. 322–3.
7 Lang, *op. cit.*, vol. I, p. 78.
8 Gosse, 'Confidential Paper', *passim*.
9 A. C. Benson, *Memories and Friends*, London, 1924, p. 90.
10 Mary Leith, *The Boyhood of Algernon Charles Swinburne*, London, 1917, pp. 13–17; Lang, *op. cit.*, vol. VI, pp. 251–3.
11 *Ibid.*, pp. 39–43.
12 *Ibid.*, pp. 43–5.
13 *Ibid.*, pp. 49–51.
14 *Fortnightly Review*, 14 July 1869; reprinted in *Essays and Studies*, 1875.

## CHAPTER THREE 1856–60 OXFORD

1 Lafourcade, *La Jeunesse*, vol. II, pp. 45–6.
2 Jean Overton Fuller, *Swinburne: A Critical Biography*, London, 1968, p. 39.
3 Lafourcade, *La Jeunesse*, vol. II, pp. 46–7.
4 Bonchurch edn, vol. 18, pp. 1–4; Lang, *op. cit.*, vol. I, pp. 15–18.
5 Collins, *Life and Memoirs of J. C. Collins*, pp. 26–8; Bonchurch edn, vol. 18, pp. 111–13; Lang, *op. cit.*, vol. II, pp. 342–3.
6 Bonchurch edn, vol. 18, pp. 5–6.
7 Gosse, *Life*, pp. 54–5. Gosse, it would appear, is wrong about the date of Swinburne's first visit to Paris, for in a letter to Lady Trevelyan of 19 January 1861 Swinburne says: 'I am in love with Paris – you know I never saw it before.'
8 *Ibid.*, p. 59.
9 Leith, *op. cit.*, pp. 51–2.
10 W. H. Hutton, *Letters and Papers of William Stubbs*, London, 1904. Quoted by Lafourcade, *Swinburne: A Literary Biography*, London, 1932, p. 75.
11 Gosse, *op. cit.*, pp. 61–2.
12 *Ibid.*, pp. 62–3, *passim*.
13 Lang, *op. cit.*, vol. I, pp. 27–9.
14 Lafourcade, *Swinburne: A Literary Biography*, p. 77.
15 Leith, *op. cit.*, pp. 53–4.
16 *Ibid.*, pp. 54–5.
17 *Ibid.*, pp. 55–7.
18 Gosse has confused his dates, for he says 'on the 21st of November 1859 Swinburne left Oxford for good, never taking a degree' (*Life*, p. 64). As we have seen, Swinburne did not leave Oxford until June 1860.
19 B.M. MS. Ashley 5073, f. 73.

## CHAPTER FOUR 1860–63 CHELSEA: A YEAR'S LETTERS: JUSTINE

1 Georgiana Burne-Jones, *Memorials of Edward Burne-Jones*, London, 1904, vol. I, pp. 215–16.
2 Bonchurch edn, vol. 18, pp. 8–11; Lang, *op. cit.*, vol. I, pp. 38–40.
3 John Gere's 'Descriptive Catalogue' in Robin Ironside, *Pre-Raphaelite Painters*, London, 1948, p. 37.
4 See *New Writings by Swinburne* (ed. C. Y. Lang), New York, 1964, pp. 119–74.
5 William M. Meredith, *Letters of George Meredith, collected and edited by his son*, vol. I, p. 55. Quoted by Lang, *op. cit.*, vol. I, p. 41*n*.
6 Lang, *op. cit.*, vol. I, pp. 103–18.
7 Sara Bailey (ed.), *John Bailey, 1864–1931, Letters and Diaries*, London, 1935, p. 174; Lang, *op. cit.*, vol. I, p. 42.
8 Bonchurch edn, vol. 18, pp. 6–8; Lang, *op. cit.*, vol. I, pp. 45–6.
9 S. M. Ellis, *A Mid-Victorian Pepys*, London, 1923, pp. 78–9.
10 Helen Rossetti Angeli, *Dante Gabriel Rossetti: His Friends and Enemies*, London, 1949, p. 195.
11 Oswald Doughty, *A Victorian Romantic: Dante Gabriel Rossetti*, London, 1949, p. 297.
12 Leith, *op. cit.*, pp. 102–3.
13 B.M. MS. Ashley 5073, f. 39.
14 *Ibid.*, ff. 72–3.
15 *Ibid.*, ff. 77–8.
16 *Ibid.*, f. 74. A large blot on the manuscript nearly obscures the last three lines.
17 *Ibid.*, f. 33.
18 *Ibid.*, ff. 1–3. Quoted (with omissions) in Lafourcade, *La Jeunesse*, vol. II, p. 294.
19 R. Hughes (ed.), *Lesbia Brandon*, London, 1952, pp. 298–300, *passim*.
20 *Ibid.*, p. 295.
21 Quoted in Lang, *op. cit.*, vol. I, pp. 87–8.
22 This poem was, of course, also written by Swinburne. It is at once a celebration of de Sade and a parody of Hugo's *La Légende des Siècles*.
23 Lang, *op. cit.*, vol. I, p. 58.
24 *Ibid.*, vol. I, p. 58.
25 *Ibid.*, p. 54.
26 *New Writings by Swinburne*, p. *x*.
27 Lang, *op. cit.*, vol. I, p. 72.
28 *Ibid.*, pp. 76–7.
29 Lafourcade, *Swinburne: A Literary Biography*, London, 1932, p. 112.
30 Gosse, 'Confidential Paper', *passim*.
31 *Ibid.*
32 *Ibid.*
33 Gosse, *Life*, p. 82.
34 John S. Mayfield, 'Swinburne's Boo'.
35 'Swinburne's Lost Love', *Publications of the Modern Language Association of America*, vol. 74, no. I.

## CHAPTER FIVE 1863–64 ITALY: 'THE TRIUMPH OF TIME': LESBIA BRANDON

1 Leith, *op. cit.*, p. 62.
2 Lafourcade, *La Jeunesse*, vol. II, p. 322; Lang, *op. cit.*, vol. I, p. 90.
3 Bonchurch edn, vol. 18, pp. 16–18.
4 B.M. MS. Ashley 1962.
5 'He was a goodnatured old fellow,' Swinburne wrote to Clement Shorter in 1908, 'but when made into a peer his title might have been "Baron Tattle of Scandal".'
6 James Pope-Hennessy, *Richard Monckton Milnes*, London, 1949, vol. I, p. 81.
7 Bonchurch edn, vol. 18, pp. 18–21; Lang, *op. cit.*, vol. I, pp. 96–8.

8 Wise, *A Swinburne Library*, London, 1925, p. 261.
9 B.M. MS. L.R. 26a, f. 15.
10 Mario Praz, *The Romantic Agony*, London, 1951, 2nd edn, p. 25.
11 Swinburne, *Essays and Studies*, London, 1875.
12 *Ibid.*
13 Daphne du Maurier (ed.), *The Young George du Maurier: A Selection of His Letters, 1860–67*, London, 1951, pp. 235–6. Miss du Maurier dates this letter April 1864, but Swinburne did not return to London until 21 May.
14 Winwood Reade, author of *The Martyrdom of Man*, a popular history from the Darwinian point of view.
15 Bonchurch edn, vol. 18, pp. 22–3; Lang, *op. cit.*, vol. 1, pp. 102–3.
16 Leith, *op. cit.*, p. 23.
17 *Ibid.*, pp. 21–3.
18 The blanks in this letter have been left by Mrs Leith, to disguise the fact that she knew the relevant passages in *Lesbia Brandon*. She describes them as 'characters in a story'.
19 Leith, *op. cit.*, pp. 25–6.
20 *Ibid.*, pp. 26–7.
21 'Swinburne's Lost Love'.
22 Fuller, *op. cit.*, pp. 221–2.
23 Bonchurch edn, vol. 18, pp. 200–2; Lang, *op. cit.*, vol. 1, p. 51.
24 After her marriage, Mary Leith wrote 'an answer to "The Triumph of Time"' in her poem 'Sketches from Recollection', using the metre of the original and some of the key words to show Swinburne that she had not forgotten him. See Frank Wilson's letter, *The Times Literary Supplement*, 16 January 1969.
25 Lafourcade (see *La Jeunesse de Swinburne*, vol. 1, p. 40) had already suggested that there was more than a fraternal affection between Swinburne and his cousin and that he resented her marriage. Dr Lang finds the evidence for this overwhelming (see 'Swinburne's Lost Love', *passim*).
26 W. Empson, *Seven Types of Ambiguity*, London, 1930; Penguin, 1961, pp. 163–4.
27 Lang, *op. cit.*, vol. 1, p. 124.
28 W. Graham Robertson, *Time Was*, London, 1931, p. 13; see 'Appendix' by Derek Pepys Whitely in Daphne du Maurier (ed.), *The Young du Maurier*, p. 300.
29 *Lesbia Brandon*, B.M. MS. Ashley 5264, F. 122.
30 *Ibid.*, f. 114.
31 *Ibid.*, ff. 32a, 41.
32 *Ibid.*, f. 129.
33 *Ibid.*, ff. 82–3.
34 E. Wilson, 'Swinburne's letters and novels'.
35 Lafourcade, *La Jeunesse de Swinburne*, vol. 1, p. 9.
36 B.M. MS. Ashley 5264, f. 1.
37 *Ibid.*, ff. 1–2.
38 *Ibid.*, ff. 2–3.
39 B.M. MS. Ashley 5264, f. 6.
40 *Ibid.*, f. 90.
41 *Ibid.*, ff. 96–100, *passim*.
42 *Ibid.*, f. 175.
43 *Ibid.*, f. 182.
44 *Ibid.*, f. 27.
45 *Ibid.*, ff. 16–19.

## CHAPTER SIX 1865–66 ATALANTA: POEMS AND BALLADS: NOTES ON POEMS AND REVIEWS

1 Bonchurch edn, vol. 18, pp. 27–30; Lang, *op. cit.*, vol. 1, pp. 115–17.
2 Bonchurch edn, vol. 18, pp. 32–3; Lang, *op. cit.*, vol. 1, p. 125.
3 Gosse, 'Confidential Paper', *passim*.
4 L. Ionides *Mémoires*, Paris, 1925.
5 Lang, *op. cit.*, vol. 1, pp. 135–6.
6 Fuller, *op. cit.*, p. 143.
7 Lang, *op. cit.*, vol. 1, pp. 122–3.
8 *Ibid.*, p. 124.

9 Fawn Brodie, *The Devil Drives: A Life of Sir Richard Burton*, London, 1967, p. 247.
10 Lang, *op. cit.*, vol. 1, pp. 138–9.
11 *Ibid.*, pp. 139–40.
12 Nicolson, *Swinburne*, pp. 13–14.
13 Bonchurch edn, vol. 18, p. 34; Lang, *op. cit.*, vol. 1, p. 143.
14 Bonchurch edn, vol. 18, pp. 11–12; Lang, *op. cit.*, vol. 1, pp. 159–60.
15 Gosse, *Life*, p. 147.
16 Swinburne, *Essays and Studies*, p. 241.
17 Swinburne was in touch with the Troubadour tradition through Rossetti's *Early Italian Poets.*
18 Ezra Pound, 'Swinburne Versus His Biographers', in T. S. Eliot (ed.), *Literary Essays of Ezra Pound*, London, 1954, p. 292, *passim.*
19 Clyde K. Hyder, *Swinburne: The Critical Heritage*, London, 1970, passim.
20 Lang, *op. cit.*, vol. 1, p. 171.
21 S. C. Chew, *Swinburne*, Boston, 1929, pp. 74–5, in facsimile.
22 Lord Lytton, *The Life of Edward Bulwer*, vol. 2, pp. 437–8: quoted by Lang, *op. cit.*, vol. 1, pp. 174–5, 175*n*.
23 Wise, *A Swinburne Library*, p. 263; Lang, *op. cit.*, vol. 1, p. 182.
24 Edward Thomas, *Swinburne: A Critical Study*, London, 1912, pp. 78–9.
25 Edmund Gosse, *Portraits and Sketches*, London, 1912, p. 4.

## CHAPTER SEVEN 1866–68 THE GROVE OF THE EVANGELIST: DOLORES MENKEN: MAZZINI

1 Gosse, 'Confidential Paper', *passim.*
2 Gosse, 'Confidential Paper', *passim.* The poems are by Swinburne.
3 Henry Maas, *The Letters of A. E. Housman*, London, 1971, p. 151.
4 Steven Marcus, *The Other Victorians*, London, 1966, p. 254.
5 *Ibid.*, p. 260.
6 From the Pines. Sold by Watts-Dunton to Thomas J. Wise and privately printed by him in a limited edition of thirty copies. For a typescript of this letter I am indebted to Professor Oswald Doughty.
7 Apart from its purely decorative qualities one's reaction to Burne-Jones's painting is bound to be ambivalent. Quentin Bell remarks: 'I find it both repulsive and admirable', *Victorian Painters*, London, 1968.
8 Quoted in Fuller, *op. cit.*, p. 146.
9 G. R. Sims, *My Life: Sixty Years' Recollection of Bohemian London*, London, 1917.
10 *Ibid.*
11 Gosse, 'Confidential Paper', *passim.*
12 *Ibid.*, Sir Walter Raleigh's comment in his letter to Gosse of 17 May 1919 is: 'I suppose A.C.S. was impotent. The flowers of the human mind grow in queer soils. . . . Adah Menken comes very well out of it. She was a gentleman, so to speak.'
13 Wise, *A Swinburne Library*, p. 266; Lang, *op. cit.*, vol. 1, pp. 276–7*n*.
14 Bonchurch edn, vol. 18, pp. 57–8; Lang, *op. cit.*, vol. 1, pp. 276–7.
15 S. M. Ellis, *The Hardman Papers*, London, 1930, p. 320; Lang, *op. cit.*, vol. 1, p. 277.
16 B.M. MS. Ashley 3482.
17 Lang, *op. cit.*, vol. 1, p. 281.
18 *Ibid.*, vol. 1, p. 286.
19 Lafourcade, *Swinburne*, p. 193; Lang, *op. cit.*, vol. 1, p. 307.
20 Lafourcade, *Swinburne*, p. 190*n*.
21 Lang, *op. cit.*, vol. 1, pp. 193–6, *passim*, 250.
22 Lafourcade, *La Jeunesse*, vol. II, pp. 324, 353–4. Typescript in Rutger Library; Lang, *op. cit.*, vol. 1, pp. 208–9.
23 Lang, *op. cit.*, vol. 1, p. 218.
24 Bonchurch edn, vol. 18, pp. 47–9; Lang, *op. cit.*, vol. 1, pp. 223–4.
25 Letter to Watts of 4 December 1876.
26 Leith, *op. cit.*, pp. 91–4.

27 Gosse, 'Confidential Paper', *passim.*
28 Leith, *op. cit.*, pp. 80–1.
29 *Ibid.*, p. 194.
30 Lafourcade, *Swinburne*, p. 154.
31 Leith, *op. cit.*, p. 96.
32 Quoted by Lang, *op. cit.*, vol. I, p. 243*n*.
33 Quoted by Lang, *op. cit.*, vol. I, p. 250*n*.
34 *Ibid.*, p. 250.
35 Gosse, *Portraits and Sketches*, p. 47.
36 Lafourcade, *Swinburne*, pp. 170, 192; Lang, *op. cit.*, vol. I, p. 295.
37 Lang, *op. cit.*, vol. I, pp. 295–6.
38 Gosse, *Life*, p. 178. In *Portraits and Sketches*, Gosse gives a more comical account of this episode, describing Swinburne as 'like some odd conception of Aubrey Beardsley, a *Cupido crucifixus* on a chair of anguish'.
39 *Rossetti Papers*, 1862–70, London, 1903, pp. 318–19.
40 Lafourcade, *Swinburne*, p. 196; Lang, *op. cit.*, vol. I, p. 305.
41 Leith, *op. cit.*, pp. 97–8.
42 Gosse, *Portraits and Sketches*, pp. 17–18.

## CHAPTER EIGHT 1868–72 LA CHAUMIÈRE DE DOLMANCÉ

1 M. Leith, *The Boyhood of Algernon Charles Swinburne*, London, 1917, pp. 198–9.
2 R. Ricatte (ed.), *Journal*, Monaco, 1956, tome x, pp. 240–8.
3 M. Praz, *The Romantic Agony*, London, 1951, 2nd edn, pp. 419–20.
4 Translated by Violette Lang, Clyde H. Hyder, *Swinburne: The Critical Heritage*, pp. 185–7, *passim.*
5 I. S. Turgenev, *Complete Works: Letters*, Moscow, 1961, vol. I, pp. ix, 125.
6 S. Usov, 'Mozaika', *Istorichevski Vestnik*, 1880, no. 12, pp. 1051–2.
7 Lang, *op. cit.*, vol. II, p. 251.
8 E. & J. de Goncourt, *Journal*, tome XIII, p. 28.
9 Lafourcade, *Swinburne*, pp. 250–1; Lang, *op. cit.*, vol. II, p. 253.
10 Bonchurch edn, vol. 18, pp. 204–8; Lang, *op. cit.*, vol. III, p. 61.
11 A. Storr, *Sexual Deviation*, London, 1964, p. 98.
12 Leith, *op. cit.*, p. 110.
13 The Spartan Artemis, at whose altar boys were flogged.
14 Cotytto's orgiastic rites culminated in self-castration.
15 Lang, *op. cit.*, vol. II, p. 312.
16 Gosse, *Life*, p. 183.
17 Lang, *op. cit.*, vol. II, pp. 18–20, *passim.*
18 James Pope-Hennessey, *Monckton Milnes: The Flight of Youth, 1851–1885*, London, 1951, pp. 17–20. Quoted by Lang, *op. cit.*, vol. II, p. 20.
19 Ezra Pound, 'Swinburne versus his Biographers', *Literary Essays*, London, 1954, p. 291.
20 Lang, *op. cit.*, vol. II, pp. 20–1.
21 Leith, *op. cit.*, pp. 100–3. 'Isabel may well have sensed ... that the real rivals for her husband's affection were likely to be men and not women,' remarks Fawn Brodie, *The Devil Drives*, p. 248.
22 Leith, *op. cit.*, p. 106.
23 *Ibid.*, pp. 238–9.
24 Lang, *op. cit.*, vol. II, pp. 51–2.
25 *Ibid.*, pp. 56–7.
26 Gosse, *Life*, pp. 168–9.
27 Reprinted in *Essays and Studies*.
28 As Prince Albert lies in the fantastic gothic chapel at Windsor Castle, though the reference here is to Tennyson's *Idylls of the King*.
29 Wise, *A Swinburne Library*, pp. 49–51; Lang, *op. cit.*, vol. II, pp. 72–5.
30 *Ibid.*, pp. 51–3; Lang, vol. II, pp. 89–90.
31 Wise, *op. cit.*, pp. 53–4; Lang, *op. cit.*, vol. II, p. 96.
32 Wise, *op. cit.*, p. 55; Lang, *op. cit.*, vol. II, pp. 101–2.
33 Lang, *op. cit.*, vol. II, pp. 107–8, *passim.*

34 Gosse, 'Confidential Paper', *passim.*
35 C. Kernahan, *Swinburne As I Knew Him*, London, 1909, pp. 41–3.
36 Gosse, *Life*, p. 199.
37 Lang, *op. cit.*, vol. II, p. 114.
38 Gosse, 'Confidential Paper', *passim.*
39 *Ibid.*
40 Gosse, *Life*, pp. 200–1.
41 *Ashley Library, A Catalogue*, 1927, 9, pp. 146–7; Lang, *op. cit.*, vol. II, pp. 124–5.
42 Bonchurch edn, vol. 18, pp. 82–3; Lang, *op. cit.*, vol. II, pp. 134–5.
43 Swinburne, *Essays and Studies*, pp. 278–80.
44 Lang, *op. cit.*, vol. II, p. 136.
45 *Ibid.*, p. 137.
46 *Ibid.*, pp. 137–8.
47 Dr Lang has revealed that Thomson lived at 7 Circus Road, St John's Wood. The house was 'sumptuously furnished', and is probably to be identified with the flagellation brothel to which Thomson had introduced Swinburne.
48 Lang, *op. cit.*, vol. II, p. 139.
49 *Ibid.*, p. 141.
50 *Ibid.*, p. 144.
51 *Ibid.*, pp. 158–9.
52 Bonchurch edn, vol. 18, pp. 84–6; Lang, *op. cit.*, vol. II, pp. 146–7.
53 H. Taine, *Sa Vie et sa correspondance*, 4 vols, Paris, 1905–14, pp. 3, 145. Quoted by Lang, *op. cit.*, vol. II, p. 150*n*.
54 Lang, *op. cit.*, vol. II, pp. 154–5.
55 *Ibid.*, pp. 157–8.
56 Bonchurch edn, vol. 18, pp. 92–3; Lang, *op. cit.*, vol. II, p. 159.
57 Lang, *op. cit.*, vol. II, pp. 160–1.
58 *Ibid.*, pp. 161–2.
59 Reprinted in Robert Peters, *Victorians on Literature and Art*, London, 1964.
60 Lang, *op. cit.*, vol. II, p. 170.
61 Leith, *op. cit.*, pp. 98–9.
62 Lang, *op. cit.*, vol. II, p. 178.
63 Leith, *op. cit.*, pp. 62–3.
64 Gordon Haight, *George Eliot*, Oxford, 1968, p. 502.
65 Bonchurch edn, vol. 18, pp. 95–6; Lang, *op. cit.*, vol. II, pp. 198–9.

## CHAPTER NINE 1872–76 A FORSAKEN GARDEN

1 Lang, *op. cit.*, vol. II, p. 210.
2 *Ibid.*, p. 253.
3 *Ibid.*, p. 261.
4 Lafourcade, *Swinburne*, p. 264*n*.
5 *Ibid.*
6 Clyde K. Hyder, *Swinburne's Literary Career and Fame*, pp. 177–9.
7 Lang, *op. cit.*, vol. II, pp. 272–3.
8 *New York Daily Tribune*, 25 February 1874; Lang, *op. cit.*, vol. II, pp. 274–5.
9 Lang, *op. cit.*, vol. II, p. 299.
10 *Ibid.*, pp. 318–21, *passim.*
11 *Ibid.*, p. 323.
12 T. Hake and A. Compton-Rickett, *The Letters of Algernon Charles Swinburne*, London, 1918, pp. 65–9; Lang, *op. cit.*, vol. II, pp. 330–2, *passim.*
13 Hake and Compton-Rickett, *Letters*, pp. 88–90; Lang, *op. cit.*, vol. II, pp. 333–5.
14 Lang, *op. cit.*, vol. II, p. 336.
15 Bonchurch edn, vol. 18, pp. 175–86; Lang, *op. cit.*, vol. III, pp. 8–14, *passim.*
16 Lang, *op. cit.*, vol. III, pp. 29–30.
17 *Ibid.*, pp. 38–9.
18 It was not till 1890, after fifteen years of friendship, that Gosse wrote to J. A. Symonds admitting that he, too, was homosexual. 'I know of all you speak of – the solitude, the rebellion, the despair.... Years ago I wanted to write to you about all this, and withdrew through cowardice. I have had a very fortunate life, but there has been this obstinate twist in it! I have reached a quieter time – some beginnings of that Sophoclean period when the wild beast dies. He is not dead; but tamer; I understand him & the trick of his claws.' Phyllis Grosskurth, *John Addington Symonds*, London, 1964, pp. 280–1.

19 Lang, *op. cit.*, vol. III, p. 55.
20 Bonchurch edn, vol. 18, pp. 210–12.
21 Gosse, *Portraits and Sketches*, London, 1912, pp. 48–51, *passim*.
22 *Ibid.*, pp. 11, 14.
23 *Ibid.*, pp. 15–16.
24 There is a reference to the poem, however, in Swinburne's letter to Watts, 22 January 1876.
25 Leith, *op. cit.*, pp. 175–7; Lang, *op. cit.*, vol. III, pp. 187–8.
26 Lafourcade, *Swinburne*, pp. 218, 247–8.
27 Gosse, *Life*, p. 234.
28 Bonchurch edn, vol. 18, pp. 258–62; Lang, *op. cit.*, vol. III, p. 211.
29 Hake and Compton-Rickett, *Letters*, pp. 131–3; Lang, *op. cit.*, vol. III, pp. 228–9.
30 The complete ballad is reprinted in *New Writings by Swinburne*, pp. 17–19.
31 Or 'Denmark Hill' – where Ruskin lived.
32 Hake and Compton-Rickett, *Letters*, pp. 133–6; Lang, *op. cit.*, vol. III, pp. 230–2.

## CHAPTER TEN 1877–79 THE LONELY YEARS

1 J. D. Rosenberg, 'Swinburne', *Victorian Studies*, XI, 1967–68.
2 Gosse, *Life*, pp. 262–3.
3 *Ibid.*, pp. 261–2.
4 Ezra Pound, 'Swinburne Versus His Biographers', *Literary Essays*, London, 1954, p. 290.
5 Hake and Compton-Rickett, *Letters*, pp. 161–3; Lang, *op. cit.*, vol. III, pp. 305–6.
6 Bonchurch edn, vol. 18, pp. 172–3; Lang, *op. cit.*, vol. III, pp. 2–3.
7 Gosse, *Life*, pp. 237–8.
8 *Ibid.*, pp. 238–9.
9 *Ibid.*, pp. 236–7.
10 Lafourcade, *Swinburne*, pp. 239–43.
11 Lang, *op. cit.*, vol. IV, pp. 10–11.
12 Gosse, 'Confidential Paper', *passim*.
13 Lang, *op. cit.*, vol. IV, pp. 21–2.
14 Ricatte (ed.), *Journal*, vol. XIII, p. 28.
15 Lang, *op. cit.*, vol. IV, pp. 31–2.
16 Hake and Compton-Rickett, *Letters* (with omissions), pp. 163–5; Lang, *op. cit.*, vol. IV, pp. 35–7.
17 Lang, *op. cit.*, vol. IV, pp. 38, 38*n*.
18 Gosse, *Life*, p. 244.
19 A. E. Housman, 'Swinburne', *Cornhill*, Autumn, 1969.
20 J. D. Rosenberg, 'Swinburne', *Victorian Studies*, reprinted as 'Introduction' to *Swinburne: Selected Poetry and Prose*.
21 Lang, *op. cit.*, vol. IV, pp. 55–6.
22 Quoted by Lang, *op. cit.*, vol. IV, p. 59*n*.
23 Lord Gower, *My Reminiscences*, London, 1883, pp. 2, 290. Quoted by Lang, *op. cit.*, vol. IV, p. 60*n*.
24 Hake and Compton-Rickett, *Letters* (with omissions), pp. 166–8; Lang, *op. cit.*, vol. IV, pp. 62–3.
25 Lang, *op. cit.*, vol. IV, pp. 66–7.
26 A reference to Charles Reade's *Drink*, an adaptation of Zola's *L'Assommoir*, produced on 2 June 1879, with considerable success; Lang, *op. cit.*, vol. IV, p. 74*n*.
27 Bonchurch edn, vol. 18, pp. 305–7; Lang, *op. cit.*, vol. IV, pp. 72–3.
28 Bonchurch edn, vol. 18, pp. 307–8; Lang, *op. cit.*, vol. IV, p. 79.
29 Lang, *op. cit.*, vol. IV, p. 86.
30 Gosse, *Life*, p. 244.
31 *A Swinburne Library*, 109; Lang, *op. cit.*, vol. IV, p. 84.

## CHAPTER ELEVEN 1879–82 AT THE PINES

1 Lang, *op. cit.*, vol. IV, pp. 88–9.
2 Leith, *op. cit.*, pp. 149–51.
3 Bonchurch edn, vol. 18, pp. 318–19; Lang, *op. cit.*, vol. IV, pp. 111–12.
4 Bonchurch edn, vol. 18, pp. 317–18; Lang, *op. cit.*, vol. IV, p. 107.
5 Bonchurch edn, vol. 18, pp. 317–18.

6 C. Kernahan, *Swinburne as I Knew Him*, London, 1919, pp. 12–16, *passim*.
7 Clara Watts-Dunton, *The Home Life of Swinburne*, London, 1922, pp. 74–5.
8 Leith, *op. cit.*, pp. 153–5. Lang, *op. cit.*, vol. IV, pp. 110–11.
9 Gosse, *Life*, pp. 255–6.
10 Thurman, L. Hood, *Letters of Robert Browning*, New Haven, Conn., 1933, p. 193.
11 Watts-Dunton, *The Home Life of Swinburne*, p. 94.
12 Fuller, *Swinburne: A Critical Biography*, p. 288.
13 Gosse, *Life*, pp. 248–9.
14 Lang, *op. cit.*, vol. IV, p. 166.
15 Leith, *op. cit.*, p. 206.
16 *Ibid.*, pp. 123–4.
17 Lang, *op. cit.*, vol. IV, pp. 213–14.
18 T. Earle Welby, *A Study of Swinburne*, London, 1926 (reprinted 1969), pp. 196–7.
19 Lang, *op. cit.*, vol. IV, p. 197.
20 *Ibid.*, p. 253.
21 *Ibid.*, pp. 239–40.
22 Welby, *op. cit.*, pp. 216–17.

## CHAPTER TWELVE 1882–1909 RELICS

1 Max Beerbohm, 'No. 2 The Pines' in *And Even Now*, London, 1920.
2 Lang, *op. cit.*, vol. V, p. 52*n*.
3 *Ibid.*, vol. IV, p. 265*n*.
4 *The Times Literary Supplement*, 10 June 1909; Lang, *op. cit.*, vol. IV, pp. 264–6, *passim*.
5 Wise, *A Swinburne Library*, pp. 199–200; Lang, *op. cit.*, vol. IV, p. 267.
6 Lang, *op. cit.*, vol. IV, p. 283.
7 Bonchurch edn, vol. 18, p. 363; Lang, *op. cit.*, vol. IV, pp. 287–8.
8 Lang, *op. cit.*, vol. IV, p. 296.
9 *Ibid.*, p. 302*n*.
10 Edward Dowden, *Correspondence of Henry Taylor*, London, 1888, pp. 407–8; Lang, *op. cit.*, vol. IV, pp. 302–3.
11 Gosse, *Life*, p. 313.
12 Wise, *op. cit.*, pp. 159–60.
13 Gosse, *Life*, p. 265.
14 Welby, *A Study of Swinburne*, p. 153.
15 Leith, *op. cit.*, pp. 64–7; Lang, *op. cit.*, vol. IV, pp. 315–17.
16 Lang, *op. cit.*, vol. IV, p. 317.
17 *Ibid.*, vol. V, p. 337*n* (quoting from the *Referee*, 18 April 1909).
18 Quoted by Lang, *ibid.*, p. 39.
19 *Ibid.*, p. 32.
20 First published in the *Spectator*, July 1862.
21 Fuller, *Swinburne: A Critical Biography*, p. 109.
22 First published in *The Spectator*, 17 May 1862.
23 Ezra Pound, 'Troubadors: their sorts and conditions', *Quarterly Review*, 1913.
24 Fuller, *op. cit.*, pp. 221–2.
25 Lang 'Swinburne's lost love'.
26 Quoted in Fuller, *op. cit.*, p. 270 (from B.M. MSS. Ashley 5752, ff. 40–1).
27 T. A. J. Burnett, letter to *The Times Literary Supplement*, 23 January 1969.
28 But see 'Freddy Thorburn' in *Trusty in Fight*.
29 *The Times Literary Supplement*, 30 January 1969.
30 Lang, *op. cit.*, vol. VI, pp. 100–1.
31 May Morris, *William Morris, Artist, Writer, Socialist*, Oxford, 1936, vol. I, p. 648.
32 Leith, *op. cit.*, p. 128.
33 Wise, *op. cit.* (extract), pp. 160–1; Lang, *op. cit.*, vol. VI, pp. 104–5.
34 Gosse, *Life*, p. 279.
35 *Ibid.*, pp. 279–80.
36 Leith, *op. cit.*, pp. 128–9.
37 This bed is now part of the collection of Lady Rosalie Mander at Wightwick Manor, Wolverhampton.
38 Alan Bell, 'Gladstone looks for a Poet Laureate', *The Times Literary Supplement*, 21 July 1972, 847. On 20 October Gladstone wrote to Lord Acton: 'On account of Swinburne's *pre*-eminence as a poet, I have been making a very careful examination

of his case. I fear he is *absolutely* impossible.... It is a sad pity; I have always been deeply impressed by his genius.'

39 *Ibid.*, p. 847.

40 Lang, *op. cit.*, vol. VI, pp. 176–7.

41 T. Hake and A. Compton-Rickett, 'Theodore Watts-Dunton and I', *The Life and Letters of Theodore Watts-Dunton*, London, 1916, p. 167.

42 *Ibid.*, p. 172.

43 Helen Rossetti Angeli, *Dante Gabriel Rossetti*, London, 1949, p. 109*n*. Watts called her 'Minaw' ('beloved one' in the gypsy tongue) and Clara called him 'Gualtiero', Rossetti's Italianization of Walter.

44 *Ibid.*, pp. 108–9.

45 *Ibid.*, p. 177.

46 *Ibid.*, p. 176.

47 Fuller, *op. cit.*, pp. 290–1.

48 Watts-Dunton, *Home Life of Swinburne*, pp. 178–9.

49 *Ibid.*, pp. 174–6.

50 *Ibid.*, p. 259, *passim*.

51 *Ibid.*, pp. 271–2.

52 *Ibid.*

53 *The Times*, 16 April 1909.

# INDEX